# Stumbling Colossus

## THE RED ARMY ON THE EVE OF WORLD WAR

David M. Glantz

Maps by Darin Grauberger and George F. McCleary, Jr.

University Press of Kansas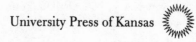

© 1998 by the University Press of Kansas

Published by the University Press of Kansas (Lawrence, Kansas 66049),
which was organized by the Kansas Board of Regents and is operated and
funded by Emporia State University, Fort Hays State University, Kansas
State University, Pittsburg State University, the University of Kansas, and
Wichita State University

Library of Congress Cataloging-in-Publication Data

Glantz, David M.
    Stumbling colossus : the Red Army on the eve of World War / by
David M. Glantz.
        p.   cm. — (Modern war studies)
    Includes bibliographical references and index.
    ISBN 0-7006-0879-6
    1. Soviet Union. Raboche-Krest 'ianskaia Krasnaia Armiia—History—
World War, 1939–1945. 2. World War, 1939–1945—Campaigns—Eastern
Front. 3. Soviet Union—History, Military. I. Title. II. Series.
D764.G556   1998
940.54'217—dc21                                              97-33277

British Library Cataloguing in Publication Data is available.

Printed in the United States of America

10  9  8  7  6  5  4  3  2  1

The paper used in this publication meets the minimum requirements of the
American National Standard for Permanence of Paper for Printed Library
Materials Z39.48-1984.

# Contents

# Maps and Illustrations

# Preface

Over fifty years ago, on 22 June 1941, the German Army inflicted a devastating surprise blow against the Soviet Union. Code-named Operation Barbarossa, the German offensive sought nothing short of the outright and total destruction of the Red Army and the Soviet state. Fresh after their striking military victories in 1939 and 1940 over the Poles and the French, which accorded Germany hegemony over continental Europe, few in the German High Command doubted they would succeed. Operation Barbarossa nearly proved them correct. Within weeks after unleashing blitzkrieg against the Soviet Union, German panzer spearheads crossed the Dnepr River into Russia proper, raced along the Baltic shores toward Leningrad, and plunged deep into Ukraine toward Kiev, leaving in their wake a Red Army in shambles. Red Army defending armies were encircled and destroyed, hundreds of thousands of Red Army soldiers died or went into German captivity, Red Army strategic reserves were gobbled up piecemeal by rapidly advancing and seemingly unstoppable Wehrmacht armored columns, and the Soviet political leadership struggled in vain to halt the German juggernaut and survive the storm. Five months later, in December 1941, the Soviets would finally do so, but only after the advancing German columns had reached the outskirts of Leningrad and Rostov, and the very gates of Moscow.

A war of unprecedented violence and savagery ensued that would endure for four more bloody years. The war on the Eastern Front was a war of "cultures," a veritable war of annihilation, that mercilessly pitted the entire mobilized power of the Soviet state against the entire German nation in a war of total destruction. Human losses on both sides were appalling. Total Soviet military casualties numbered in the tens of millions, including at least 29 million soldiers, and civilian casualties more than matched that gruesome number. Economic devastation gripped the Baltic region, Belorussia, Ukraine, the Caucasus, and vast regions of Russia proper, as armies swept to and fro across the map inflicting damage unparalleled in Europe since the scourge of the seventeenth-century Thirty Years War.

The searing effect of war touched the soul of every family in the Soviet Union. Husbands, fathers, brothers, and sons all perished on the battlefield in unprecedented numbers. Unlike more civilized conflicts, mothers, wives, and daughters also felt the ferocity of the war and died alongside their menfolk in a struggle whose horrors knew no bounds. The conflict left scars on the Russian soul that will persist for generations to come, personified by the oft-repeated slogan, "No one is forgotten, nothing is forgotten."

Like their predecessor Soviets, the Russians will not be able to forget the struggle still known to them as the Great Patriotic War. Unlike their predecessors, however, they can now ask with greater candor, "Why did the conflict occur?" and "Why was initial defeat so severe?" Also unlike their predecessors, they can now receive an honest answer. For fifty years, the Soviet propaganda machine vividly portrayed Germany as a vicious, predatory, and militarily effective power whose ruthlessness and deceptiveness conditioned initial victory over the Soviet Union in Operation Barbarossa. Soviet propaganda emphasized the keen attention paid by the Party and the government to defensive preparations and admitted some failures on the eve of and during the initial period of war but insisted that those progressive policies ultimately permitted mobilization of the power of the state and the achievement of ultimate (and inevitable) victory. Moreover, it steadfastly portrayed that victory as the triumph of socialism over aggressive capitalism (fascism).

Beneath the surface of the stifling Soviet system, more complete answers to those two critical questions existed but lay dormant. Hundreds of thousands of veterans who suffered through the war and survived knew more but prudently held their tongues. So did many senior officers who survived to write their memoirs. Although occasionally truth did seep through, the censor generally prevailed. Political change within the system also often permitted bursts of historical candor. N. S. Khrushchev's early 1960s experiment in glasnost occasioned the release of liberal doses of truth, but these were as much associated with de-Stalinization as with a real search for truth. Again, in the late 1980s, Gorbachev revived Khrushchev's program of glasnost in a vain attempt to reform a decayed Soviet system before collapse ensued. In the end, however, Gorbachev could not stave off collapse, and history caught up with and destroyed the Soviet state.

Historical truth, so long held hostage by the Soviet regime, has now been partially liberated. Now historians can provide answers for the Russians to questions associated with 1941 that have for so long tortured their collective soul. It is somewhat ironic, however, that as the archives doors are slowly opening to reveal greater truth, the Russians and others who suffered so intensely in the war are being subjected to new theories whose effects are more damaging than those embraced and propounded by the Soviet system. To the former writings of Soviet apologists have been added new theories about the advent of war that place responsibility for the war squarely on Stalin and the Soviet Union.

In short, these new theories categorically blame the Soviet Union for planning preemptive war against Germany in July 1941. Enunciation of this theory further condemns the Soviet regime and, more importantly, justifies the German invasion and absolves Germany of blame for the ensuing human suffering. Quite naturally, a host of German historians have gravitated to this view. More frighteningly, a growing number of Russian reformers have embraced the theory as if to cleanse totally the postcommunist Russian soul by laying the blame for all of the ills of humanity at the feet of Stalin and the Communist Party.

As interesting, sensational, and salable as this new theory is, the ultimate question for any responsible historian must be, "To what extent is the new theory correct?" Most who support the theory of preemptive war assume that the Red Army was both powerful and ready for war in 1941. That assumption underlies their descriptions of Stalin's subsequent political, diplomatic, and military actions prior to the outbreak of war. This volume exploits both German and Soviet archival evidence to question that vital assumption, which, following the evidence, this book finds to be totally unfounded.

# Abbreviations

| | |
|---|---|
| A | Army |
| AABn | Antiaircraft artillery battalion |
| AAD | Assault aviation division |
| AAR | Assault aviation regiment |
| AAR | Antiaircraft artillery regiment |
| ABn | Artillery battalion |
| AbnB | Airborne brigade |
| AbnC | Airborne corps |
| AR | Aviation regiment (miscellaneous) |
| ATB | Antitank brigade |
| B | Brigade |
| BAC | Bomber aviation corps |
| BAD | Bomber aviation division |
| BAR | Bomber aviation regiment |
| BF | Briansk Front |
| CAR | Corps artillery regiment |
| CASqdn | Artillery correction squadron |
| CavGp | Cavalry group |
| CC | Cavalry corps |
| CD | Cavalry division |
| CF | Central Front |
| DBA | Long-range bomber aviation |
| EngBn | Engineer battalion |
| EngR | Engineer regiment |
| FAD | Fighter aviation division |
| FAD, PVO | Fighter aviation division, air defense |
| FAR | Fighter aviation regiment |
| FAR, PVO | Fighter aviation regiment, air defense |
| FR | Fortified region |
| GAR | Gun artillery regiment |
| GAU | Main Artillery Directorate |
| Gds | Guards |
| Gp | Group |
| GrenRB | Grenadier rifle brigade |

| | |
|---|---|
| GRU | Main Intelligence Directorate |
| HAR | Howitzer artillery regiment |
| HGABtry | Heavy gun artillery battery |
| HPHAR | High-powered howitzer artillery regiment |
| KF | Kalinin Front |
| LIB | Light infantry brigade |
| LR | Long-range |
| MAB | Mixed aviation brigade |
| MAD | Mixed aviation division |
| MAR | Mixed aviation regiment |
| MBn | Mortar battalion |
| MC | Mechanized corps |
| MD | Mechanized division |
| MilRD | Militia rifle division |
| MotArmB | Motorized armored brigade |
| MotEngBn | Motorized engineer battalion |
| MRB | Motorized rifle brigade |
| MRD | Motorized rifle division |
| MRR | Motorized rifle regiment |
| MtCD | Mountain cavalry division |
| MtRD | Mountain rifle division |
| MVO | Moscow Military District |
| MvrAbnB | Maneuver airborne brigade |
| NCMD | North Caucasus Military District |
| NF | Northern Front |
| NIB | Naval infantry brigade |
| NRB | Naval rifle brigade |
| NWF | Northwestern Front |
| OKH | High Command of Armies |
| OMD | Odessa Military District |
| PBR | Pontoon-bridge battalion |
| PV | Border forces |
| PVOB | Antiaircraft defense brigade |
| PVOC | Antiaircraft defense corps |
| PVOD | Antiaircraft defense division |
| RAR | Reconnaissance aviation regiment |
| RAT | Mobile radio station |
| RB | Rifle brigade |
| RC | Rifle corps |
| RD | Rifle division |
| RecR | Reconnaissance regiment |
| Res. AB | Reserve aviation brigade |

| RF | Reserve Front |
| RGK | Reserve of the High Command |
| RGKA | Reserve of the High Command Artillery |
| RVGK | Reserve of the Supreme High Command |
| SA | Shock army |
| SBn | Sapper battalion |
| SepA | Separate army |
| SepMRB | Separate motorized rifle brigade |
| SepRB | Separate rifle brigade |
| Sep TBn | Separate tank battalion |
| SF | Southern Front |
| SPABn | Special-power artillery battalion |
| SR | Sapper regiment |
| StuRB | Student rifle brigade |
| SV | Ground forces |
| SwF | Southwestern Front |
| TB | Tank brigade |
| TBn | Tank battalion |
| TcF | Transcaucasian Front |
| TD | Tank division |
| TR | Tank regiment |
| VV | Internal Forces |
| VVS | Air forces |

Red Army troops on Red Square

# Introduction

During the almost half century that has passed since the end of World War II, historians and the reading public alike have agreed that the war was the product of the evil geopolitical designs of Adolf Hitler, the *Fuehrer* of the vaunted German Third Reich. Volumes document the march of German political and military power during the 1930s, from Hitler's seemingly innocent accession to power as the democratically elected political head of the German Weimar Republic, through the conversion of that ill-fated republic into the fiercely militaristic Third Reich, to the inexorable drive of Hitler's Third Reich to a position of European and, perhaps, global political and military domination that propelled Europe and the world into the most terrible war mankind has endured.

Traditionally, historians have generally agreed that Hitler's insatiable appetite for conquest, which was fed by his dream of German hegemony over Europe, was encouraged by a generation of Western political leaders whose memories of the last terrible world war and whose warped consciences and feelings of guilt conditioned them to greet German ambition with a devastating policy of appeasement. Like a pampered schoolyard bully, Hitler interpreted appeasement as weakness and so accelerated his drive for European domination. The crises of the 1930s, replete with dashed Western hopes and unbridled German victories, culminated in war in September 1939. Within two years the war had spread across the expanse of Europe, and in summer 1941 German armies marched into the depths of the Soviet Union.

Nor was the question of war guilt after World War II as controversial as it had been in the wake of World War I. By means of a thoroughly legal process, the Nuremberg trials, the victorious Allies placed responsibility for waging "aggressive war" directly at the feet of Hitler and his regime. That responsibility encompassed the entire war, from August 1939 and the host of illegal German acts extending back through the 1930s. Finally, the Allies documented the accusations and Hitler's deeds with his own words and writings.

Historians have long acknowledged the passive complicity of Western leaders in Hitler's march toward war and the often insidious and cynical role the Soviet Union played in that drama as it sought to reach accommodation with its ideological nemesis. Thus, most Western historians, beginning with William L. Langer and S. Everett Gleason, have recognized that Stalin gave

Hitler a "blank check" in August 1939 by negotiating and signing the Molotov-Ribbentrop Pact. Although they have often differed regarding why Stalin did so, they nevertheless have highlighted the pact's cynical and destructive nature. For nearly five decades after war's end, Soviet authorities and historians themselves did nothing for their image by denying that they had signed a secret protocol with Hitler, dividing up Eastern Europe between Germany and the Soviet Union. Gorbachev's 1980s perestroika finally ended that nonsense and brought Soviet historiography on that question in line with Western views.

When all was said and done, however, the same historians, while viewing the ensuing war through the prism of its awful consequences, unequivocally blamed Hitler. The litany of successive German aggressive acts, from the invasion of Poland, through the attack on the Soviet Union, to the declaration of war on the United States and all the horrors that ensued, they concluded, were all a consequence of Hitler's unbridled and unprincipled ambition. The world public rested comfortable in this judgment as postwar generations attempted to elucidate and eradicate the causes of the horrible struggle in the service of fashioning a new and lasting peace.

In 1990 the comfortable certainties of the past were severely shaken by the publication of a short volume that challenged accepted historical judgments concerning war guilt. Furthermore, the new volume threatened to make the issue of guilt for World War II as contentious and potentially damaging an issue as had been the issue of assessing guilt for World War I. In short, the book accepted the June 1941 arguments by Hitler's propaganda minister, Joseph Goebbels, that Germany was fighting a preventive war when it invaded the Soviet Union. Furthermore, it postulated, by planning to attack Germany preemptively in summer 1941, Stalin shared with Hitler the guilt for the ensuing war between Germany and the Soviet Union. In fact, the book directly challenged the validity and conclusions of the entire Nuremberg process by assigning almost all blame for the war to Stalin, who, it claimed, had manipulated Hitler. Diplomatically speaking, the new book asserted that the Molotov-Ribbentrop Pact gave Stalin a "free hand," which Stalin then used to plan his aggression against Germany and, by extension, the West.

This argument runs counter to the facts. Even if Stalin could be accused of manipulation, that manipulation in no way accorded him a free hand through summer 1941. In summer 1939 Stalin was nearly at a state of declared war with Japan on the Mongolian-Manchukuo border, and Germany and Japan were allies in the Anti-Comintern Pact. The German ambassador in Moscow, Count Friedrich Werner von Schulenburg, told V. M. Molotov on 15 August that Germany would attempt to influence Japanese policy toward better relations with the USSR, which amounted to a de facto admission that Germany did not intend to support Japan. Although Stalin obtained his sphere of influence in

Eastern Europe and a free hand in the Far East, the "free hand" was tenuous at best and depended entirely on Germany's future actions in Europe. Hitler's subsequent conquest of the bulk of Western Europe in May and June 1940 fundamentally altered the entire strategic situation. Hitler's new aggression granted Germany hegemony over Europe, defied Stalin's original intent in sanctioning the nonaggression pact, and inalterably negated Stalin's "free hand" in the Far East. From that point on and through much of the ensuing Soviet-German war, Stalin worried about the security of his eastern flank. Meanwhile, from 1940 through June 1941, Stalin clung grimly to his gains and prepared stoically for the inevitable German blow, which Hitler began planning in summer 1940 and intended to begin after driving Britain from the war.

This starkly revisionist book, which was first published in France in 1988 and then in Great Britain in 1990, was written by a former Soviet Army major, Viktor Rezun. Writing under the pseudonym "Viktor Suvorov," apparently in emulation of imperial Russia's great military captain, Rezun's book was chillingly entitled *Icebreaker* (Ledokol).[1] It was not Rezun's first book. After defecting to the West, the former Soviet Army major wrote a series of exposés on the Soviet Army, beginning with *The Liberators,* which described parts of his army career and, most notably, the Soviet invasion of Czechoslovakia, and a series of "insider" books that dealt with the contemporary Soviet Army and Soviet intelligence organs. In these earlier works, Rezun alternately portrayed the Soviet military as imposing and inept, depending on the book and the period in which it was written. Sensationalism aside, while tickling the interest of Western readers, these Cold War volumes summoned mixed reactions but had no lasting impact.

However, the appearance of *Icebreaker* and its subsequent companion volume, *M-Day* (Den'-M), which was published in 1994, prompted quite different reactions.[2] Given the contents of the two books, the reactions were perhaps understandable. *Icebreaker's* jacket text starkly enunciates Rezun's brazen new claim:

Who started the Second World War? The question has been asked count-less times. Allowing for some variations in the formula, the answer has always been, unequivocally, Adolf Hitler.

Germany's acceptance of blame for the war and her openness on the matter lies in marked contrast to the muted, patently propagandist state-ments issued by the Soviet Union over the years. For the Soviet Union, the war was and still is the "Great Motherland War"; the triumph over fascism was a victory for communism, not just on a Soviet but on a Euro-pean scale. The Continent has been divided ever since.

For the first time, a historian—Soviet defector Viktor Suvorov—shows that the USSR's part in starting the war was very much greater, and much more sinister, than has been hitherto assumed. His starting thesis is that Stalin, like Hitler, was intent on world domination; but that Stalin used Hitler as a stepping-stone—an "Icebreaker"—to ensure Soviet participation and eventual victory in a war meant for one purpose only: the exporting and imposition throughout the world of communism. The great Soviet dictator would stop at nothing to see this aim through and had had it in preparation for many years.

Suvorov's book is a direct and often harrowing challenge on accepted history. Its achievement is to force us all to revise radically our ideas about the origins of—and the reasons for—the most destructive war mankind has ever experienced.

Thus, Rezun resurrected the hitherto muffled and generally discounted argument, which in the past circulated in some German circles (mostly right-wing and nationalistic), that Stalin and his cronies were directly responsible for fostering the outbreak of the war. "From the 1920s on," stated Rezun, "sparing neither resources nor effort, nor indeed time, Stalin revived the strike power of German militarism. . . . For what purpose? So that war would be declared on the rest of Europe." According to Rezun, Stalin in effect encouraged and exploited German militarism and ensuing German military action as an "icebreaker for the Revolution." Further, Rezun argued, Stalin was prepared to attack Germany in the summer of 1941, on the presumption that "war is won by the side which enters it last and not by the one who goes into it first."

In *Icebreaker,* Rezun documented his contentions with personal recollections and material culled from a host of Soviet open sources with questionable regard to context. While claiming to have had access to classified archival materials while serving as a captain and major in the Soviet Army over twenty years ago, he undercut the possible arguments of those who might use such material in the future to refute his claims by asserting that the most controversial information in the archives has been suppressed or removed. At the least one can validly question how an officer of his lowly rank could have had access to such material in the first place and, if he had access, how he could recall the minute details of such an extensive collection after so long a period.

In his exposé, Rezun wove a complex mass of credible facts taken from Soviet memoirs and postwar studies into a less credible web of intrigue surrounding the circumstances associated with the outbreak of war. His documentary evidence was sufficient to defend his thesis regarding Stalin's strategic intent prior to June 1940, but he presented considerably less evidence to support his more radical contentions concerning Stalin's war plans for 1941. Specifically, and among a multitude of other claims, he contended that Stalin planned offensive action in the summer of 1941 (specifically, on 6 July), that he deliberately mobilized and deployed a massive strategic second echelon to achieve victory, that this echelon consisted of imposing "black-shirted" NKVD formations and crack shock armies (such as the 16th and 19th), that Stalin deliberately dismantled existing defensive fortifications to facilitate his impending offensive, and that General A. M. Vasilevsky and not General G. K. Zhukov was the architect and designated implementer of Stalin's cunning plan. Using the same historical methodology, Rezun expanded in *M-Day* upon the startling theses he had presented in *Icebreaker*.

Although Rezun's contentious and explosive theses have had little impact on scholarship in the Anglo-American historical community, they have had a major impact in Germany and the former Soviet Union. As justifiable and necessary as well-founded historical revisionism is, the effects of ill-conceived and less well-founded revisionism can be profound and, ultimately, damaging. As after World War I, it can open old wounds and inflict unwanted or unwarranted new ones. In extreme cases, it can undermine peace by igniting older suspicions and hatreds. At the least, it can pervert balanced and rational perspectives on the past.

The rippling disruptive effects of Rezun's work can already be seen in continental Europe and, in particular, in the German and Russian historical community. Prominent German historians have embraced his theses, and the ensuing personal and legal arguments have torn the German historical community and venerable historical institutions apart. Even post-Soviet Russia has yielded fertile soil for Rezun's brand of revisionism. A new generation of anti-Soviet historians has emerged whose ideological hatred of socialism and communism has conditioned them to accept any and all arguments against their former oppressors, however tenuous. In short, resentment and even hatred has conditioned them to accept and propagate even the most extreme claims of heinous behavior on the part of the Soviet Union. Furthermore, under assault from those who agree with Rezun, some members of the more traditional mainline Russian historical community have broken ranks and, in varying degrees and for varied motives, have accepted some of Rezun's arguments. Because revisionism in this form and for these motives can be so damaging, it must be tested or, if necessary, challenged. That is the purpose of this book.

As well constructed as Rezun's arguments are and as credible as the individual facts may be, the whole of his case regarding Soviet intentions in 1941 is incredible for a number of reasons. First, it is not consistent to reject in advance the validity of Soviet classified archival materials while basing one's arguments, in part or in total, on extensive unclassified memoirs and studies. Second, Rezun exploits memoir material, which in the main is accurate at least regarding time, place, and event but often contains subjective interpretation, by considering it wholly out of context and using it adroitly to support his arguments. Finally, and most important, the validity of Rezun's arguments is challenged by three fundamental types of sources: newly released and extensive Soviet declassified documents and studies on the war (all secret or top secret); German archival materials; and other materials that document the parlous state of the Red Army in 1941 and indicate that any offensive operations contemplated by the Soviets in 1941 would have bordered on the lunatic. Stalin may well have been an unscrupulous tyrant, but he was not a lunatic.

Extensive Soviet declassified reports, orders, and plans released within the past several years and recent books dealing with Soviet strategic plans in the year 1940–1941 clearly indicate that after the fall of France in June 1940 the Soviets frantically sought to defend themselves against what they increasingly believed was the threat of an inevitable (and probably successful) attack by Nazi Germany. This involved a Soviet declaration in early 1941 of a "war imminent" state, which entailed extensive covert force mobilization, mobilization that was under way but only partially complete on 22 June. Soviet desperation was vividly underscored by the publication in the General Staff journal *Military Thought* (Voennaia mysl') and other Soviet operational journals of articles detailing the stark German threat and a variety of defensive topics. The records of Soviet *fronts*, armies, corps, and divisions in the days immediately preceding and following the outbreak of war fail to provide any direct evidence to support Rezun's claims and instead substantiate the reverse conclusions.

German records, as well, contradict Rezun's arguments. They too underscore the appalling state of Red Army preparedness for war, although the Germans woefully underestimated the mobilization potential of their foe and eventually paid the price. According to both Soviet and German classified sources, the formidable Soviet strategic second echelon, to which Rezun refers, including the vaunted 16th and 19th Armies and their associated mechanized corps, was considerably less than formidable, as attested to by its subsequent combat performance when its forces were committed to action between August and October. Second strategic echelon Soviet mechanized corps almost totally lacked modern medium and heavy tanks, and their combat performance was typified by the example of the 5th and 7th Mechanized Corps, which went into combat near Lepel' in July and were quickly decimated. The mechanized corps in the western border regions, which did have some modern tanks, fared little better.

In fact, it was the poor performance of the Red Army before 1941 in Poland and Finland and during 1941 that renders Rezun's arguments even less credible. Stripped of the bulk of its command cadre by four years of catastrophic purges and in the midst of a badly managed force expansion and rearmament program, the Red Army was clearly not suited to the conduct of large-scale offensive operations in summer 1941. The course and results of the secret Moscow war games of January 1941 underscored that fact for Stalin. Consequently, when in May 1941 an anxious Zhukov proposed to Stalin that the Soviet Union launch a preemptive attack against the mobilizing Germans, Stalin rejected the idea, and for good reason.

Finally, in a military-technical sense, as this book will clearly indicate, there are cogent reasons why the Soviet Union was unprepared for war in summer 1941. Fundamental differences distinguish a mobilized, combat-tested army that only has to redeploy before launching a war (like the 1941 armies of Germany and Japan) from a mass-conscript army that has both to mobilize and deploy before doing so. A wealth of newly available archival materials and older classified and newer unclassified studies clearly indicates that both the 1941 Soviet Army and the prewar U.S. Army fell inexorably into the latter category. Hindered by the harsh social realities and constraints associated with its inherently "peasant rear" and subjected to unprecedented turbulence produced by major force expansion, reorganization, and reequipment programs, the Red Army was incapable of mounting large-scale war in 1941. It could and did fight "small wars" in Finland, at Khalkhin-Gol, and in Bessarabia in 1939 and 1940, but its lackluster performance in those conflicts only underscored its incapability for conducting the larger war. Thus, like the United States in the prewar years, the Soviet Union was condemned to "creep up to war." As the chief of the Red Army General Staff, Marshal B. M. Shaposhnikov, noted, mobilization was the doorstep to war; cross it and you take responsibility for aggressive war. Hitler did so in Europe in September 1939, and Japan did so in China in 1937. Soviet mobilization of a few armies in 1941 was an act of prudence and not the full mobilization so indicative of an intention to conduct aggressive large-scale war.

It is relatively easy to postulate startling revisionist concepts concerning such dramatic events as the beginning of the Soviet-German war. The very drama and emotional content of such events guarantee notoriety for the claims and fertile soil for their sustenance. Consequently, it is less easy and certainly far less dramatic to refute these claims, particularly when they have been so warmly received in some quarters. Nevertheless, at the least, the claims demand close examination and, in the last analysis, refutation, if history requires it.

Much work has already begun to test the validity of Rezun's arguments, from both a diplomatic and a military perspective. In January and February 1995, a conference on this theme, sponsored jointly by the World History Institute of the Russian Federation's Academy of Science and Tel Aviv University's Cummings Center for Russian and East European Studies, was held in Moscow. More than thirty-five American, European, Russian, and Israeli scholars delivered papers on Rezun's theses and a host of associated themes, and the conference papers are scheduled for publication. Subsequently, Russian historians have prepared studies, articles, and anthologies of papers investigating the same general theme for publication in a wide range of Russian journals. The latter is best exemplified by an anthology prepared and published by the Association of Researchers of Twentieth Century Russian Society.[3]

Several years before, the U.S. Army's Foreign Military Studies Office sponsored a symposium with German war veterans on the subject of the initial period of the Soviet-German war. The symposium combined scholarly analysis of the circumstances associated with the outbreak of war and the nature of operations during the initial period of war with the personal perspectives of German army participants. A major work, *The Initial Period of War on the Eastern Front: 22 June–August 1941*, was published to disseminate the results of this symposium.[4] The synthesis of this in-depth research, along with the observations of a dwindling number of war participants and ongoing work in the field by many other historians, promises to cast the events of spring and summer 1941 in a critical and more revealing light. So also will continuing releases of materials from the Soviet archives. Tragically, the time has passed when we can interview those who lived through the period and endured its privations. There are, however, increasing opportunities for gathering and exploiting the written letters and personal memoirs of those who survived those times, if the political climate remains favorable.

This book continues the essential process of examining the circumstances surrounding the outbreak of the Soviet-German war by objectively studying the readiness state of the Red Army in summer 1941 on the basis of Soviet and German archival materials.

# CHAPTER 1

# Red Army Forces

Within the context of a sharply more threatening European political situation after 1935 and the outbreak of general European war in 1939, the Soviet Union prepared its armed forces for war. Prudently, the Soviet political and military leadership reformed and greatly expanded the size of its peacetime military establishment in an attempt to improve its combat capabilities. The General Staff studiously altered its war plans to meet newly perceived threats, and it changed the Red Army force generation and mobilization system to accord with these new war plans. Between 1937 and 1939, to increase the size and improve the readiness of peacetime forces and facilitate their transition to war, the Soviets converted their traditional territorial-militia force-manning system to a regular-cadre system. The 1 September 1939 Law on Universal Military Service provided manpower resources necessary for the new system to achieve its ends. These measures permitted the Red Army to "creep up to war" by expanding the army's peacetime strength from 1.5 million men on 1 January 1938 to over 5 million men in June 1941 and enabled the mobilization system to expand the peacetime Red Army cadre force to well over 500 divisions of various types in wartime.

During the series of European crises that occurred between 1937 and 1939, the Soviets extensively exercised their mobilization system. Exploiting these experiences, the General Staff refined its mobilization and war plans throughout 1940 and right up to 22 June 1941 by continuously analyzing evolving geopolitical conditions and conducting high-level strategic planning conferences and strategic-operational war games. The revised plans estimated the size and deployment potential of threat (primarily German and Japanese) forces and adjusted Soviet peacetime and mobilized force levels to meet these projected threats.

While the Soviet leadership prepared its armed forces for general war, it tested the Red Army's combat readiness in limited conflict in Poland, Mongolia, Finland, and Rumania. In the majority of cases, the Red Army failed the test. Embarrassing Red Army battlefield failures and striking force readiness deficiencies lent a new sense of urgency to the work of strategic planners and accelerated their attempts to reform, restructure, and reequip the Red Army before it was forced to participate in a general European war. The ensuing extensive "Timoshenko reforms" were in progress when war broke out on 22 June 1941.

Prompted by intelligence indicators of a growing German threat, between April and June 1941 the Soviet government partially implemented a "special threatening military period" and accelerated "creeping up to war" by conducting a concealed strategic deployment of forces. This was, in essence, the first stage of a precautionary mobilization process that would accelerate in wartime and continue through early 1942. This first stage began in late April, when forces from the Trans-Baikal and Far East regions moved west, and continued in early May, when smaller forces moved west from the Ural and Siberian Military Districts. Meanwhile, in April the People's Commissariat of Defense (NKO) approved an expanded wartime establishment for rifle divisions (14,483 men) and ordered 99 rifle divisions to be brought up to full wartime strength. Despite this order, only 21 of these divisions had reached full manpower strength by 22 June.[1] On 13 May the NKO issued a decree for mobilization and formation of a seven-army (67-division) strategic reserve and for deployment of this reserve along the Dvina-Dnepr River line within the first ten days of July. This reserve included 16th, 19th, 21st, and 22d Armies from the Trans-Baikal, North Caucasus, Volga, and Ural Military Districts, which began movement in May, and 20th, 24th, and 28th Armies, made up of formations from the Moscow, Orel, Volga, Siberian, Arkhangel'sk, and Far Eastern Military Districts, which began deploying only after 22 June.

In early June, under the cover of "large-scale war games" and in accordance with the State Defense Plan, the NKO conscripted 793,500 men to fill out about 100 existing divisions and fortified regions. By 22 June, 9 divisions of the 19th Army had completed deployment forward, and 19 divisions of 16th, 21st, and 22d Armies were en route to their deployment regions. When fully implemented (after 30 days), the Soviet mobilization plan (MP-41) was to produce a total force of 344 divisions and 7.85 million men, 6.5 million of whom would be deployed in the Western Theater.[2] Many of these mobilized divisions, however, were not at full strength. These were to complete their mobilization during the initial period of war. In actuality, by 22 June 1941, MP-41 had produced an initial combat force in the west of 2,901,000 men organized into 171 divisions out of a total Soviet mobilized strength of 4,826,900 men.[3]

By 22 June 1941, the Soviet government had implemented many, but not all, of the military requirements of the "special threatening military period." Long-term preparedness programs were well under way, partial mobilization was proceeding apace, forces were converting to their wartime establishments, and strategic and operational force concentration and deployment were in progress. These measures extended into forward military districts, but because Stalin was concerned about German perception of provocations, he severely restricted similar measures at the operational and tactical levels.[4] The ongoing mobilization raised three major questions: "How large would the force become?" "What was the force's actual combat capability?" and, given that combat capability, "How did the Soviets intend to employ it?" The first two questions can now be answered, and the answers have considerable bearing on the third question.


## SIZE AND CONFIGURATION

In summer 1941 the armed forces of the Soviet Union consisted of the Workers' and Peasants' Red Army (RKKA), the Workers' and Peasants' Military-Naval Fleet (RKVMF), Border Forces (PV), and Internal Forces (VV). Total strength was 5.7 million men. The Red Army included ground forces (SV), air forces (VVS), and national air defense forces (PVO-strany).

On 22 June 1941, Red Army ground forces consisted of 4 *fronts*, 27 armies, 29 mechanized corps, 62 rifle corps, 4 cavalry corps, 5 airborne corps, 303 divisions, 57 fortified regions, and 5 separate rifle brigades, supported by 10 antitank brigades, 94 corps artillery regiments, 75 RGK (Reserve of the High Command) artillery regiments, and 34 engineer regiments, with a total strength of about 5 million men (see Appendix A).[5] By type, the 303 divisions consisted of 198 rifle, 61 tank, 31 mechanized, and 13 cavalry. Field forces in the Western Theater included three *fronts* (Northwestern, Western, and Southwestern), formed on 22 June from the Baltic, Western, and Kiev Special Military Districts, a separate army (the 9th), and a fourth *front* (Northern) created on 24 June from the Leningrad Military District. These field forces ("operating armies," *deistvuiushchie armii*) contained 15 armies, 20 mechanized corps, 32 rifle corps, 3 cavalry corps, 3 airborne corps, 163 divisions (97 rifle, 40 tank, 20 mechanized, and 6 cavalry), 41 fortified regions, 2 separate rifle brigades, 10 antitank brigades, 87 artillery regiments (52 corps and 35 RGK), and 18 engineer regiments with a total strength of about 2.9 million men (see Table 1.1, p. 18, and Map 1.1).

The High Command (Stavka) reserve consisted of 6 armies, 14 rifle corps, 5 mechanized corps, 57 divisions (42 rifle, 10 tank, and 5 mechanized), and 17 artillery regiments (13 corps and 4 RGK) (see Table 1.2).[6] The remaining military districts and Far Eastern Front counted 6 armies, 16 rifle corps, 4 mechanized corps, 83 divisions (59 rifle, 7 cavalry, 11 tank, and 6 mechanized), 16 fortified regions, 3 separate rifle brigades, 65 artillery regiments (29 corps and 36 RGK), and 16 engineer regiments (see Table 1.3).

In accordance with prewar planning, the Red Army was echeloned strategically in depth. The first strategic echelon, formed from field forces in the western (border) military districts, including 9th Separate Army in the Odessa Military District, consisted of 171 divisions (104 rifle, 40 tank, 20 mechanized,

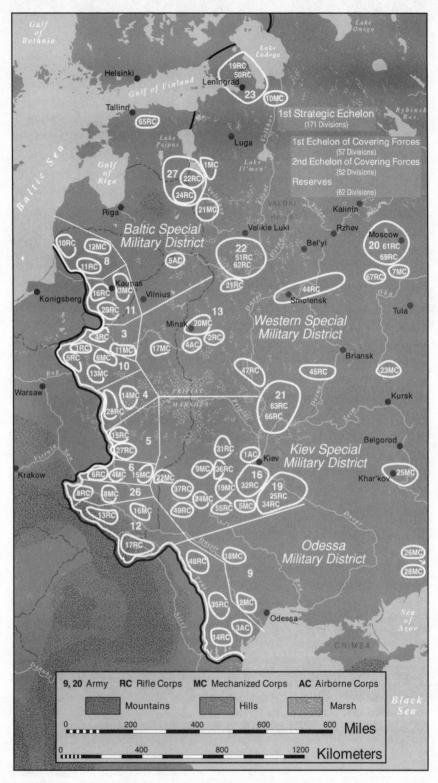

Map 1.1. Field Forces in the Western Theater, June 1941

and 7 cavalry) arrayed along a front of 4,500 kilometers from the Barents Sea to the Black Sea. Within these field forces, 56 divisions and 2 brigades were in the first echelon of border military district covering armies, 52 divisions were in army second echelon, 50 to 100 kilometers to the rear, and 62 divisions were in border military district reserve, deployed 100 to 400 kilometers from the state borders. Fortified regions were positioned along the 1941 border, in the depths along the pre-1939 Soviet-Polish border, and on the approaches to major cities such as Kiev.

The second strategic echelon consisted of 57 divisions from six Stavka reserve armies, which by 22 June were beginning to deploy along the Dvina-Dnepr River line. Finally, the strategic reserve consisted of all forces existing or mobilizing in other military districts and the Far Eastern Front.

The Red Army Air Force provided support to all ground forces in the field, in the military districts, and in nonoperating *fronts*. The Air Force consisted of long-range bomber aviation (DBA), *front*, army, and force aviation (see Table 1.4.). Long-range aviation was consider a strategic asset and therefore was directly subordinate to the chief of the Air Force command. *Front* aviation was subordinate to the military district (or *front*) commander, army aviation to army commanders, and force aviation (*voiskovaia aviatsiia*) served corps commanders. Long-range bomber aviation numbered 5 bomber aviation corps, each of two bomber aviation divisions, and 3 separate bomber aviation divisions. *Front* and army aviation fielded 61 mixed, fighter, and bomber divisions. Of this total, 31 were positioned with field forces and 30 with military districts and nonoperating *fronts*. In addition, the Air Force fielded a wide range of separate aviation regiments, generally supporting more remote forces. These included 7 reconnaissance aviation regiments, 5 mixed aviation brigades, 2 mixed aviation regiments, 2 fighter aviation regiments, 1 bomber aviation regiment, and 7 artillery correction aviation regiments.[7]

On 22 June 1941, total Soviet Red Army air strength numbered 19,533 combat aircraft (see Tables 1.5 and 1.6). An additional 1,445 aircraft were under fleet control. Of the total Red Army aircraft strength, 2,311 planes were assigned to long-range bomber aviation and 13,288 aircraft to air forces in the military districts. The remaining 3,934 aircraft served schools and training installations. The NKO allocated the preponderance of aviation forces to the western military districts, where it deployed 61 percent of its aviation formations, 53 percent of its aircraft, and 45 percent of its Air Force personnel. A total of 7,133 aircraft were stationed in these military districts, distributed as follows: Leningrad Military District, 1,270; Baltic Special Military District, 1,211; Western Special Military District, 1,789; Kiev Special Military District, 1,913; and Odessa Military District, 950.[8] Other military districts possessed 6,155 aircraft.

A portion of Red Army air assets was assigned to the Air Defense Command (PVO). These consisted of 40 fighter aviation regiments, which had a paper establishment strength of 2,520 aircraft but actually totaled fewer than 1,500 planes. According to aviation type, aircraft distribution in the western military districts was as shown in Table 1.6 (p. 21).

Assisting the Red Army in the defense of the Soviet Union's borders were 165,000 border guards troops of the Border Guards Forces, who were primarily deployed along the western borders of the country from the Barents Sea to the Black Sea and in the Far East. These light security forces made up 8 border districts (okrug), which, in turn, consisted of 49 numbered border detachments, 10 separate border *komendatura*, 7 border guard boat detachments, 8 district junior officer schools, and supporting special units and subunits.

Special formations and units of NKVD internal security forces provided security for key governmental installations, rail lines, and industrial centers and sites. A 62,100-man railroad security force organized into 9 NKVD divisions and 5 brigades provided security for 1,697 objectives. NKVD operational forces included 11 regiments stationed in the western military districts and the F. E. Dzerzhinsky division, 7 regiments, and 3 separate battalions scattered about the internal military districts. In addition, a specialized NKVD force was created in October 1940 for local antiaircraft defense of cities, population points, and economic objectives. By June 1941, the new Main Directorate for Local Antiaircraft Defense (MPVO) fielded 3 engineer-antichemical regiments (in Moscow, Leningrad, and Baku) and 4 engineer-antichemical battalions. The remaining MPVO structure, which was in the process of forming, consisted of 1 division and 5 brigades, numbering 29,900 men defending 145 objectives.[9]

A final NKVD force provided convoy security for prisoners of war during their transport to POW camps and security for the camps. These forces and internal security forces were also responsible for running labor camps within the Soviet Union, which were commonly known by the acronym GULag (Main Administration of Corrective-Labor Camps). By June 1941 this force numbered 38,311 men organized into two divisions and seven brigades. Total NKVD strength on 22 June amounted to 171,900 men.[10]

## ACTUAL FORCE GENERATION AND MOBILIZATION

The German 22 June 1941 invasion of the Soviet Union obviously interrupted and disrupted the Soviet armed forces' mobilization. Despite the invasion, the NKO proceeded as planned, and although German military action hindered mobilization in the border military districts, it probably accelerated the overall mobilization process. By 1 July 1941, the total Soviet call-up of military manpower had reached 5.3 million additional men, and the count of mobilized armies, corps, and divisions rose steadily thereafter.[11] By 10 July the newly formed State Defense Committee (GKO) had completed the mobilization of 56 additional divisions, which reinforced existing armies, filled out the Western and Southern Fronts' 13th and 18th Armies, completed formation of 28th Army, and began forming a new wave of reserve armies, including the new 31st Army (see Table 1.7). Both 28th and 31st Armies joined 24th Army in a new Stavka reserve, replacing other reserve armies that had already joined battle with operating *fronts*. All the while, German forces were destroying Soviet 3d, 10th, and the better part of 4th Army in fighting around Bialystok and Minsk.[12]

By 1 August, the number of newly mobilized divisions had grown to a total of 144, including 8 100-series tank divisions formed primarily from tank divisions of mechanized corps deploying from the internal military districts. From this wave of mobilization emerged the reformed 3d and new 29th, 30th, 32d, 33d, 34th, 35th, 36th, 43d, 44th, 45th, 46th, and 47th Armies. The 3d Army joined the new Central Front, and 29th and 30th Armies (together with 28th) reinforced the Western Front. The Stavka formed a new Reserve Front from 32d, 33d, 34th, and 43d Armies (with the existing 24th and 31st Armies), assigned 35th Army first to the Reserve Front and then to the Far Eastern Front, formed 36th Army in the Trans-Baikal Military District, and created four new armies (44th, 45th, 46th, and 47th) in the Transcaucasus Military District. Meanwhile the weakened 4th Army disappeared from the Red Army order of battle.

By 1 August Red Army strength stood at 401 divisions, despite the loss of about 46 divisions incurred since the beginning of hostilities. Subsequently, during August, the Stavka formed 37th, 38th, 40th, 42d, 48th, 49th, 50th, 51st, 52d, and 55th Armies, all of which it assigned to operating *fronts*.

Thus, the Soviet mobilization system added 4 armies and 56 divisions to the Soviet force structure by 10 July and a total of 17 armies and 144 divisions by 1 August (see Map 1.2). The additional 9 armies created in August brought total Red Army strength on 1 September to 50 armies, 450 divisions (356 rifle, 31 tank, 5 mechanized, and 58 cavalry), 7 rifle brigades, and 37 fortified regions. Throughout August and September, the Stavka began abolishing rifle corps' headquarters, disbanded those older mechanized corps that German forces had not destroyed, and created from their remnants new 100-series tank divisions and separate tank brigades. Most of the new tank divisions would be short-lived. By October most had been destroyed or reformed into smaller separate tank brigades. Meanwhile, mobilization continued at a frenzied pace, producing by 31 December 1941 a total of approximately 285 rifle divisions, 12 re-formed tank divisions, 88 cavalry divisions, 174 rifle brigades, and 93 tank brigades.

Mobilization of Air Force formations and units lagged behind the growth in ground force strength because of the technological complexities associated

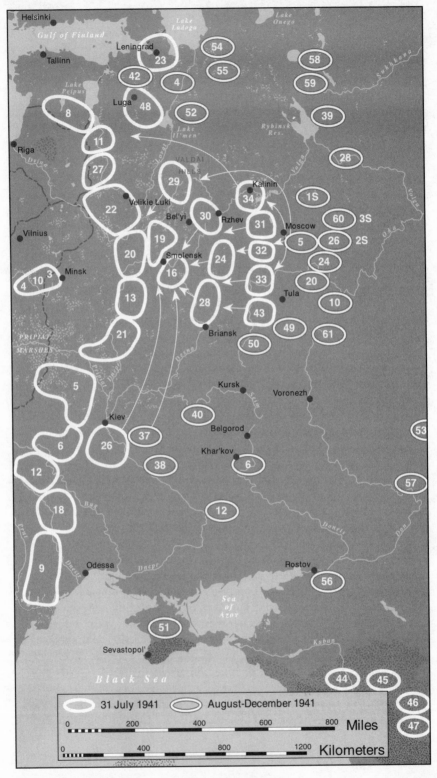

Map 1.2. Soviet Mobilization, 31 July to December 1941

with fielding and equipping trained and capable aviation forces and the heavy Soviet air losses incurred during the initial days and weeks of war. In a sense, Soviet deployment of air formations resembled their experience with mechanized and armored forces. Heavy initial wartime losses, poor troop training, and massive command and control difficulties forced the Soviets to truncate the size of mobilizing forces and delayed the growth of Soviet air power (see Tables 1.8 and 1.9).

In December 1941 the Soviets fielded five aviation groups, each consisting of from four to five regiments of various types, whose regiments are included in Table 1.8. Not shown on the table are the long-range aviation bomber corps and divisions of long-range bomber aviation (DBA). On 22 June, these consisted of four corps in the western military districts and one corps in the Far East, each with two bomber aviation divisions. In addition, long-range bomber aviation fielded two separate fighter and one bomber aviation divisions. The corps were abolished in August 1942, and seven long-range bomber aviation divisions remained under DBA control after 1 October.

Mobilization also embraced NKVD internal security forces. The 1941 Mobilization Plan called for the expansion of operational forces in the western military districts. Regiments located in the Baltic, Western, and Kiev Special Military Districts were to form three motorized rifle divisions (the 21st, 22d, and 23d), and of the 41,500-man increase in NKVD strength, 16,000 were to be concentrated in the border military districts. This mobilization plan was carried out, and, in addition, NKVD troops in the internal military districts played a considerable role during the initial period of war by fielding and filling out numerous NKVD formations and, from late July on, by providing the nucleus of many new Red Army rifle divisions.[13]

In total, counting initial Red Army ground forces on 22 June and those mobilized to 31 December, during the first six months of war the Red Army fielded approximately 483 rifle divisions, 73 tank divisions, 31 mechanized divisions, and 101 cavalry divisions, for a total of 688 divisions. If brigades are tallied in the total on the basis of 2 brigades (rifle and tank) per division, another 133 divisions can be added, for a grand total of 821 divisional-size formations. Of this number, 447 divisions were in the field by 1 August. One must bear in mind, however, that the mobilized strength of these divisions was roughly half that of their more experienced German counterparts.

As imposing as this force may seem on paper, simple numbers are one-dimensional and misleading. The true capability of this massive Red Army must be measured by its combat readiness. One significant indicator of Red Army combat readiness on 22 June 1941 was the losses it suffered during the first six months of war, which amounted to at least 229 division equivalents (147 rifle, 40 tank, 11 mechanized, and 10 cavalry, plus 21 rifle and tank brigades) (see Table 1.9, p. 24).

## STATISTICAL DATA

Table 1.1. Field Forces in the Western Theater, 22 June 1941

| Front | Army | Rifle Corps | Mechanized Corps | Cavalry Corps | Airborne Corps | Fortified Regions |
|---|---|---|---|---|---|---|
| Northern | 7th, 14th, 23d | 19th, 42d, 50th | 1st, 10th | | | 21st, 22d, 23d, 25th, 26th, 27th, 28th, 29th |
| Northwestern | 8th, 11th, 27th | 10th, 11th, 16th, 22d, 24th, 29th, 65th | 3d, 12th | | 5th | 41st, 42d, 44th, 45th, 46th, 48th |
| Western | 3d, 4th, 10th, 13th (headquarters only) | 1st, 2d, 4th, 5th, 21st, 28th, 44th, 47th | 6th, 11th, 13th, 14th, 17th, 20th | 6th | 4th | 58th, 61st, 62d, 63d, 64th, 65th, 66th, 68th |
| Southwestern | 5th, 6th, 12th, 26th | 6th, 8th, 13th, 15th, 17th, 27th, 31st, 36th, 37th, 49th, 55th | 4th, 8th, 9th, 15th, 16th, 19th, 22d, 24th | 5th | 1st | 1st, 2d, 3d, 4th 5th, 6th, 7th, 8th, 10th, 11th, 12th, 13th, 15th, 17th |
| | 9th Separate | 14th, 35th, 48th | 2d, 18th | 2d | | 80th, 81st, 82d, 84th, 86th |

Table 1.2. Stavka Reserves, 22 June 1941

| Army | Rifle Corps | Mechanized Corps |
|---|---|---|
| 16th | 32d | 5th |
| 19th | 25th, 34th | 26th |
| 20th | 61st, 69th | 7th |
| 21st | 63d, 66th | 25th |
| 22d | 51st, 62d | |
| 24th | 52d, 53d | |
| | 20th, 45th, 67th | 21st |

Table 1.3. Military Districts and Nonoperating Fronts, 22 June 1941

| Military Districts | Army | Rifle Corps | Mechanized Corps | Cavalry Corps | Airborne Corps | Fortified Regions |
|---|---|---|---|---|---|---|
| Moscow | | 41st | | | | |
| Volga | | | | | | |
| Orel | | 30th, 33d | 23d | | | |
| Ural | | | | | | |
| Siberian | | | | | | |
| Khar'kov | 18th (headquarters only) | | | | 2d | |
| North Caucasus | | 64th | | | | |
| Odessa | | 7th, 9th | | | 3d | 83d |
| Trans-Caucasus | | 3d, 23d, 40th | 28th | | | 51st, 52d |
| Central Asian | | 58th | 27th | 4th | | |
| Arkhangel'sk | | | | | | |
| Trans-Baikal | 17th | 12th | | | | Trans-Baikal |
| Far Eastern Front | 1st, 2d, 15th, 25th | 18th, 26th, 59th, Special | 30th | | | 101st, 102d, 103d, 104th, 105th, 106th, 107th, 108th, 109th, 110th, 111th, Ust'-Bureisk |

Table 1.4. Red Army Aviation Forces, 22 June 1941

| Formation | Force Aviation | Air Defense |
|---|---|---|
| **Field Forces** | | |
| Northern Front | | |
| 7th Army | 55th MAD | |
| 14th Army | 1st MAD, 42d CASqdn | |
| 23d Army | 5th MAD, 41st BAD, 15th, 19th CASqdn | |
| Front | 2d MAD, 39th FAD, 311th RAR, 103d CASqdn | 3d, 54th FAD, PVO |
| Northwestern Front | 57th FAD, 4th, 6th, 7th, 8th MAD, 312th RAR | 21st FAR, PVO |
| Western Front | 43d FAD, 12th, 13th BAD, 9th, 10th, 11th MAD, 313th, 314th RAR. 59th, 60th FAD (forming) | 184th FAR, PVO |
| Southwestern Front | 44th, 64th FAD, 19th, 62d BAD, 14th, 15th, 16th, 17th, 63d MAD, 315th, 316th RAR | 36th FAD, PVO |
| 9th Separate Army | 20th, 21st, 45th MAD, 317th RAR. 65th, 66th FAD (forming) | 131st FAR, PVO |
| Long-Range Bomber Aviation | 1st BAC (40th, 51st BAD), 2d BAC (35th, 48th BAD), 3d BAC (42d, 52d BAD), 4th BAC (22d, 50th BAD), 56th, 61st FAD, 18th BAD | |
| **Military Districts** | | |
| Moscow | 24th FAD, 23d, 46th MAD. 77th MAD, 78th FAD (forming) | |
| Volga | 58th BAD (forming) | |
| Orel | 47th, 67th FAD, 68th BAD, 1st Res. AB (two regiments) | |
| Ural | | |
| Siberian | 30th BAD | |
| Khar'kov | 75th, 76th FAD, 49th BAD | |
| North Caucasus | 73d FAD, 74th BAD | |
| Odessa | | |
| Trans-Caucasus | 25th, 72d MAD, 26th BAD (LR), 27th, 71st, FAD, PVO, 68th FAD, 320th RAR, 3d, 23d CASqdn | |
| Central Asian | 4th MAB (116th FAR, 34th BAR) | |
| Arkhangel'sk | 1st MAB | |
| Trans-Baikal | 38th FAD, 30th BAD (LR), 28th, 37th MAD, 9th FAR, PVO 2d MAB, 51st FAR, 64th MAR, 318th RAR | |
| Far Eastern | 5th BAC (33d, 53d BAD), 29th FAD, 5th MAB, 71st MAR, 18th FAR, PVO, 168th RAR | |
| 1st Army | 32d, 34th MAD. 79th FAD (forming) | |
| 2d Army | 31st FAD, 319th RAR | |
| 15th Army | 69th MAD, 18th CASqdn | |
| 25th Army | 70th MAD, 39th, 59th CASqdn | |

Note: For abbreviations, consult List of Abbreviations, p. xv.
Source: *Boevoi sostav Sovetskoi armii* [ Combat composition of the Soviet Army], pt. 1 (Moscow: Military-Scientific Directorate of the General Staff), 7–14.

Table 1.5. Soviet Armed Forces Aviation Strength, 22 June 1941

| Force | Aircraft |
|---|---|
| Military districts | 13,288 |
| Western | 7,133 |
| Other | 6,155 |
| Long-range bomber aviation | 2,311 |
| Schools and training installations | 3,934 |
| Red Army total: | 19,533 |
| Naval forces (fleets) | 1,445 |
| Armed Forces total: | 20,978 |
| | (16,502 serviceable and 13,211 combat-ready) |

Source: "Spravochnik boevogo i chislennogo sostava chastei i soedinenii Vozdushnykh sil SA 1941–1954 gg." [Handbook of the combat and numerical composition of Soviet Army Air Force units and formations, 1941–1945], *Tsentral'nyi arkhiv Ministerstva Oborony (TsAMO)*, inv. 962, 5–10. Cited in an unpublished manuscript by N. M. Ramanichev. Hereafter cited as "Spravochnik." See also *Nachal'nyi period Velikoi Otechestverroi voing* [Initial period of the Great Patriotic War] (Moscow: Vorosh lov Academy of the General Staff, 1989), 57–59.

Table 1.6. Composition and Strength of Soviet Air Forces in the West, 22 June 1941

| Aviation Grouping | Number of Aircraft | | | | |
|---|---|---|---|---|---|
| | Bomber | Assault | Fighter | Reconnaissance | Total |
| Air Force (western military districts) | 2,212 | 317 | 4,226 | 378 | 7,133 |
| High Command long-range bomber aviation | 1,339 | 0 | 0 | 0 | 1,339 |
| Total Red Army in the West | 3,551 | 317 | 4,226 | 378 | 8,472 (7,133 serviceable) |
| Northern, Baltic, and Black Sea Fleets | 217 | 120 | 763 | 345 | 1,445 |
| Total Armed Forces in the West | 3,768 | 437 | 4,989 | 723 | 9,917 (8,727 combat-ready) |
| Percent of the total force | 38 | 4.4 | 50.3 | 7.3 | 100 |

Source: "Spravochnik," 5–10.

Table 1.7. Armies Mobilized, 10 July to 1 September 1941

| Army | Subordinate Formation |
|---|---|
| **By 10 July 1941** | |
| 13th | 45th RC (148th, 187th RDs), 20th RC (132d, 137th, 160th RDs), 61st RC (53d, 110th, 172d RDs), 4th AbnC (7th, 8th AbnBs), 20th MC (26th, 38th TDs, 210th MD), 24th RD |
| 18th | 17th RC (96th MtRD, 164th, 189th RDs), 55th RC (130th, 169th RDs), 60th MtRD, 30th CD, 39th TD, 10th, 11th FRs |
| 28th | 30th RC (89th, 120th, 149th RDs), 33d RC (145th, 217th, 222d RDs), 27th MC (9th, 23d TDs, 221st MD) |
| 31st | 244th, 246th, 247th, 249th RDs |
| **From 10 July to 1 August 1941** | |
| 3d | 66th RC (75th, 232d RDs), 214th AbnB, 65th FR |
| 29th | 243d, 252d RDs, 1st MRR (NKVD), 50th, 53d CDs |
| 30th | 242d, 250th, 251st RDs |
| 32d | 220th RD, 2d, 7th, 8th, 13th, 18th MilRDs |
| 33d | 1st, 5th, 9th, 17th, 21st MilRDs |
| 34th | 245th, 257th, 259th, 262d RDs, 25th, 54th CDs |
| 35th | Initially in Reserve Front with 194th, 220th, 248th RDs; subsequently in Far Eastern Front with 35d, 66th, 78th RDs, 109th FR |
| 36th | 65th, 93d, 94th, 114th RDs, 61st TD, 82d MD, 31st, 32d FRs |
| 43d | 53d, 217th, 222d RDs, 105th TD |
| 44th | 20th, 77th MtRDs, 17th CD |
| 45th | 31st, 136th RDs, 138th MtRD, 1st MtCD, 55th FR |
| 46th | 4th RD, 9th, 47th MtRDs, 51st FR |
| 47th | 236th RD, 63d, 76th MtRDs |
| **From 1 August to 1 September 1941** | |
| 37th (Southwestern Front) | 27th, 64th RCs (headquarters only), 28th MtRD, 87th, 124th, 146th, 147th, 165th, 171st, 175th, 206th, 228th, 284th, 285th RDs, 1st FR |
| 38th (Southwestern Front) | 97th, 116th, 196th, 212th, 297th, 300th, 304th RDs |
| 40th (Southwestern Front) | 135th, 293d RDs, 10th TD, 2d AbnC |
| 42d (Leningrad Front) | 2d, 3d Gds MilRDs, Krasnogvardeisk FR |
| 48th (Leningrad Front) | 128th, 311th RDs, 21st TD, 1st Gds RB |
| 49th (Reserve Front) | 194th, 220th, 284th RDs, 4th MilRD |
| 50th (Briansk Front) | 217th, 258th, 260th, 278th, 279th, 290th, 299th RDs |
| 51st Separate (Crimea) | 9th RC (106th,156th RDs), 271st, 276th RDs, 1st, 2d, 3d, 4th Crimean MilRDs, CavGp (40th, 42d, 48th CDs) |
| 55th (Leningrad Front) | 70th, 90th, 168th, 237th RDs, 1st, 4th MilRDS, RR (3d Gds MilRD), Slutsk-Kolpinsk FR |

Note: For abbreviations, consult List of Abbreviations, p. xv.

Table 1.8. Soviet Air Force Mobilization, 22 June to 31 December 1941 (not including long-range aviation)

| Formation | 22 June | 10 July | 1 August | 1 September | 1 December | 31 December |
|---|---|---|---|---|---|---|
| Fighter aviation division | 19 | 11 | 9 | 10 | 15 | 12 |
| Bomber aviation division | 11 | 20 | 16 | 18 | 20 | 17 |
| Mixed aviation division | 31 | 26 | 33 | 40 | 49 | 57 |
| Assault aviation regiment | 0 | 0 | 0 | 0 | 1 | 1 |
| Total divisions | 61 | 57 | 58 | 68 | 84 | 87 |
| Fighter aviation regiment | 5 | 8 | 12 | 25 | 47 | 84 |
| Bomber aviation regiment | 1 | 5 | 7 | 11 | 33 | 125 |
| Mixed aviation regiment | 2 | 1 | 1 | 1 | 2 | 1 |
| Reconnaissance aviation regiment | 7 | 6 | 6 | 6 | 4 | 4 |
| Assault aviation regiment | 0 | 0 | 2 | 3 | 11 | 29 |
| Aviation regiment | | | | | | 6 |
| Total regiments | 15 | 20 | 28 | 46 | 97 | 249 |
| Mixed aviation brigade | 5 | 5 | 5 | 3 | 1 | 1 |
| Total brigades | 5 | 5 | 5 | 3 | 1 | 1 |

Source: *Boevoi sostav Sovetskoi armii*, 7–14.

Table 1.9. Red Army Strength and Losses, 22 June to 31 December 1941

| Date | Strength | | Losses (cumulative) | |
|---|---|---|---|---|
| | Personnel | Formations | Personnel | Formations |
| 22 June 1941 | 5,373,000 | 303 | | |
| 31 August 1941 | 6,889,000 | 450 | 2,500,000 (est.) | 80 (est.) |
| 31 December 1941 | 8,000,000 (est.) | 592 | 4,308,094 | 229 |

Note: Formations include two brigades counted as one division.
Source: Strength as of September 1941, according to *TsPA, UML* [Party archives], f. 644, op. 1, g. 9, 1. 50. Similar records for March 1942, show ration strength as 4,663,697 for field forces and 4,934,105 in nonoperating forces (less hospitalizations). Formation count from *Boevoi sostav Sovetskoi armii.*

CHAPTER 2

# Command and Control
# and Command Personnel

Although the Soviet strategic command and control system met peacetime demands, in no way did it meet the demands of war.[1] No Stavka or High Command or any other strategic system of command posts or communications centers existed in peacetime. Three organizations bore responsibility for implementing partial mobilization, insuring force readiness, and carrying out strategic deployment of forces on the eve of war. The People's Commissariat of Defense (NKO), under Marshal S. K. Timoshenko but closely supervised by Stalin and the Communist Party Politburo, articulated overall military defense policy and approved or rejected specific force readiness measures. The General Staff, headed by Army General G. K. Zhukov, which had drafted formal mobilization, deployment, and war plans, had a key role in their implementation but could only act with NKO approval. Finally, the Military Councils in the military districts were responsible for maintaining the readiness of district forces and fulfilling General Staff plans, but only when specifically ordered to do so by the NKO.

On the eve of war, the NKO was in the midst of carrying out an extensive and complex military reform program in concert with the General Staff and military district commanders. The General Staff was actively working on equally complex revisions of mobilization and war plans. Both organizations functioned within an immensely complex political context at a time when the military policy of the Soviet Union as defined by Stalin was charting a treacherous course between peace and war. Stalin's political guidance during 1940 and 1941, which often reflected conflicting policies, sharp political turns, and perhaps even confusion as to what security situation those policies would ultimately produce, constrained the work of both the NKO and the General Staff. In fact, these political uncertainties produced noticeable paralysis and confusion in the military reform programs themselves and in many ways negated the presumed benefits of the reforms.

Nowhere was this paralysis clearer than in the western border military districts. There, the military district commanders and their Military Councils were directly responsible for maintaining force readiness, carrying out all aspects of the reform programs, implementing current defensive and mobilization plans, and insuring the security of the Soviet Union's borders. These conscientious leaders were burdened with multiple responsibilities, and

25

confusion and uncertainty at the top made the accomplishment of their tasks that much more difficult. In 1941, because their forces occupied relatively exposed positions along the Soviet Union's borders, these commanders were keenly aware of growing external threats and appreciated the urgency of completing reform, increasing force readiness, and implementing necessary defensive plans. Starkly aware of the combat capability of their forces and equally cognizant of the capabilities of their prospective foes, these commanders struggled to fulfill their missions within the constraints imposed from above.

Although partial mobilization was under way in the Soviet Union in spring 1941, the mobilization plan functioned poorly and was full of defects, and the war plans which governed that mobilization were equally flawed. In addition, frequent changes in command personnel at the highest level of military leadership fostered uncertainty in planning and lowered the overall quality of strategic leadership.

Operational force command and control organs, prospective wartime *fronts* and armies, were also insufficiently prepared for war, both in terms of their organizational structure and in terms of personnel training and readiness. Since 1937, the military purges had created immense turbulence in command personnel, and most who occupied command positions were neither trained nor experienced enough to perform their assigned functions effectively. Prepared to command regiments and battalions, they were now called upon to command *fronts*, armies, and corps. The same conditions reduced the effectiveness of staffs at all levels.

Finally, on the eve of war, most formations lacked complete and up-to-date mobilization and operational plans, since those plans were constantly being revised. Military district staff sections, constrained by higher authorities, had not thoroughly analyzed the existing military situation and had not established necessary command and control organs. They were unable to conduct proper intelligence collection and analysis, establish required command communications nets, or knit troops from various arms and services into a single combat effective force. Consequently, when war broke out, command organs were forced to improvise against the most experienced army in Europe, with understandably disastrous results.

## THE CONTINUING PURGES

Nothing had a more debilitating effect on the prewar Red Army than the military purges that commenced in 1937 and continued unabated through 1941. These purges were part of a continuous "cleansing" process that dated back to the end of the Civil War and that sought to eradicate "old thinking" from the ranks of the Red Army. After its formation in 1918, the Red Army contained a high percentage of "military experts" whose service with the old tsarist army provided an essential leavening of experience necessary for the Red Army to operate successfully. Debates had raged throughout the 1920s and early 1930s over the presence of these officers in an army that was, supposedly, in the "vanguard" of revolution. After the expulsion from the Soviet leadership of Commissar of War L. D. Trotsky, who had been the principal defender of the "military experts," and the rise to power of I. V. Stalin, the cleansing of the army began.

It was a slow and increasingly violent process. From the mid-1920s through the mid-1930s, 47,000 officers, most of them with previous service in the tsarist army, were forced from service, and more than 3,000 of these were "repressed," a euphemism for being found guilty of criminal behavior or performance.[2] As the political and economic purges seized hold of the Soviet leadership in the 1930s, largely related to Stalin's consolidation of power, it was inevitable that the purges would ultimately engulf the military. They did so with a vengeance when military purge trials suddenly commenced in 1937.

The official announcement of the first secret military purge trials came as a surprise. Less than two years before, the military seemed to be riding high. On 22 September 1935, and on 30 December for the Navy, a Council of People's Commissars decree reintroduced ranks into the armed forces from marshal of the Soviet Union through army, corps, and brigade commander (first and second rank), to lieutenant. In November, V. K. Bliukher, S. M. Budenny, K. E. Voroshilov, A. I. Egorov, and M. N. Tukhachevsky received the rank of marshal, and I. P. Belov, S. S. Kamenev, I. P. Uborovich, B. M. Shaposhnikov, and I. E. Iakir became army commanders first rank. By 1936 the Red Army contained 16 army commanders (5 first and 11 second rank), 62 corps commanders, 201 division commanders, 474 brigade commanders, 1,713 colonels, 5,501 majors, 14,369 captains, 26,082 senior lieutenants, and 58,582 lieutenants.[3]

All of these senior and many junior commanders were experienced combat veterans, and not a few were preeminent military theorists in their own right who had orchestrated an intellectual revolution in the Red Army and made it one of the largest and, at least potentially, most technically advanced armed forces in Europe. In early 1937, as NKVD arrests of political leaders "for propagandizing counterrevolutionary Trotskyite views" accelerated, the first lesser military figures disappeared without announcement in the press. These arrests, however, in no way prepared the military for what was about to follow.

On 1 June 1937, a statement appeared in the "Chronicle" section of several newspapers that the chief of the RKKA Political Directorate and the first deputy people's commissar of defense of the USSR, Ia. B. Gamarnik, "having become entangled in his ties with anti-Soviet elements and, obviously, fearing disclosure, on 31 May ended his life by suicide."[4] Days later, on 11 June, the USSR procurator issued a press release:

> The investigation of the case of Marshal of the Soviet Union M. N. Tuk-hachevsky, Army Commanders 1st Rank I. E. Iakir and I. P. Uborovich, Army Commander 2d Rank A. I. Kork, Corps Commanders V. M. Primakov, V. K. Putna, B. M. Feldman, and R. P. Eideman, who had been arrested at various times by NKVD organs, has been completed and turned over to the courts. The named were accused of violating military duty (oath), of betraying their motherland, betraying the peoples of the USSR, and be-traying the RKKA. On the same day, a closed court session was held of the Special Court appointed by the USSR Supreme Court. All the defendants were stripped of their military ranks and sentenced to the highest criminal punishment of execution.[5]

A report from the U.S. Army military attaché in Moscow, Lieutenant Colonel Philip R. Faymonville, confirmed this:

> The Soviet press of 11 June 1937 carried announcements to the effect that eight important commanders of the Red Army had been arrested, charged with treason in maintaining communication with the espionage agencies of a foreign government. The announcement was unexpected, although rumors of secret investigations had been current in Moscow for weeks. The foreign government whose espionage agents were alleged to have been in touch with the accused was not named. From editorials and unmistakable references, however, it became clear that the accused were charged with treasonable dealings with the German secret police. . . .
> The entire case appears to have been settled in the secret session of 11 June. At 11:45 p.m., 11 June, radio broadcasts announced that all the accused had pleaded guilty and had been condemned to be deprived of all military rank and shot. The Soviet press of this morning, 12 June, re-peats this information. While no announcement has yet been made that the sentences have been carried into effect, there can be little doubt that the accused have already been executed.[6]

On 14 June, the People's Commissariat of Defense (NKO) published Order No. 96, dated 12 June, which addressed all RKKA personnel and stated that from 1 through 4 June, a military council was held in the presence of the NKO and government members. During the session they heard and discussed a report by the People's commissar of defense, K. E. Voroshilov, about the "traitorous counterrevolutionary military fascistic organization" uncovered by the NKVD. The organization was "strictly conspiratorial and had existed for a long time and had conducted ignoble subversive wrecking and espionage work in the Red Army."[7] A 17 June report by the U.S. military attaché in Moscow succinctly summarized the potential effects of the new purge. In a preface to a new report, he wrote, "The recent execution of eight former commanders of high rank in the Red Army and the suicide of a ninth are evidence of a crisis in the military forces of the Soviet Union which is probably more serious than any disturbance in the Red Army since the Revolution."[8]

The ensuing purge did not end in June 1937. Instead, it broadened to encompass all those in the former circles of the initially condemned. The effect on the army was catastrophic, especially in light of the wholesale expansion of the armed forces, which was occurring at the same time as the purges. So serious and rapid were the losses that the Voroshilov General Staff Academy class of 1937 had to be released early to fill command and staff vacancies. Of the 138-man class, 68 were assigned to key command and staff positions; another 60 were themselves purged and shot.

The Soviets attempted to make up for the losses through accelerated promotion of junior officers. From 1 March 1937 through 1 March 1938, the Red Army promoted 39,090 officers, including 12 to military district command, 35 to corps command, 116 to divisional and brigade command, and 490 to regimental and squadron command. After this wholesale shift to new commanders, the average age of regimental commanders was 29 to 33 years, divisional commanders 35 to 38 years, and corps and army commanders 40 to 43 years.[9] At the same time, the promotion rate to higher command positions increased markedly. From 1 March 1937 through 1 March 1938, promotions amounted to 1 army commander 1st rank, 5 army commanders 2d rank, 30 corps commanders, 71 division commanders, 257 brigade commanders, 1,346 colonels, and 5,220 majors. On the other hand, from 9 February 1939 through 4 April 1940, 20 corps commanders received promotion to army commander 2d rank (admittedly during the Finnish War). On 7 May 1940, the NKO appointed S. K. Timoshenko, G. I. Kulik, and B. M. Shaposhnikov as marshals of the Soviet Union.[10] Aside from the new marshals, few of the new commanders had any combat experience.

The purges also created tremendous command turbulence, which inevitably had a catastrophic effect on planning and force combat readiness. For example, Air Force commander Army Commander 2d Rank Ia. I. Alksnis was executed in 1938, and his successor, Colonel General A. D. Loktionov, was arrested in 1939. His successor, Lieutenant General P. V. Rychagov, was also arrested, and the two were shot without trial in October 1941.[11] On the very eve of war, a distinguished group of senior officers was arrested (and shot in October). In addition to Loktionov, then commander of the Baltic Special Military District, Rychagov, this group included Lieutenant General Ia. V.

Smushkevich, deputy chief of the Red Army General Staff, Colonel General G. M. Shtern, chief of the Red Army's Air Defense Directorate, Major General G. K. Savchenko, deputy chief of the Red Army Artillery Directorate, Lieutenant General F. K. Arzhenukhin, chief of the Air Academy, Major General I. F. Skrier, deputy chief of Weaponry of the Main Air Force Directorate, and Major General I. I. Proskurov, former chief of the Red Army's Main Intelligence Directorate (GRU).

The roster of purged commanders included two deputy commissars of defense (Tukhachevsky and Egorov); chiefs of the Red Army training, air defense, intelligence, air force, artillery, signals, mobilization, education, and medical directorates; all 16 military district commanders; 90 percent of the military districts' deputy and assistant commanders, chiefs of staffs and chiefs of arms and services; 80 percent of corps and division commanders; and 91 percent of regimental commanders, their deputies, and chiefs of staff. This grisly toll amounted to 3 of 5 marshals of the Soviet Union, 2 of 4 army commanders 1st rank, 12 of 12 army commanders 2d rank, 60 of 67 corps commanders, 136 of 199 division commanders, and 221 of 397 brigade commanders.[12] Even the NKVD did not escape the wrath of Stalin, for more than 20,000 of these select men were purged, including 10,000 men from the internal and border forces.[13]

Some commanders miraculously escaped, only to be immediately engulfed in the Soviet-German war. On 17 August 1937, K. K. Rokossovsky, commander of the Leningrad Military District, was arrested, presumably because of his association with the purged Marshal Bliukher, and initially charged with sabotage and impairing combat readiness. Later Rokossovsky was accused of working for Polish and Japanese intelligence organs, but the absurdity of the charges was so evident at his trial that he avoided execution. Nevertheless, Rokossovsky sat for three years in NKVD internment, until his release on 22 March 1940. In an astonishing but characteristic turnabout, the NKO then appointed Rokossovsky to command 5th Cavalry Corps and, in 1941, the newly formed 9th Mechanized Corps. Future Army General A. V. Gorbatov, Corps Commander L. G. Petrovsky, and several others shared Rokossovsky's good fortune and escaped Stalin's grim reaper.

The purges were still under way when war began in 1941. The bizarre and now well-known case of General Merestkov is illustrative. K. A. Meretskov, a veteran of the Spanish Civil War, chief of staff of a number of military districts, and chief of the Red Army General Staff itself in fall 1940, was arrested in July 1941 for being a friend of the discredited and shot Western Front commander, General D. G. Pavlov. Meretskov was more fortunate than most. Although treated roughly in NKVD captivity, like Rokossovsky, fate smiled on Meretskov and he escaped the firing squad. Moreover, in September 1941 he was rehabilitated and returned to the front. Meretskov survived both Stalin and the war, and by 1945 he had been promoted to *front* command with the rank of marshal of the Soviet Union.

The continuing purge also consumed officers from states annexed into the Soviet Union (for example, Latvia, Lithuania, and Estonia). These officers had received Red Army commissions after Soviet seizure of the Baltic states. This number included Major General A. N. Krustyn'sh, commander of 24th Territorial Rifle Corps' 183d Rifle Division, Major General I. K. Chernius, another division commander, and Lieutenant General R. I. Kliavin'sh, the corps commander. Other former Baltic states military commanders were consumed by the purge during wartime.[14]

The final toll the purges exacted on the Red Army officer's corps is still unknown. At a 29 November 1938 NKO meeting, Voroshilov is recorded as saying, "During the course of the cleansing of the Red Army in 1937–1938, we purged more than 40,000 men"[15] This, of course, included every penalty from being shot to being personally censored. More recent assessments based on the records of the USSR Supreme Court and associated military tribunals place the total figure of repressed from 1937 to 1941 at 54,714.[16]

The impact of the purges on Red Army morale and combat readiness was devastating. Relatively unbiased foreign observers were forthright in their judgments and, as subsequent events would show, accurate. Faymonville, the U.S. military attaché in Moscow, wrote, "The execution of the eminent former leaders of the Red Army and the suicide of Gamarnik have produced in the Red Army a feeling of surprise amounting almost to stupefaction. Morale has received a serious blow. . . . It is probable that an entirely new draft of recruits will be required for the Red Army before it regains the high level of morale which it had attained before the trial."[17]

The U.S. military attaché in Riga quoted from a Latvian intelligence assessment that "the combat efficiency of the Soviet Army has suffered so heavily from the recent investigations and executions that the Soviet Regime realizes that it cannot become involved in a war and will make unlimited concessions to prevent a major war at this time."[18] The Latvians were correct in their judgment that the Soviets would avoid a war with a major power (like Germany) at all costs, but the purges did not deter Soviet action against lesser powers like Poland and Finland or local Soviet action against Japan. To the Latvian's consternation, the purges did not deter action against them in 1940 either. As they believed, however, and as the Finnish War would demonstrate, Red Army combat performance would be impaired.

The purges also clearly encouraged the Germans to act militarily against the Soviet Union. According to one retrospective Soviet assessment, "Hitler's military was ecstatic. The chief of the German General Staff, General von Beck, in assessing the military situation in the summer of 1938, said that the Russian Army could not be considered an armed force, for the bloody repressions had sapped its morale and had turned it into an inert military machine."[19] Subsequent Red Army performance in Poland and Finland did nothing to dispel this impression.

Within the Red Army, there were clear indicators that morale was in a parlous state. According to Red Army data, the suicide and accident rate among officers and soldiers rose precipitously in the second quarter of 1937, as compared with the previous year: 26.9 percent in the Leningrad Military District; 40 percent in the Belorussian Military District; 50 percent in the Kiev Military District; 90.9 percent in the Separate Red Banner Far Eastern Army; 133 percent in the Black Sea Fleet; 150 percent in the Khar'kov Military District; and 200 percent in the Pacific Fleet. Accident rates rose accordingly.[20] In addition, by 1938 drunkenness had become such a problem in the Red Army that, in December of that year, the NKO had to issue a special order "On Combating Drunkenness in the RKKA." The order required all regiments to convene conferences of all command and supervisory personnel to describe "forcefully" all drunken disorders and to condemn drunkenness and drunks as an inadmissible and shameful phenomenon.[21]

A letter later sent to the Soviet writer Ilia Ehrenburg by the famous publicist Ernst Genri captured the feeling of many: "No defeat has ever led to such monstrous losses in command personnel. Only the complete surrender of a nation after a lost war could have such a rout as a consequence. Precisely on the eve of the crucial clash with the Wehrmacht, on the eve of the greatest of wars, the Red Army was decapitated. This was done by Stalin."[22]

There is no doubt but that Stalin and the Soviet political hierarchy were well aware of the damage to the Red Army caused by the purges. At a May 1940 Moscow meeting chaired by the newly appointed people's commissar of defense, Marshal S. K. Timoshenko, Deputy Commissar I. I. Proskurov stated courageously, "However hard it is to do so, I must say directly that such laxness and a low level of discipline exist in no other army as ours (voices: Right!)."[23] It was not coincidental that Proskurov himself joined the ranks of the purged shortly before the outbreak of war. To counter some of the adverse consequences of the purges, on 12 August 1940 the Presidium of the USSR Supreme Soviet issued a decree, "On Strengthening One-Man Command in the Red Army and Navy." The decree abolished the hated institution of military commissars, which had been introduced in May 1937, and entrusted "full responsibility for all spheres of life and activity of subunits, units, and formations, including political work and political education and the state of discipline, into the hands of commanders."[24] One must note, however, that in the event the thoroughly cowered commanders deviated from proper performance, the position of deputy commander for political affairs was retained at all levels of command.

Undoubtedly the purges produced a Red Army whose loyalty to Stalin was unquestioned. That loyalty, however, was based largely on abject and paralyzing fear, which stifled any creativity, initiative, or flexibility within the Red Army's ranks. While ridding the Red Army of its most creative military thinkers and its most experienced practitioners of war, the purges also smothered the revolutionary traditions that had fired the enthusiasm of Red Army commanders and soldiers alike. Thereafter, a lifeless and wholly mechanical Red Army struggled ineptly and bled profusely on the battlefields of the Finnish War. It would do so again and in like fashion in the western Soviet Union in summer 1941. Ultimately, only German arrogance, ignominious Soviet defeats, and the threat of national destruction would ignite renewed Red Army combat enthusiasm, and that only after catastrophic losses and suffering. Even then the purges would leave an indelible mark on Soviet souls, a mark that could not be fully expunged until the ultimate demise of the Soviet state.

## COMMAND CADRE AND TRAINING

The purges and wholesale expansion of the Red Army between 1937 and 1941 placed immense strain on the Red Army combat training system. Not only did the tens of thousands of purged experienced officers and soldiers have to be replaced, but cadre had to be prepared to command, control, and man an army that more than doubled in size. Many of the new troops possessed only rudimentary training, which they had received while serving in the reserve or territorial units. A report prepared in December 1939 by the U.S. military attaché in Helsinki summed up Western impressions of the new Soviet soldiers based upon the lessons of the Finnish War:

> The morale of the Russian troops at the present time is a difficult thing to analyse. The soldiers are practically all peasants or common laborers, accustomed to a meager existence which would itself be unbearable to almost any other white race. They are fed with a constant stream of propaganda extolling the virtues of Communism and assuring them that they are making some sacrifices in the present in order that it may eventually triumph throughout the world. Being unbelievably simple-minded and kept in total ignorance of conditions outside Russia, many of them are actually almost fanatical in their zeal for what they have been led to believe is a holy crusade to rescue their own class from villainous oppressors. . . .
>
> The Finnish GHQ reports that Russian troops encountered to date have been of two distinct classes. More than half of them have been of inferior quality, badly clothed and equipped and poorly trained. These I

believe to be the so-called trained reserves recently mobilized and these reports are corroborated by reports previously received of Soviet troops fighting against the Japanese in Outer Mongolia. Certain Russian regiments, on the other hand, are reported to be well-trained and equipped. These are being used as shock troops in the more important attacks, or main efforts, and are said to conduct themselves very well in action, attacking bravely and skillfully and showing considerable tactical ability in their expedients to take the Finns by surprise.[25]

A particularly perceptive recent study by a Russian scholar noted the training deficiencies of both officers and men: "The main mass of enlisted recruits in a partial mobilization consisted of those who had undergone military training in territorial units and did not have firm professional skills. An inexperienced command element, and the rank and file's extended breaks from combat training for economic purposes, told extremely negatively on the results of combat and operational training. Figuratively speaking, there was no one to teach, no one to be taught, and nothing to teach with."[26] This wholesale force expansion would have been a daunting task under normal circumstances. The dangerous international climate, the extraordinary combat performance of the German Army, the less than stellar involvement of the Red Army in war, and the fear that gripped the Red Army made it even more difficult.

From 1939 through mid-June 1941, the number of Red Army ground force divisions increased from 98 to 303, and the overall size of the armed forces grew from 1.6 million to 5.3 million men. In 1937, 69,000 officers were replaced, in ten months of 1938, 100,000 received new assignments, and in 1939 246,626 officers (68 percent of the total) were reassigned.[27] In many instances, battalion commanders rose to command divisions and squad leaders rose to regimental command. In a speech to the Party Central Committee on the consequences of the Finnish War, Commissar of Defense Voroshilov noted that "many senior commanders did not prove to be at the required high level. The Stavka of the Main Military Council was forced to remove many higher commanders and chiefs of staff."[28]

A lengthy and thorough 20 March 1940 report by E. A. Shchadenko, the chief of the Red Army Cadres Directorate, to the NKO vividly outlined Red Army cadre problems. Shchadenko assessed the situation in 1938:

The Red Army began its expansion from 1932, the tempo of expansion has quickened, and by 1939 it grew almost four times. This expansion was not supported by normally prepared army cadres, since the capacity of training institutions remained as before. These conditions compelled us to turn to the reserves, which consist of:

a. 31 percent of junior lieutenants of the reserves, who formerly were trained for one year in the forces;

b. 24.3 percent of junior lieutenants who were trained in civilian military training in civilian schools, whose entire course of study consisted of 360 hours of theoretical studies and two two-month camps in the RKKA (four months—768 hours), and who have absolutely no practice in commanding;

c. 13.2 percent of junior lieutenants, who were trained in two-month reserve courses from junior command personnel in a 384-hour program; and

d. 4.5 percent of commanders, who completed a short-term course in school during the period of the Civil War.

In general, 73 percent of the reserves are junior lieutenants, that is, commanders with short-term training, who have not had the opportunity for systematic retraining.

In schools, as it is now apparent, study time has been criminally wasted; only 66 percent has been devoted to studies and necessary types of activities, and the remaining time (127 days per year) passed without organization, on interruptions, leaves, and holidays. . . . Students were left without required field exercises and training. As a result one must admit that the training of cadre, especially infantry, was extremely unfavorable. . . . Such a situation also exists with the training of junior officers in the army.

For six years (from 1932 to 1938), 29,966 men were taken from the reserves, and 19,147 junior lieutenants were retained in the cadre from former one-termers [soldiers] for a six-year total of 49,113 men, that is, as many as were produced by military schools during that time. These measures have not covered the rapidly growing army requirements either in a quantitative or, especially, in a qualitative respect.

A large shortage has formed, which on 1 January 1938 has reached 39,100 men, or 34.4 percent of the establishment requirements for command personnel. Organizational measures in 1938 demanded 33,900 men and another 20,000 men to replace those expelled from the RKKA and a total of 93,000 men. Thus, it is completely clear that in 1938 the army is lacking almost 100,000 men.

The call-up of a great quantity of reserves with short-term training completely fails to meet the growing demands for the technical reequipping of the army and has led to a sharp decrease in the quality of army cadres, which cannot fail to turn out to be adverse for the training of soldiers and junior officers, particularly in the infantry.[29]

Having shaped the problem the Red Army faced, Shchadenko reviewed the graduation record of military training institutions and focused directly on the adverse impact of the purges: "During these ten years [1928–1938], 62,000 men left the army (death, invalided, tried in court, or for other reasons), and 5,670 were taken away or transferred to the Air Force. Altogether, 67,670 commanders left the ground forces. It follows that the output of schools hardly covers the actual losses and has not created any sort of reserve to support the growth of the army and its reserves."[30]

Shchadenko underscored the particularly disturbing shortages in infantry commanders. He pointed out that infantry school output actually fell, while army requirements had risen sharply and would accelerate. Moreover, "If you take into account that during 1937–1938 35,000 were arrested, expelled from the Party, and thus left the RKKA in connection with the cleansing of the army, including 5,000 political workers, the situation with the infantry becomes still more aggravated."[31]

According to Shchadenko, the condition of the reserves was even more dangerous because it threatened to disrupt mobilization should it become necessary:

The situation with command personnel of the reserves is still more acute, and there are not sufficient infantry [in the reserves] even for a partial mobilization. At the same time, as the experience of combat at [Lake] Khasan, at Khalkhin-Gol, in western Belorussia and Ukraine, and on the Finnish front has shown, the quality of reserve commanders is very low. Moreover, 14.5 percent of the 73 percent of reserve commanders with short-term training and even 23 percent of the infantry [commanders] are 40 years old or older. The latter cannot be used in line units as platoon or company commanders, which they were in the reserves.

Regarding personnel in the reserves, they completely have not and, at present, do not cover losses of the first year of war and new formations during the course of war.

In summary, by 1938 the Red Army, as regards the provision of trained cadre, finds itself in an exceptionally difficult situation; the army is short 93,000 cadre and the reserves 300–350,000.[32]

Shchadenko then proposed a series of detailed measures to remedy the situation during 1939, 1940, and 1941. The three-year plan that he proposed was designed to produce a fully complete and competent cadre for the Red Army and its reserves, but not before 1942.

On 5 May 1939, Shchadenko presented another report to the NKO that described in detail the work done by his Cadres Directorate during 1939. He began the report by summarizing the major changes that had taken place within the Red Army during the year:

During the reporting period, and especially during August and September, a considerable number of new formations were introduced into the army, namely, 4 *front* administrations, 2 military district administrations, 8 armies, 19 rifle corps, 111 rifle divisions (containing 333 rifle regiments, 222 artillery regiments, and 555 separate battalions), 16 tank brigades, 12 reserve rifle brigades, 42 military schools, 52 courses for officer improvement, 85 reserve regiments, 137 separate battalions, not included in corps and divisions, 345 evacuation hospitals, and a number of rear service installations (forward warehouses, workshops, medical trains, medical detachments, etc.).

To conduct these measures required 117,188 command cadre or an increase of 40.8 percent over the strength on 1.1.1939. . . .

The bringing up to full strength of new formations, as well as the filling up of field army units in the east, west and northwest, required a large quantity of appointed and reassigned command personnel, whose total number amounted to 246,626 men, or 68.8 percent of establishment requirements.[33]

To satisfy this demand, school output had increased to a total of 101,147 personnel per year (from 13,995 in 1937 and 57,000 in 1938). Although shortages still existed, the system's efficiency had improved. Contrasting with these figures were the numbers of officers purged: 18,658 in 1937 (4,474 arrested); 16,362 in 1938 (5,032 arrested); and 1,878 in 1939 (73 arrested).[34] Shchadenko concluded, "The missions assigned by you [Voroshilov] to the Red Army Cadres Directorate in 1939 in the main are basically fulfilled."[35] He claimed that the 1939 plan for cadre training and filling out field units had been successful, and the directorate was prepared to work on the 1940 plan. Given the figures, however, it was clear that the Red Army would not be ready for combat in 1941, nor was there any assurance that the quality of officers produced by the accelerated training courses met required standards.

The proof of Shchadenko's excessuve optimism is found in a document produced a year later under the name of the outgoing people's commissar of defense in conjunction with his successor. On 8 May 1940, the outgoing people's commissar of defense, K. E. Voroshilov, presented an *akt o prieme* (document of reception) to his successor, S. K. Timoshenko. The *akt* was a formal document detailing the condition of the Red Army (armed forces) when it was transferred into Timoshenko's hands. Although signed by Voroshilov, the report was clearly prepared by his critics in the service of the incoming commissar. Under the rubric of "Operational Preparations," the *akt* began with scathing criticism:

1. At the moment of the handover and reception of the People's Commissariat of Defense, there was no operational war plan, and both

general and partial operational plans were not worked out and were absent.

The General Staff had no information about the state of covering the borders. The decisions of the military district, army, and *front* military councils on this question were unknown to the General Staff.

2. The direction of operational training of senior command personnel and staffs is expressed only in planning for it and in directives. From 1938 the People's Commissariat of Defense and the General Staff, themselves, have not conducted work with senior command personnel and staffs. Control over operational training in the districts was almost absent. The People's Commissariat of Defense lost touch with the working out of questions on the operational use of forces in modern war.

3. The preparation of the theater of military operations in war was weak in every respect. As a result:

   a. The VOSO [military communications service] did not demonstrate required flexibility [maneuverability] in the matter of exploiting existing rail means for troop transfers. . . .
   b. The construction of main roads goes on slowly and is conducted by many organs. . . .
   c. The construction of communications along NKS [People's Commissariat of Communications] lags, and along NKO lines in 1940 was completely absent as a result of delivery of construction materials by representatives of the General Staff and Communications Directorate.[36]

On and on went the *akt*, condemning the poor work of Voroshilov's commissariat. It criticized the "extremely weak" airfield network in the border military districts, the lack of a "clear and precise plan for preparing the theater in an engineer sense," the lack of directives to implement the 1940 plan for constructing fortified regions, and the absence of requisite maps to support operations in the theater.

Even more damning were the comments on the Red Army force structure, mobilization planning, and the state of Red Army cadre. The *akt* admitted that "the commissariat had no exact determination of the factual strength of the Red Army," "the calculation of personnel, through the fault of the Red Army Main Directorate, was in an exceptionally neglected state," the personnel composition of forces was unclear, and the plan to expel personnel was in the process of being worked out.[37] It noted that all recent plans to replace cadre and construct forces were incomplete and badly administered.

Mobilization plans were in similar disarray. Thus, "in connection with the war and the significant restationing of forces, the mobilization plan has been violated." The *akt* identified many shortcomings in mobilization plans and concluded that the People's Commissariat of Defense had not "reworked instructions for mobilization work in forces," and that existing instructions were obsolete.[38] Regarding Shchadenko's optimistic reports on the formation of Red Army cadre, the *akt* stated that "the army had a considerable shortage of command personnel, especially infantry, reaching 21 percent of establishment strength on 1 May 1941."[39] Moreover, it judged that yearly accessions would not create necessary reserves to support necessary Red Army growth. It went on to confirm suspicions about officer quality: "The quality of command personnel training is low, particularly at the level of platoon and company, where up to 68 percent have only the short-term six-month training course for junior lieutenants." After condemning other aspects of the system, the *akt* concluded, "There was no plan for training and filling up reserve command personnel for full mobilization of the army in wartime."[40]

Contradicting Shchadenko's claims for improved training, the *akt* then listed the legion of shortcomings in force training, noting "low quality training of mid-level officers," "weak tactical training for all types of combat and reconnaissance," "unsatisfactory field training," "extremely poor coordination of forces in combat," "faulty camouflage . . . , fire control . . . , and tactics for attacking fortified regions, overcoming obstacles and forcing rivers."[41] Finally, the act catalogued in detail the many deficiencies found in all types of forces and in rear services.

Although the *akt* was prepared in 1940, and the new commissar of defense, Timoshenko, subsequently instituted a sweeping reform program designed to eradicate the problems, the detailed list of Red Army deficiencies that it contained precisely presaged the difficulties the Red Army would encounter in June 1941, in particular regarding the strength, condition, and training state of Red Army cadres.

In the wake of Voroshilov's and Timoshenko's joint report and during the course of the Timoshenko reforms, the NKO attempted to improve the Red Army education and training system. At its highest level, it continued efforts to beef up instruction at the Voroshilov Academy of the General Staff. A series of short higher commanders' courses, which the NKO added to the curriculum between 1938 and 1940, produced 400 graduates in 1939 and 1940 alone. In addition, a 25 February 1941 NKO order expanded the Zhukovsky Air Academy, created the Mozhaisky Air Academy in Leningrad, and formed a new PVO school. By May 1941, 18 military academies existed, supplemented by hundreds of lower-level military schools. The total establishment strength of military academy faculties grew from 9,189 officers in 1937 to 20,315 in 1940.[42]

During the period 1937 through 1940, the total number of military educational and training institutions rose from 49 to 114, and the number of graduates increased from 36,085 to 169,620.[43] Despite, and perhaps because of, this increased production of trained officers and accelerated promotions due to the purges, few officers had combat experience, and most were fresh to their new tasks. Thus, in 1941, 5.8 percent of command personnel had Civil War experience (which often was of questionable value), and 29 percent had combat experience from 1938 to 1940. Table 2.1, p. 55, shows the relative command experience of commanders in June 1941.

Based on these data concerning command military experience, one recent Russian assessment concluded:

> Immense work was done in the prewar years to prepare military cadres in all specialties. As a result, a large number of officers had fair professional training and were committed to the Communist Party and Socialist Homeland. Among these were distinguished military leaders and commanders who, during the war, covered themselves with the unfading glory of victory. At the same time, the massive repression against military cadres and the death of many higher-level military leaders led to a weakening of the officer's corps, had a telling effect on the combat capability of the armed forces, and was one of the reasons for the defeat in the initial period of war. It was also felt throughout the entire duration of the war.[44]

The training program for Red Army cadre and soldiers, which had received lip service in 1938 and 1939, accelerated thereafter, largely due to dismal Soviet combat performance in the Finnish War. The looming international threats and the resulting expansion of the Red Army lent urgency to the task. The Timoshenko programs were ambitious and well thought out, but they were also too late. Human and technical resources were insufficient to support the program, and the dislocations produced in the Red Army during 1940 and 1941, first by the occupation of Polish, Baltic, and Rumanian territory and then by the partial mobilization of spring 1941, destroyed coherent training and all scale of exercises.

As a result, commanders were unfamiliar with their forces and modern tactical and operational techniques, staffs were understrength and unaccustomed to performing as teams, units and formations had not been welded together into coherent combat forces, and service arms were not able to function together. Combat and combat support personnel had not mastered the new equipment coming into the inventory (tanks, aircraft, artillery) and were not prepared to function in the partially formed new combat and combat support systems. Compounding these problems, because they were imbued with the traditional offensive spirit of the Red Army, all levels of command had little notion of the requirements of defensive battle. This they would learn, but at tremendous cost and personal sacrifice. In short, in the words of one perceptive critic, "The Soviet military and political leadership, having considered a military clash with world imperialism inescapable and having equipped the army with a huge quantity of the basic means of armed struggle, had not troubled themselves about the creation of a necessary reserve of command cadres and, instead, concerned themselves with the slaughter of them, which led not only to a deficit of them, but also created in the army an atmosphere of fear, suspicion, distrust, and a dread of any display of independence and initiative."[45]

## KEY COMMAND AND STAFF PERSONNEL

In June 1941 the Red Army was commanded and staffed largely by cronies of Stalin and inexperienced or partially experienced survivors. The former owed their careers and well-being to their long association with the autocrat. The survivors, knowing full well the fate of their former comrades, lived in a perpetual state of anxiety. Undoubtedly, many among them were thoroughly competent and despised the circumstances in which they lived, and many of these would demonstrate their competence and loyalty during war. Others, like A. A. Vlasov, would avail themselves of the first opportunity to strike back at the regime. But all shared a common state in June 1941, a fatalistic determination to survive their times, at whatever cost.

It was perhaps ironic that in 1941, in spite of the purges, the Red Army officer corps was blessed with a modest number of talented, if only partially experienced, staff officers and a nucleus of capable combat commanders who survived the initial bloodletting and subsequently led the Red Army to victory. It is important to remember that for each of these who achieved fame, there were many others of equal talent who perished and many other sycophants (or less competent commanders) who made the job that much more difficult and costly for the Red Army. Most of the competent ones began their rise to prominence during and because of the Timoshenko reforms.

At the apex of the Soviet military hierarchy in June 1941 was Marshal of the Soviet Union Semen Konstantinovich Timoshenko, who had succeeded the talentless K. I. Voroshilov as people's commissar of defense on 8 May 1940. Timoshenko earned his spurs as commissar (and as a Hero of the Soviet Union) in the embarrassing Finnish War. As the organizer of the February 1940 offensive that drove the Finns from the war, he partially restored the badly tarnished reputation of the Red Army. A former cavalryman and crony of Stalin during the Civil War, Timoshenko received the daunting task of reinvigorating the Red Army on the eve of war. He attempted to carry out the reforms that have since born his name amid paralyzing purges and immense international uncertainties and plagued by the personal vicissitudes of Stalin.

G. K. Zhukov, then Timoshenko's chief of the Red Army General Staff, later defended Timoshenko as an old and experienced war leader, stubborn, strong-willed, and well versed in tactical and operational terms. "He was," said Zhukov, "far better than Voroshilov as defense commissar, and in the short time that he held that post the army started to improve."[46] Zhukov added that Timoshenko had never fawned on Stalin, and despite the series of fiascoes Timoshenko later presided over in 1941 and at Khar'kov in May 1942, Timoshenko survived and, at war's end, received the Order of Victory for his services to the state.

Timoshenko was assisted by the deputy people's commissar of defense, Boris Mikhailovich Shaposhnikov. This former tsarist officer, well known for his theoretical prowess and independence, had been instrumental in creating the post–Civil War Red Army and had clashed with Tukhachevsky over the interpretation of the latter's failed Vistula campaign in 1920. This, plus his reputation as a "top-notch military commander . . . unequaled for erudition, professional skill and intellectual development" and his love for cavalry, conditioned his survival and rise to prominence as chief of the Red Army General Staff in spring 1937, a post he held with brief interruptions until August 1940, when he became deputy defense commissar. Shaposhnikov had been admitted to the Communist Party in 1930, and the XVIII Party Congress had elected him a candidate member of the Communist Party Central Committee.[47] Shaposhnikov's massive work, The Brain of the Army (Mozg armii), had prompted creation of the Red Army General Staff in 1935. Never ideological (he was admitted into the Party in 1939), Shaposhnikov often disagreed with Stalin regarding Soviet defense strategy, including prewar Soviet defense planning, but nevertheless survived, probably because Stalin did not fear the erudite staff officer and, in fact, respected his nonthreatening candor. Shaposhnikov enjoyed a strange relationship with Stalin; he was one of the few whom Stalin addressed by his first name and patronymic.

Shaposhnikov returned to the post of chief of the Red Army General Staff in July 1941, and thereafter, until his replacement for health reasons in May 1942, he served as architect of the newly organized General Staff, which provided wartime victory. During wartime he proved to be a moderating influence on Stalin, and although he was associated with the Kiev disaster of September 1941, his influence ultimately caused Stalin to defer to General Staff leadership of the war effort.

The chief of the Red Army General Staff in June 1941 was Army General Georgi Konstantinovich Zhukov, a veteran cavalry officer in the World and Civil Wars, former commander of the Kiev Special Military District, where Vatutin served as his chief of staff, and hero of the August 1939 battle against the Japanese at Khalkhin-Gol. Zhukov had rocketed to higher command after 1937 despite his respect for such purged commanders as Uborovich and Egorov, under whom he served. He became Kiev Special Military District commander in June 1940 and played an influential part in the January 1941

Moscow war games, at the end of which, due to his vigorous and skilled performance, he replaced K. A. Meretskov as chief of the Red Army General Staff. Thereafter, under Shaposhnikov's attentive tutelage, Zhukov worked closely with his deputies Vatutin and G. K. Malandin and with A. M. Vasilevsky, first deputy chief of the Operations Directorate, to develop more coherent war and mobilization plans. Despite the threatening example of the purges, Zhukov dealt as forcefully as possible with Stalin, and it was at his urgings that Stalin undertook the partial secret mobilization prior to the war. Apparently, Zhukov advocated more active measures, but these Stalin rejected.

Zhukov was an energetic but stubborn commander. He approached war with dogged determination. His force of will, tempered with occasional ruthlessness and utter disregard for casualties, carried Soviet forces through their trials in the initial period of war and ultimately to victory. Like the American Grant, he understood the terrible nature of modern war and was psychologically prepared to wage it. He demanded and received absolute obedience to orders, he identified and protected key subordinates, and, at times, he stood up to and incurred the wrath of Stalin. There was little finesse in his operations, and he skillfully used the Red Army as the club it was to its full operational effect. His temperament was perfectly suited to the nature of the war on the Soviet-German front, and Stalin knew it. For this reason alone, he, Stalin, and the Red Army emerged victorious, despite immense casualties.

Zhukov's first deputy was Lieutenant General N. F. Vatutin, graduate of the truncated General Staff Academy class of 1937, former chief of staff of the Kiev Special Military District, and former chief of the General Staff's Operations Directorate. Described by his contemporaries as the quintessential staff officer, Vatutin cherished a desire to command. The energetic Vatutin had planned the incursion into Poland in September 1939 and Rumanian Bessarabia in June 1940. Because of his stellar performance, he was then brought into the General Staff, where he was instrumental in war and mobilization planning under Zhukov's, Timoshenko's, and Shaposhnikov's guidance and reworked Red Army regulations. When war broke out, over Vatutin's protests, Stalin used him as his personal representative in key threatened sectors.

Zhukov described Vatutin "as a man of exceptional industry and broad strategic thinking." When Vatutin finally rose to *front* command, Vasilevsky noted his enormous skill in handling combined operations. Vatutin, who proved to be one of the Red Army's most competent and audacious field commanders, was mortally wounded in spring 1944.

The chief of the General Staff's Operations Directorate was a 1938 graduate of the General Staff Academy, Lieutenant General German Kapitonovich Malandin, a professional staff officer who had served as chief of staff in infantry units at all levels of command, finally serving for four years as corps chief of staff in the Far East (1930–1935). After graduating from and teaching at the General Staff Academy in 1938 and 1939, Malandin was appointed Zhukov's deputy chief of staff in the Kiev Military District (under Vatutin), where he helped plan the military operations in Poland and Bessarabia in 1939 and 1940. Thereafter, in February 1941, Malandin went with Zhukov to the General Staff, where he worked closely with Vatutin and Vasilevsky on Red Army prewar planning. When war began, Timoshenko took Malandin with him as Western Direction chief of staff. Later, Malandin served as Zhukov's chief of staff during the defense of Moscow.

We best know of this professionally competent staff officer's work from the surviving reports he prepared while serving as Western Direction and Western Front chief of staff during the trying combat of 1941. Future Chief of the General Staff S. M. Shtemenko described Malandin as "a very balanced and very courteous person, exceptionally modest and cordial. He devoted himself to his work utterly and completely and was able to cope with the most difficult task. He enjoyed great respect at the General Staff for his unfailing punctuality and the depth of his analysis of the situation. He too became one of our top military scientists and headed the General Staff Academy."[48] Although he needed these qualities to survive, they did not grant him lasting fame.

Malandin's deputy in the Operations Directorate was Aleksandr Mikhailovich Vasilevsky, perhaps the most skilled officer the Red Army produced during the war. An infantryman who did not enjoy the benefits of belonging to the "cavalry clique," Vasilevsky rose through merit alone and joined the General Staff after his graduation from the General Staff Academy in the truncated class of 1937. He too worked on defense plans and mobilization plans in the months preceding war. Rising from colonel to colonel general in four years, Vasilevsky was essentially Shaposhnikov's favorite and his heir apparent in the General Staff. Vasilevsky's even temperament and intellectual keenness balanced the sheer power and crudeness of Zhukov, and throughout the war the two made a superb team of effective Stavka troubleshooters, representatives, and commanders.[49] At war's end, Vasilevsky was elevated to theater command and planned and conducted the Manchurian operation against the Japanese. Among staff officers, no one contributed more than Vasilevsky, Vatutin, and their protégé, A. I. Antonov, to the defeat of Nazi Germany.

Whereas Vatutin, Malandin, and Vasilevsky began the war in key staff positions, Alexei Innokentievich Antonov, the future leading figure in the Red Army General Staff, began the war in relative obscurity. A veteran of the World and Civil Wars, Antonov remained relatively obscure until his attendance at several Frunze Academy courses in the early 1930s, where he was recognized as "an excellent operations staff worker."[50] His superb performance as chief of the Khar'kov Military District's Operations Department during the 1935 Kiev maneuvers earned for Antonov the praises of Defense Commissar Voroshilov and an appointment to the General Staff Academy, where he too graduated in the class of 1937. Upon graduation Antonov briefly became Moscow Military District chief of staff under Stalin's favorite, Budenny, and was then posted to the Frunze Academy to replace purged faculty members.

Promoted to major general in June 1940 (with Vasilevsky and many others), during the wholesale command changes of January 1941, Antonov replaced Malandin as Kiev Military District deputy chief of staff, where he was serving when war began. After Antonov took part in the ignominious defeats in 1941 and at Khar'kov in May 1942, in December 1942 Vasilevsky brought Antonov into the General Staff as chief of the Operations Division, where his work would earn him everlasting fame and praise from all who knew or worked with him.

The tragic course of the initial period of war severely tested prewar Soviet military district commanders, and as victims of fate, few survived the test. Colonel General Mikhail Petrovich Kirponos rose from 70th Rifle Division commander during the Finnish War to command the Kiev Special Military District in January 1941. A World War I veteran, Kirponos had been chief of staff of the famous 51st Rifle Division during the storming of the Crimea in the Civil War, attended the General Staff Academy in 1923, and was chief of the Kazan' Infantry School from 1934 to 1939. After service in combat at Lake Khasan and Khalkhin-Gol in the Far East, and in the Finnish War, Kirponos commanded a corps, the Leningrad Military District, and in February 1941 the Kiev Special Military District, where he was serving when war began.[51]

Zhukov praised Kirponos in his memoirs: "I was pleased that the Kiev Special Military District was entrusted to such a worthy commander. Naturally, like many others, he still lacked the knowledge and experience essential to command such a big frontier district, but, nonetheless, his past experience, industriousness, and resourcefulness were a guarantee that Kirponos would be a first-class field commander."[52] Kirponos proved Zhukov correct. He struggled (largely in vain) with the High Command to increase preparedness for war, and when war began his forces acquitted themselves better in often futile combat than the forces of other *front* commanders. Kirponos died in the Kiev encirclement with much of his *front* in September 1941 and was denied the fame he so richly deserved.

Kirponos's colleague in command of the Western Special Military District was Army General Dmitri Grigor'evich Pavlov, also a World War I and Civil War veteran (and prisoner of war). Pavlov was a cavalry officer who attended the Frunze Academy in 1928 and the Military-Technical Academy in 1931, where he is reported to have "actively combated Trotskyites."[53] Upon graduation, Pavlov commanded one of the Red Army's first mechanized units, the 4th Mechanized Brigade, and then, in 1937, rose to head the Red Army's Armored Directorate, where he earned the misplaced sobriquet, "the Soviet Guderian." During the Spanish Civil War, Pavlov was sent to Spain to experi-

The Red Army High Command (clockwise): Marshal of the Soviet Union S. K.
Timoshenko, People's Commissar of Defense; Marshal of the Soviet Union B. M.
Shaposhnikov, Deputy People's Commissar of Defense; Army General G. K. Zhukov, Chief
of the Red Army General Staff; and Lieutenant General N. F. Vatutin, First Deputy Chief
of the Red Army General Staff.

The Red Army High Command, *continued:* Lieutenant General G. K. Malandin, Chief of the Operations Directorate, Red Army General Staff (left); and Major General A. M. Vasilevsky, Deputy Chief of the Operations Directorate, Red Army General Staff (right).

Military district commands: Colonel General M. P. Kirponos, Commander, Kiev Special Military District (left); and Major General A. I. Antonov, Chief of Staff, Kiev Special Military District (right).

Military district commands, *continued* (clockwise): Lieutenant General M. F. Lukin, Commander, 16th Army, Kiev Special Military District; Colonel General F. I. Kuznetsov, Commander, Baltic Special Military District; and Army General D. G. Pavlov, Commander, Western Special Military District.

Military district commands, *continued* (clockwise): Lieutenant General P. P. Sobennikov, Commander, 8th Army, Baltic Special Military District; Lieutenant General V. I. Morozov, Commander, 11th Army, Baltic Special Military District; Major General N. E. Berzarin, Commander, 27th Army, Baltic Special Military District; and Lieutenant General V. I. Kuznetsov, Commander, 3d Army, Western Special Military District.

Military district commands, *continued* (clockwise): Lieutenant General A. A. Korobkov, Commander, 4th Army, Western Special Military District; Lieutenant General K. D. Golubev, Commander, 10th Army, Western Special Military District; Lieutenant General P. A. Kurochkin, Commander, Orel Military District and 20th Army; and Lieutenant General I. N. Muzychenko, Commander, 6th Army, Kiev Special Military District.

Military district commands, *continued* (clockwise): Major General P. A. Rotmistrov, Chief of Staff, 3d Mechanized Corps, Baltic Special Military District; Brigade Commissar N. V. Shatalov, Commissar, 2d Tank Division, Baltic Special Military District; Colonel M. E. Katukov, Commander, 20th Tank Division, 9th Mechanized Corps, Kiev Special Military District; and Colonel S. I. Bogdanov, Commander, 30th Tank Division, 14th Mechanized Corps, Western Special Military District.

ment with the combat use of armored forces, and he returned with a more sober view of the utility of armor in modern combat, a view that contributed to the Red Army's abandonment of large mechanized formations in late 1939. In 1940 Pavlov received command of the Western Special Military District and later participated in the January 1941 Moscow war games, where his performance was rated as less than stellar.

When war began, Pavlov fell victim to Stalin's wrath after he lost control of a situation that perhaps no one could have controlled. Stalin accused Pavlov of treachery, removed him from command, and had him shot. The tragic fate of Pavlov remains a wartime vestige of the unrelenting purge.

Colonel General Fedor Isidorovich Kuznetsov was the third major border military district commander on the eve of war. A World War I and Civil War veteran infantry officer, in 1926 Kuznetsov attended the Frunze Academy, where he was recognized for his combat skill and potential. In July 1938, after service on the faculty of the Moscow Infantry School and Frunze Academy, he was appointed deputy commander of the Belorussian Special Military District and helped orchestrate the invasion of eastern Poland. Later in the year he commanded a corps in the Finnish War. A case study in Soviet command turbulence, in 1940 Kuznetsov briefly headed the General Staff Academy, then took command of the North Caucasus Military District, and finally the Baltic Special Military District late in the year.

Rewarded with the rank of colonel general in February 1941, Kuznetsov also struggled in vain with the High Command to improve district force readiness and, on the eve of war, undertook measures of his own to improve district defenses. Although his forces were routed in June and July 1941, and Kuznetsov was relegated to army command, he survived the ordeal and later served as deputy *front* commander and head of the General Staff Academy.[54]

Army command in the Red Army of 1941 was a thankless and often fatal task. Among the surviving army commanders, two examples must suffice. On 22 June 1941, Lieutenant General Mikhail Fedorovich Lukin commanded Soviet 16th Army, a Stavka reserve army raised in the Far East in June 1940 and transferred West in April and May 1941 as part of an initial strategic reserve. Lukin's career is representative of many army commanders' preparation and combat fate. An NCO in World War I, Lukin had commanded a rifle regiment and brigade in the Civil War, was deputy commander of the 7th and 99th Rifle Divisions in the early 1920s, and attended the Frunze Academy in 1926. After Frunze graduation, he commanded the 23d Rifle Division and the Moscow garrison. In 1937 the purges propelled him to the post of assistant chief of staff and chief of staff of the Siberian Military District and, in 1939, deputy commander of the military district.

In June 1940 Lukin was entrusted with raising and commanding 16th Army, and in April 1941 he led that army when it was transferred to the west. First deployed in support of the Kiev Special Military District, when war began

Lukin's army deployed northward and entered battle in the blazing cauldron west of Smolensk. Lukin's surviving reports poignantly capture the frustrating hegira of his army and the travails it suffered before being surrounded and destroyed at Smolensk. Fortuitously, Lukin escaped his army's fate. Later, in equally harrowing combat around Viaz'ma, Lukin himself was severely wounded and captured, and, although initially denounced by Stalin, he survived both German captivity and Stalin's wrath to earn the respect of his wartime comrades and nation.[55] Zhukov credited the courageous defense of Smolensk by Lukin and his forces with contributing to the ultimate German defeat at Moscow.

Lukin's counterpart in the reserve 20th Army was Lieutenant General Pavel Alekseevich Kurochkin, a participant in the 1917 storming of the Winter Palace and also a Civil War veteran of combat on the Western Front. A cavalry officer, Kurochkin attended and taught at the Frunze Academy and commanded a cavalry brigade and division. During the Finnish War, he commanded the 28th Rifle Corps and in 1941 graduated from the General Staff Academy. After graduation he was appointed commander of, first, the Trans-Baikal and then, only hours before the outbreak of war, the Orel Military District. In his words, he "entered the war from the march."[56] Kurochkin received word about the outbreak of war while en route from Chita to his new headquarters. When he paused in Moscow, the General Staff ordered him to raise 20th Army from military district forces and "conduct defensive operations along one of the decisive axes in the Western Front."[57]

Kurochkin did so and within a week his new army, now serving for the first time in the field and under an unfamiliar commander, deployed forward to the Dnepr line west of Smolensk to engage the spearheads of two German panzer groups. Kurochkin's army fought bravely but was largely destroyed in the Smolensk encirclement. Kurochkin survived to command armies and a *front*, and in the postwar years he became a prolific and talented writer on military force structure and theory.

These are but two examples of many that illustrate the frightening adjustment to the shock and rigors of war that *front* and army commanders experienced. Many others perished, but some lived through the experience to rise to higher command later in the war. The shock was similar at lower command levels, where the losses were even higher. It was from these lower levels that many of the finest corps and army commanders later emerged. For example, Pavel Alekseevich Rotmistrov, a cavalry officer with Civil War service and command at lower levels in the 1930s, began the war as chief of staff of newly formed 3d Mechanized Corps in the Baltic Special Military District. He survived to command a tank brigade at Moscow, a tank corps at Stalingrad, and 5th Guards Tank Army later in the war, ending the war as deputy chief of the Soviet Army's Armored and Mechanized Forces. Mikhail Efimovich Katukov, who began the war as a colonel commanding 20th Tank Division, rose to command 1st Guards Tank Army, and Colonel Semen Ilich Bogdanov similarly rose from command of 30th Tank Division to 2d Guards Tank Army command. The same pattern was apparent in all arms and branches of services. The survivors of the purges and the bloody initial months of war rose to the occasion and prevailed. To Timoshenko's credit, his reforms and the protection he and others accorded to these officers enabled them and the Red Army to survive and emerge victorious in the war.

For each of these victors, however, there were also equally incompetent commanders or creatures of Stalin, whose position and influence tortured the competent and impeded victory. The inept Voroshilov set the pattern, and even after his replacement by Timoshenko, he continued to serve Stalin and spread his ineptness at the *front*. Most damaging, however, were the vicious and vindictive political officers who surrounded Stalin and whom Stalin used as his personal "inspectors" to insure continued loyalty and obedience to his every desire. Only the strongest commander could resist them, and then only at considerable risk. One example will suffice.

Lev Zakharovich Mekhlis, who rose to the rank of colonel general in 1944, had served as a Party activist in the Red Army since the Civil War, when he developed a close relationship with Stalin. A 1930 graduate of the Institute of Red Professors, from 1937 through 1940 as army commissar first rank, he was chief of the Red Army's Main Political Directorate, which oversaw the conduct of the purges. Appointed as USSR commissar of state control in 1940, he soon also became deputy commissar of defense. During wartime, although he served incompetently as Stavka representative (in the Crimea in 1942) and was removed as chief of the Main Political Directorate, he retained Stalin's favor as a Party watchdog and continued to plague commanders.

Although few commanders felt confident to criticize Mekhlis even in the postwar years, Zhukov had few kind words about him, and Shtemenko later wrote:

> His reports often passed through my hands and always left a bitter aftertaste; They were as black as night. Taking advantage of the great powers that had been granted to him, he would dismiss dozens of people from positions of command and at once replace them with people he had brought with him. He demanded that Division Commander Vinogradov be shot for losing control of his division [in 9th Army during the Finnish War]. Later on, I came into contact with Mekhlis more than once and formed the conclusion that this man was always predisposed to adopt the most extreme measures.[58]

The fact that Shtemenko could address this and other instances of Mekhlis's machinations so candidly even in a time of heavy Soviet censorship is a measure of the unbridled hatred of Soviet commanders for tormentors like Mekhlis.

There were those, however, who validated Stalin's worst fears and whose revulsion over the state of the Red Army and the nation caused them to reject the Soviet state. Also products of the purges, they responded differently from their colleagues, and because they did, only a few are remembered. Principal among them was Andrei Andreevich Vlasov, another World War I and Civil War cavalry veteran, whose career record paralleled that of his comrades. He joined the Communist Party in 1930, before it was necessary to do so, served under Timoshenko in the Kiev Military District, and then in China in 1938 and 1939 as Soviet adviser to Chiang Kai-shek. In late 1939 he returned to command the Kiev Special Military District's 99th Rifle Division, where he was decorated for bringing order to the notoriously badly behaved outfit. For his performance he was appointed to command the new 4th Mechanized Corps, and he commanded that strong force during the initial weeks of war.

After escaping encirclement with his corps and subsequent encirclement at Kiev with 37th Army, which he then commanded, Vlasov took part in the defense of Moscow as 20th Army commander. For his outstanding performance, the Stavka appointed him lieutenant general, and in March 1942 he was sent to the Leningrad region to help restore the fortunes of recently encircled 2d Shock Army. In the ensuing Soviet disaster, Vlasov and the army he was sent to save were destroyed, and Vlasov went into German captivity, where he founded the Russian Liberation Movement.[59] Although few others seem to have followed Vlasov's path, it was true that he, too, and his actions were, at least in part, a product of the purges.

Thus, on the eve of war, the competent and the incompetent served side by side, the purge and those who orchestrated it endured, and all, whether experienced or inexperienced, together with the partially reformed Red Army, faced the rigorous test of war.

## STATISTICAL DATA

Table 2.1. Command Experience (duration) of Red Army Commanders in June 1941

| | Time in Command | | | | | |
|---|---|---|---|---|---|---|
| Command Level | To 3 Months | 3–6 Months | 6–12 Months | 1–2 Years | 2–3 Years | Over 3 Years |
| Military district | 3 | 4 | 5 | 3 | 2 | 0 |
| Armies | 10 | 3 | 5 | 1 | 1 | 0 |
| Corps | 19 | 28 | 26 | 11 | 5 | 6 |
| Rifle divisions | 59 | 10 | 51 | 65 | 10 | 3 |
| Tank divisions | 0 | 59 | 2 | 0 | 0 | 0 |
| Motorized divisions | 0 | 22 | 9 | 0 | 0 | 0 |
| Regiments | 50 | 12 | 40 | 47 | 14 | 9 |

Source: N. Ramanichev, "The Red Army, 1940–1941," 192–193, citing archival material in TsAMO, f. 32, op. 15823, d. 547, l. 444. See also F. B. Komal, "Voennge kadry nakanune voiny" [Military cadres on the eve of war], *VIZh* 2 (February 1990): 27–28.

# CHAPTER 3

# The Soviet Soldier

To a greater extent than in any other previous or subsequent war, the human dimension has been largely absent from most combat accounts of World War II on the Soviet-German front. This is particularly ironic given the war's unprecedented brutality and the catastrophic human suffering on both sides. Although true to a lesser extent on the German side, it is particularly true of the Soviet soldier. This wholesale suffering embraced generals, other officers, soldiers, and civilians alike, and the toll of dead, maimed, and psychologically scarred numbered in the tens of millions. It is no small wonder that the war has lacked a human face, for it has taken over forty years for the subject of losses to be addressed to any degree at all. In short, it took the collapse of the Soviet Union to liberate losses as a valid subject of discussion. Even now, that discussion revolves around total numbers, which, although almost beyond human comprehension, are still the subject of heated controversy. Nor does this discussion remotely touch upon more than the gross fate of the Soviet soldier. He or she still lacks a human face or personality.

This unpleasant reality reflects the very nature of the state that the Soviet soldier served. Ideologically, the totalitarian Soviet Union viewed man, in general, as a cog in a system whose importance transcended the worth of men as individuals. The individual suffered and sacrificed for the greater good of society, in this case the socialist collective, and the collective responded by according the sacrificed an officially sanctioned epitaph, which, in turn, glorified the dead and maimed by concealing their pain under a radiant cloak of glorious service to Party and motherland. Carried to the extreme, individual human suffering was lost amid countless tales of soldiers throwing their bodies into pillbox machine-gun embrasures and into the path of invariably black, swastika-bearing German tanks. In almost Calvinist fashion, the ill-fated soldier justified himself through his deeds, in this case by his personal sacrifice to the Party and the state.

Of course, in reality, politics played a far more sinister and cynical role. Totalitarianism required unquestioned obedience and perfect performance at all levels and scarcely tolerated failure. With the purges as a backdrop, Stalin and the Party demanded sacrifice by all from general to private. Quite understandably given the system, while suffering themselves, the generals and subordinate officers passed the overwhelming weight of that sacrifice to the lower ranks. A significant majority of generals, as one recent Russian observer noted, "were an integral part of Stalin's totalitarian system, which regarded men as merely 'cogs.' They fought as the popular song stated, 'The cost did not stop us.' Army General N. G. Lashchenko later wrote, 'Indeed, despite the excuses, the deaths in the war were many. We encountered many military leaders and commanders who strove to achieve success without any regard to costs.'"[1]

In his memoirs, former Soviet General P. G. Grigorenko echoed these views. Grigorenko joined the Red Army's officer ranks in the early 1930s, served with distinction during World War II, and after Stalin's death in 1953 eventually joined the ranks of anti-Soviet critics. In 1964, for his outspoken criticism and advocacy for reform, he was stripped of his rank, imprisoned, and committed to a psychiatric hospital. Persecuted along with the more famous dissident Andrei Sakharov, who won a Nobel Prize for Peace, Grigorenko finally emigrated to the United States, where he wrote memoirs that revealed a stark portrait of life in the prewar Red Army.

Grigorenko's portrait included a scathing assessment of Soviet performance at the Battle of Khalkhin-Gol, where in August and September 1939 Red Army forces under Zhukov defeated a Japanese force that had occupied disputed territory in Mongolia. Although then and now official Soviet accounts of the fighting lauded Zhukov's and the Red Army's performance, Grigorenko qualified that assessment while revealing the inherent flaws in the Red Army and callous command attitudes toward the fate of the common soldier: "We suffered enormous losses mainly because of our commander's inexperience. In addition, Zhukov did not care about any losses we suffered. . . . He was a cruel, vengeful person and throughout the war I was afraid that I might have to serve under him again."[2] Generalizing, Grigorenko added: "The battles at Khalkhin-Gol were studied by a large group of specialists in operations from the staff of the front group and the First Army Group [Zhukov's command]. Their report, which was released as a book, disclosed deficiencies in the preparation of enlisted men and officers. Military actions were described and thoroughly analyzed. Zhukov was not directly attacked nor Schtern [Zhukov's superior] praised, but anyone who read the book could draw his own conclusions."[3]

Although, in Grigorenko's words, the Red Army General Staff "warmly approved" the report, after Zhukov became chief of the General Staff "he read it and relegated it to the archives."[4] More tellingly, Grigorenko added, "Thus a book that revealed through the study of one small military episode the basic defects in the battle preparation of enlisted men and officers was hidden from commanding officers. Consequently, these defects manifested themselves again in World War II."[5]

A. M. Samsonov, the preeminent Soviet military historian, seconded Lashchenko's and Grigorenko's harsh judgments, adding:

On the whole, the Stavka of the Supreme High Command treated human losses with inexcusable thoughtlessness. Otherwise, it is not possible to explain the obstinacy with which at times, without regard to losses, we frontally assaulted points of insignificant strategic importance instead of enveloping them. . . . Evidently, Stalin believed that our human resources were inexhaustible. That was completely not the case. In 1942 and 1943 we were forced to call up to the front seventeen year olds and those who had recently turned fifteen. . . . We withdrew from the reserves hundreds of thousands of peoples from Ural and Siberian enterprises, among them were many unique specialists, and we dressed them in soldiers' greatcoats.[6]

At considerable risk, field soldiers also recorded the often callous attitude of senior commanders to the human cost of war. Lieutenant Colonel A. K. Konenenko, chief of intelligence of General P. A. Belov's vaunted 1st Guards Cavalry Corps, wrote eloquently but bitterly about his experiences during the cavalry corps' raid into the German rear from January through June 1942: "How many victims did we suffer because of the *front* commander's [Zhukov's] desire to take Viaz'ma!" Further, he recorded: "But although they fulfilled their missions, G. K. Zhukov repeatedly reproached P. A. Belov that the corps was not able to take Viaz'ma. In his telegrams he constantly displayed a kind of rage, cruelty, ruthlessness, mercilessness, and complete contempt for thousands of peoples and for their needs and lives."[7]

Another postwar analyst added his candid assessment of the attitudes of individual generals:

As the analysis of documents, publications, and memoirs demonstrate, a considerable number of senior commanders, including the well-known G. K. Zhukov, I. S. Konev, N. F. Vatutin, F. I. Golikov, A. I. Eremenko, G. I. Kulik, S. M. Budenny, K. E. Voroshilov, S. K. Timoshenko, R. Ia. Malinovsky, V. D. Sokolovsky, V. I. Chuikov, and some of lower ranks, who considered soldiers as "cannon-fodder," fought with maximum losses. On the other hand, K. K. Rokossovsky, A. A. Grechko, A. V. Gorbatov, E. I. Petrov, I. D. Cherniakhovsky, and several others fought with minimum casualties but still at the required professional level. Unfortunately, the latter were in the minority. Therefore, V. Astef'ev was correct when he declared, "We simply did not know how to fight. We finished the war without knowing how to fight. We poured out our blood and threw back the enemy with our bodies."[8]

Although it is clear that, in part, Astef'ev's bitter judgments reflected his and an entire society's frustration over its ignored and forgotten sacrifices, his remarks certainly captured the reality and horror of the initial period of war. Other more official sources have also captured the impersonal nature of the system and written of its utter inability to quantify the scope of the human sacrifice. A current member of the Department for the Individual Registration of Irrevocable Losses among Soviet Army Sergeants and Soldiers (of the Central Archives of the Russian Federation's Ministry of Defense) described the impersonal methods of wartime casualty recordkeeping:

> From the initial days of war, reports began to be received with lists of lost, missing in action, dead, etc., military service men from field army units, formations, large formations, and other institutions. Simultaneously, lists arrived from medical departments of rear area military districts about losses of service men who died of wounds, illness, and other causes.
>
> One should add that the complex military situation at the front did not always allow for the conduct of a full accounting of losses. Often they were accounted for by document *[akt]* quantitatively, rather than by name. Therefore, already from 1942, they began to accept registration of service men [losses] based on the statements of relatives.[9]

Chaotic and callous Soviet wartime casualty recordkeeping did nothing to ameliorate the anonymity that shrouded the soldier's existence and his very soul:

> Bear in mind that millions of soldiers still remain unburied today and, during the reburial of communal graves during the postwar years, these calculations were done very inexactly. Usually, when burial sites were excavated, only the corpses on top were considered. In addition, commands at all levels underestimated losses. . . . Commissariat of Defense (NKO) Order No. 138, dated 15 March 1942, abolished the well-known soldiers [identification] medallions, although that covered far from everyone. The NKO gave up registering casualties by name on 12 April 1942. Therefore, such a name count constitutes only about one-third of the total number of Soviet military dead. This permitted millions of dead and living to be written off with the introductory notation, "missing in action."[10]

Conditioned by the political and ideological proclivities of the Stalinist regime and the chaotic and harrowing course of combat, the Soviet soldier remained, and largely remains, a faceless facet of the war. Quite naturally, this facelessness has permitted and even encouraged the growth and persistence of stereotypes.

STEREOTYPES

Given Soviet postwar silence concerning the character and fate of the Red Army soldier, it was also natural and inevitable that we should be introduced to this subject through the pens of the Soviets' foes. Just as they predominated in postwar historiography about the war, it was the German memoirists who provided Westerners with their first portraits of the anonymous Soviet soldier. Conditioned by ideology, national perspectives, wartime hatreds, and Cold War perceptions, the emerging image was not a favorable one.

Describing the Soviet soldiers as the "essential foundation on which to build up a serious appreciation of Russia's military power," the premier German memoirist, General F. W. von Mellenthin, provided Western readers with their most thorough and lasting description of the Red Army soldier. Qualifying his description with the statement that "no one belonging to the cultural circle of the West is ever likely to fathom the character and soul of these Asiatics, born and bred on the other side of the European frontiers," Mellenthin nevertheless did his best to create a comprehensive psychological profile:

> There is no telling what the Russian will do next; he will tumble from one extreme to the other. With experience, it is quite easy to foretell what a soldier from any other country will do, but never with a Russian. His qualities are as unusual and many-sided as those of his vast and rambling country. He is patient and enduring beyond imagination, incredibly brave and courageous—yet at times he can be a contemptible coward. . . . The Russian is quite unpredictable; today he does not care whether his flanks are threatened or not, tomorrow he trembles at the idea of having his flanks exposed. . . . Perhaps the key to this attitude lies in the fact that the Russian is not a conscious soldier, thinking on independent lines, but is the victim of moods which a Westerner cannot analyze. He is essentially a primitive being, innately courageous, and dominated by certain emotions and instincts. His individuality is easily swallowed up in the mass, while his powers of endurance are derived from long centuries of suffering and privation. . . .
>
> A feature of the Russian soldier is his utter contempt for life or death, so incomprehensible to a Westerner. The Russian is completely unmoved when he steps over the dead bodies of hundreds of his comrades; with the same unconcern he buries his dead compatriots, and with no less indifference he faces his own death. For him life holds no special value; it is something easy to throw away.
>
> With the same indifference the Russian soldier endures cold and heat, and the pangs of hunger and thirst. Unheard-of hardships make no impres-

sion on his soul. He lacks any true religious or moral alliance, and his moods alternate between bestial cruelty and genuine kindness. As part of a mob he is full of hatred and utterly cruel, but when alone he can be friendly and generous. These characteristics apply to the Asiatic Russian, the Mongol, the Turkoman, and the Uzbek, as well as to the Slavs west of the Urals.

The Russian soldier is fond of "Little Mother Russia," and for this reason he fights for the Communist regime, although generally speaking he is not a political zealot. . . .

The Russian soldier is independent of season or environment; he is a good soldier everywhere and under any conditions; he is also a reliable tool in the hands of his leaders who can unhesitatingly subject him to sufferings far beyond the conception of the European mind. . . .

The ration problem is of secondary importance to the Russian Command, for their soldiers are virtually independent of army food supplies. . . . The nearness to nature is also responsible for his ability to become part of the soil. . . . The Russian soldier is a past master of camouflage, of digging and shoveling, and of digging earthworks. In an incredibly short time he literally disappears into the ground, digging himself in and making instinctive use of the terrain to such a degree that his positions are almost impossible to locate. . . .

To some extent the good military qualities of the Russians are offset by dullness, mental rigidity, and a natural tendency towards indolence. . . . Among the rank and file the gregarious instinct is so strong that the individual fighter is always submerged in the "crowd." Russian soldiers and junior commanders realized instinctively that if left on their own they were lost, and in this herd instinct one can trace the roots of panic as well as deeds of extraordinary heroism and self-sacrifice.[11]

Left in possession of an abandoned field, von Mellenthin's comprehensive portrayal remained unchallenged and, in later years, was even augmented by the recollections and perceptions of a host of other memoir writers. So durable was this image that another writer could note in the mid-1980s:

From a private soldier's point of view based on about 2½ years of close combat we could make the distinction [between Soviet ethnic groups]. We knew exactly if this company was obviously composed in the majority of what we called Tartars. Not Islamic, but peoples with slit eyes different from the normal Russian face. Indeed, we could see that. We captured them, and what was the difference? In many respects these people were even tougher and more ruthless. Not a single bit of Western type of morals. They shot everybody—the wounded, and so did we because we knew that the Tartar at the last moment would fire or throw a hand grenade, while the flat-faced Russian perhaps wept or cried.[12]

As is the case with all stereotypes, these are mixtures of truth and fiction, colored by personal recollections and prejudices. At times, to the obvious joy of his opponent, the Soviet soldier has lived up to this stereotype. At other times, however, he has confounded his opponent by violating the stereotype, usually to his opponent's surprise and everlasting regret.

The sadder truth, however, is the fact that the Soviets themselves were partially responsible for the triumph of these and other stereotypes about the Soviet soldier. Soviet authorities neither made nor permitted any serious effort to portray the nature, role, suffering, or fate of their own wartime soldiers. While Stalin concealed Soviet wartime personnel losses within an impenetrable cloak of secrecy, he, his political successors, and two generations of Soviet military historians, who worked under his strict guidance, created their own stereotypical images of the individual and collective combat sacrifices of Soviet soldiers.

The image was one of unsurpassed soldierly heroism against the well-trained and well-equipped combat hordes of a hitherto unvanquished Nazi Germany. Motivated by their dedication to socialist ideals, soldiers routinely threw themselves selflessly in the paths of advancing massed German armor, exacting an incredible toll on their foe. They fell on grenades to save their comrades, and they threw their bodies into the embrasures of enemy pillboxes, rushed headlong into threatening machine guns, and sacrificially rammed their aircraft into enemy planes. Common soldiers, all of worker and peasant stock, heroes of the Soviet Union, Komsomol and Party members alike, all side by side, routinely faced nearly insurmountable enemy numbers, and more often than not they prevailed, despite the daunting odds against them.

The blatant propagandistic tone of Soviet literature in the Stalinist years persisted into the post-Stalinist era, even after Khrushchev's de-Stalinization and the first round of glasnost permitted and even encouraged greater candor about the war. However, the suffering that Khrushchev's generation revealed was still of the impersonal sort, implying loss but devoid of numbers or real feeling. Memoirs, unit histories, and operational studies, even the many that were accurate in the main, still skirted the human factor and left the wartime Red Army faceless. Compounding this situation was the Soviet policy of strictly editing all memoir literature to insure continued secrecy regarding the human face of war and of discouraging the preparation or publication of real wartime personnel diaries or letters. In short, the Soviet regime would and could never come to terms with the real horror of the war in human terms. It would take a revolution and the destruction of the regime for the Soviet peoples to be able to do so—and even then it would be difficult.

SOURCES

Today, over 40 years since the end of the war, historians are just beginning
to restore a human face to the wartime Red Army soldier. It is a still a slow
and painful process, in part because of the lingering reluctance of Russian
authorities to reopen old wounds and in part because of the paucity of available sources with which to do so. Interestingly enough, the raw materials
necessary to re-create the Soviet soldier's human face do exist, although quite
natural official inhibitions still prevent their full revelation. However, despite
the fear of compromise or worse, and in spite of the prohibitions against them,
a surprising number of wartime soldiers and officers maintained diaries. Many
others prepared notes on their experiences and wrote letters that defied fate
and escaped the censor's eye. These materials are just now appearing and
will undoubtedly do so in greater numbers in the future. Together with these
materials are the censored versions of existing memoirs, which are now slowly
appearing and which reveal more truths regarding the human dimension of
the war, particularly at higher command levels.

Despite these emerging materials, the largest remaining gap concerns the
collective and individual origins, nature, and fate of the common soldier, for
he had neither the time, the occasion, nor the will to set his experiences to
paper. Here we must rely on the words of those in higher ranks or the few
memoirs and recollections written by common soldiers in the relative security of the postwar years. Fortunately, some of this memoir material is now
also appearing in print. Unfortunately, its authors are waging a losing race
against time.

There are many as yet largely unexploited official documents that can cast
some light on the origin, nature, and fate of the common soldier. These fall
into two general categories: Soviet classified studies; and German archival
materials. In characteristic fashion, the few existing examples of the former
are didactic in nature, matching the intellectual intent of virtually all Soviet
military analytical work. Sanctioned by the Party and the General Staff, their
authors wrote simply to better understand the past in order that the military
perform better in the future. Such descriptions as survive in these works are
surgical in their approach; they record the quality and state of the Soviet soldier at various stages of the war to test the ability of the state to mobilize,
deploy, and fight. In short, rather than lamenting the past, they are designed
to serve the future.

In addition, in the archives of various military manpower directorates there
are volumes of records that fully survey the origins (primarily social), capabilities, and general fate of enlisted soldiers. The slowly opening Soviet archives have and will continue to speak volumes about the Soviet soldier of
1941. Soviet authorities were inveterate recordkeepers, sometimes to their

regret. The Russian State Archives and the various People's Commissariat of Defense directorates associated with manpower questions (for example, the Main Cadres Directorate and the Main Directorate for the Formation and Manning of the Red Army), likely contain answers to all relevant questions about Red Army soldiers and officers. A few Western and Russian historians, including Roger Reese and A. A. Maslov, have just begun to mine and exploit this immensely valuable material. Once their work proves that these revelations are positive rather than a threat to the state, even more materials will likely become available for examination.

The second category, which encompasses German archival materials, is also vast but largely unexploited. The German intelligence service, Foreign Armies East (Fremde Heere Ost) collected, recorded, catalogued, maintained, and studied data on Soviet manpower to better understand the capability of the Soviet Union to sustain the war. Most of this material is in the form of card files and summary reports on the personnel in specific Red Army units. The data, much of which was collected by debriefing prisoners of war and processing the bodies of Soviet dead, are comprehensive and, when fully analyzed, will provide sound social data on the origins, training, and morale of the Soviet soldier.

The primary weakness of this material derives from the fact that it was collected seriously only from mid-1942, after Foreign Armies East was reorganized and reinvigorated under its famous head, Lieutenant Colonel Reinhardt Gehlen. Records on the Soviet soldier in 1941 are substantially less thorough, and most German intelligence estimates were based on Soviet performance in the Polish and Finnish wars. Moreover, by 1942 much of the Red Army of 1941 had perished and along with it up to two-thirds of the soldiers in the Red Army's "Class of '41."

## THE EVOLVING OFFICIAL IMAGE

Based upon the fragmentary materials now at hand, one can form a tenuous mosaic of the origins and personal qualities and qualifications of the Soviet soldier who participated in Operation Barbarossa. Official records and documents invariably describe the Soviet soldier as from either worker or peasant stock. In general terms this was true, since truth (and ideology) dictated that there was no middle or upper class (or classes at all) in the Soviet Union. Regardless of the ostensibly classless society, however, the sons of political and economic officialdom (the *nomenklatura*) were more likely to be found in the officer ranks. An unofficial class system existed based in part on one's origins, ethnic background, and, at times, religion. The combat arms were dominated by Slavs, particularly in the western border military districts. Farther east, in the military districts of the Caucasus, Central Asia, Siberia, and the Far East, the commanding heights in military formations were generally held by Slavs (with some notable exceptions), but the ranks had a higher percentage of non-Slavic peoples. Certain groups (classes, ethnic minorities, and religions) of soldiers, whose loyalty was in question, were relegated to service in noncombat formations (such as railroad and labor troops). Other could not serve at all.

Loyalty, education, ideological fervor, and intelligence also determined soldierly assignments. For example, elite formations, such as airborne brigades and NKVD units, had a higher percentage of Komsomol and Party members than other combat arms. Artillery, mechanized and antitank forces, and Air Force units drew the most intelligent and capable soldiers, and, obviously, border forces and other NKVD troops, of necessity, were considered more ideologically dedicated than soldiers in other combat arms. Generally speaking, regulars measured up to these requirements better than former territorials or the vast mass of semi-trained reserves.

An official assessment of troop combat readiness in the western border military districts in June 1941 was prepared in the late 1980s by the eminent military-academician A. G. Khor'kov for the Voroshilov General Staff Academy. A product of Gorbachev's glasnost, it revealed both the impersonal tone of official assessments, even at the height of glasnost, and some interesting facts about the quality of Red Army inductees. Khor'kov described the process for mobilizing inductees and their demeanor:

> Immense work was done during the prewar years on the registration for call-up of young replacements for the ranks of the Red Army. During the preparatory period, *raion* [district] meetings, conferences, and gatherings of those men due for call-up took place in all military districts. During the course of these measures, questions of registration, the missions of those called up, and their training for these missions was examined, lectures were heard, and meetings were held on the international situation. The political-moral state of those to be called up was characterized by exceptionally great political enthusiasm and desire to serve in the ranks of the Red Army. A great number of declarations were made to the registration commissions about the desire to enter service ahead of schedule and voluntarily.[13]

Khor'kov noted the "constantly rising Party-Komsomol and worker-peasant" stratum among the replacements and quoted the following archival figures to substantiate his claim:[14]

| Military District | Called Up | Communist Party | Komsomol Members | Workers |
|---|---|---|---|---|
| Leningrad | 79,985 | 182 | 22,886 | 43,278 |
| Western Special | 61,235 | 87 | 21,015 | 16,730 |
| Kiev Special | 145,720 | 197 | 48,860 | 31,671 |

These replacements were then integrated into existing units and formations in piecemeal fashion (for example, a company per regiment). Thereafter, they were subjected to a distinct phased training program, including youth programs (three months) and regimental schools (ten months). Upon completion of this program, some were appointed as second lieutenants, but the bulk remained common soldiers.

Despite this concerted education effort, by Khor'kov's own admission, "The level of training of replacements in the western military districts was very low:

This was explained first of all by the fact that, until their Red Army service, they had no preinduction training, and many were semi-literate or required medical treatment. Thus, according to a report by the Kiev Special Military District commander, among the replacements called up in 1941 were the following number of men liable for call-up who did not meet the requirements of Soviet Army service:

|  | Total | In the Western District |
|---|---|---|
| Illiterate | 19,042 | 18,167 |
| Semi-literate | 79,118 | 65,494 |
| Ill or sick | 10,782 | 6,951 |
| Total | 108,934 | 90,612 |

They strove to find a solution for this situation by dispatching young replacements to other districts. Thus, among the 14,411 new replacements for the Central Asian Military District, 50 percent arrived from the Western and Kiev Military Districts and the remainder from other districts. In fall 1940, 15,838 men arrived in the Trans-Baikal Military District from the western districts.[15]

Nor did reality justify the description of the Red Army as a totally worker and peasant force. Although the Party and government mandated intensified political education during the period of Red Army expansion and reform, official sources grudgingly admitted that problems existed. According to one relatively critical source:

The fact that, during the prewar years, there were a great number of young Red Army men, as well as military service men from the reserves of the western regions of Ukraine and Moldavia and the former bourgeois Baltic republics, had a telling effect on the level of training of western military district forces. This circumstance required additional attention to these categories of military service men from all political organs and unit political apparatus' and commanders (combined military-political commanders). Party-political work with them was shaped taking into account

Soldiers on maneuvers.

Marshal of the Soviet Union S. M. Budenny inspecting Baltic Special Military District troops.

Mobilizing troops.

Troops of the 6th Rifle Division's 16th Rifle Regiment, 28th Rifle Corps, 4th Army, Western Special Military District.

Prewar mobilization poster.

that the service man spent a distinct period of life in capitalist conditions and, therefore, was still only vaguely familiar with our Soviet life.[16]

Intensive reeducation by political and party cadres, claimed the author, overcame these problems and accomplished its ends:

The personnel of the western border military districts, united around the Communist Party and the Soviet government, selflessly attached to their socialist Motherland, were "ready to fulfill their sacred duty, to justify the love and faith of the Soviet people."
The military district Military Councils reported to the People's Commissariat of Defense that the main mass of soldiers were healthy in a political respect and displayed great interest in all types of combat and political training, and were disciplined.[17]

This description of the nature, capabilities, and morale of the 1941 Soviet soldier, when compared with other official accounts, is as critical and candid as any. Other than hinting at the gnawing problems that beset the Red Army ranks, however, these accounts do little to put a face on anything but a minority of Red Army soldiers.

THE EMERGING HUMAN DIMENSION

Fortunately, new materials are now appearing that help fill that void. These materials indicate that the Soviet soldier defied stereotyping. He reflected the complexities of Soviet society as a whole and, hence, was a far more diverse breed than official sources have indicated. First and foremost, he had many faces. He was a peasant fresh from the state or collective farm. He was a worker who could be spared from the burgeoning industrial base. He was a Komsomol member or, in rarer cases, a member of the Bolshevik Party. He was a dedicated and idealistic Communist. He was a disaffected peasant seeking through his service upward mobility and a place in the Soviet Union's expanding cities. Although many were Russians, Belorussians, or Ukrainians, he could also be a member of countless other peoples inhabiting the Soviet Union. Sometimes he was a Latvian, Lithuanian, Estonian, or Rumanian, from the territories incorporated into the Soviet Union after 1939. Unlike his counterpart of 1942 and the later war years, however, there was less chance that he was of Asiatic origin. He was an orphan or ward of the state because his parents had perished in the countless purges or had been displaced or killed in the ruthless collectivization program. In short, he was representative of the diverse population of the massive Soviet state that he enthusiastically, passively, or reluctantly served. His dedication, ideology, sincerity, and national fervor were, in the last analysis, irrelevant, for he was a Soviet soldier. Furthermore, there was a better than 60 percent chance he would be either dead or in captivity within six months.

A recent Russian analysis of the initial period of war, written to restore accuracy to accounts of military operations in 1941 and 1942, tangentially adds to our understanding of the soldier's condition. While describing the life of Soviet aviators during the chaotic prewar period, it boldly admits an emerging truth: "The unceasing organizational changes in RKKA units, the participation in local wars and armed conflicts, the mobilizations and demobilizations that were carried out, and the instability in command cadres all had a negative impact on the army's combat readiness."[18] Given these adverse circumstances, the author argues that discipline and law and order deteriorated throughout army ranks: "Thus, by 1 January 1941, the number of extraordinary occurrences alone (without consideration of instances of desertion and absence without leave) reached the huge figure of 14,058, and the number of dead and severely wounded among these comprised 10,048 men. In a number of units, the quantity of extraordinary occurrences reached threatening proportions."[19]

In response to this continuing problem and prompted by Stalin, military commands adopted draconian measures to root out the causes of this turbulence. For example, on 22 December 1940, the Air Force command issued Order No. 0362 in an attempt to restore flagging discipline. The order, which applied to all Air Force pilots and technical troops who had served for less than four years, required that they be "transferred to a barracks-like situation with the rights and responsibilities of fixed-term servicemen."[20] As a result, "36,953 Air Force commanders (around 40 percent) were transferred to barracks." More importantly, this order prescribed that the serviceman's family members be evicted from aviation cantonments: "For a short period 8,049 families were in fact deported from the birthplace of the husband or wife."[21] Shortly thereafter, the Air Force commander, P. V. Rychagov, evaluated the importance of this order with some cynicism: "The young pilot and technician, who was burdened with his family, lost any maneuverability in the event his unit was transferred. Moreover, the pilot who was constrained by a large family lost combat readiness and bravery and prematurely aged physically. The order of the People's Commissariat of Defense [No. 0362] removed existing shortcomings in this respect and created normal working conditions and the growth of the VVS [Air Force]. . . . It was not long," noted the author, "before the results of such an immoral cadre policy as was instituted in the Air Force had a telling effect."[22] Faced with an existing cadre shortage, students soon requested release from training schools. Additional harsh NKO orders were met with only increased resistance by the student-officers: "The consequences of Order No. 0362 had a negative influence on the combat training of aviation units. The situation of the transfer to barracks of aviation units increased the numbers of flying accidents and was marked by depression, slackness, and a fall in discipline, and the pilots expressed discontent with nutrition and living conditions. The low indices of combat training were accompanied by a significant increase in accidents and crashes."[23] Although it dealt only with officer personnel, this order and the reaction of the men to it symbolized an entire range of morale problems that the Red Army faced in 1940 and 1941.

The wholesale expansion of the Red Army also produced other hardships that adversely affected the soldiers' morale. Existing shortages of foodstuffs and fodder led to the introduction of "vegetarian days" to economize on supplies and to create necessary wartime food reserves. Food deficiencies were accompanied by shortages in food service support for Red Army units and by a lack of the requisite number of trained cooks and field kitchens. As in other areas, the food situation was not to stabilize until summer 1942.[24] The same problems existed in clothing Red Army troops.

A host of recent and even older works catalogue training deficiencies in the Red Army, both among officers and, to a lesser extent, among enlisted soldiers. As detailed as these are, however, most focus on the combat capability of the soldier, individually, or collectively, in his unit.[25] As a rule, they do not zero in on such essential questions as the soldier's origins, his personal traits, and most importantly, his disposition toward the state and the army.

A new study written by Roger R. Reese goes a long way toward filling this void. Validly claiming that "to appreciate the causes of the Red Army's failure in June 1941, the army must be understood as a society in and of itself, but one cut from the whole cloth of the larger society that produced it," Reese examined "the social composition of the enlisted ranks and officer corps, as well as the elements of social mobility, education, morale and discipline, party membership patterns, and the social and political factors external to the military that affected the dynamics of military life."[26] His conclusions, based in large part on Soviet archival materials, make immense strides in placing a human face on the Soviet soldier.

What does Reese conclude? First, agreeing with many Soviet critics, he underscores that the single most important factor in the defeat of the Red Army in 1941 was its rapid peacetime expansion. This, in turn, was exacerbated by rapid economic expansion, which placed unmanageable strain on Red Army cadres:

> Changes in the Soviet economy affected the organization of the armed forces which in turn affected manpower policies. The industrialization of the Soviet Union . . . created the necessary conditions for the Red Army

to expand . . . but expanding the army in the early thirties brought mixed blessings. It contributed to both discipline problems and the shortage of officers. Because the army continually grew, it constantly needed more officers, but because it could not get as many as needed, the ratio of officers to men decreased. Thus, fewer leaders attempted—unsuccessfully—to exercise control over more men. The army was forced to adopt traditional authoritarian practices [like Order No. 0362] to lead the soldiers because the leaders it got were by and large socially and educationally unprepared for their positions of responsibility. To make matters worse, many conscript soldiers served very reluctantly due to a variety of social factors. In short, the expansion made the military susceptible to the same social chaos evident in a civilian society characterized by labor indiscipline, work turnover, and shortages of competent and trained managers.[27]

While challenging the traditional claim that the military purges were the principal and often sole cause of future Red Army misfortunes, Reese admits that they clearly exacerbated the bad situation. In reality, however, like many other critics, Reese claims that the Red Army did poorly in June 1941 because "it suffered from flawed organization and poor training."[28] Unlike these critics, however, he argues that these problems were "systemic," that is, they resulted from the inherent nature of the Soviet soldier.

What, then, did that soldier look like? First, right up to 1939, official policies stressed the induction of as many workers and nonpeasants as possible into regular forces (in border military districts and urban areas), whereas peasants were more likely to be assigned to territorial forces (in rural areas and internal military districts). This approach was designed to increase the educational level of soldiers by recruiting more literate workers and to insure greater ideological reliability. On the other hand, "Wealthy peasants, former noblemen, and middle-class men were neither conscripted nor allowed to volunteer for the military. To keep the army free of these 'class enemies,' conscription commissions checked (though often poorly) the social background of conscripts to weed out undesirables."[29]

As the pressures of army expansion increased after the mid-1930s, it became more difficult to adhere to these conscription requirements. Consequently, the draft age range expanded, exemptions became fewer, and more ethnic minorities were permitted to serve. By 1941, these pressures required that non-Russian-speaking minorities be assigned throughout the entire force structure. Although the non-Slavic representation in Red Army ranks declined from 25 percent in the tsarist army of World War I to 13.7 percent in the 1941 Red Army, Soviet authorities did not welcome this unpleasant reality; clearly it was necessitated by the circumstances of the Red Army expansion.[30] Most important, during the late 1930s, the Red Army was forced by the army's expansion to abandon its older manning criteria and to absorb millions of soldiers from its "peasant rear":

> The eve of the German invasion found the Red Army, for the most part, unprepared for war. . . . As a social unit, the army was riven by fault lines, some of its own making, others not. Poorly trained officers led unmotivated men. The army had begun reequiping, but in such a way as to disorganize training and maintenance. The RKKA continued to expand, furthering the breakdown of cohesion and continuity in major units. Finally, the regime had not clearly stated the mission of the armed forces in the newly acquired western territories, thus leaving the army leadership, as well as the rank and file, to assume the normal peacetime laxity, complacency, and incompetence remained the order of the day."[31]

This was so, in Reese's view, first and foremost because of the Red Army's "rapid and incoherent expansion" and, secondarily, because of the "social disruption of civil society characteristic of the Stalin era."[32] Emerging from a turbulent society, the officers and their men could not and would not cope with the task at hand: "The USSR, as a predominantly backward rural society with peasant values, was in most respects unable to create a modern mass army that required people with urban skills and values." Worse still, enlisted men were "disinterested in soldiering at best. . . . Soldiers often proved uncooperative and sometimes demonstrated outright hostility to their leaders. This resulted primarily from their disaffection with the communist regime and anyone identified as its agents. The large number of men who eventually joined the Germans attests to the anger over collectivization and de-kulakization."[33]

In short, just as A. A. Svechin had presciently highlighted the effects of the "peasant rear" on the nation's ability to wage war in an economic sense, it also rang true in a social sense. Reese concluded:

> The problem with the Red Army in June 1941 was a human problem. . . . The armed forces had outrun the capacity of a still predominantly peasant society to provide (on a mostly volunteer basis) cadres capable of leading and managing a modern mass army. Soviet society was no different from Tsarist society in that the majority of its members showed aversion to military service in any capacity. What was different was that the Soviet regime, contrary to its intentions, had created a reservoir of ill will among potential conscripts through its social and economic policies of collectivization and de-kulakization and had disrupted normal patterns of social development through rapid industrialization and urbanization. These policies hindered the assimilation of such state-promoted values as patriotism, obedience, and self-discipline, all necessary to a stable military.[34]

It would take the searing experience of war and the death of the prewar Red Army for a new Red Army to emerge victorious after four years of unprecedented combat. How this transformation of the soldier and army took place still requires thorough examination.

Reese's description of the social nature of the Red Army is the most convincing assessment yet to be advanced. Although his arguments are cogent, however, they are not definitive. The archival base for such conclusions is still incomplete and, sadly, may remain so. In addition, a wealth of other materials, some of which are now appearing, require detailed examination. These include suppressed memoir materials, thousands of diaries, letters, and personal memoirs and recollections of wartime soldiers, which their authors have fearfully hidden for these many years, and hundreds of other still unavailable archival files in the Russian State Archives and other archives that relate to personnel affairs of Red Army cadres and enlisted men.

Among the most notable of these other materials are the first of the published "new model" memoirs and semi-fictional works portraying the service life of Red Army soldiers. Typical of these newly emerging genres are the personnel recollections of the dissident general Petro Grigorenko and of Georgi Arbatov, who is the current director of the Russian Federation's Institute of the USA and Canada, and the fictional writings of the Russian satirist Vladimir Voinovich.

For years after their publication in 1982, Grigorenko's pioneering memoirs remained the only personal exposé of Red Army life and the human side of the Red Army soldier and officer. His account, although dealing primarily with officers, on the whole substantiates Reese's ground-breaking analysis. Writing of his initial training at the Khar'khov Technical Institute, he spoke of the appalling conditions at the institute and the lackluster preparation of the students. "More than half of the first-year students in this institute," he recorded, "consisted of special recruitment, most of whom had very little education and were unaccustomed to mental labor."[35] Grigorenko then provided vivid descriptions of Red Army life and combat readiness in the turbulent decade of the 1930s, ending with the disastrous effects of the purges on Soviet command cadres:

I saw for myself the aftermath of the destruction of officers cadres in the Far East. . . . Two years had passed since the mass arrests had come to an end, but the command pyramid had not yet been restored. Many positions remained unfilled because there were no men qualified to occupy them. Battalions were commanded by officers who had completed military schools less than a year before. Some battalion commanders had completed only courses for second lieutenants and their experience had been limited to several months of command of a platoon and a company. How could anyone have thought that such a gap could be filled?[36]

Grigorenko offered an equally devastating portrait of the readiness of Soviet divisions mobilized in the Far East once war had begun:

> In place of each division sent west . . . [we] formed a local replacement division of our own. . . . There were no men; there were no weapons; there was no transportation equipment; there was, in fact, nothing at all. . . . Opanasenko [the commander in the Far East] mobilized all men through age fifty-five, including those in all concentration camps located on highways or railways. He even got a certain number of recruits from Magadan [a notorious prison camp], including officers. Thus he solved the problem of men. . . . True, the reinforcements were totally unsuited to combat.
>
> So second-string divisions were formed to replace all the dispatched divisions. In the end, two or three more divisions were formed than we had originally. When the new formations became a reality, the General Staff at long last "made itself heard." All were confirmed and given numbers. And suddenly Moscow had so much faith in these new formations that it took four of the second-string units to the western front.[37]

Georgi Arbatov was the son of a member of the Communist *nomenklatura,* a worker who had risen in Party service during the mid-1930s to a position in the People's Commissariat of Foreign Trade. Stripped of his position in the purges, he nonetheless survived to fill lower-level administrative positions.[38] Son Georgi, a student when war broke out, was swept by the tide of war into Red Army service as a common soldier. Arbatov served in combat for three years until felled by tuberculosis and mustered out in summer 1944.

Arbatov framed his description of army life with an old army joke that to Arbatov captured the dilemma of army service and the definition of personal courage. When asked, "Are you afraid of the Germans, soldier?" the answer was "No." However, when asked, "Then who are you afraid of?" the soldier would invariably respond, "My sergeant." Arbatov matured in service, realizing that one's daily well-being depended on sergeants for "an extra ration of bread or a portion of kasha, new leggings, or, if you're really lucky, a new pair of boots. . . . In the end," concluded Arbatov, "the 'sergeant's' attitude to you in a society like ours could mean your survival."[39]

While serving in a Katiusha [multiple rocket] unit, which Arbatov admitted was "an easier life than in the infantry," he rose to officer rank and later served in the Battle for Moscow and subsequent combat in the Smolensk region and across the Dnepr into Ukraine. In assessing his military service and the overall military condition, he lamented what he described as the "awful and often unjustifiable losses" and recorded the personal transformation that seized him during the postwar years:

Naturally, I sometimes recall my wartime experiences with a sense of nostalgia for duty, for camaraderie in battle, and the knowledge that you are prepared to fight as long as you have any strength left. But what I went through also demystified the army and the Great Patriotic War and stripped them of that super-romantic aura that was nurtured in us for years. I discovered for myself the great opportunities that existed for petty tyranny, for a superior to humiliate a subordinate, for bullying, for mediocre and untalented people to flourish and succeed, for nepotism. I also learned how the operations of our army were managed; how many mistakes were made and at what tremendous cost! This made me quite skeptical towards the top brass, and allergic to all kinds of militarism.[40]

Arbatov's memoirs provide the necessary context for what is perhaps the most poignant and accurate portrayal of Red Army life, Vladimir Voinovich's novel *The Life and Extraordinary Adventures of Private Ivan Chonkin*. The sergeant, the political commissar, commanders in the chain of command, common citizens, and, above all, the Red Army soldier come to life in the novel's pages: "The news that war had broken out caught everyone napping, because no one had been paying war the least bit of mind," Voinovich admitted, then shaped his description of the eternal Russian soldier: "Chonkin did not learn about what happened immediately, because he was sitting in the outhouse, in no hurry to leave. Chonkin's time had not been apportioned and allotted for any noble purpose; it was only for living and for him to contemplate the flow of life without drawing any conclusions: simply to eat, drink, sleep, and to answer the call of nature, not only in those moments determined by the regulations on guard and garrison duty, but as the needs arose."[41]

Although reflecting eternal truths that apply to many private soldiers in most armies, this description and those that follow are particularly relevant to human conditions that prevailed in the prewar Red Army. Mixing satire, harsh irony, and uplifting farce in a most simple tale, Voinovich articulates an unsurpassed mosaic that juxtaposes the simple earthy existence of the Red Army soldier to the depressing context of immensely complex human tragedy. Once again, Reese's conclusions seem vindicated.

Other fragmentary recollections of Red Army soldiers have emerged that add flesh and bones to this emerging image. Speaking at a symposium on Red Army wartime operations, former Private L. Tarassuk recorded his impressions of life in the Red Army. His service began in 1943, but his description echoes those of his predecessors. Although admitting that "we were properly trained, mostly spiritually," he related the initial "depersonalization" process, which Red Army soldiers inevitably experienced, the so-called "disinfection ritual":

That was my first great shock of the realities of army life. Disinfection involved taking off one's civilian clothes and working on them in special rooms. You remember well that it was war and every piece of clothing or shoes was very precious for our families. So we were told that after disinfection we would make packages and send them to our families to sell or to live on. After the shower we were shown to a room containing some uniforms and then were led to a courtyard where some—it is hard to describe—garbage had been put in piles. We were told to select our items, package them, and send them home. But there was nothing at all that belonged to us. All had been taken by our company sergeants and sold at the local bazaar.[42]

Tarassuk also noted the ethnic animosities that afflicted Soviet ranks:

The next thing that struck me most was the incredible animosity between personnel. I don't mean between sergeants and enlisted men, but rather between enlisted men themselves. You see, the regiment was located near the town of Fergana in Central Asia (Uzbek Republic). So roughly half the enlisted men were local people and minorities. The rest were Ukrainians and Russians. There was terrible animosity that resulted in beatings, and in very harmful things like "making a fox trot." That was when you put strips of paper between the toes of a sleeping man and burned them—as a joke.[43]

Tarassuk went on to record the widespread and endemic instances of theft in the ranks, adding, "If such a thing happened in our company, we were encouraged to go to a neighboring company to steal the same thing from them—just as a replacement. It was a method of education—to become courageous up to a point of being insolent."[44] Tarassuk recalled the perpetual state of hunger among common soldiers while his division was in reserve and the improved conditions among front-line units, although he was careful to say that this hunger never matched that prevalent in the civilian rear. Before his division entered Rumania, he recalled receiving a "sermon" on proper soldierly behavior and then, after his division had plunged deep into the country, he saw the man who had given the sermon, together with two sergeants, liberating a local woman of a bag and watch.

Finally, amid his many impressions, he recalled the great impact on the Russian soldier of what he saw while liberating Eastern and Central Europe. This, more than anything else, sharply underscored the essential difference between the Soviet soldier and his Western counterparts and, not coincidentally, explained why Stalin instituted his postwar program, "Against Servility to the West," to eradicate those dangerous impressions.[45]

Thus, although a beginning has been made in describing the human condition of Red Army service and putting a human face on the Red Army soldier, much remains to be done. These fragmentary glimpses of the soldier and his existence help fill in the gaps in current archival research. The gaps will be adequately filled, however, only when the archives are fully open and exploited and when the thousands of likely personal memoirs see the light of day. In the meantime, we must be satisfied with these fleeting glimpses.

Finally, although many of these descriptions are universal in the sense that they apply to service in many armies, their sheer scope and persistence seem to distinguish the Red Army from other national armies. Given the immense political and ideological pressures on the Soviet soldier, the social nature of the prewar Soviet Union, the class and ethnic rifts in Soviet society, and the grim realities of life in the totalitarian Soviet state and the even more totalitarian Red Army, this was understandable. Moreover, and perhaps more importantly, the emerging image in no way detracts from the sacrifice, pain, and suffering experienced by the Red Army soldier in his quest for ultimate victory.

# CHAPTER 4

# Strategic Deployment Planning and Mobilization

Soviet military planning in the 1930s, and particularly after 1935, reflected two fundamental and disturbing realities. The first was the clear Soviet understanding of their own strategic posture and, specifically, their vulnerabilities associated with the vast expanse of the Soviet Union and the nation's economic, technological, and social weakness relative to the West, in general, and Germany, in particular. The preeminent military theorist A. A. Svechin and others had considered this matter in detail in the 1920s on the basis of their study of past Russian conflicts and, in particular, German conflicts. In his massive tome, *Strategy*, which was published in 1927, and in which he initially articulated the new theory of operational art, Svechin described the political-economic preparations for war so necessary as the foundation of any nation's military strategy.[1] Given the young Soviet Union's vast territorial expanse, the underdeveloped nature of its communications system and industrial base, and its lagging technological prowess, Svechin believed that it was necessary to exploit foreign technology and "prepare the nation's rear in service to the front" for success to be achieved in any future major conflict. These grim realities of the 1920s Soviet state impelled Svechin to stress the necessity of peacetime and wartime unity of the front and rear and to advocate a strategy of attrition that would recognize and, at the same time, exploit the Soviet Union's inherent strengths and weaknesses.

In short, Svechin believed that a socially and economically backward country such as the post–Civil War Soviet Union, with its weak industrial base, sparse and tenuous communications systems, and largely peasant population, had what he and others referred to as a "peasant rear." The term "peasant rear" applied as much to the efficiency of Soviet political institutions, to social cohesion or the lack thereof, and to public morale as it did to the country's lagging economic infrastructure and technological base. Considering both its material and spiritual aspect, in Svechin's view, the Soviet Union with its "peasant rear" could not hope to sustain war with any more advanced major Western European power unless it devised special methods for doing so. Specifically, Svechin argued that the Soviet Union had to achieve unity of front and rear in peacetime, create sound plans for military mobilization (with a strong economic component) in peacetime, and wage an attrition rather than an annihilation struggle during war. Although eschewing rapid victory, commitment to a strategy of attrition would also avoid early catastrophic defeat at the hands of a more proficient military machine and, at the same time, would capitalize on the Soviet Union's vast expanse and imposing human and natural resource base.

Svechin's strategic concepts were directly and forcefully challenged by leading Civil War leader and postwar theorist M. N. Tukhachevsky and others. They argued for adoption of a more aggressive strategy of destruction, which postulated the "complete militarization of the national economy to create the tools necessary to wage modern mechanized warfare." Tukhachevsky's concepts, which seemed to be more in tune with the revolutionary ideals of the 1920s Soviet state, emerged supreme, and amid the turbulent political infighting of the 1930s, Svechin and his writings disappeared into obscurity until rediscovered over 40 years after World War II. Ironically, although Tukhachevsky's concepts emerged victorious, he too was consumed by the conflagration in 1937. As a result, the Soviet Union approached war in 1941 armed with neither Svechin's nor Tukhachevsky's strategic vision. The ensuing strategic vacuum would exact a terrible toll on the armed forces and state.

The realities of which Svechin spoke plagued Soviet military planners throughout the late 1930s. Deprived of the best strategic planners by the purges, the surviving planners sought to formulate plans to guarantee the security of the Soviet state. The difficulties these planners encountered during the Polish and Finnish Wars only underscored the fact that despite Tukhachevsky's strategic victory, the mobilization of the rear so essential for victory was not and would not be an easy task. That stark reality, more than any concrete prewar mobilization plan, suggested what sort of war the Soviet Union was preparing to fight.

The second disturbing reality was the growing perception on the part of Soviet political leaders and planners alike, based on political, ideological, and military considerations, that "sooner or later fascist Germany would attack the Soviet Union," either alone or in concert with the Japanese empire.[2] As the European political situation deteriorated after 1935 and a series of crises ensued, Soviet military planners were forced to tailor their threat assessments, Soviet strategic posture, and mobilization planning to satisfy the new and more threatening realities. The Czech crisis of September 1938 was just such a situation. During the crisis the Soviet Union attempted to cooperate with Great Britain and France to provide political and military guarantees to the Czechs against German aggression. In addition to undertaking diplomatic measures, the Soviet government partially mobilized and deployed its armed forces to demonstrate solidarity with Czechoslovakia, Great Britain, and France against German actions.[3]

Although Soviet actions were futile and the Munich Agreement settled the fate of the Czech state, the Soviet strategic deployment exercise was instructive. Soviet mobilization and deployment plans proved inadequate, and command and control of the mobilized force was immature. Coming as it did at the height of the purges, this was understandable. The affair prompted the Soviet government to take corrective measures and accord some attention to preparing a new set of plans.

In November 1938 the Main Military Council approved a strategic deployment plan developed by the chief of the Red Army General Staff, B. M. Shaposhnikov, despite the turbulence within the staff because of its recent formation and the ongoing purges. The plan "considered the most probable enemies, their armed forces and possible operational plans, and the basic strategic deployment of the Red Army in the West and the East."[4] Although the General Staff had no real documentary evidence of hostile enemy plans, the postulated threat seemed realistic. The plan identified Germany and Italy, possibly supported by Japan, as the most likely and most dangerous enemies. Although it assumed Germany would ultimately wage war on the Soviet Union, it judged that, at that time, Germany was not yet materially capable of launching such an attack. Nor were political conditions suitable for Germany to do so.

The Shaposhnikov plan assumed that the Soviet Union would face a two-front war, in the west against Germany, Italy, Poland, and possibly Rumania, Finland, and the Baltic states, and in the east against Japan (see Maps 4.1 and 4.2). The postulated combined threat amounted to 194 to 210 infantry, 4 motorized, and 15 cavalry divisions equipped with 13,077 guns, 7,980 tanks, and 5,775 aircraft. Over one half of these forces threatened the western Soviet Union. In the event of crisis, the Soviets assessed the Germans and Poles would jointly occupy Lithuania.[5]

Consistent with earlier plans, Shaposhnikov and the General Staff accorded priority to the Western Theater of War, where he planned the main Soviet force concentrations. The location of the Pripiat Marshes in the center of the front forced the staff to address the controversial dilemma as to whether the enemy would make his main effort north or south of the marshes. Shaposhnikov skirted the issue by planning scenarios that would meet either circumstance.[6] In either case, the staff presumed Finnish forces and those of the Baltic states could assist the Germans in any attack on Leningrad.

In response to these postulated threats, the General Staff planned force concentrations that could defeat the enemy sequentially, first in the west and then in the east. This implied the reliance on covering forces to defend in the east while Soviet forces dealt with the western threat and similar forces to defend in less threatened western sectors (the Pripiat flank). General Staff adoption of this strategy required maintenance of well-equipped covering armies in the most threatened border sectors and the construction of fortified regions along the entire border. The Soviet presumption was that these

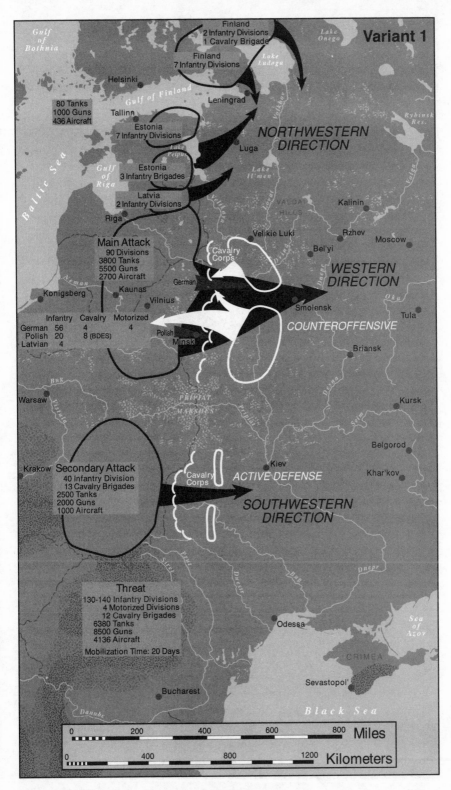

Map 4.1. The Shaposhnikov Plan, November 1938: Variant 1

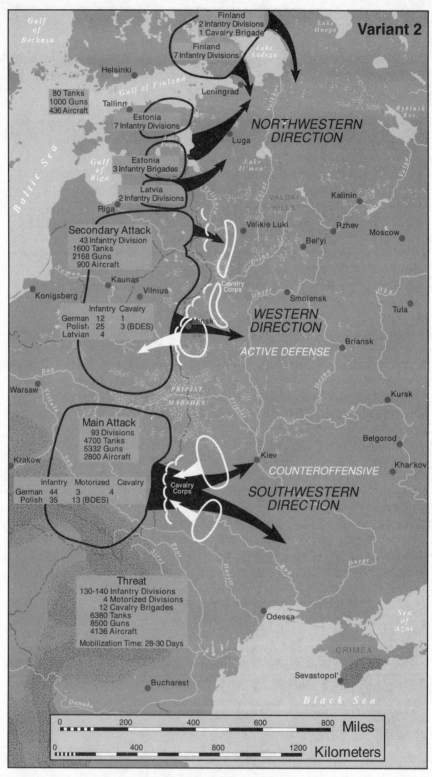

Map 4.2. The Shaposhnikov Plan, November 1938: Variant 2

forces could cope with enemy first echelon invading armies while mobilization generated "main" forces that could then conduct "decisive" counteroffensives to repel enemy main forces.

Shaposhnikov's 1938 plan resembled pre–World War I plans in the sense that it postulated full Soviet mobilization before hostilities commenced and assumed that existing covering forces and fortified regions would be adequate to cope with any forces the enemy was able to field in preliminary (secret, prewar) mobilization. Indicating the immature nature of these plans, the Soviets did not designate creation of a specific number of wartime *fronts*, although they did foresee operations along three "strategic directions [axes]," the most important of which was the Western.

The international crises of 1939 and Soviet reactions to them complicated the work of the General Staff and, at the same time, vividly underscored the inadequacies of Soviet war, mobilization, and strategic deployment planning. During the Polish crisis of August, the General Staff first contemplated strategic cooperation with Western powers, and then, after they signed the Molotov-Ribbentrop Pact with Germany, the Soviets partially mobilized and invaded eastern Poland. The ensuing mobilization was fraught with problems, and Soviet forces performed poorly in the operation. To conduct the operation, the General Staff formed two *front* commands (Belorussian and Ukrainian), each containing armies and tailored mobile operational groups. Although the command structure was more elaborate than that used during the Czech crisis the year before, the number of mobilized divisions was roughly the same. Because of a wide variety of command and control, logistical, and even morale problems, Soviet forces only muddled through the operation.[7] Moreover, Soviet occupation of eastern Poland rendered obsolete all existing Soviet war and mobilization plans.

The westward movement of the Soviet frontiers into Poland posed strategic planners with two new dilemmas. First, since Soviet-gauge railroads differed from gauges used in Central Europe, and specifically in Poland, all material, equipment, and supplies destined for the new border regions would have to move through transshipment points along the old border, where they would have to be reloaded on rail for transport to forces in the new border region. This process would materially slow any and all mobilization plans. In response, Soviet authorities planned to construct new depots in the new border regions. However, not only did the construction of these depots move forward too slowly, but these new depots themselves, as well as the bottlenecks along the old borders, were also vulnerable to any precipitous enemy advance or deep air attack.

The movement of the Soviet frontier westward also raised the question of what was to be done with the older fortified regions along the former frontier. Obviously, Soviet faith in the utility of such fortifications dictated the erection of defenses along the new border, which would be an expensive and time-consuming process. A question then arose as to whether both the new and old system should be manned. Given the scarcity of resources, although priority was accorded to the erection of defenses along the new border, neither set was fully prepared or manned in June 1941.[8]

The planning experiences for the Finnish War, as well as subsequent dismal Soviet combat performance, were even more sobering and embarrassing. Shaposhnikov's General Staff worked out the initial plan for operations against Finland in a realistic international context and concluded that fulfilling the mission "was far from an easy matter" and would require "several months of intense and difficult war."[9] Stalin rejected the plan for overestimating Finnish military capabilities and ordered the commander of the Leningrad Military District, K. A. Meretskov, to prepare a new plan. Meretskov's plan, which "practically ignored real conditions" and was accepted by Stalin, foresaw defeat of the Finns by powerful initial attacks along numerous axes that would force the Finns to scatter their forces and subject them to piecemeal defeat. Of course, in the initial phase of war, just the reverse occurred.

Generation of forces necessary to conduct such extensive operations required extensive partial mobilization, and coming as it did on the heels of planning disruptions caused by the occupation of eastern Poland, this also turned out to be chaotic and further disrupted existing strategic plans. Consequently, in addition to mobilizing the 7th Army from the Leningrad Military District, the Soviets had to move 8th and 9th Armies from the Baltic Military District and deploy 14th Army in the Polar region. In addition, to assemble necessary combat ready forces initially and after the disastrous first phase of the operation, the General Staff had to shift other divisions to the Finnish border from other military districts.[10] The subsequent course of combat clearly demonstrated

> that the Red Army was not ready for that war, particularly in its offensive form. . . . Our forces were unable to fulfill their combat missions on any axis and first of all along the Karelian Peninsula. . . . Formations transferred to the Leningrad Military District from the Ukraine and Belorussia found themselves in a particularly difficult situation. A large portion of them were not dressed and equipped to a required extent to operate in the severe climatic conditions of the north. Many other major deficiencies appeared, especially in the functioning of rear services. From the first days of the war, resupply of forces broke down. Multi-kilometer traffic jams tied up road traffic. The forces experienced acute shortages of not only ammunition and fuel, but also provisions. . . .
>
> But the main problem was that the command cadre of the army, weakened by the massive repression of 1937 and 1938, operated timidly and

passively. The majority of hastily promoted junior commanders who replaced the repressed did not possess sufficient habits of controlling forces in combat. Many officers were incapable of skillfully organizing cooperation, correctly resolving questions of reconnaissance, camouflage, and engineer and material combat support, and exploiting technical means of communications. All of this led to failure and great losses, and, moreover, it permitted the well-trained Finnish forces, operating in a familiar theater with fewer forces, to repulse our attacks successfully and steadfastly hold on to a great front in the course of the first months of war.[11]

After extensive command changes, sizable reinforcements, additional mobilization, and extensive new preparations, the damage was undone, and during the second phase of the war, the Soviets finally prevailed.

The dismal Soviet performance in eastern Poland and Finland prompted removal of Voroshilov as defense commissar and his replacement by Timoshenko. It also forced wholesale Soviet reevaluation of defense and mobilization planning and force preparedness. Not coincidentally, it also encouraged German aggressive plans against the Soviet Union. Soviet operations in eastern Poland in September 1939, in Finland in winter 1939–1940, and later in Bessarabia in June 1940, significantly altered the Soviet Union's borders and rendered existing strategic plans irrelevant. At the same time, Soviet military performance, especially compared with ongoing and subsequent German combat performance in Poland and the West, indelibly indicated that reform of the Red Army was necessary. Stalin tasked Timoshenko with carrying out those reforms and with adjusting strategic plans to meet new strategic realities.

The *akt* prepared jointly by Voroshilov and Timoshenko on 8 May 1940 clearly stated the problem. Its section on "Operational preparations" began by stating: "At the moment of the handover and reception of the People's Commissariat of Defense, there was no operational war plan, and both general and partial operational plans were not worked and were absent. The General Staff had no information about the state of covering the borders. The decisions of the military district, army, and *front* military councils on this question were unknown to the General Staff."[12] Although Timoshenko then detailed planning deficiencies of the General Staff and Commissariat of Defense, it was clear that he and those political figures who endorsed and co-signed the *akt* (A. A. Zhdanov, G. M. Malenkov, and N. A.Voznesensky) blamed Voroshilov and not Shaposhnikov for the failures. They understood the external and internal conditions that precluded effective planning and permitted Shaposhnikov to continue his important work.

While Timoshenko implemented his extensive new reform program (his first act was an order to create nine new mechanized corps), a new planning team consisting of N. F. Vatutin, chief of the Operations Directorate, and

G. F. Malandin and A. M. Vasilevsky, his deputies, assembled and began their planning work under Shaposhnikov's tutelage.[13]

## WAR AND STRATEGIC DEPLOYMENT PLANNING
## ON THE EVE OF WAR

German conquests in western and northern Europe in spring 1940 lent an air of urgency to General Staff planning. The unsettling course of the European war, Soviet military actions and ensuing Soviet territorial annexations, and chaos within the Red Army had destroyed the utility of any existing plans. The new planning team worked hard and by July produced results. Late that month Shaposhnikov approved a new strategic deployment plan, largely prepared by Vasilevsky. Like its predecessor, the plan postulated an attack by Germany supported by Italy, Finland, Rumania, and possibly Hungary against the western Soviet Union and by Japan against Soviet Far Eastern territories. Vasilevsky's plan assessed a total threat of 270 infantry divisions supported by 11,750 tanks, 22,000 guns, and 16,400 aircraft, the bulk of which would be committed in the critical Western Theater.[14]

The July plan assessed that the enemy would launch his main attack north of the San River in eastern Poland along the Vilnius-Minsk and Brest-Baranovichi axes (see Map 4.3). A second less likely scenario had German and Polish forces attacking from the Lublin region of southern Poland through Ukraine toward Kiev. In conclusion, the plan stated, "The chief, most politically favorable course for Germany and, consequently, the most probable is the first variant of her action—with deployment of the main force of the German Army north of the San River."[15]

In accordance with this plan, the General Staff anticipated formation and deployment of three *fronts* in the Western Theater: the Northwestern and Western covering the main strategic axis toward Moscow, and a secondary axis toward Leningrad and the Southwestern, defending the strategic axis south of the Pripiat Marshes. They also planned to form the Trans-Baikal and Far Eastern Fronts to deal with the Japanese threat in the Far East. The only apparent weakness in the new plan was its concentration on the Moscow axis to the detriment of the Leningrad and Kiev axes. Soon this would become a major bone of contention between Stalin and the General Staff.

After the appointment of K. A. Meretskov as chief of the General Staff in August 1940, in accordance with a 16 August Main Military Council decree, the General Staff reevaluated the July Shaposhnikov plan in a study entitled "Considerations of the Principal Bases of Strategic Deployment of the Armed Forces of the Soviet Union in the West and the East in 1940 and 1941."[16]

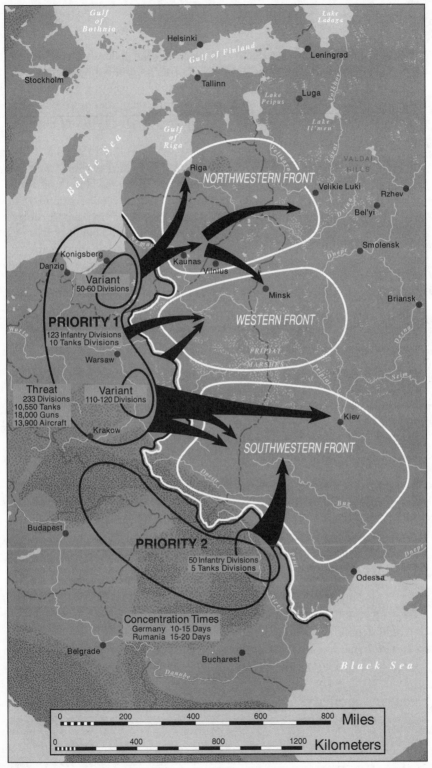

Map 4.3. The July 1940 Strategic Plan.

Once again Vasilevsky took the lead in preparing the document, and by mid-September he had completed his work. On 18 September Vasilevsky submitted the final "Considerations," a position paper whose conclusions resembled those found in Shaposhnikov's earlier plan, to Timoshenko and Meretskov for approval. Timoshenko then passed it to Stalin and the Party for final review and approval.

Vasilevsky's "Considerations" once again maintained that the Soviet Union had to be prepared for war on two fronts, against Germany and her allies in the West and against Japan in the East. It increased the size of the overall threat and assessed that Germany and her allies could commit up to 243 divisions, 10,000 tanks, and 15,000 aircraft against the Soviet Union.[17] Therefore, it mandated deployment of the bulk of the Soviet armed forces in the West (189 division and 2 brigades, or 61 percent of all formations), organized into four wartime *fronts* (Northern, Northwestern, Western, and Southwestern). The plan called for the maintenance of 5 High Command reserve armies (with 51 divisions), all of which were earmarked for operations in the West. Thus, the General Staff proposed that 240 Red Army divisions (80 percent of the Red Army) be committed in the West, 33 in the Far East, 30 in the Transcaucasus and Central Asia, and 1 in the White Sea region.[18] The plan accorded 60 percent of *front* and long-range bomber aviation to the West, 16 percent to the Far East and Trans-Baikal, and 24 percent to the Transcaucasus and Central Asia.

Further, the plan assumed that "both sides would begin combat operations with only part of their forces, and both the main forces of the Red Army and the main enemy forces would complete their deployment in not less than two weeks." In any event, Red Army forces were to "strike a powerful answering blow [counteroffensive] against German-fascist forces and carry combat operations to his territory."[19] The "Considerations" again suggested two possibilities for Soviet strategic deployment in the West. The first (and secondary) required deployment of the principal strategic grouping south of Brest to repel the enemy offensive and deliver a strong counterthrust toward Lublin, Krakow, and Breslau to cut Germany off from the Balkans and deprive her of her economic base.

The first (main) planning scenario placed the bulk of Soviet forces north of Brest with the mission of repelling the enemy and attacking his main grouping in East Prussia. The final decision as to which scenario would be followed would depend on conditions at the beginning of war. This meant that the General Staff had to prepare fully for both in peacetime.

On 5 October Timoshenko and Meretskov presented the "Considerations" and concurrent war plans to Stalin and the Soviet political leadership for approval. Stalin objected to its contents:

I don't fully understand the General Staff's insistence on concentrating our forces on the Western Front. They say Hitler will try to send his main attacking force in the direction of Moscow by the shortest route. But I think the most important thing for the Germans is the grain in Ukraine and the coal of the Donbas. Now that Hitler has established himself in the Balkans, it's all the more likely he'll launch his main attack from the southwest. I want the General Staff to think again and submit a new plan in ten days' time.[20]

In all likelihood, Stalin's experience as military commissar in Ukraine during the Civil War, his familiarity with Hitler's geopolitical and economic views, and the influence of "Southerners" like Zhukov in his strategic thinking influenced his decision to reject Timoshenko's and Vasilevsky's arguments. In any event, he gave the General Staff ten days to prepare a new plan based on the southern variant.

On 14 October Timoshenko presented Stalin with his revised plan, which, unlike its predecessor, flatly declared that the Western Theater was the principal theater of war and mandated having "the main grouping in the West in the Southwestern Front," specifically south of Brest (see Map 4.4).[21] As a result of the review process, Stalin and Timoshenko decided to strengthen the composition of the Southwestern Front forces to an even greater extent. Although the second scenario for deployment of larger forces north of the Pripiat was not categorically rejected, "it did not receive particular support." As a consequence, "there occurred a full reorientation and reassessment of the basic strength of our forces from the Northwestern (as proposed by Shaposhnikov) to the Southwestern axis."[22]

This strategic assessment and plan did not fundamentally change before the outbreak of war, first and foremost because Stalin had decreed it. In addition, most leading military figures were products of the "Southern School." As Stalin's biographer D. Volkogonov has pointed out:

The top posts in the General Staff . . . were now occupied by men "promoted" from the Kiev Special Military District: S. K. Timoshenko as defense commissar, G. K. Zhukov, who became chief of the General Staff in February 1941, N. F. Vatutin, Zhukov's first deputy, and S. K. Kozhevnikov, head of the political section of the General Staff. It was natural that these people, who had been long involved in operational matters in the Kiev Special Military District, would, in some degree, consider the southwest axis to be of primary importance. Stalin's point of view was well known to them. . . . The Military Counsel of the Kiev Special Military District held to the point of view that "one must expect the main strike of combined

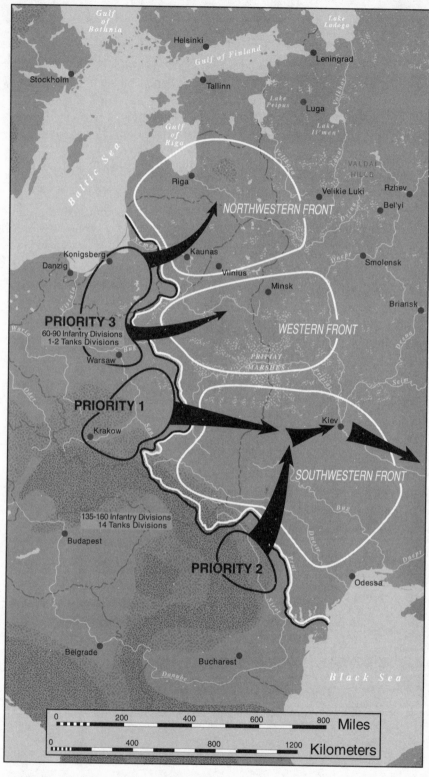

Map 4.4. The October 1940 Strategic Plan.

enemy forces in [our] zone of responsibility." A document on deployment for 1940, prepared by the new chief of the Kiev Special Military District, M. A. Purkaev, stated simply that the sharpest attacks of the German army must be expected along the southwestern axis.[23]

Subsequently, the General Staff planned for war, mobilization, and strategic deployment on the basis of the October decisions. In December 1940 and January 1941, the General Staff held a conference and war games in Moscow to investigate current war-fighting concepts and test war plans in a variety of scenarios. Both the conference and the war games raised as many questions as they answered and, not surprisingly, indicated flaws in war planning. As a result of the war games, Zhukov replaced Meretskov as chief of the General Staff.[24] On 1 February 1941, Deputy Chief of the General Staff Lieutenant General Vatutin prepared a "Plan for the Elaboration of Operational Plans," which Chief of the General Staff Army General Zhukov approved with slight amendments. According to that "plan of plans," all planning was to be completed by 1 May 1941. Such, however, was not the case.

The continued rapid expansion of the Soviet armed forces and changing threat assessments complicated the planning process, and "the General Staff constantly introduced changes into its calculations on strategic concentration and deployment. The latest information about their deployment in the event of war in the West and about the composition of district forces was assembled by General Vatutin on 13 and 14 June 1941."[25] Throughout the period of heightened tensions, the General Staff undoubtedly prepared many draft contingency plans, and military district commanders made proposals as well. Although most of these have remained buried in Russian archives, one notable proposal, which has attracted public attention, has surfaced: a 15 May proposal prepared by Zhukov for a preemptive Soviet attack on German forces concentrating in eastern Poland. The plan has been published in part and thoroughly analyzed; it did not accord with Soviet mobilization capabilities and force readiness, and there is no direct evidence that Stalin ever saw it. (See chapter 8 for the details of Zhukov's proposal.) Even if he had, given his known actions in 1941, it is fairly certain he would not have approved it.[26]

The most important aspect of planning strategic deployment was formulation of plans for covering (defending) the borders of the Soviet Union. This was the responsibility of the western border military districts, each of which prepared a "Plan for Defending the State Borders." For example, the Western Special Military District presented its plan to the General Staff on 31 December 1940, and the Kiev Special Military District did likewise on 7 February 1941. Changing internal and international conditions, however, demanded that these plans be revised. Thus, in early May 1941, the General Staff worked out a more refined plan, "The 1941 Plan for Defending the State

Borders," and sent it, along with directives from the People's Commissariat of Defense, to the five western border military districts. (See Appendix B for an example of the planning guidance and completed plans.)[27] The directives ordered the districts to submit new defense and PVO (air defense) plans by 25 May 1941. They also designated specific regions the districts were to defend, assigned forces and equipment for their defense, and specified coordination measures with naval and neighboring forces, and other appropriate questions.[28] The districts, in turn, submitted their plans to the General Staff between 10 and 20 June. This work was complicated and delayed by the partial mobilization that began in April 1941.

The plans for both strategic deployment and the defense of the state border were deficient in several respects. Most important, although they were hastily prepared by a competent group of staff officers, there was great turbulence among the command cadre designated to carry them out. Compounding the situation, the international climate was volatile, and through fall 1940 Soviet military interference in the affairs of its neighbors (such as Belorussia in July 1940 and the Baltic states in fall 1940) added to international tension and further disrupted General Staff planning.

The strategic deployment plans themselves were based upon false Soviet assumptions about the period required to deploy. The General Staff believed the German Wehrmacht required 10 to 15 days to mobilize and deploy, therefore the Soviets would have time to deploy fully its covering armies. It did not consider the possibility that the German Army could deploy sufficiently in peacetime to launch an attack. Nor did they think that the Germans could exploit military circumstances in the west to conceal concentration in the east.

Consistent with longstanding interwar views, the General Staff ignored the possibility of a surprise attack by enemy main forces before routine mobilization had taken place. They felt that covering armies were fully sufficient to repulse an enemy attack while Soviet main forces were mobilizing and deploying to launch a counteroffensive. More important, they failed to insure that covering armies and the most ready of the reserves were properly manned and equipped to perform their critical mission.

More catastrophic was the failure of the Soviet political leadership, particularly Stalin, to appreciate the increased degree of threat. The military leadership, cowed by the looming presence of the purges, acted timidly and generally acquiesced to Stalin's views. Right up to 22 June, and despite ample intelligence warnings, Stalin could not believe he did not understand Hitler's psyche and credited German offensive preparations to disinformation and the machinations of Western powers. When convinced to undertake a precautionary partial mobilization, the mobilization took place in slow motion. "Therefore, practical measures for strategic deployment of the armed forces on the eve of war proceeded slowly and, in certain cases, were of a local nature and failed to touch upon such critical issues as movement, deployment, and the bringing to combat readiness of first echelon covering armies and the deployment of air defense, aviation, and naval forces."[29]

The overall General Staff state border defense plan and individual *front* plans for defense of the state borders were also deficient in terms of the timeliness of their preparation and the specific contents of each plan. Many military district plans were still incomplete when war began, and programs mandated from above, like the fortified region construction plan, were inconsistent with these plans. Because military districts did not forward their proposed plans to the General Staff until 25 May, on 22 June the comprehensive General Staff plan was still far from complete.

Neither the overall state nor the district defense plans created buffer regions between the state border and the forward defensive positions of covering armies. Most army defenses were anchored on the border defenses of forward fortified regions and border guard detachments. This placed all forward forces in jeopardy if surprised and prevented army commanders from responding flexibly to any attack. In essence, any attack would immediately carry into the depth of the army defense. Often, the grouping of defending forces was so far forward, in particular the covering armies and mechanized corps in the key Bialystok and L'vov salients, that no space was available for Soviet commanders to organize coherent counterattacks or counterthrusts.

In several front sectors, the deployments called for by the plans facilitated rapid defeat. For example, the majority of Western and Kiev Special Military District divisions were located 30 to 60 kilometers from sectors that the plan designated as most threatened. Therefore, at the commencement of hostilities, many formations had to move laterally across the front to occupy their assigned defensive positions. The plan "did not envision a variant where first echelon divisions could occupy defenses in depth close to their home stations."[30] Given these realities, effective defense was difficult in the best of circumstances. It was suicidal against the well-trained German Army.

The state defense plan also presumed all commanders would know about an impending enemy attack in timely enough fashion to undertake relatively simultaneous deployment of their forces. All alert commands for implementing the plan were to be passed to headquarters by enciphered telegrams. The time necessary to encode, transmit, and decode messages inhibited timely reaction, and in reality many headquarters never received their alert orders. The combination of a German surprise attack, a Soviet alert system geared to slow mobilization, Soviet deployment plans that presumed a certain degree of advanced warning, and flawed state border defense plans guaranteed that all Soviet plans would abort the moment war began.

## MOBILIZATION PLANNING

The changing, more threatening political atmosphere of Europe in the 1930s, as well as the demands of changing technology, altered Soviet strategic concepts and rendered the existing force generation system ineffective in meeting potential future threats. Svechin's enjoinder that the Soviet Union should achieve "permanent mobilization" by building a civilian economy that maximized support for the military economy based upon a unity of the front and the "state rear" had not been realized. No Soviet mobilization plan could cope with, alter, or overcome this stark reality.

The territorial-cadre force, which postulated the employment of regionally based reserves to supplement the peacetime cadre army, had served the Soviets well in the 1920s. After 1935, however, it had become apparent that the growing threat required a wartime force that was larger and more technically competent than the territorial system could produce. The peacetime force simply could not be expanded sufficiently to meet the demands of future war:

> It is important to note that by the mid-1930s the mixed territorial-cadre system of completing and organizing forces had already exhausted itself and become a brake on the path of their combat growth. There matured an actual necessity for the transformation to the unified cadre principle of formation. One of the main reasons was that the temporary manpower of territorial units and formations at short muster were already not in a state to master the new complex technology and to learn how to employ it in ever-changing conditions. . . . The transformation to a cadre system, to a considerable degree, was dictated by the growing demands for increased combat and mobilization preparedness, since the danger of war with fascist Germany was growing.[31]

The transformation process began in 1937 and was supposed to be completed by January 1939, although conversion of some formations lagged until later in the year.[32] Officially, during the period from 1 January 1937 to 1 January 1939, the total number of Soviet rifle divisions increased from 97 to 98. The number of cadre divisions increased from 49 to 84, and the 35 territorial divisions disappeared from the Red Army force structure. (The precise pace and extent of this conversion process is shown in Table 4.1, at the end of this chapter.) In addition, during 1938 the NKO also abolished the few existing Soviet nationality-based formations and military schools.

To provide an increased supply of manpower for these divisions and for future mobilization, on 1 September 1939, the Supreme Soviet of the USSR passed a new law on Universal Military Service that increased the term of military service for enlisted men and NCOs to three years and provided for more thorough military training. At the same time, the NKO reformed the military district system to improve its efficiency in processing military manpower and increased the number of districts to 16.[33] The new force-manning system and the reorganized administrative structure made possible expansion of the Red Army as it "crept up to war" between 1939 and June 1941. The Red Army grew from a total strength of 1.5 million men on 1 June 1938 to just over 5 million men in June 1941. The Red Army force structure expanded from 27 to 62 rifle corps and from 106 mixed cadre and regular rifle divisions to 196 regular rifle divisions. In addition, the Soviets created 31 motorized (motorized rifle) and 61 tank divisions, 16 airborne brigades, and over 100 new fortified regions. (See Table 4.2 for the details of Red Army expansion.)

By June 1941 the wartime establishment strength of rifle divisions was set at 14,483 men, and peacetime divisions were supposed to be maintained at several levels of cadre strength. In early 1939 the strongest divisions (1st line), deployed in border military districts, numbered 6,959 men; those in the interior (2d line) had a paper strength of 5,220 men; and other reserve divisions (3d line), with insignificant numbers of cadre personnel in peacetime, would form during mobilization and wartime from existing divisions.[34] After 1939 the NKO increased these peacetime strengths, and by June 1941 most border military district divisions were at 60 to 85 percent of their new strength (8,500 to 12,000 men). Divisions in the interior, however, were closer to 1939 requirements.

The deteriorating European political situation and ensuing crises, which resulted in the wholesale strengthening of the active armed forces and prospective wartime mobilization, placed an immense strain on the Soviet mobilization system. The incessant redrafting of war and strategic deployment plans abruptly and frequently raised the projected size of the wartime Soviet armed forces at a time when crisis and war experience underscored the weaknesses and inadequacies of current mobilization systems.

Quite understandably, these factors impelled the General Staff to produce new revised mobilization instructions and plans, which it hoped would satisfy the demands of new strategic deployment plans. These new instructions, patterned after those of the early 1930s, sought to refine the mobilization system. The 1940 mobilization Instructions, unlike those of 1930, began with a striking warning: "War against the USSR, which is in capitalist encirclement, can begin unexpectedly. Today wars are not declared. They simply begin."[35] The 1940 Instructions and its 1941 counterpart reeked of an increased sense of urgency and concern for mobilization detail. Understandably, they added secret mobilization procedures to existing procedures for conventional mobilization.

Within the parameters laid out by the Instructions, on 16 August 1940, the Main Military Council issued orders for the preparation of a new mobilization plan, the Mobilization Plan, 1941 (MP-41). The new planning team on the General Staff, headed by Vasilevsky, prepared the plan, and the NKO approved it in February 1941. Like strategic deployment plans, however, it soon required revision. Consequently, in March 1941 the General Staff decided to revise the plan and ordered the military districts to present new plans so that a new MP-41 could be prepared by 1 May. According to one assessment, "This period was clearly insufficient, and as a result, the military districts and forces were not able to work out the whole complex of measures according to the new scheme of mobilization deployment thoroughly. Therefore, a number of [strategic] axes prolonged the working out of a mobilization plan until 20 July 1941."[36]

The Communist Party Central Committee added its encouragement to the military districts. In an order accompanying the General Staff instructions to the districts, it wrote, "The weight of all of our people is needed to support the state of mobilized readiness in the face of the danger of military attack."[37]

Force mobilization was the most critical element of the mobilization plan. According to MP-41, it consisted of "the planned and timely transition of each separate force unit, headquarters, directorate, organization, and the whole Red Army from a peacetime establishment organization to a wartime establishment organization during a period prescribed by the mobilization deployment scheme."[38] The border military district deployment schemes encompassed a variety of readiness states, including peacetime units mobilized to full wartime state, secondary units mobilized on the basis of cadre allocated from peacetime units, secondary units that lacked cadre in peacetime, and units that remained on a peacetime establishment. Mobilization was to be announced by order of the Presidium of the USSR Supreme Soviet, and conscription upon mobilization and subsequent call-ups took place on the basis of Council of People's Commissars decrees and accompanying orders of the NKO. This process encompassed all military district units included in the district's mobilization scheme according to a strict time schedule.

By June 1941 the new mobilization plan was incomplete and "was not well thought out."[39] In addition, military district plans were only partial and did not include all force formations. The plan did not contain provisions for elevating all forces to full combat readiness simultaneously. All forces in a theater could either be brought to full readiness or left at the lesser state of "constant readiness." The mobilization period was also staggered depending on force importance and location. Formations of first echelon covering armies were to mobilize within 2 to 3 days, and remaining formations, rear service units, and other organizations were to mobilize in 4 to 7 days. Full mobilization and deployment of the armed forces in a theater of military operations was to require 15 to 30 days of mobilization. All of this, of course, corresponded to General Staff assumptions as to how war would commence.

According to MP-41, mobilization could be either secret or open. The former anticipated use of large-scale exercises as a cover for mobilization and applied primarily to partial mobilization. Secret mobilization involved use of a so-called mobilization telegram scheme for alerting units. Enciphered telegrams were sent to formation commanders in the military districts who had special sealed packets marked "top secret" and "open only on receipt of a telegram about mobilization." By regulation, these packets were kept in the safes of the formations' chiefs of staff.[40]

Alert notification for open mobilization was to take place through normal communications channels and did not require disclosure of the reasons for the mobilization. This mobilization was called "large training exercises" (bol'shie uchebnye sbory, or BUS) and was of two types, designated by the letter "A" or "B." During "A" mobilization, units and formations were filled with establishment personnel. Military districts, which had centralized methods for supply of mobilization rescues and which had to conduct the BUS, provided units and formations with command personnel, soldiers, transport, and horses. During "B" mobilization, forces were to be filled out by mobilization resources obtained from the surrounding territory of the military district, and material support was based upon peacetime norms at the expense of routine allowances and reserve stores.[41]

Despite the apparent deficiencies of MP-41 and, in particular, the unfavorable conditions surrounding mobilization and the compressed time frame for its implementation, the mechanics of the process permitted mobilization to occur in June 1941. According to the mobilization plan, although the quantity of rifle corps and divisions would remain unchanged (at 62 and 198, respectively), the number of fronts and armies would increase from 1 and 16 to 8 and 29, respectively. Furthermore, there would be a major expansion of supporting RGK (High Command Reserve) artillery and aviation regiments and aviation divisions. (See Table 4.3 for the full scope of the mobilization envisioned in MP-41.)

Full implementation of MP-41 involved the call-up of almost 5 million reservists, including up to 600,000 officers and 885,000 NCOs, and transfer from the civil economy of 248,000 vehicles, 36,000 tractors, and 730,000 horses.[42] The total quantity of mobilized and deployed formations was 344 division equivalents, 25 divisions more than called for by the January mobilization plan. Since many of these formations were not at full combat strength, the plan envisioned their being filled out during the initial stages of hostilities. Although the mobilization plan allocated 6.5 million of the total mobilizable force of 7.85 million men to the western military districts, by 22 June 1941 western military district strength had reached only 2,901,000 men.[43]

Despite the large-scale organizational expansion called for by the plan, the Soviet material base and production potential in 1941 was insufficient to support such a large-scale mobilization. In the beginning of 1941, cadre formations and units possessed 76 percent of their artillery, and 31 percent of their heavy, 74 percent of their medium, and 100 percent of their light tanks, and the Red Army aircraft park had few modern aircraft. Vehicles and tractors were in short supply, and civilian mobilization resources covered 81.5 percent of necessary vehicles and 70 percent of required tractors. Much of this equipment, however, was in poor repair and was available for distribution to the military only after the declaration of mobilization. Finally, these key mobility assets had to move long distances before joining their parent forces. Rear service support was also very weak, and the General Staff estimated existing supplies were capable of supporting only two to three months of wartime operations.[44]

Although on paper the mobilization plan provided requisite forces and weaponry to form the operational-strategic force groupings mandated by war and deployment plans, associated plans for the material support of operating forces were woefully inadequate. The Red Army lacked mobilizable emergency strategic reserves necessary to replace initial wartime losses until Soviet industry had geared up to meet wartime needs: "The considerable growth in demands for weapons and military equipment under the new mobilization plan, especially in tanks, aircraft, and antiaircraft systems, given existing resources, caused an increase in force shortages. Thus, for example, mechanized corps forming in the Western and Odessa Military Districts were supplied with 35 to 40 percent of their tanks and were equipped with chiefly four to five types of light tanks. Aviation, antiaircraft, and other units were in roughly the same situation."[45] Thus, according to retrospective Soviet critiques, during the period of the Timoshenko reform program and the development of strategic deployment and mobilization plans, the NKO and General Staff "violated the important demand for coordinating deployment of the armed forces with the economic potential of the country, especially in the production of means of armed struggle. It would have required around five years to provide the Red Army with weaponry and military equipment called for by the new mobilization plan. Mobilization in the USSR went on at an extremely slow tempo. As a result, war found the forces of the border military districts not fully mobilized and, consequently, not fully combat ready."[46]

## MOBILIZATION AND STRATEGIC DEPLOYMENT PRIOR TO 22 JUNE 1941

Between April and 22 June 1941, during what they called a "specially threatening military period," the Soviet government and NKO accelerated "creeping up to war" by conducting a concealed strategic deployment of forces. This was, in effect, the first stage in a prolonged mobilization and deployment process that would continue into wartime and, ultimately, through early 1942. From 26 April 1941, on the instructions of the General Staff, the Trans-Baikal Military District's and Far Eastern Front's Military Councils dispatched to the West one mechanized corps, two rifle corps, and two airborne brigades. On 10 May the Ural Military District received instructions to send two rifle divisions to the Baltic Special Military District, and five days later the Siberian Military District received similar orders to transport single divisions to the Western and Kiev Special Military Districts.[47]

On 13 May 1941, the People's Commissariat of Defense and Zhukov, the chief of the General Staff, directed the military districts to move 28 divisions, 9 corps headquarters, and 4 army headquarters (16th, 19th, 21st, and 22d) from internal districts to the border districts. These forces were to assemble in positions along the Western Dvina and Dnepr Rivers, with the 16th and 19th armies reinforcing the Kiev Special Military District and the 21st and 22d the Western Special Military District. Movement of these armies began in May with orders to adhere to a strict camouflage regime and to deploy carefully and slowly so as not to portray abnormally high traffic on the rail net. These armies were to complete their concentration in designated assembly areas between 1 and 10 June 1941 and were to constitute a second strategic echelon.[48]

The 13 May directive also ordered the redeployment of formations from the Moscow, Volga, Siberian, Arkhangel'sk, Orel, and Far Eastern Military Districts for the formation of three additional armies (20th, 24th, and 28th). Although the bulk of 20th Army, primarily from the Orel Military District, had begun to assemble west of Moscow, the remaining armies had not started to move when war began on 22 June. Initially, all of these armies were designated for use as a strategic reserve, but when hostilities broke out they became the nucleus of a *Front* of Reserve Armies, under Marshal S. M. Budenny's command. Thus, the mobilization involved a total of seven armies and one mechanized corps. (See Table 4.4 for the origin and destination of each mobilized force.)

Most of the formations in these reserve armies were not at full strength. Up to 80 percent of the divisions were at reduced peacetime manning (6,000 rather than 14,800), and only when war actually began did they begin receiving reservists and additional weapons, equipment, and transport from wherever they could obtain it. Ultimately, most divisions reached 60 percent manning but still lacked much of their weaponry and, in particular, necessary vehicles for movement and for transporting supplies. The inability to fill out the divisions to wartime strength was caused by shortages of equipment in the military districts and inaccurate assessment by the General Staff and military districts of rail transport capacity.

Underestimation of rail capacity was the most serious of the problems:

According to plan, the overall volume of force transport consisted of 939 trains, including 759 trains for rifle forces, 105 for tank, 50 for aviation units, and 25 for artillery.

According to their status on 22 June, of the planned 939 trains, 538 were loaded, 455 of these were still en route, and 83 had unloaded at their designated points. The loading of the remaining trains continued until 2 July, and the unloading was fully completed on 14 July. By the beginning of war, only 9 divisions of the second strategic echelon had concentrated in their designated regions (19th Army), and 19 divisions were en route (16th, 21st, and 22d Armies).[49]

To supplement these secret troop movements, by 1 to 10 June the NKO and General Staff had called up 793,500 conscripts under the guise of "large training exercises" (BUS). In fact, this amounted to a partial secret mobilization.[50] This permitted filling out to a considerable extent about half of the existing rifle divisions as well as fortified regions, RGK artillery regiments, Air Force, engineer, signal, air defense, and rear service forces. Since priority went to combat divisions, the support forces had to absorb the worst manpower shortages. Although these orders provided valuable manpower resources, full force readiness depended greatly on weaponry and combat equipment, which were in short supply.

Wholesale failures due partly to the German surprise attack and partly to planning failures and inefficiencies of the procurement system occurred in the provision of combat forces with requisite weaponry and other key equipment. The failure of the transport mobilization system was particularly catastrophic. Military requisitions of civilian trucks and tractors simply were not filled. As a consequence, alerted formations had to move to assembly areas by whatever means possible (usually rail or foot), and they could not bring heavy weapons, artillery, fuel, ammunition, or critical foodstuffs with them. This particularly hurt divisions fielding from the internal military districts to the *front*. Most had to leave behind their equipment and supplies, which never caught up with them. Virtually all divisions went into battle without the necessary equipment or supplies.

While forces in the internal military districts were mobilizing men and raising and redeploying forces, in late May, within severe constraints imposed by Stalin, the western border military districts finally carried out limited regrouping. This regrouping, however, was limited to forces in the depths of the districts, lest the Germans take the movements to be a provocation. For example, on 19 June the Leningrad Military District commander transferred 1st Tank Division (1st Mechanized Corps) from the Pskov region to Kandalaska in central Karelia. The same day Leningrad Military District transferred 11th Rifle Division to Baltic Special Military District's 8th Army along the border.

On 15 June district commanders received permission from the NKO and General Staff to shift forces from deep in the district to positions further forward in accordance with existing defense plans. Some deployed by rail, but most did so on foot and at night in order to maintain secrecy. During this movement the NKO categorically prohibited military district commanders from redeploying first echelon forces or improving their forward defenses.

At least one brave military district commander violated these instructions. On 15 June General F. I. Kuznetsov, Baltic Special Military District commander, alarmed by intelligence reports that described a threatening enemy buildup along the borders, issued a lengthy order increasing force readiness along the border. Without specifically mentioning the German offensive preparations, Kuznetsov criticized specific division commanders for laxness and sloppiness in maintaining combat readiness: "Today, as never before, we must be fully combat ready. Many commanders do not understand this. But all must firmly and clearly understand that at any moment we must be ready to fulfill any combat mission."[51] Kuznetsov then ordered commanders to implement specified passive measures to improve combat readiness and defenses.

Later the same day, the district Military Council reiterated combat alert procedures in a directive that began, "In the event of enemy violation of the border, a surprise attack by large [enemy] forces, or an overflight of the border by aviation formations, I am establishing the following notification procedures."[52] Finally, on 18 June, after receipt on 17 June of a lengthy, detailed, and threatening intelligence summary, Kuznetsov ordered his forces to full military readiness. The order, which began, "With the aim of rapidly bringing the district theater of military operations to combat readiness, I order," specifically mandated full combat readiness on the part of district air defense, signal, and ground transport systems, instructed 8th and 11th Army commanders to prepare engineer bridging and minelaying, and provided instructions to all other force commanders to make appropriate defensive preparations.[53] Despite these courageous actions on Kuznetsov's part, there is no evidence that the additional preparations made any difference in district combat performance when war began.

These measures designed to beef up the defensive capability of the border military districts failed. In the period immediately preceding the German attack, although 33 divisions began moving from internal military districts into the border districts, only 4 to 5 divisions succeeded in reaching their new concentration areas. This, combined with the dispersion of district forces to a depth of up to 400 kilometers, set up these forces for sequential and piecemeal defeat. Meanwhile, in the strategic depths, the Soviet command failed to back up forward forces in timely fashion with ready reserves. The planned formation and deployment of the strategic reserve of seven armies with 67 divisions was also chaotic and late. This, combined with the General Staff's misassessment of where the German main attack would occur, condemned forward forces and strategic reserves alike to subsequent rapid defeat.

Mobilization also encompassed the vast mass of rear service necessary to sustain forces in combat and preparation of the theater of operations, particularly in an engineer sense. On the eve of war, there were little or no rear services in *fronts* and armies, and these services in subordinate field units and in military districts were maintained at reduced peacetime state. Therefore, MP-41 laid out service support mobilization parameters that required army rear service organs to mobilize in 7 days, *front* organs in 15 days, and Air Force organs in 5 days. This required formation in each *front* of 400 to 500 rear service units and organizations and more than 100 in each army.[54]

The mobilization plan required that "stable and stationary" *front* organs maintain large reserves amounting to 9 to 10 combat loads of ammunition, up to 10 refills of fuel, and 30 days of food to complement the 3 to 6 days of supply for these items in force units. Although the overall mobilization plan contained a separate "Plan for Deployment of the Rear," the confused command responsibilities for planning and directing rear services (see chapter 6) reduced the effectiveness of the plan. Shortages of key materials and, in particular, transport and mal-deployment of reserve stocks resulted. In essence, the rear services plan and how it was implemented did not meet the requirements of force mobilization and strategic deployment plans. As a result, rear service support became a major Achilles' heel for the Soviets when war began.

Preparation of the theater of military operations for combat (in an engineer sense) also fell short, in part because of faulty planning and in part due to the shift of the Soviet border westward in 1939 and 1940. The plan for the formation of fortified regions and defensive fortifications along the border was not timely enough for defense in 1941, and the haste in preparing border defenses disrupted other aspects of the general defense plans. Special plans to revitalize the Soviet rail system and extend it to the new western borders were also incomplete in summer 1941, and Soviet industry did not produce the required quantities of rail rolling stock. The same applied to theater wire and radio communications, which by June 1941 were only 75 percent complete.[55] "Thus, by the beginning of war, the theater of military operations was not well prepared, and that considerably hindered the strategic deployment and combat readiness of forces in the border military districts and had a negative effect on the conduct of the defense during the initial period of war."[56]

Although mobilization and deployment plans were severally flawed and contributed to the ensuing series of military disasters during the initial period of hostilities, by 1941 the Soviet manpower training system had produced an overall manpower reserve pool of 14 million men. The General Staff mobilization system, as flawed as it was, permitted the Red Army to produce a massive number of new armies, divisions, and other military units during the initial period of war. In the last analysis, this system and the forces it produced in 1941 and later, in 1942, enabled the Red Army and Soviet state to survive the initial period of war and emerge victorious in 1945.

## STATISTICAL DATA

Table 4.1. Cadre and Territorial Formations and Units in the Red Army

| Formation and Unit | 1 January 1937 | 1 January 1938 | 1 January 1939 |
|---|---|---|---|
| Cadre rifle divisions | 49 | 50 | 84 |
| Mixed rifle divisions | 4 | 2 | 0 |
| Territorial divisions | 35 | 34 | 0 |
| Cadre mountain rifle divisions | 9 | 10 | 14 |
| Separate brigades | 0 | 0 | 5 |
| Separate territorial regiments | 2 | 2 | 0 |
| Total | 97 divisions | 96 divisions | 98 divisions |
|  | 2 regiments | 2 regiments | 5 brigades |

Source: I. G. Pavlovsky, *Sukhoputnye voiske SSSR* [Ground Forces of the USSR] (Moscow: Voenizdat, 1985), 65.

Table 4.2. Red Army Expansion, 1939 to June 1941

| Formation | 1 June 1938 | 1 September 1939 | December 1940 | June 1941 |
|---|---|---|---|---|
| Armies | 1 | 2 | 20 | 20 |
| Rifle corps | 27 | 25 | 30 | 62 |
| Rifle divisions (regular) | 71 | 96 | 152 | 196 |
| Rifle divisions (cadre) | 35 | 0 | 0 | 0 |
| Motorized rifle and mechanized divisions | 0 | 1 | 10 | 31 |
| Cavalry corps | 7 | 7 | 4 | 4 |
| Cavalry divisions | 32 | 30 | 26 | 13 |
| Rifle brigades | 0 | 5 | 5 | 3 |
| Tank divisions | 0 | 0 | 18 | 61 |
| Tank corps | 4 | 4 | 0 | 0 |
| Fortified regions | 13 | 21 | 21 | 120 |
| Airborne brigades | 6 | 6 | 12 | 16 |
| Airborne corps | 0 | 0 | 0 | 5 |
| Red Army strength | 1,513,000 | 1,520,000 | 4,207,000 | 5,373,000 |

Sources: I. Kh. Bagramian, ed., *Istoriia voin i voennogo iskusstva* [A history of wars and military art] (Moscow: Voenizdat, 1970); V. A. Anfilov, *Proval blitskriga* [The failure of blitzkrieg] (Moscow: Nauka, 1974); A. Ryzhakov, "K voprosu o stroitel'stve bronetankovykh voisk Krasnoi Armii v 30–e gody" [Concerning the question of the formation of Red Army armored forces in the 1930s], *VIZh* 8 (August 1968).

Table 4.3. Mobilization Required by MP-41

| Deploying Unit and Formation | Quantity in Peacetime | New under MP-41 | Total Deployed |
|---|---|---|---|
| *Front* headquarters | 1 | 7 | 8 |
| Army headquarters | 16 | 13 | 29 |
| Rifle corps headquarters | 62 | 0 | 62 |
| Rifle divisions | 198 | 0 | 198 |
| Separate rifle brigades | 3 | 0 | 3 |
| Mechanized corps | 29 | 0 | 29 |
| Tank divisions | 61 | 0 | 61 |
| Motorized divisions | 31 | 0 | 31 |
| Cavalry corps | 4 | 0 | 4 |
| Separate airborne brigades | 16 | 0 | 16 |
| Corps artillery regiments | 72 | 22 | 94 |
| RGK artillery regiments | 56 | 18 | 74 |
| Separate antitank artillery brigades | 10 | 0 | 10 |
| Aviation corps | 5 | 0 | 5 |
| Aviation divisions | 53 | 26 | 79 |
| Aviation regiments | 247 | 106 | 353 |

Note: The 26 aviation divisions and 106 aviation regiments were in the process of forming, and they were to be mobilized based on their preparedness.
Source: *Nachal'nyi period Velikoi otechestvennoi voiny: Vyvody: uroki* [The initial period of the Great Patriotic War: Conclusions and lessons] (Moscow: Varoshilov Academy of the General Staff, 1989), 40.

Table 4.4. Planned Mobilization of Strategic Reserves, May to June 1941

| Formation | Origin | Destination |
|---|---|---|
| 16th Army | Trans-Baikal Military District | Proskurov, Khmel'niki (Kiev MD by 22 June) |
| 19th Army | North Caucasus Military District | Cherkassy, Belaia Tserkov' (Kiev MD by 22 June); 34th RC, Rzhishchev by 22 June; 25th RC, Korsun' by 22 June; 67th RC, Tarashcha by 22 June |
| 25th Mechanized Corps (19th Army) | Orel Military District | Mironovka (Kiev MD by 7 July) |
| 20th Army | Orel Military District | 61st RC, Mogilev by 22 June; 69th RC, Smolensk by 22 June; 20th RC, Krichev by 22 June; 41st RC, Dorogobuzh by 22 June (Moscow MD by 3–5 July) |
| 7th Mechanized Corps | Orel Military District | Orsha (Moscow MD by 5 July) |
| 21st Army | Volga Military District | 66th RC, Chernigov by 22 June; 63d RC, Gomel' by 22 June; 45th RC, Ostera by 22 June; 30th RC, Bakhmacha by 9 July; 33d RC, Gordnia by 10 July |
| 22d Army | Ural Military District | 62d RC, Sebezh by 2 July; 51st RC, Vitebsk by 2 July |
| 24th Army (52d, 53d RC) | Siberian Military District | Nelidovo, Belyi (Moscow MD by 15 July) |
| 28th Army (30th, 31st RC) | Arkhangel'sk Military District | Dorogubuzh, Elnia, Zhukovka (Moscow MD by 15 July) |

Source: M. V. Zakharov, *General'nyi shtab v predvoerrye gody* [The General Staff in the prewar years] (Moscow: Voenizdat, 1989), 258–262. Note that some corps (30th) shifted subordination during deployment.

# CHAPTER 5

# Combat Readiness: Ground Combat Forces

In 1941 the Red Army was struggling to overcome the consequences of internal political strife at home and military embarrassment abroad. The internal political power struggle within the Soviet Union associated with Stalin's consolidation of dictatorial powers had led directly to the savage purges of the Red Army's leadership in the late 1930s. Between 1937 and 1941, the cream of Soviet military talent perished, including those visionaries who had begun transforming the Red Army from a foot- and hoof-bound mass army into a modern force capable of and willing to exploit the fruits of twentieth-century technology. The Soviet senior officer corps of June 1941 consisted largely of political hacks, sycophants, and cronies of Stalin, as well as a host of less senior and surviving junior officers, some skilled, but all cowed to some degree by the grisly fate of their predecessors.

The incompetence or inexperience of this truncated and fearful officer corps contributed, in part, to the less than stellar performance of Soviet arms during the occupation of eastern Poland in September 1939 and during the ensuing Finnish War of 1939–1940. At the same time, the surviving senior military leadership, at Stalin's urging, undid many of the reforms of their purged predecessors (e.g., the abolition of the mechanized corps in fall 1939). The French Army's debacle of May and June 1940, which repeated the lesson in mobile warfare the Germans had taught the world in Poland in September 1939, stunned the Soviets further and later prompted them to note bitterly that "fascist Germany used the methods of deep operations that we developed earlier. The Germans borrowed the achievements of Soviet military-theoretical thought and with great success used them in the war with Poland and the West."[1] The fact was that in 1940 the Germans were embracing advanced military reform vigorously, while in the Soviet Union military reform had atrophied.

The Soviets responded to the shock of their own failures and German successes by embarking on a crash program to reinvigorate their armed forces. The ensuing reforms, which bore the name of Commissar of War S. K. Timoshenko, affected virtually every facet of the Red Army. Beginning in haste in mid-1940, the Soviets attempted to rebuild their mechanized force structure, expand and modernize their artillery and airborne troops, modernize and strengthen their rifle forces, and create a logistical structure sufficient to sustain so large and modern a force. The ambitiousness and grandeur of the reform program and the frenetic haste of its implementation vividly demonstrated Soviet concern for the looming threat. The chaotic results of the attempted reforms likewise underscored the utter futility of the effort.


## GROUND FORCES

Red Army ground forces consisted of rifle forces, armored and mechanized forces, cavalry, air assault (airborne) forces, artillery, engineer forces, chemical defense forces, and signal forces. In peacetime the ground forces were organized into 16 military districts and the Far Eastern Front. When war broke out, the western border military districts (Leningrad, Baltic Special, Western Special, and Kiev Special) would immediately become wartime *fronts*. Each *front*, in concert with associated air forces, was designated to operate along a key strategic axis, which was defined as an axis where forces could achieve war-winning objectives. Each *front* consisted of three to four combined arms armies, mobile forces consisting of from two to eight mechanized corps and sometimes a cavalry corps, *front* aviation, and *front* artillery, engineer, and signal forces. Within the *front*, armies were designated to perform operational missions along wartime operational axes.

The highest-level ground force tactical formations were rifle, mechanized, and cavalry corps. The basic building block tactical formation was the division, which, according to its composition, could be rifle, mountain rifle, motorized rifle, cavalry, tank, or motorized.


## RIFLE FORCES

Beginning in 1939, because of the growing threat of war in Europe and the Far East, the Soviet government steadily expanded their armed forces structure. This expansion was most apparent in the ground and rifle forces. (See the detailed breakdown in Table 5.1 at the end of this chapter.) In June 1941 traditional rifle forces predominated in the Red Army force structure. The 62 rifle corps, 198 divisions (177 rifle, 19 mountain rifle, and 2 motorized rifle), and 3 brigades of rifle forces comprised 65 percent of the total number of Soviet formations and 56.6 percent of ground force manpower.[2]

On 5 April 1941, the NKO had adopted a new rifle division establishment that ostensibly replaced the former dual peacetime manning level of the division (6,000 and 12,000), increased rifle strength, up-gunned divisional artillery, improved antitank and antiaircraft capability, and added a light tank battalion of 16 tanks to each division. The new division consisted of three rifle regiments, two artillery regiments (one artillery and one howitzer), and re-connaissance, antitank, antiaircraft, sapper (engineer), signal, and tank battalions. On paper, the new rifle division fielded 14,483 men, 78 artillery pieces (over 50mm), 66 mortars (82mm and 120mm) (plus 84 50mm mortars), 54 45mm antitank guns, 12 antiaircraft guns, 16 light tanks, 13 armored cars, 558 vehicles, and 300 horses. On the eve of war, however, most divisions in the internal military districts were still organized under the older establishment or were in the process of effecting a transition to the new. The new Soviet rifle division contained 2,376 fewer men than its counterpart German infantry division, but on paper its weaponry more than matched the German division except in the realm of antitank defense. (See Table 5.2 for a comparison of German and Soviet divisions.) In June 1941, however, most Soviet rifle divisions lacked vehicles and tanks, which were used in the formation of new mechanized corps.

Soviet infantrymen in rifle divisions (and tank formations) were theoretically equipped with the most modern of infantry weapons. These included the DP-27 light machine gun, the DS-39 heavy machine gun, the PPD submachine gun (developed by V. A. Degtiarev), and the SVT self-loading rifle (developed by F. V. Tokarev). However, the introduction of these new rifle weapons into the infantry force structure was slow and by 1941 amounted to only 50 percent of requirements. The submachine guns had been added to the weapons inventory largely due to the experiences of the Finnish War, which indicated that the infantry required heavier firepower. Although the 1941 rifle division establishment required the fielding of 1,204 submachine guns in each rifle division, divisions in the Western Special Military District averaged 550 such weapons per division and those in the Kiev Special Military District averaged 267 per division. In the meantime, Soviet infantry were armed with the older "Mosin" rifle (1891–1930) and the 1940 model "Maksim" machine gun.

Most rifle divisions were organized into rifle corps, which contained two to three rifle divisions, two corps artillery regiments, separate antiaircraft and sapper battalions and smaller signal and rear service units. The paper strength of a three-division rifle corps was 51,061 men, 306 field guns (76mm or higher), 162 45mm antitank guns, 48 antiaircraft guns, 198 mortars (over 50mm), 48 light tanks (T-38), and 39 armored cars.[3] The rifle corps and its component divisions were designed to fulfill, independently, basic tactical missions such as tactical defense and penetrating enemy tactical defenses (to a depth of about 30 kilometers).

The basic operational-level formation in the Red Army was the combined arms (rifle) army, which consisted of from one to three rifle corps, one mechanized corps, a mixed aviation division, artillery regiments, and an antitank brigade provided by the Reserve of the (Supreme) High Command (R[V]GK), engineer-sapper regiments, signal battalions, and rear service units.[4] Armies performed operational defensive and offensive missions (to depths of up to 100 kilometers), which were defined as missions contributing to the achievement of ultimate strategic aims. Finally, *fronts,* which contained multiple armies and RGK reserves, were the basic Red Army strategic-level formation. Fielded only in wartime on the basis of military districts, each *front* was to perform strategic (war-winning) missions along a single strategic direction (axis) to depths of up to 300 kilometers.

On 22 June 1941, most Soviet rifle forces were well below full wartime strength in manpower and, most important, in firepower and critical logistical support. In April the NKO ordered 99 rifle divisions in the border military districts to be brought to full strength. By 22 June only 21 had reached requisite manning, and even these lacked a full complement of weaponry. Divisional manpower, depending on military district, ranged from 70 to 82 percent of required fill. (See Table 5.3 for representative division strengths.) Weaponry shortages and deficiencies in corps and divisional support structures were even more severe. Production of the new Maksim machine gun and machine pistols lagged, depriving Soviet infantrymen of critical firepower against their German opponents. In addition, most rifle corps and divisions had only one artillery regiment instead of the required two, and antitank and antiaircraft artillery units were either entirely absent or sparsely equipped with antiquated weapons. Divisional tank battalions had not been formed, since all tank resources were allocated to the formation of the new mechanized corps, and for the same reasons vehicles were either absent or in short supply. In short, most corps and divisions were deficient in manpower, firepower, logistical support, and mobility.[5]

Like other forces, rifle forces suffered greatly from the debilitating effects of the purges on command personnel. Most commanders filled positions and performed duties one to two levels above their training and experience, and inexperienced officers predominated at regimental and battalion level. This situation was exacerbated by the wholesale mobilization and fielding of new formations. According to one assessment: "As indicated by Inspectorate inspections in spring 1941, vital deficiencies existed in the training of rifle forces. Thus, in the best case, corps, divisional, and regimental staffs satisfactorily coped with their responsibilities on exercises, but many did poorly. Still greater time and effort was required to elevate the combat training of rifle forces to levels the situation required."[6] Rifle divisions dispatched to the front from internal military districts were not fully mobilized and often lacked rear service units and transport. Separated from their mobilization base, they were never able to mobilize fully. Their readiness condition was far worse than that of their counterparts in the border military districts.

A Baltic Special Military District report of 15 June 1941 recorded, "An inspection of combat readiness of military district forces indicated that, to date, some unit commanders criminally do not devote required attention to combat readiness and are not able to control their units and subunits." Alert and assembly procedures often did not work, and the soldiers were badly prepared for combat. The report criticized 90th and 125th Rifle Division senior commanders for "negligence and thoughtlessness" while on exercises and all officers for failing to improve the division's dismal readiness state during May and June.[7] At the very hour of the German attack, another Baltic Special Military District report sent from Lieutenant General P. S. Klenov, military district chief of staff, to the General Staff lamented poor communications within the district, including the weakness of *front* and army signal units and the absence of requisite internal communications and key communications equipment, presumably due to internal shortages and the partial mobilization.[8] Later, on 22 June, the military district (now Northwestern Front) commander, Colonel General F. I. Kuznetsov, admitted that the 184th, 181st, and 81st Rifle Divisions were woefully understrength and consequently "unreliable" and requested dispatch of manpower from the NKO to fill out the former territorial divisions.[9]

A 23 June report from Major General P. Belov, Northwestern Front chief of artillery, complained about the shortage of ammunition and the absence of any army artillery repair facilities above division level.[10] A similar report on the condition of Northwestern Front communications noted that, when war began, the district signal regiment and army, corps, and division signal battalions were in peacetime configuration, lacked transport, and could not establish required wartime communications. The appalling condition of *front* communications units, coupled with the destruction wrought by advancing German forces, hindered communications at all levels and paralyzed communications below army level. Although radio communications "functioned without interruption during the first days of war, . . . staffs used these means reluctantly and unskillfully." Even more catastrophic, *front* and army lacked means to create mobile communications.[11]

Matters were scarcely better in the realm of other supporting arms. For example, on 20 August, Colonel Ivin, 8th Army chief of artillery, reported retrospectively:

> Army artillery deployed to the front and entered combat operations with great shortages in peacetime establishment both in personnel and in transport, communications, and observation equipment. Not only were units not ordered to draw stocks up to wartime establishment, they were also not informed about the possibility of combat operations. . . .

The great shortages in personnel, transport, communications and reconnaissance means and, at times, in weaponry had a great influence on the combat activities of artillery.[12]

The absence of transport vehicles and the shortages of communications equipment curtailed ammunition resupply and evacuation of damaged equipment and made delivery of effective artillery fire impossible. Corps artillery regiments had no target acquisition equipment and could not mass their fires on enemy objectives. In addition, corps and divisional artillery staffs were short of trained personnel and functioned poorly. A detailed 7 July report by the 27th Army chief of staff, Colonel Voloznev, bitterly catalogued deficiencies in Army, corps, and division staff operations during the first days of combat.[13] Voloznev's report typified similar criticisms found throughout Northwestern Front's combat correspondence during the initial period of war.

In fact, existing records from all operating *fronts* contain similar refrains regarding personnel and equipment shortages and unit and officer training deficiencies. A particularly scathing critique by the Western Front Military Council prepared on 23 June began by stating, "The experience of the first day of war demonstrates disorganization and carelessness by many commanders, including senior commanders."[14] Periodic situation reports from Western Front's subordinate armies clearly illustrated how inadequate combat readiness quickly sapped the strength of all combat formations. Lieutenant General V. I. Kuznetsov, the 3d Army commander, reported on the evening of 23 June, "We are holding out without transport, fuel, and sufficient ammunition. Nikolaev [divisional commander] alone, has only 3,500 rifles."[15] Major General A. N. Ermakov, commander of Western Front's 2d Rifle Corps, reported on 25 June that his corps' headquarters and units were mobilizing at Minsk. By evening on 24 June, only 10 percent of his divisional personnel had assembled, although the influx resumed normal levels the following day. Corps units, however, had no auto transport, and many soldiers lacked uniforms.[16] Four days later, as German forces approached Minsk, Ermakov reported: "At the present moment the corps' position is rather difficult: (a) no ammunition; (b) no fuel; (c) no food; (d) no transport for resupply or evacuation; (e) no communications with the 161st Rifle Division, and the corps separate signal battalion is greatly understrength; (f) no hospitals (the corps hospitals were not mobilized)."[17] These and many similar reports clearly explain why the German attack utterly collapsed the Western Front in a matter of days.

Soviet war planners had emphasized the importance of the Southwestern Direction (axis) in the event of war. Yet, even in this most critical of sectors, Red Army formations displayed many of the same deficiencies that plagued the combat performance of Soviet forces in other sectors. Four days after the outbreak of war, the Southwestern Front chief of staff, Lieutenant

General M. A. Purkaev, reported to Stavka that *front* shortages in tractors, combat and transport vehicles, and ammunition "lowered his forces' combat capability." "This," he said, "related, in the first place, to the new formation of rifle and especially mechanized forces."[18] On 29 June the*front* commander, Colonel General M. P. Kirponos, criticized the performance of 36th Rifle Corps and associated formations stating, in part, "When fired upon in combat, subunits lacking materiel support do not advance, and block up the rear area and roads." He too mentioned communications problems, poor reconnaissance, lackluster commanders, inadequate unit control, and "instances of panic (140th and 146th Rifle Divisions) when, even without seeing the enemy or seeing an insignificant number of enemy, subunits run to the rear, casting away everything in their path, and subunit and unit commanders fail to undertake required measures to restore order."[19]

An assessment of Kiev Special Military District artillery units on the eve of hostilities noted that "the provision of rifle-mortar weaponry, especially in forming units was low. There were insufficient overall, large-caliber and submachine guns, revolvers, pistols, pistol-machine guns, 82mm mortars, etc."[20] Accompanying lists underscored the severe shortages in all weapons categories. The same report went on to note that, in particular, formations created from March through June (including 2d Rifle Corps and 5th Mechanized Corps) had insufficient weaponry and, consequently, went into battle largely unprepared, as did regular formations such as the 206th, 227th, and 147th Rifle Divisions and 5th Fortified Region. Another detailed assessment of Southwestern Front artillery, prepared shortly after war began, echoed the earlier report, pointed out that existing weapons were often old and in need of repair and underscored the lack of transport necessary to maneuver weapons and resupply them with ammunition. A host of other archival reports detailed the parlous combat readiness of *front* formations.

A retrospective detailed account of the readiness of rifle forces in Southwestern Front's 5th Army confirmed the shortage of manpower and key command personnel: "The rifle divisions, which were maintained at wartime establishment, had an average of 10,000 men, or 70 percent of their required personnel strength. The fill of command cadre (generals and officers) on average amounted to 68–70 percent, sergeants 70 to 72 percent, and privates 66 percent. There were sufficient drivers in the rifle divisions to man 60 to 70 percent of the vehicles."[21]

Although 5th Army's forces had adequate quantities of basic rifle weaponry, shortages in other types of weapons included 65 to 70 percent of required submachine guns (PPD), 85 percent of heavy caliber machine guns, and 94 percent of heavy antiaircraft machine guns. Artillery shortages included 50 percent of requisite 37mm antiaircraft guns, 60 to 67 percent of corps 76mm antiaircraft guns, and 50 to 60 percent of artillery tractors. Similar shortages existed in ammunition stocks for these weapons. After 20 May 1941, reserve call-ups occurred that by 22 June had added an average of 2,500 conscripts and 150–200 sergeants to each division. Although this brought divisional strengths up to 12,000–12,500 men, most of these men had not been fully integrated into combat subunits when war began.[22]

Therefore, on paper, Soviet rifle forces in the border military districts appeared numerous and strong. The sheer number of divisions, however, was misleading. In reality, most elements of the force lacked their full manpower complement, and critical shortages in key weaponry, communications equipment, transport, and logistical support, together with the dearth of trained, experienced, and skilled leaders, rendered the force hollow and presaged rapid Soviet defeat.

## MECHANIZED FORCES

Shocked by the sensational performance of German armored forces in the 1940 French campaign, in mid-1940 the Soviets frantically attempted to atone for the mistakes they had made in fall 1939 when they had abolished their previous five tank corps.[23] An assessment jointly prepared in early May 1940 by the outgoing commissar of defense, K. E. Voroshilov, and his successor, S. K. Timoshenko, succinctly defined the problem:

> The development of the weaponry of tank units lags behind modern requirements owing to the late introduction of modern, heavily armored tanks into the weapons inventory.
>
> In the use of tank units, the organization of cooperation with other types of forces is not being worked out to a sufficient degree.
>
> Repair of armored vehicles is dragged out even when there are sufficient repair bases.
>
> Both in terms of quantity and their specifications, existing repair complexes are badly placed. . . .
>
> The matter of capital and mid-level repair of combat vehicles in field conditions has been improperly resolved. . . .
>
> The exploitation of the existing automobile and tractor park is unsatisfactory, and as a result the armies have a large number of vehicles requiring repair.
>
> The existing tractor park is inadequate and does not fully support artillery requirements for mechanized hauling.[24]

Consequently, to improve Red Army mechanized capabilities, on 6 July 1940, the NKO ordered the creation of 9 new mechanized corps and, in

February and March 1941, began forming an additional 20.[25] Significantly larger than their predecessors, on paper each new corps consisted of two tank divisions, one mechanized division, a motorcycle regiment, signal and motorized engineer battalions, an aviation troop, and small logistical elements.[26] The corps' component tank division contained two tank, one motorized rifle, and one artillery regiment, antitank, antiaircraft, signal, reconnaissance, and pontoon-bridge battalions, and small logistical elements with a strength of 11,343 men (10,940 in 1941), 60 guns and mortars, and 375 tanks (including 63 heavy KVs and 270 medium T-34s). The motorized division consisted of two motorized rifle, one tank, and one artillery regiment, plus supporting subunits similar to those found in the tank division. Its strength was 11,650 men, 98 guns and mortars, 275 light tanks, and 49 armored cars.

The total paper strength of each new mechanized corps was 36,080 men, 1,031 tanks (including 126 new KVs and 420 new T-34s), 358 guns and mortars, 268 armored cars, 5,165 vehicles, and 352 tractors. These new corps were the armored heart of the Red Army, and the Soviets correctly felt they were vital to achieving offensive or defensive success in modern war. The paper strength of these mechanized corps was far stronger than those of their German counterparts. (See Table 5.4 for a comparison of the strength of Soviet and German tank and motorized divisions.)

The Soviets hoped to complete creation of their immense new armored and mechanized force by summer 1942. Despite hasty attempts to accelerate the program, however, by 22 June 1941 most of these corps were still woefully understrength in manpower, equipment, and logistical support, and the officers and men who manned them were largely untrained. The original nine corps, which were stationed in the border military districts, were most complete, but even these suffered from major readiness deficiencies, which included manpower shortages, poor personnel and unit training, inadequate quantities of supporting equipment (particularly radios), and a woefully inadequate logistical system. (See Table 5.5 for the strength of all Soviet mechanized corps.) Despite these weaknesses, 2 of the corps (1st and 6th) were overstrength in tanks (although not new models) and 2 corps (4th and 6th) had over 75 percent of their required new models. The remaining 20 were scarcely ready for any sort of combat and possessed only 53 percent of their required tank strength. New KV heavy tanks and T-34 medium tanks were in especially short supply, with only 1,861 in service on 22 June.[27] Of this total, 1,475 were distributed unevenly to corps in the western military districts. These corps had an average of only 19 percent of their required heavy tanks and 11.2 percent of their medium tanks. An additional 16,500 new model tanks were required to bring all mechanized corps up to full combat strength, and the NKO anticipated that industry would require not less than three years to meet this requirement. In the meantime, the corps were equipped largely with lesser numbers of older light BT and T-26 models. Soviet commanders permitted many of these older models to fall into disrepair in the expectation that new models would soon replace them. On 15 June 1941, 29 percent of the older model tanks required capital repair and 44 percent lesser maintenance.[28]

The new mechanized corps also lacked 39 percent of their vehicles, 44 percent of their tractors (for towing artillery), and 17 percent of their motorcycles (for reconnaissance).[29] Overall, corps manning ranged from 22 to 40 percent fill in enlisted personnel and from 16 to 50 percent fill in junior officers. Shortages of experienced senior commanders and staff officers were even more pronounced. Corps in the western border military districts averaged 75 percent personnel fill and 53 percent of equipment fill on 22 June. Half of the mechanized corps in the western districts had only 50 percent of their required tanks, and the modern tanks were distributed in uneven fashion. (For precise tank distribution, see Table 5.6.)

Many corps also had vacant staff sections and missing support elements, logistical organs were weak, ammunition was in short supply, and few officers had any experience in how to sustain forces logistically in mechanized warfare. For example, the 15th, 16th, 19th, and 22d Mechanized Corps had no operational or intelligence staff sections. A report by the 9th Mechanized Corps commander, Major General K. K. Rokossovsky, noted that on 28 April 1941 that corps' units possessed only 3 percent of its engineer complement (5 of 165 men) and 22 percent of its required material support technicians (110 of 489 men).[30]

Compounding these deficiencies, since the corps were formed on the basis of existing cavalry corps and divisions, many of its new officers and men had no familiarity with the basics of armored warfare. Hastily organized remedial courses failed to solve this problem. Moreover, since the new model KV and T-34 tanks were secret, training in their use was limited, and by 22 June only 20 percent of corps personnel had any experience operating with them.

The varied subordination of these mechanized corps generated some confusion regarding their prospective wartime use. Part of the corps were subordinate to covering armies along the borders and others were subordinate directly to military district commanders. In the event of war, the corps in the Baltic Special Military District served under the military district commander. However, when the enemy advance had been halted, they were to be subordinated to the 8th Army commander to participate in planned counterstrokes. In the Western Special Military District, four of the six corps were an integral part of covering armies and two were under military district command. Corps located in covering armies were generally to be employed in second echelon to launch counterattacks against penetrating enemy forces along preplanned deployment routes and attack axes. On the other hand, mechanized corps under district control had no preplanned missions to perform. Although use of mechanized corps under army control permitted early delivery of tactical counterattacks, it deprived the military district commander of the ability to mass his armor to perform more important operational missions.

Complicating these organizational and subordination problems, on 22 June the mechanized corps in the western military districts were mal-deployed and could conduct neither defensive nor offensive operations effectively (see Map 5.1). They were based from 40 to 180 kilometers from one another, their component divisions were also scattered in a fashion that prevented rapid concentration, they were often remote from their logistical support bases (where they existed), and they lacked transport necessary to provide adequate resupply of critical fuel and ammunition. (See Table 5.7 for the geographical distribution of Soviet mechanized corps.)

In general terms, despite these organizational, structural, and equipment problems, in addition to being more numerous, both the old and the new model Soviet tanks were clearly superior to their German counterparts. German light tanks (the PzKpfw I and PzKpfw II) were inferior to the Soviet BT-series and the T-26, and medium tanks like the PzKpfw III and IV were outstripped by the medium T-34 and heavy KV.[31] The new Soviet T-34 and KV tanks were superior to any models the Germans fielded in terms of firepower, armor, and mobility. Their diesel engines were less prone to fire than the German tanks' gasoline engines, the frontal armor of the T-34 could be penetrated only by 50mm antitank shells (within a range of 500 meters), and the KV was invulnerable to all existing enemy antitank weaponry. In addition, the older model Soviet tanks could defeat any existing German tank. The Soviet diesel-driven T-26, BT-5, and BT-7 tanks could destroy all German tanks, and even the 45mm guns on Soviet light tanks could defeat all German armor except the PzKpfw IV.

However, poor training and abysmal Soviet logistical and service support negated the Soviet numerical and technological advantage, as did frequent problems with the technical automotive and drive systems (engines and transmissions) on the Soviet models. Numerous archival documents indicate that, on the eve of war, many of the older Soviet model tanks had been allowed to fall into disrepair and the new Soviet tanks often were not even bore-sighted and, hence, could not fire. Furthermore, many tank crews had not received requisite driver and crew training. All of this, together with the surprise nature of the German offensive, negated any Soviet numerical or qualitative advantages. Numerous German combat reports verified this fact. In the end, superior German training, organization, and logistics negated these Soviet advantages. So successful and overconfident were the Germans that they did not fully appreciate the new Soviet armored vehicles and begin developing countermeasures against them until fall 1941.

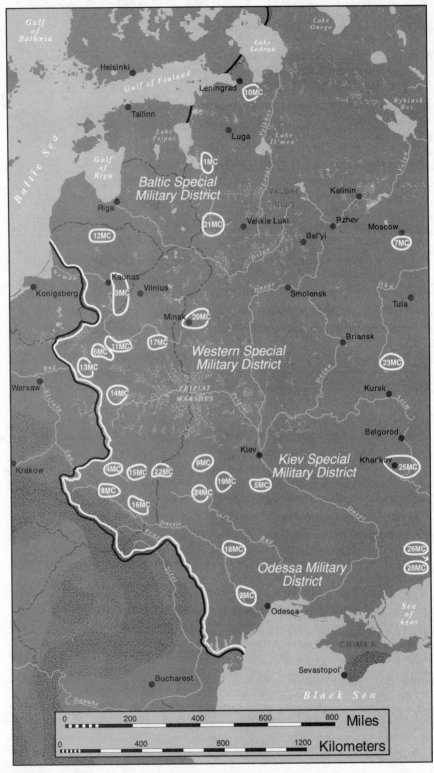

Map 5.1. Mechanized Corps Dispositions, 22 June 1941.

A Soviet TB-3 bomber.

Soviet tanks on exercise in the late 1930s.

Soviet bombers overflying Red Square.

Marshal of the Soviet Union S. K. Timoshenko and Army General G. K. Zhukov, commander of the Kiev Special Military District, supervise 1940 maneuvers in the Kiev Special Military District.

122

Marshal of the Soviet Union S. K. Timoshenko and Army General K. A. Meretskov, commander of the Leningrad Military District, supervise 1940 maneuvers in the Leningrad Military District.

Marshal of the Soviet Union S. K. Timoshenko instructs the troops during 1940 maneuvers in the Western Special Military District.

Numerous Red Army and German combat reports attest to the deplorable state of the mechanized corps. On 27 June, Major General N. M. Shestopalov, commander of 12th Mechanized Corps, reported to the Northwestern Front command on the condition and combat readiness of his corps before the German attack and after five days of combat. He began by stating that "before the beginning of war, separate orders and instructions had torn units away from their training, and, on the first day of battle, it became clear that they did not represent the motor-mechanized units that they wished to be."[32]

Subsequently, by order of the *front* commander, corps units had been committed to combat in piecemeal fashion: "From the first days of combat, we began to receive operational orders or combat instructions two to three times daily which contradicted one another. As a result the forces 'twitched' in vain, and this situation prevented the capability of using the forces and weaponry expediently to fulfill orders and deprived us of the ability to employ large formations."[33]

Regarding the state of corps equipment and resupply, Shestapalov stated:

4. The combat equipment in the formations was old and used up, in particular the "BT" tanks that had participated in the march to liberate western Belorussia, in the march into Lithuania, and etc.

After the first day's march and especially after the first day's battle, entire "tens" of tanks rapidly broke down. Because of the absence of reserve units, both on the march and during combat actions these vehicles were not restored, and, if they were restored, it had to be on the field of battle since the lack of tractors did not permit their towing to the damaged vehicle collection points. For this reason much of the equipment was left on enemy territory.

5. The antiaircraft battalions were poorly supplied with shells. Thus, for example, the batteries had only 600 37mm shells (this insignificant quantity was expended during the first two days of operations), and the total absence of 85mm antiaircraft shells at the very moment the units were placed on alert provides a complete picture of the state of the corp's antiaircraft defense. . . . This situation, as well as the absence of our fighter aviation along this axis, provided full air superiority to the enemy. Therefore, enemy bombers completely did what they wished. They smashed units on the march, in crossings and while stationary, and, while destroying equipment and putting people out of action, they lowered the combat readiness of the same units. While completing one march in the course of a single day, enemy aviation succeeded in carrying out bombing on this or that unit two to three times. On 26.6.41 enemy aviation destroyed and burned 17 combat and around 20 transport vehicles. . . .

6. Shells for 152mm guns are completely lacking for the divisions in spite of repeated demands for them before the beginning of war. It was necessary to consider equipment reinforcement, since the older existing equipment could hardly have been considered combat capable (BT and old T-26s).

7. Material supply of the troops was satisfactory. Provision of dry rations was normal. The matter of feeding command personnel was bad.

8. During combat operations command personnel demonstrated exceptionally low "exactingness" and instances of cowardliness occurred. . . .

11. Deaths have been very great among the command staff personnel. Thus, for example, in the course of one battle, one of 28th Tank Division's tank regiments lost, as killed or wounded, the deputy regimental commander, two battalion commanders, and one commissar.

12. The unwillingness of command personnel to eradicate fraternization is noted.

13. Fatigue is apparent among personnel as a consequence of fulfilling daily missions.

14. Command and control of forces was weak because of the lack of radios. There was no constant wire communications. In light of the scattered nature of the divisions, the establishment means of wire communications were not adequate. Radio communications almost completely did not work. The only means of communications during the course of the operation were liaison officers.[34]

On 29 June, Major General D. D. Leliushenko, commander of 21st Mechanized Corps, reported that his corps had gone into action near Dvinsk and admitted that the corps consisted only of the corps headquarters and "mixed groups formed from the 42d, 46th Tank, and 185th Motorized Divisions, which carried the division's numbers." Further, he explained, "Corps units, in fact, represented motorized groups which were formed at the expense of long-serving and often young troops. There are no tanks in the corps besides the few machines in the temporary training park since, at the beginning of the war, the corps had not completed its formation and specialist training." He ended his report by stating, "The mood of the soldiers and commanders is excellent, despite the absence of equipment and the shortages of fuel, ammunition, and food."[35]

On 11 July 1941, Major General Vershinin, deputy commander of Northwestern Front Armored Forces, wrote to Lieutenant General Ia. N. Fedorenko, chief of the Red Army Armored Forces, "Only today is it possible for me to make my first report to you on the tank forces of the Northwestern Front." Vershinin began his report:

My overall impression is that tanks were used improperly, without infantry and cooperation with artillery and aviation. Worst of all, the mechanized corps do not exist, since Colonel General Kuznetsov [Northwestern Front commander], totally expended them bit by bit, which led to huge equipment losses unprecedented in their scope. [Colonel] Poluboiarov [chief of the Northwestern Front Armored Directorate] is providing detailed figures, and I am indicating only what remains in units. Thus, for example, [Major General] Leliushenko [21st Mechanized Corps commander] has 25 KVs, 10 T-26s, 4 BTs, and 2 T-34s remaining. Only 35 BTs remain in 1st Mechanized Corps' 3d Tank Division. All tanks require repair, but conditions force us to leave them in battle.[36]

Vershinin complained about the lack of logistical support and evacuation means for tanks and the deplorable command and control of tank units. As a consequence, "often our troops withdraw without seeing the Germans, only under the influence of aviation, small groups of tanks, and, often, only as a result of German artillery fire."[37]

The same day Colonel P. P. Poluboiarov sent Fedorenko a terse report on his mechanized corps' condition, outlining the consequences of the corps' lack of readiness. In part it read:

Briefly regarding the operations of mechanized corps formations.

a. 3d Mechanized Corps (Kurkin) has completely perished. Kukushkin reports in detail. At present, those led out and already assembled are 400 remaining men who escaped from encirclement with 2d Tank Division (Soliankin) and one BT-7 tank.

5th Tank Division also perished in a series of encirclements. No personnel at all remain. It seems that the survivors can be found among Western Front forces.

84th Motorized Division has, in essence, not been in battle, and withdrew and was encircled several times together with units of 16th Rifle Corps.

b. 12th Mechanized Corps has been in constant combat for 12 days. At first Kuznetsov introduced large groups into battle, but without infantry and without cooperation with artillery and aviation. Subsequently, he conducted local counterattacks tens of times. . . . Up to 80 completely worn out tanks and 15 to 17 armored cars remain in both divisions. . . .

c. 21st Mechanized Corps is no longer a mechanized formation. Its motorized infantry are most often simple infantry reinforced by a few tanks. . . .

d. 1st Mechanized Corps . . . at the present moment has fewer than 100 tanks. . . .

e. From 10.7.41 the 21st Tank Division of 10th Mechanized Corps was put at the disposal of the *front*. It consisted of one tank regiment, a motorized rifle regiment, an artillery battalion, and other divisional units. It had around 100 old T-26 tanks. . . .

The situation with reservists is very difficult. . . . As a matter of fact normal resupply only began on 11–12.7.41.[38]

Poluboiarov then listed the causes for the series of disasters, which included premature commitment of the mechanized corps into battle without cooperation with other types of forces, complete loss of command and control by higher headquarters, poor command and control within tank formations, an absence of any air support, the parlous technical operating condition of the older tank park (T-26s and BTs), and superb German use of antitank weapons and reconnaissance. Poluboiarov concluded, "There are no longer any mechanized formations in the *front*, we only have anemic tank units and can no longer perform any sort of serious missions." Further, "*Front* mechanized formations and forces lack minimally necessary transport. During mobilization, the civilian economy provided the *front* with about 200 of the required 10,000 vehicles."[39]

On 23 July 1941, Leliushenko, commander of Northwestern Front's 21st Mechanized Corps, provided a complete report on the state of his corps when war began and its performance during the initial stage of war:

[The corps] began forming in only April 1941 with the estimate (according to the General Staff plan) of completing its combat materiel fill not earlier than 1942. . . . At the beginning of war the corps was at 80 to 90 percent personnel fill, [but] of these, 70 percent came from the April–May conscription. . . . Corps material units were at 10 to 15 percent fill (wheeled and special vehicles). . . . The corps deployed to the front with considerable shortages of artillery, mounted and hand machine guns, automatic rifles, and even mortars. The majority of 76mm guns were without panoramas (sights), and small caliber antiaircraft guns lacked range-finders (they were provided two days before and after war broke out).[40]

Leliushenko complained about poor officer and troop training and stated that because of the lack of training and weapons shortages he was forced to leave 17,000 men in winter quarters for remedial training. He stated that at the time of his report the 17,000 were making their way to Ostashkov in the rear area "while experiencing extreme difficulties both in feeding and in training: neither 22d Army nor any other supply organ wish to supply the corps second echelon, considering it to be someone else's problem and, at the same time, [they] undertake the most decisive measures to pilfer away its cadre and equipment, thus depriving me of any prospects for reforming the mechanized corps."[41]

According to Leliushenko, during the first month of combat, the corps suffered 6,284 casualties, or 60 percent of its combat strength. These losses, in part, were due to the problems the corps encountered, which he then described:

> While experiencing extreme shortages in artillery, heavy and light machine guns, automatic rifles and mortars, all types of communications equipment (existing communications means were insufficient even for the control of artillery fires), and with considerable shortages in command and political personnel and with understrength staffs, the corps is continuing to struggle, and while its combat spirit has not flagged, it cannot last long both because of the absence of personnel and material reinforcements, and while its cadre are suffering considerable losses.

Colonel Grinberg, temporary commander of 12th Mechanized Corps after the death of the corps' original commander, Major General N. M. Shestopalov, reported on 29 July that his 28th Tank Division entered combat without its motorized rifle regiment (due to corps mal-deployment and military district orders). Reconnaissance information about the enemy was nonexistent, radio communications failed because of a shortage of radios, resupply was ineffective, and fuel and ammunition shortages paralyzed subsequent force operations. As a result, his corps' strength fell from 28,832 men to under 17,000 in the first two weeks of combat.[42] Companion reports vividly described the failure of old equipment, in particular tanks, poor command and control, and the disastrous logistical situation.

On the other hand, on 2 August Colonel Limarenko, chief of staff of 1st Mechanized Corps, described his corps as "filled with personnel and combat material units and fully combat ready." Despite this initial comment, Limarenko went on to state that the corps lacked full signal and engineer complement and possessed no KV or T-34 tanks (20 T-34 were delivered after combat began).[43] The day before, however, Limarenko had dispatched instructions to subordinate corps units that identified a long list of combat deficiencies and demanded that they be corrected.[44] Among those deficiencies, he listed excessive "formalism" in staff work, which reduced unit effectiveness, incompetent staff work, poor or altogether absent intelligence collection, and chaotic communications, all of which damaged corps' combat performance.

Combat reports regarding Western Front mechanized force combat readiness and combat performance in the initial stages of combat are fewer in number because of the rapid and total defeat of Soviet forces in the region and the destruction or capture of their records. Some reports, however, have survived.

One of the few surviving division-level reports was prepared on 28 July 1941 by Major General of Tank Forces S. V. Borzilov, commander of 6th Mechanized Corps' 7th Tank Division. Borzilov stated that "6th Mechanized Corps . . . was generally not employed as a mechanized formation; it was thrown from one direction to another while [constantly] under the blows of enemy aviation."[45] Borzilov complained about the piecemeal commitment of his and other divisions and the division's inability to cope with the small tailored groups of German tanks, infantry, and artillery.

Borzilov's frustration echoed the problems encountered by Soviet 6th and 11th Mechanized Corps as they tried in vain to orchestrate an effective counterattack against the southern flank of German forces attacking from East Prussia through Vilnius toward Minsk. Unbeknownst to the Soviet mechanized force, the German armor of Third Panzer Group had raced deep toward Minsk, leaving only infantry formations reinforced by artillery and a few tanks to counter the Soviet counterattack south of Grodno. Adding to the Soviets' mortification, their mechanized attack was mauled by German aviation and German antitank guns, and their attack utterly failed. A message from Western Front to the commander of 10th Army, which was supposedly controlling the mechanized counterattack, captured the growing Soviet frustration:

> Why are the mechanized corps not attacking? Who is guilty? Activate your operation quickly, do not panic, and take charge of things. You must strike the enemy in organized fashion, but do not run out of control.
>
> You must know where every division is, when and what it is doing and what are the results.
>
> Why did you not give the mechanized corps the order to attack?
>
> Find out where the 49th and 113th Rifle Divisions are and lead them out.
>
> Correct your mistakes. Bring up fuel and ammunition. It is better to take care of rations on the spot.
>
> Remember, if you do not operate actively, the Military Council will tolerate it no longer.                [signed] Pavlov, Fominykh[46]

The order was symptomatic of similar command and control problems across the breadth of Western Front's three forward armies. Soon Western Front lost all control, and separate formations were left to their own devices. In the ensuing melee, within days all of the mechanized corps perished together with the bulk of other *front* forces. Surviving fragmentary Soviet documents recorded the carnage. A 25 June situation report from the Western Front to the Red Army General Staff gave an indication of the mechanized corps' heavy initial losses: "The 4th Tank Division and 6th Cavalry Corps are in the Indura region and to the west. 4th Tank Division [6th Mechanized

Corps] reports that it has no ammunition. The corps commander reports losses reaching 50 percent."[47] Another report later that day noted that "the remains of Northwestern Front's 5th Tank Division are concentrated 5 kilometers southeast of Molodechno; 3 tanks, 12 armored cars, and 40 trucks are present." The same report recorded the demise of 14th Mechanized Corps: "14th Mechanized Corps, having actively defended all day and having repeatedly launched counterattacks, suffered heavy personnel and material losses. By 25.6.41 the corps is no longer combat capable."[48]

A Western Front situation report on 27 June recorded that 6th Mechanized Corps' 4th Tank Division had lost 20–26 percent of its tank strength but ended with the optimistic note that "the KV tanks did not always suffer losses, even from direct bomb hits."[49] The same report referred to the "remains" of 13th Mechanized Corps and said that "by 2000 hours 26.6.41, 20th Mechanized Corps was concentrating in its defense regions . . . on foot."[50]

A 29 July report from Colonel Ivanin, chief of the Western Front's Armored Directorate, to the chief of the Red Army's Armored Directorate provided a succinct view of the condition of the *front*'s mechanized forces and the degree to which *front* headquarters was out of touch with the situation:

> As a whole, 6th, 17th, and 20th Mechanized Corps are operating as rifle [units]; there is no information about 11th Mechanized Corps, and 14th Mechanized Corps is proceeding to Smolensk.
>
> Overall material losses are at 70 to 80 percent. Units of 7th Mechanized Corps are arriving from the Trans-Baikal Military District. One forward warehouse for armored stock is working, and two are preparing to deploy. Repair and evacuation facilities are being organized and are working in the rear. . . . Up to 29.6.41, no information has been received from the chiefs of army armored forces.[51]

Reports later that day noted the worsening fuel and ammunition situation in the remaining mechanized corps, but thereafter *front* daily operational summaries noted total loss of communications with 3d and 10th Armies and their supporting mechanized corps. A 1 July report from Colonel Ivanin reflected this situation:

> The condition of armored forces is: 6th Mechanized Corps—its rear services have been destroyed and its equipment is in combat. Presumably, its losses are 30 to 40 percent. There is no news of 11th and 13th Mechanized Corps. 14th Mechanized Corps lost all of its equipment and is being pulled back to Smolensk for re-forming. 17th and 20th Mechanized Corps are holding at the front as rifle corps, and their losses are not known. New types of equipment with crews are essential, at first for 14th Mechanized

Corps and then for 17th and 20th. . . . At the present time, despite repeated attempts, it is impossible to receive exact information about the
presence and losses of equipment. I will report when accurate information is received.[52]

Subsequent reports noted that remnants of 3d and 10th Army had reached
Soviet lines east of Minsk, but that the bulk of the armies' forces, including
6th and 11th Mechanized Corps, were presumed lost.

On 5 August 1941, Colonel Ivanin submitted a detailed summary report
to the deputy people's commissar of defense for armored forces, Major General Ia. N. Fedorenko, in which he reviewed the condition of Western Front
mechanized forces on 22 June.[53] In it he stated that, with the exception of
5th, 6th, and 7th Mechanized Corps, *front* corps (11th, 13th, 14th, 17th, and
20th) had only 15 to 20 percent of their combat and supporting equipment,
10 to 15 percent of their required artillery and tractors, and insufficient quantities of 76mm and 45mm artillery ammunition. The tank park, which consisted exclusively of older models, had an average of only 75 to 100 motor
hours remaining, and equipment shortages forced adoption of an infantry
rather than a tank force training program. Thus, "The tactical training of
mechanized corps was conducted according to the program of all tank forces,
however, in a majority of instances, they had to serve as infantry since they
did not have sufficient quantities of required equipment."[54]

Although fuel and oil supplies were sufficient to support initial operations, enemy action and lack of transport caused subsequent serious resupply problems in most units. This, combined with the mal-deployment of
mechanized formations, led to the corps' early combat destruction. The
report went on to catalogue material and training deficiencies that rendered
these and subsequent armored operations costly and futile. Among the most
serious of noted weaknesses were the absence of aerial reconnaissance, poor
cooperation between tanks and supporting arms, and an utter lack of adequate artillery support.

Ivanin then went on, with a misplaced air of confidence, to describe specific mechanized corps problems:

At the moment combat operations on the Western Front began, of all of
the mechanized corps, only 6th Mechanized Corps was at full strength.
    14th Mechanized Corps had two tank divisions, which had 50 percent
of their light tanks, and 11th Mechanized Corps had only one tank division with 50 percent of its light tanks. The remaining corps (17th and 20th)
lacked combat equipment and constituted separate units of unarmed tank
troops that grouped themselves around several vehicles from the training equipment park. The commander of 6th Mechanized Corp's 7th Tank

Division, Major General of Tank Forces Borzilov, wrote in his assessment: "At the current stage we do not need to have corps, but [we should] limit ourselves to tank divisions and separate regiments, which will be better suited to the tactics of the German Army." The position of the latter is entirely incorrect. We do not need to accommodate ourselves to the enemy's tactics but to force the enemy to accommodate to our tactics.

The mechanized corps, when fully equipped with material, can resolve missions of army, and even *front* scale. However, the operations of 6th Mechanized Corps at the beginning of war and the subsequent actions of 5th and 7th Mechanized Corps did not provide significant results.

The reasons for their lack of success are as follows:

1. The absence of air reconnaissance and aircraft observation led to blind operations.

2. The absence of accompanying combat aviation and the weakness of their own artillery led to unprepared attacks on completely unsuppressed defenses.

3. The absence of cover by fighter aviation allowed enemy dive bombers to bomb and pour down upon tanks with phosphorus mixtures [napalm].

4. The incorrect use of mechanized corps on difficult terrain without any communications with the infantry, artillery, and aviation in offensive operations in the context of a front-wide defensive operation.

Conclusion: Mechanized formations, of course, have not lost their importance and are a powerful shock means in the hands of army and *front* commands; however, they must not be used in isolation from the actions of remaining forces, but rather in full coordination with the concept of overall operations and with the obligatory support of powerful aviation.[55]

Another report that assessed the operations of Western Front armored and mechanized forces during the period 22 June through 13 July echoed Ivanin's complaints: "Within three days, 14th Mechanized Corps was put out of action due to [its] lack of readiness, insufficiently skillful action, the absence of air support, the lack of antitank and antiaircraft weaponry, weak cooperation with the infantry, poor rear service organization and support, as well as the suddenness of the enemy attack and the strong actions of his aviation."[56]

During early July 1941, the Western Front committed its fresh 5th and 7th Mechanized Corps to combat at Lepel', southwest of Vitebsk, in an attempt to halt the German armored spearheads. On 6 and 7 July, the two corps, under 20th Army control, engaged lead elements of German XXXIX and XXXXVII Panzer Corps, and in two days of heavy battle the two Soviet corps were badly mauled and forced to retreat. Unlike the other Soviet western military district mechanized corps, 5th and 7th had time to assemble and plan their attack. However, this made no difference in the outcome of the engagement.

Among the many critiques of the mechanized corps' performance was an 8 July assessment by 20th Army commander, Lieutenant General P. A. Kurochkin. He criticized the two corps for clumsy operations:

> The experience of the two-day battle of the mechanized corps showed the following shortcomings in the conduct of the tank battle:
>
> 1. Small tank subunits (companies and platoons) during the offensive moved primarily on the roads and in column, one tank after another. When meeting with antitank artillery the lead tank was usually knocked out, and the remaining, instead of rapidly deploying to attack and destroy the enemy, became flustered, marked time in place, and often withdrew to the rear.
>
> 2. During the operations, maneuver by individual subunits and units was absent. Having met antitank positions or obstacles, the tanks attempted to attack them frontally or withdraw, while neither availing themselves of their maneuverability nor bypassing the enemy antitank fortifications nor seeking bypass routes.
>
> 3. The absence of cooperation between tanks, infantry, and artillery . . .
>
> 4. Instead of massive and decisive attacks on the opposing enemy, regimental and division commanders, without need, sent out many different reconnaissance and security groups, dissipating their forces and weakening the tank blow.
>
> 5. The matter of reports and information was criminal. Unit and formation commanders were situated in tanks and lost their radios for communications with higher headquarters. None bore the responsibility for informing higher headquarters. Often they distorted and confused news about the enemy, the condition of their own units, and the nature and form of battle and brought harm. . . . No one answered for that severe responsibility.
>
> 6. Orders concerning obstacle detachments and establishing order in the rear area were not fulfilled. March discipline was not observed. Individual tanks by the hundreds, without direction and without concrete necessity, rolled along the road, while passing one another and destroying normal movement. Soldiers by themselves and entire crowds roamed throughout the rear area, not in their [proper] place.[57]

Kurochkin ended with a searing series of instructions designed to correct the shortcomings. Numerous orders and reports by Major General V. I. Vinogradov, 7th Mechanized Corps commander, and Major General I. P. Alekseenko, 5th Mechanized Corps commander, elaborate on Kurochkin's complaints, including a scathing condemnation by Vinogradov of his com-manders' "criminal" neglect of tank evacuation measures on the battlefield.[58]

Major General A. V. Borzikov, chief of the Red Army's Armored Direc-torate's Combat Training Section, later summed up the staff appreciation of the two corps' effectiveness: "The corps [5th and 7th Mechanized] . . . staffs operated poorly and sluggishly, and, still worse, many machines [tanks] fell to the enemy because of tolerated disrepair. Neither the divisions, the mecha-nized corps, the armies, nor the front organized repair and evacuation. There were no reserve units and no rubber [tires], and they were supplied poorly. The mechanized corps had no aviation, and, as a consequence, they were blind and sometimes . . . lacked communications."[59]

On 4 August 1941, Major General B. S. Vasil'evich, then titular com-mander of 6th Mechanized Corps' 7th Tank Division, reported to the Red Army Armored Directorate about his division's performance during the first five weeks of war. Unlike many other divisions, Vasil'evich's was at nearly full strength, with 98 percent of its required enlisted strength and 60 to 80 per-cent of its senior and junior officers. Its 348 tanks included 51 KVs and 150 T-34s. The 7th Tank Division's 'Achilles' heel' was its supply condition. When it began its march into battle it possessed only one to one and a half combat loads of 76mm ammunition, no armor-piercing ammunition for its tanks, three refills of gasoline, and a single fill of diesel fuel. Confused orders required the division move to three new assembly areas during the first two days of war. Given these excessive movements, the fuel ran out quickly, and the di-vision was soon immobilized south of Grodno.[60]

These fragmentary situation reports and retrospective analyses more than adequately record the fate of Western Front's mechanized corps. They clearly describe the condition of the corps on 22 June and chronicle the combat capability of the corps, which ultimately led to their virtual total destruction in less than two weeks of battle.

Extensive reports from Southwestern Front forces reverberate with similar problems, even though Soviet mechanized forces there were far more suc-cessful than their counterparts in other *front* sectors. A fairly complete file of combat reports by individual mechanized corps and divisions during the ini-tial period of war documents the performance and travails of the formations. For example, the first Southwestern Front mechanized corps to enter com-bat was Major General I. I. Karpezo's 15th Mechanized Corps, which struck the south flank of German First Panzer Group on 23 and 24 June north of Brody. A combat assessment on 28 June by Colonel F. G. Anikushkin, commander of 15th Mechanized Corp's 37th Tank Division, described his division's condition during the unsuccessful Soviet counterattacks. After reviewing the week of combat, he concluded, "37th Motorized Regiment was not ready to fulfill its mission," and the "combat equipment [of the corps], as a result of its incorrect use during the period from 22 through 26.6.41 and its initial number of technically inoperable vehicles, required inspection."[61]

Subsequently, a thorough report by Major General D. I. Riabyshev, commander of 8th Mechanized Corps, chronicled his corps' extensive but unsuccessful operations during heavy counterattacks north of Brody against German XLVIII Panzer Corps. Riabyshev noted that his corps "marched an average of 495 kilometers before joining battle and abandoned more than 50 percent of its combat vehicles along the road."[62] Riabyshev's report ended with the following conclusions:

1. At the beginning of war, the corps did not have its full establishment complement of equipment. (For example, the establishment required 126 KV tanks and 420 T-34 tanks, and on 22.6.41 the corps had 71 KVs [5 in repair] and 100 T-34s. The provision of new model tanks was at 25 to 30 percent.)

The majority of KV and T-34 drivers had from three to five hours of service driver training. Throughout the entire period of its existence, the corps' equipment and personnel had taken part in practically no tactical exercises and had not been tested either in the matter of march training or in actions in the principal types of combat. Tactical unit cohesiveness existed no higher than company, battalion, and, partly, regiment. This was the main cause for weakness in the organization of command and control on the march and in combat at the division and regimental level.

2. During the period from 22 through 26 June, the corps completed intensive "super forced" marches without observing the normal demands of regulations . . . , and, because of this, 40 to 50 percent of the combat vehicles broke down for technical reasons. . . .

5. The absence of cooperation between the corps and aviation . . . deprived the corps of air cover and prevented knowledge of the situation and nature of enemy action at the most critical moments on the main axes.

9. The absence of corps evacuation means and the disorganization in *front* and army evacuation services led to extensive unnecessary equipment losses, and the lack of reserve march units forced a great amount of equipment to be abandoned on the spot without required technical assistance.

10. The weak knowledge of the tactical employment and use of motor-mechanized units, as well as the poor notion about the technical capabilities of combat equipment and weaponry on the part of some portion of the command cadre, which assigned missions to the corps, often led to the assignment of excessive missions regarding both objective and time and space.[63]

On 13 July 1941, Colonel V. S. Ermolaev, who became temporary commander of 15th Mechanized Corps when General Karpezo was wounded, prepared an extensive analysis of his corps' condition on 22 June, its performance during the first three weeks of war, and its condition by mid-July. He graphically presented the corps' initial strength (see Tables 5.8 and 5.9).[64] Although the corps' subordinate formations and units averaged 50 percent of their senior command cadre and between 16 and 75 percent of their junior commanders, they possessed from 63 to 131 percent of their required enlisted personnel. The corps' tank divisions had 318 and 272 tanks, respectively, including 69 T-34s and 64 KVs, but as was the case with most corps, its motorized division lacked most of its required combat weapons and transport. Ermolaev then described the corps' combat readiness:

The 15th Mechanized Corps entered the war not completely formed. . . .
[37th Tank Division's] motorized rifle regiment was incompletely formed, unfilled out, and untrained, and was located 150 kilometers from the division and did not have means of movement.

The artillery regiment consisted of 12 122mm guns without sights, 4 152mm guns, and 5 tractors in all. The remaining guns had no tractors and were located in the Kremenchug region. Only one 122mm battery was deployed, and after four days another 4 152mm guns were brought up on tractors provided by the civilian economy.

The bridge battalion was located in a camp on the Dnestr River south of L'vov and was subjected to enemy bombing on the first day of war. . . .
The 10th Artillery Regiment, 10th Antiaircraft Artillery Battalion, and regimental artillery of the 10th Motorized Rifle Regiment were located in a training area in the Ianuv region.

The 212th Motorized Division, with an almost full complement of Red Army soldiers, completely lacked vehicles for transporting personnel and could not even secure auto-transport for supply of ammunition, foodstuffs, and fuel and lubricants and also for the transportation of weapons.

The artillery regiment had 8 76mm guns, 16 122mm guns, and 4 152mm guns, but there were means for towing only one battalion without any rear services. . . .

The corps' motorcycle regiment had 100 percent of its personnel and 30 percent of its command cadre . . . [but] 5 armored cars, 74 motorcycles, 5 45mm guns, 1,039 rifles, and 4 machine guns.

Personnel were not trained and had even never shot.

The remaining corps' units, the signal battalion and engineer battalion, were filled with young conscripts who had gone through first degree training, but mid-level command cadre were in such short supply that noncommissioned officers commanded companies. . . . Both units were completely unformed and could not perform their combat missions.[65]

The detailed report by Ermolaev provided a superbly candid day-by-day account of the corps' operations, and a running tally of the corps' combat losses and tank strength vividly documented the terrible and rapid disintegration of the corps in combat (see Table 5.10).

Ermolaev added an extensive critique of his corps' combat performance. The piecemeal forward deployment of the corps along too broad a front and delays incurred when one tank regiment was delayed in swampy terrain permitted the Germans to engage and defeat corps' elements one by one. The lack of six of the corps' required radios made communications tenuous at best, and poor reconnaissance caused the corps to operate blindly. Most important, the long road marches, general lack of march discipline, and absence of any repair or evacuation capability and resupply of critical fuel and ammunition led to rapid erosion of corps' tank strength. Confused and altered orders and frequent changes in corps subordination to higher headquarters just added to the confusion and hastened defeat.

A series of overall assessments of mechanized corps' performance prepared by Major General Morgunov, chief of Southwestern Front Armored Forces, catalogued the problems *front* forces encountered. In a 30 June report to the *front* Military Council, Morgunov reviewed the distance the mechanized corps had traveled since the outbreak of war and the heavy toll that movement took on tank and vehicle engines. He described the adverse effect of that movement on equipment combat readiness and the logistical system:

> For the entire period, the mechanized corps, while completing marches and conducting battle with the enemy, did not have and could not have a single day for equipment inspection, adjustment, or repair. The absence of evacuation means, the distance of stationary repair bases, and the lack of repair means in formation repair and reconstruction units and of type "A" and "B" mobile repair equipment led to huge numbers of equipment breakdowns for technical faults.
>
> Up to now, the absence of reserve KV and T-34 tanks in all units have made it impossible to carry out routine and mid-term repairs in units.
>
> The completion of a great number of marches in difficult forested and swampy terrain conditions under enemy air, antitank, and artillery attack without the conduct of technical inspections and the ability to restore [equipment] because of the absence of reserve equipment has led to the great percentage of tank losses during the first nine days of war. These

losses, based upon far from complete data, constitute 25 to 30 percent of tank formations' combat equipment.[66]

On 1 July Morgunov sent to the *front* Military Council a situation report that summarized the condition of *front* mechanized formations after one week of combat and requested the Military Council seek Stavka assistance in restoring the *front*'s mechanized capability:

1. 8th Mechanized Corps is not combat capable. In battles in the Brody and Dubno regions, 80–90 percent of [its] combat equipment was destroyed on the field of battle and not evacuated, since the territory was occupied by the enemy. . . .
2. 4th Mechanized Corps—unit positions and the corps' condition are being clarified.
3. 15th Mechanized Corps has suffered great losses in battles in the Stanislavchik, Lopatin, Radzekhuv, and Toporuv regions, and its combat capability on 1.7.41 is 25 to 30 percent. Its remains are withdrawing to the Zalozhtsy-Nove, Dobrovody, and Kobyla regions.
4. 22d Mechanized Corps' 41st Tank Division is covering the Kovel' axis. 215th Motorized Rifle Division is withdrawing to the Stokhod River as a part of 15th Rifle Corps. We are establishing its combat capability and materiel losses.
5. 9th Mechanized Corps is functioning as a rifle corps and defending along the Stuba River in the Klevan' region.
6. 19th Mechanized Corps is operating as a rifle corps and defending along the Zamchisko River in the Kostopol' region.
7. 24th Mechanized Corps is preparing cutoff positions on a front from Iampol' to Zhesniuvka. It is not yet conducting battle. I request:
Accelerate the withdrawal of 4th, 8th, and 15th Mechanized Corps with the mission of rapidly restoring their equipment, filling them up, and bringing them to full combat readiness. . . .[67]

Morgunov then added, "Speed up the equipping of existing corps (4th, 8th, 9th, 15th, 19th, 22d, and 24th)" and, in the future, "form mechanized corps in internal military districts and send them to the *front* fully formed."[68]
Another report from Morgunov, prepared on 3 July, read:

The absence of evacuation means and reserve equipment for KVs and T-34s; the presence of factory defects; the lack of familiarity [with the tanks]; insufficiently trained personnel; weak antitank reconnaissance of the enemy; systematic bombing on the march, in concentration areas, and during attacks; extensive maneuvering over 800 to 900 kilometers without aviation cover and artillery coordination over almost prohibitive (for tanks) forested-swampy terrain; strong opposition by a predominant enemy; and the absence of armor-piercing shells for KVs and T-34s; has led to huge mechanized corps losses and lack of combat readiness on the part of those which remain.[69]

Morgunov complained about the absence of tractors for moving artillery and trucks for ammunition resupply and proposed an extensive list of remedies for the logistical problems. Curiously enough, even at this stage of the war, he noted that KV and T-34 tank armor needed to be augmented for defense against German antitank guns.

As was the case in the Northwestern and Western Fronts, organizational and command and control difficulties plagued the mechanized corps in their early operations. A 3 July message from the *front* commander, Colonel General M. P. Kirponos, to his subordinate armies noted: "Ten days of experience in the use of mechanized formations demonstrates that the Military Councils and army staffs weakly organize and control mechanized formations in combat."[70] Kirponos specifically mentioned poor coordination of mechanized forces with cooperating arms, lack of logistical support and vehicle evacuation, and faulty unit reporting procedures.

Morgunov prepared his most thorough report on 17 July. In it he presented a graphic and disturbing picture of mechanized corps combat readiness in the Southwestern Front:

On 22.6.41 Southwestern Front contained eight mechanized corps and one armored train battalion. The mechanized corps organization had not yet been "shaken out" organizationally and filled out with combat equipment. The most fully blooded mechanized corps were the 4th, 8th, and 15th, but, even in these, the tank regiments of motorized divisions had only training vehicles [park]. There were no combat vehicles in the motorized divisions.

The readiness condition of the remaining mechanized corps is as follows: in 16th Mechanized Corps, the 15th Tank Division was the only combat-capable division, but it had only older weapons; the remaining divisions had only limited quantities of training equipment and weaponry [park]. 19th Mechanized Corps had only the combat-capable 43d Tank Division, but with old materiel. In 22d Mechanized Corps, the only combat-capable division was 41st Tank Division, which was equipped with T-26 tanks and 31 KV tanks; the remaining divisions had only training equipment. 9th Mechanized Corps had the combat-capable 35th Tank Division armed mainly with T-26 one- and two-turret tanks in one regiment; the remaining divisions had limited quantities of training equipment. The armored train battalion had two light and one heavy armored trains. At the beginning of combat operations, in total, the Southwestern Front mechanized corps contained: tanks—4,297; armored cars—1,014.

By type, the tank park consisted of: 265 KV, 496 T-34, 1,486 BT, 1,962 T-26, 44 T-35, 195 T-28, 88 T-40, 749 BA-10, and 365 BA-20.

Front-wheeled and auxiliary vehicles totaled 12,506 and were only in the mechanized corps.

Such mechanized corps armament led to the fact that on the first day the tank regiments of 9th, 16th, 19th, 22d, and 24th Mechanized Corps, since they lacked specialized equipment, were armed with 45mm and 76mm guns and operated as antitank regiments.

Southwestern Front armored forces deployed to the front with this materiel.[71]

Regarding the corps' combat performance, Morgunov wrote:

During the course of 25 days of combat, in fulfilling missions to destroy the enemy, all mechanized corps suffered considerable equipment losses. . . .

The principal reasons for the great quantities of losses are: insufficient personnel training, especially among the conscripts of spring 1941; enemy antitank artillery fire; air strikes; technical failures; and operations in forested-swampy terrain.

Moreover, the absence in formations as well as in armies of direct means of evacuation and the untimely provision of trains for evacuation of damaged machines from army collection points to the center [rear] led to a great percentage of the combat vehicles being abandoned in technical disrepair.[72]

Thus, according to Morgunov, "all mechanized corps on 17.7.41 were not combat ready as mechanized corps because of equipment shortages."[73]

A lengthy 5 August report from Major General B. T. Vol'sky, deputy commander of the Southwestern Front for Armored Forces, to Deputy Commissar of Defense Ia. N. Fedorenko reiterated problems experienced by the mechanized corps. Vol'sky succinctly summarized the creation and state of the corps on 22 June: "The Kiev Special Military District, subsequently reorganized as the Southwestern Front, consisted of the following mechanized corps: 4th, 8th, 9th, 15th, 19th, 22d, and 24th, and since the 4th and 8th were formed in fall 1940 and the remaining corps in April 1941, thus, the time for assembling them was extremely insufficient, especially since combat material units lacked a long period of time in the new mechanized corps."[74] Vol'sky added, "As of 1 August, the Southwestern Front has no mechanized corps in its makeup that are combat-welded units, equipped with combat equipment, but it has cadre."[75]

Vol'sky criticized the improper combat employment of the corps, the absence of reconnaissance, inadequate logistics, the appalling lack of command and staff preparedness, poor communications, lack of individual initiative on the part of all commanders, and a host of lesser problems, which, taken together, formed a dismal mosaic of the corps' preparedness for war.

A host of Soviet documents elaborate upon Vol'sky's lament. Colonel P. P. Pavlov, the commander of 41st Tank Division, wrote on 25 July that he received no orders from his parent 22d Mechanized Corps for four to five days after the commencement of hostilities, although the corps commander "knew the division's concentration area."[76] When assembled, the division's artillery regiment "had not even a single tractor. Thirty-one KV tanks . . . had not a single shell. The antiaircraft battalion . . . had not a single shell. The wheeled vehicle park was missing 700 vehicles, which, to that time, we had not received from the economy." Although the division's two tank regiments had 95 percent of their required tanks, including 31 KVs (and 312 T-26s), "the drivers for these tanks had still not been trained since the tanks were received only seven to eight days before the war began." To make matters worse, the existing tanks did not work properly.

Colonel E. G. Pushkin, commander of 4th Mechanized Corps' 32d Tank Division, reported on 14 July that his division had been created in April and May from the 30th Light Tank Brigade, and when war began it had 50 percent of its personnel strength, 77 to 78 percent of its modern tanks, 110 percent of its older model tanks, and 42 percent of its armored cars. However, the division's tank drivers were untrained, and it had only 22 percent of its required transport, 13 percent of its repair facilities, 2 percent of its required reserve supplies, 30 percent of its radios, and 50 percent of its required engineer support. Between 22 June and 31 July, the division lost 307 of its original 361 tanks.[77]

The nearly full-strength 10th Tank Division of 15th Mechanized Corps also lacked most of its vehicular transport, and its personnel were inadequately trained. According to its temporary divisional commander, Lieutenant Colonel Sukhoruchkin, "The material support of the division as well as the shortages of auto transport in carry-weight and specialized vehicles lowered somewhat the combat effectiveness of the division."[78] Of the division's 355 tanks on 22 June, 310 were combat capable. Between 22 June and 15 July, the division lost 307 tanks, 151 due to maintenance problems or an inability to evacuate them properly. The commander's lengthy report clearly demonstrated that the division's combat performance was severely denigrated by support deficiencies and inadequate training of command personnel and soldiers.

A similar summary report by Colonel Anikushkin of 37th Tank Division, also of 15th Mechanized Corps, stated: "On the basis of People's Commissariat of Defense of the USSR's Directive No. OPG/1/521114, 15th Mechanized Corp's 37th Tank Division was to be fully formed by 1.7.41 (filled with personnel, equipment, weaponry, and all kinds of property)."[79] On 22 June the division was manned and equipped at the following levels:[80]

*Personnel*
| | |
|---|---|
| Command personnel | 41.2% |
| Junior command personnel | 48.3% |
| Soldiers | 111.0% |

*Establishment Equipment*
| | |
|---|---|
| KV tanks | 1 (1.6%) |
| T-34 tanks | 34 (11.4%) |
| BT-7 tanks | 258 (nonestablishment) |
| T-26 tanks | 22 |
| T-26 tanks (flamethrower) | 1 |

*Artillery Weaponry*
| | |
|---|---|
| 37mm antiaircraft guns | 33.3% |
| 122mm howitzers | 56.0% |
| 152mm howitzers | 33.3% |

About 60 percent of the enlisted personnel had joined the Army in May 1941, and none had any general or specialized training. Six hundred new recruits assigned to the motorized rifle regiment were unarmed because of the corps' shortage of weapons. The motorized rifle regiment, which was located 150 kilometers from its sister tank regiments, had no vehicles and hence could not operate with the division. Because of the shortage of artillery, when the division marched into combat it had only 1 122mm and 1 152mm artillery battery. Instead of its required 12 guns (3 batteries), the divisional antiaircraft artillery battalion had a single battery of 4 guns. Finally, the division's pontoon-bridge battalion was located in camp along the Dnepr River and also could not accompany the division into battle.

When the division answered the alert notice and began movement, it mustered 70 percent of its personnel and 315 tanks (of which 258 were BT-7 models). The tanks had to operate without accompanying infantry and with only limited artillery support. Regardless, according to the division commander, "In spite of the [shortages], the division considered itself to be a stable combat entity, and as the future would show, it could successfully resolve all missions assigned to it."[81] The 37th Tank Division fought south of Dubno until 29 June and later served as rear guard as Soviet forces withdrew to the east. Extensive records show how the division's strength eroded in subsequent combat from 10,900 men and 316 tanks on 22 June to 2,423 men and 6 tanks on 15 July (for details, see Table 5.11). This erosion of combat strength typified the fate of those divisions not destroyed outright.

Relatively complete records also illuminate the experience of 19th Mechanized Corps' 43d Tank Division. On 28 August the division commander,

Colonel I. G. Tsibin, prepared a thorough after-action report that detailed the state of the division on 22 June and its fate in subsequent combat through early August. The division numbered 8,434 men of its required 9,876 men and was equipped with 237 of its required 373 tanks (and only 7 of 273 new models). Most important and debilitating, the division had only 655 of its necessary 1,720 trucks and tractors (see Table 5.12).[82]

Colonel Tsibin's division headquarters was staffed with trained personnel inherited from the 35th Tank Brigade, upon whose base the division was formed. Senior and mid-level commanders had seen service during the Finnish War, as had many of the tank crews. On the other hand, lower-level command personnel and NCOs, in particular those serving in the division's motorized rifle regiment, had been transplanted from other units and were largely "green" and untrained. Although the tanks and crews were combat capable, the tanks had seen considerable service and were nearly worn out. Around 150 of the division's 571 trucks were not serviceable, and reserve parts stock were at 40 to 45 percent fill. Thus, because of the severe shortage of vehicles:

> The basic mass of personnel of the motorized rifle regiment and other nonspecialists could not be transported. In addition, the troops of the first battalion of the two tank regiments, who lacked equipment, could not be deployed.
>
> Thus, in the beginning of combat actions, the division consisted of two groups: (a) a mobile group—the tank regiments, each of two battalions (before the battle at Dubno united into a single regiment), and two battalions of the motorized regiment riding on trucks; and (b) a foot-bound group of around 1,500 men, consisting of motorized rifle regiment units and the remaining specialists without vehicles (recon, sappers).[83]

Tsibin noted that there were shortages of 37mm ammunition, the 122mm and 152mm artillery had only one combat load, and 10 to 15 percent of the infantry lacked automatic weapons. He added, "In spite of the fact that the division was still in the state of forming and lacked a full complement of weapons, equipment, and personnel, it was prepared for combat operations and could conduct combat in the condition it was in on 22.6.41."[84]

The 43d Tank Division subsequently took part in heavy fighting throughout the remainder of June and into July, and by 7 July the formation, down in strength to 20 light tanks, fought basically as an infantry formation. The case of this division was not atypical. By early July the strength of most mechanized formations had eroded to a shadow of their former selves. On 7 July Colonel General Kirponos, the *front* commander, reported to the General Staff on the condition of his once formidable mechanized force. He reported the following strength returns:[85]

```
4th Mechanized Corps:    126 tanks
8th Mechanized Corps:     43 tanks
9th Mechanized Corps:    164 tanks
15th Mechanized Corps:    66 tanks
19th Mechanized Corps:    66 tanks
22d Mechanized Corps:    340 tanks
24th Mechanized Corps:   100 tanks
      Personnel losses in all at 25 to 30%
```

A subsequent report on 15 July from Southwestern Front to General Federenko at the Red Army Armored Directorate showed accelerated degeneration of the formations' tank strength:

| Mechanized Corps | Tank Strength |
|---|---|
| 4th | 68 tanks (6 KVs, 39 T-34s, and 23 BTs), and 36 armored cars |
| 8th | withdrawn from battle |
| 9th | 32 tanks (7-BTs and 25 T-26s), and 30 armored cars |
| 15th | withdrawn from battle |
| 19th | 33 tanks (4 KVs, 7 T-34s, and 22 T-26s), and 2 armored cars |
| 22d | 30 tanks (2 BTs and 28 T-26s), and 17 armored cars |
| 24th | operating as a rifle corps |

In an operational summary prepared on 8 July, Major General D. S. Pisarevsky, the 5th Army chief of staff, vividly described the deplorable condition of his army's two mechanized corps:

Since 22.6.41, the corps [22d Mechanized], while in constant battle, has suffered great losses in personnel and equipment. Because of the lack of transport, the motorized rifle regiments' regiments and the crews of machines put out of action have completed long marches on foot. As a result the personnel are tired and worn down. The boots of 70 percent [of the men] are worn out and require exchange (in motorized rifle regiments).

On 7.7.41, 55 percent of the personnel, 21 tanks, 8 antitank guns of various calibers, and 4 armored cars remain in service. Remaining tank and artillery crews who lack equipment are operating as infantry, which is incomprehensible while there is insufficient cadre. . . .

The [19th Mechanized Corps], being short of personnel and equipment, during the course of 13 days of battle along an axis of active operations, has been tossed about by the enemy and has suffered great losses. The inconsiderable amount of equipment remaining is not suitable for combat and requires restoration.

On 6.7.41 the corps' first echelon, consisting of 1,500 men (40th and 43d Tank Divisions), withdrew from battle armed only with rifles and possessing one antiaircraft artillery battery and three tanks. Because of the lack of required material, the corps lost a great number of specialists who were serving as riflemen. Now new equipment is reaching the regiments, but the personnel cannot cope with it. The corps headquarters is short 50 percent of its command personnel. The corps does not have its required communications means. All of this influences the control of battle.[86]

This litany of problems revealed by Soviet archival sources is substantiated by German combat reports. A lieutenant in 6th Panzer Division's reconnaissance battalion vividly described combat against Soviet 3d Mechanized Corps' 2d Tank Division on the outskirts of Raseinai in Lithuania on the second day of war.[87] The Soviet KV tanks rammed his unit's lightly armored vehicles and, without firing a shot, ran over and crushed the German recce vehicles in the mud of a nearby riverbed. After hours of desperate combat, the Soviet tanks suddenly ground to a halt in an array of menacing but immobile pillboxes. Over a period of two days, German sappers engaged the immobile iron monsters one by one, blowing them up with satchel charges. Once the brave occupants of the tanks had been killed or captured, the Germans discovered the tanks had run out of fuel and ammunition and had been ordered to "ram" the opposing German tanks. Moreover, the guns on the Soviet KVs had not even been bore-sighted prior to battle.

German reports from this and other sectors reiterate Soviet lack of fuel and ammunition and repeatedly report Soviet tank crews unable to drive and maneuver their armored vehicles. Reports by prisoners of war from Soviet 41st Tank Division, and others, indicate that Soviet tank drivers had not received requisite driver training and their officers were totally unfamiliar with the terrain or the consequences of leaving the road in swampy regions. Consequently, entire battalions became helplessly mired in the mud and swamps.[88] A Soviet 8th Mechanized Corps report prepared by the corps commander, Major General D. I. Riabyshev, confirmed that KV and T-34 tank drivers had only three to five hours' driving training.[89] This explains why German infantry of XXXVIII Army Corps, without tank support, could successfully counter 12th Mechanized Corp's counterattack in Lithuania, and XX and VIII Army Corps could do likewise against the formidable (on paper) force of 6th and 11th Mechanized Corps south of Grodno.

Thus, on 22 June 1941, the Soviet mechanized corps in the border military districts and throughout the entire armed forces' force structure were not combat ready. They were understrength by 25 percent in enlisted personnel and short even greater numbers of command cadre and NCOs. Training of those personnel was poor, especially in the corps that had been formed in 1941. Corps' equipment strength, in particular tanks, averaged 53 percent, and most tanks were older models that required repair or reconditioning. Compounding these problems, the corps were mal-deployed and lacked clear missions.

The Soviet's immense mechanized force did possess considerable combat potential. That potential, however, would take months or perhaps a full year to realize. As subsequent combat and the reports of its command personnel vividly indicated, the corps were simply not prepared to fight the world's most experienced army in the summer of 1941.

## CAVALRY

Other branches of Red Army forces shared the same deficiencies as rifle and mechanized forces. The favorite combat arm of Stalin, the cavalry, was one of the few exceptions. In 1939 cavalry forces made up 10 percent of Red Army ground forces, a greater proportion than armored forces or RGK artillery considered together. Cavalry forces shrank considerably in size in 1940 and 1941, however, since the NKO used many cavalry corps and divisions as the nuclei for the new mechanized corps. By June 1941, of the 7 cavalry corps and 32 cavalry divisions that had existed in 1937, only 4 corps and 13 divisions (including 4 mountain cavalry divisions), numbering 80,000 men, remained in the force structure.[90]

On paper, the cavalry division consisted of four cavalry regiments, one tank regiment, artillery and antiaircraft battalions, and support subunits, for a total strength of 9,240 men, 68 guns, 64 mortars, 64 light tanks, 18 armored cars, 555 vehicles, and 7,940 horses. The mountain cavalry division was somewhat lighter than a line division. It had three cavalry regiments, armored and artillery battalions, and lighter support and counted 6,574 men, 14 guns, 42 mortars, 19 tanks, 17 armored cars, and 6,853 horses. The cavalry corps contained two divisions and supporting corps units and numbered 19,430 men, 136 guns, and 128 tanks. (See Table 5.13 for the precise corps and division organization.)

Because they had not been subjected to wholesale reorganization by the Timoshenko reforms, the 4 cavalry corps and 13 cavalry divisions were more combat ready than rifle forces. On 22 June cavalry formations in the border military districts were at 85–90 percent personnel and equipment fill, and those in the internal military districts numbered closer to 6,000 men each. The command cadre of these divisions were experienced veterans of the Civil War, and most of the cavalrymen were also highly experienced. Without their required complement of tanks, however, all the experience in the world meant nothing, for the divisions were vulnerable anachronisms on the modern field of battle. In addition to lacking any sort of armor, the divisions possessed only

45–50 percent of their required vehicles, they lacked any antiaircraft defense, and they had few tanks, since all existing armor went to the newly forming mechanized corps. This, in large part, explained why 6th Cavalry Corps' 36th Cavalry Division was put out of action so quickly, before it could join battle south of Grodno.[91]

Few records exist that document the precise composition and combat performance of the cavalry divisions during the first few days of war. This is because they normally operated in tandem with mechanized corps and were overshadowed by their more powerful companions or because they were quickly consumed in combat or fought in relative obscurity as dismounted infantry.

## AIRBORNE FORCES (AIR ASSAULT)

Among the most elite of Soviet combat forces were the 5 Soviet airborne corps, which formed by 1 June from the 6 existing prewar airborne brigades and personnel from 11 rifle divisions.[92] The airborne brigades had been formed in the early 1930s, and according to theory, they formed the vertical dimension of deep battle and the deep operation. In theory, during war they performed a variety of combat, reconnaissance, and diversionary missions in the enemy tactical and operational rear area. Their most important mission was to operate in brigade configuration in cooperation with deeply operating ground mobile groups (tank, mechanized, or cavalry corps) to encircle or chop up major enemy formations. At the other end of the spectrum, operating in small teams, they could conduct diversionary missions under *front* or army control.

The 1941 airborne brigade as configured tactically consisted of a parachute group, a glider group, and an airlanding group. The brigade as a whole contained four 546-man parachute battalions, an artillery battalion (4 45mm and 4 76mm guns), a mortar company (9 82mm mortars), an air defense company (12 heavy machine guns), a light tank company (11 T-40 or T-38 tanks), a reconnaissance-bicycle company, and a signal company, for a strength of over 3,000 men, 11 tanks, and 4 field guns.[93] The personnel in these corps were among the best trained and most highly motivated troops in the Red Army.

In April 1941, after close observation of 1940 German airborne operations in Belgium, the Soviet NKO decided to expand their airborne structure drastically through the formation of new airborne corps. On 1 April 1941, the order went out to form five new corps. The new 10,400-man corps consisted of three air assault brigades of 2,634 men each and a separate light tank battalion. The subordinate brigades had three parachute assault battalions, an artillery battalion, and reconnaissance-bicycle and antiaircraft companies. The corps was supposed to cooperate closely with a designated air transport unit. Again, lack of fire and logistical support and, in particular, dedicated air delivery units when war broke out forced the corps to be employed primarily as infantry "fire brigades."

When war broke out, the new airborne corps were in the midst of forming. In addition to lacking much of their heavy equipment and supporting air transport, many of the brigades were untrained in basic airborne procedures. Many personnel had received only rudimentary parachute training, and 10 of the 16 brigades had received no training in jumping and operating as a unit. The 5th Airborne Corps in the Baltic Special Military District was undergoing this training in the field as war broke out.

According to an NKO directive of 5 June 1941, air transport for the airborne corps was supposed to be provided by two assault-landing bomber aviation regiments subordinate to each airborne corps. These aviation regiments were to be equipped with older, specially modified TB-3 bombers, whose quiet operations at slow speeds would facilitate safe delivery of the paratroopers to their objectives. However, on 22 June none of these units had formed.

After 22 June the Soviet commands attempted to employ at least two of their airborne corps in missions for which they had been configured. On 28 June, as German forces were racing forward toward Minsk and the Dnepr River beyond, Colonel General D. G. Pavlov, Western Front commander, ordered 4th Airborne Corps to conduct an air landing west of Bobruisk in tandem with a 20th Mechanized Corps assault southward from Minsk to halt the German advance:

> Upon receipt of this order, bring the 214th Airborne Brigade to full combat readiness and, having loaded its personnel and equipment on all available corps' transport, transfer it for a subsequent air landing at Lubnishche and Tumanovka (12 kilometers northwest and southwest of Mogilev) in the forests near these points. . . .
>
> At first light on 29.6,41, the 214th Airborne Brigade, under the control of the Western Front Airborne Force commander, will conduct a parachute assault in the Slutsk region with the mission of cutting the roads running from Baranovichi, Timkovichi, and Siniavka to Bobruisk and preventing the approach of reinforced enemy forces from the west to forward units at Bobruisk. Subsequently, the brigade will cooperate with 210th Motorized Division, which is being transferred to the Slutsk region to destroy the enemy Bobruisk group, while disrupting work in the rear and command and control by blowing up bridges, destroying lines of communications, and diversionary activity. All attempts by the enemy to

penetrate back to the west toward Slutsk will be thwarted by all means available to the brigade.[94]

No sooner had 4th Airborne Corps reached the Berezina River late on 28 June than the planned assault went awry. Sufficient aircraft were not available to lift the brigade into combat. Hence, on 29 June the 214th Brigade received orders from Pavlov to "travel by trucks along open march routes in the general direction of Slusk and secure the Grusha, Slutsk, Staraia Doroga regions. Deprive the enemy of all lines of supply, destroy crossings and bridges and, by night actions, smash [enemy] transport and separate vehicles and burn and destroy tanks. . . . Remain in that area until the full destruction of the enemy Bobruisk group and, upon the fulfillment of these missions, independently rejoin our forces, depending on conditions."[95]

Subsequently, the 214th Brigade failed to accomplish its original mission but operated in the German rear area for several weeks before it dissolved, with some of its soldiers joining partisan formations and a few making their way back to Soviet lines, which by that time were far to the east.

This ill-fated attempt to use the fledgling airborne force aborted, as did a similar attempt in the Southwestern Front. The two incidents were indicative that the airborne brigades, although well motivated, were not combat ready.

FORTIFIED REGIONS

The final component in the June 1941 Soviet army ground force combat structure was the fortified region (FR, *ukreplennyi raion*), a formation strong in firepower but modest in manpower that was designed to provide the backbone for Soviet fortified defense lines. First created as a separate Red Army type formation in 1923, by the mid-1930s a string of fortified regions defended major segments of the USSR's western borders in tandem with regular border troops. In 1938 the Soviets constructed 13 fortified regions along their western border manned by 25 machine-gun battalions totaling 18,000 men. In late 1938 and early 1939, they added 8 more fortified regions to their existing force structure. After the Soviet seizure of eastern Poland in 1939 and the Baltic states in 1940, fortified regions were also created along the new western border.

Soviet interest in fortified regions grew precipitously after the Soviet-Finnish War because of the impression Finland's strong defenses made on the Red Army General Staff. Consequently, in late 1940 the Soviets began a program to expand their development and deployment. Soviet intent was to use the new fortified regions to create a strong defensive barrier and help cana-

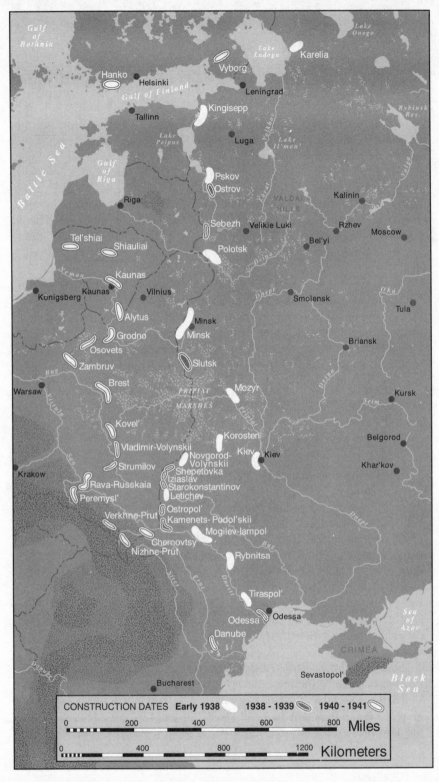

Map 5.2. Fortified Regions on the Soviet Western Frontiers, June 1941.

lize attacking enemy forces into regions where they could be destroyed by counterattacking mechanized forces. During 1940 and 1941, the Soviets formed 20 new fortified regions along the new border, each consisting of two defensive belts to a depth of 15–20 kilometers (see Map 5.2).

Each fortified region contained several machine gun–artillery battalions, separate machine-gun companies, which would form battalions at the outset of war, separate artillery battalions or artillery regiments, and service sub-units for an average wartime strength of about 4,000 men.[96] Groups of deployed fortified region formations created larger territorial entities also called fortified regions and named after a specific location (e.g. Polotsk, Vladimir-Volyinskii). By 1941 the fortified region system embraced all of the Soviet Union's border regions.

On 21 May 1941, the NKO ordered the fortified regions in the West to begin full deployment on 4 June 1941, and mandated measures for their reinforcement by the addition of 17 new fortified regions, 110 battalions, 16 companies, 6 artillery battalions, 16 artillery batteries, and other smaller units totaling 120,695 men to the existing force structure. The augmentation was to be completed by 1 July for fortified regions along the new border and by 1 October for those along the old border. During this period the number and total strength of fortified regions was to double in number, and the size and strength of each battalion was to rise to 1,000 men. However, none of these measures were complete by 22 June. Moreover, in the haste to reinforce the fortified regions along the new border, fortifications along the old border were stripped bare.

The 57 fortified regions existing in June 1941, 42 of which were located in the West, contained 192,240 men organized into 7 regiments and 160 artillery and machine-gun battalions equipped with 1,700 guns and mortars and 9,800 light and heavy machine guns.[97] These fortified regions were positioned in prepared defenses along the border and in the depth near the old 1939 border and on the approaches to major cities. On the eve of war, the fortified regions were manned with 34 percent of their required officers, 27.7 percent of their NCOs, and 47.2 percent of their enlisted men.[98] Only 50 percent of their required fortifications had been constructed, and all formations experienced severe shortages of modern model machine guns. Thus, on 22 June the fortified regions were not fully combat capable, and neither of the defensive lines they manned was fully combat ready.

# STATISTICAL DATA

Table 5.1. Rifle Force Expansion, 1939–1941

| Type of Formation | 1 January | | | 22 June 1941 |
|---|---|---|---|---|
| | 1939 | 1940 | 1941 | |
| Rifle corps | 25 | 48 | 50 | 62 |
| Divisions | 97 | 168 | 179 | 198 |
| Rifle | 86 | 155 | 166 | 177 |
| Mountain rifle | 11 | 11 | 10 | 19 |
| Motorized rifle | 0 | 2 | 3 | 3 |
| Separate rifle brigade | 3 | 3 | 3 | 3 |
| Separate rifle regiment | 0 | 0 | 44 | 44 |

Source: *Nachal'nyi period*, 43.

Table 5.2. Comparison of the Wartime Strength of Soviet Rifle and German Infantry Divisions

| Division Units and Subunits | Soviet Rifle Division | German Infantry Division |
|---|---|---|
| Personnel | 14,483 | 16,859 |
| Rifles and carbines | 10,420 | 11,500 |
| Heavy machine guns | 166 | 142 |
| Light machine guns | 392 | 434 |
| Antiaircraft machine guns | 33 | 0 |
| Submachine guns | 1,204 | 787 |
| Antitank rifles | 0 | 81 |
| Guns | 144 | 161 |
| Mortars | 66 | 54 |
| Vehicles | 558 | 902 |
| Horses | 3,039 | 6,358 |
| Light tanks | 16 | 0 |
| Armored cars | 13 | 16 |
| Tractors | 99 | 62 |

Source: *Nachal'nyi period*, 44; Ramanichev, 80–84, quoting from archival citation TsAMO, f. 16a, op. 2951, d. 264, l. 2–6.

Table 5.3. Combat Readiness of Selected Soviet Rifle Divisions on 22 June 1941

| | Men | Guns (>76mm) | Mortars | Antiaircraft Guns | Light Tanks | Vehicles | Tractors |
|---|---|---|---|---|---|---|---|
| Rifle division peacetime establishment (5 April 1941) | | | | | | | |
| 12,000 level | 10,298 | 140 | 66 | 32 | 16 | 414 | |
| 6,000 level | 5,864 | 126 | 48 | 8 | 16 | 155 | |
| Mountain rifle | 8,829 | | | | | | |
| Rifle division wartime establishment | 14,483 | 132 | 66 | 12 | 16 | 558 | |
| German wartime infantry division strength | 16,859 | 74 | 54 | | | 902 | |
| Average strength on 22 June 1941 | | | | | | | |
| Leningrad Military District | 11,985 | | | | | | |
| Baltic Special Military District | 8,712 | | | | | | |
| Western Special Military District | 9,327 | | | | | | |
| Kiev Special Military District | 8,792 | | | | | | |
| Odessa Military District | 8,400 | | | | | | |
| Kiev Special Military District: | | | | | | | |
| 45 RD (5 Army) | 8,373 (10,010) | 78 (84) | | | | 127 | 50 |
| 62 RD (5 Army) | 9,546 (9,973) | 70 (82) | | | | 63 | 86 |
| 87 RD (5 Army) | 9,973 (9,872) | 85 (82) | | | | 328 | 58 |
| 124 RD (5 Army) | 9,471 (9,426) | 75 (82) | | | | 229 | 8 |
| 135 RD (5 Army) | 9,232 (9,911) | 44 (80) | | | | 194 | 0 |
| 41 RD (6 Army) | 9,912 | 74 | | | | 222 | 17 |
| 97 RD (6 Army) | 10,050 | 86 | | | | 143 | 78 |
| 159 RD (6 Army) | 9,548 | 69 | | | | 395 | 40 |
| 72 Mountain Rifle Division (26 Army) | 9,904 | 62 | | | | 433 | 44 |
| 99 RD (26 Army) | 9,912 | 69 | | | | 345 | 28 |
| 173 RD (26 Army) | 7,177 | 59 | | | | 251 | 50 |
| 43 MtRD (12 Army) | 9,159 | 56 | | | | 189 | 30 |
| 192 MtRD (12 Army) | 8,865 | 56 | | | | 134 | 1 |
| 60 MtRD (12 Army) | 8,313 | 56 | | | | 10 | 1 |
| 96 MtRD (12 Army) | 8,477 | 56 | | | | 138 | 17 |
| 58 MtRD (12 Army) | 10,279 | 56 | | | | 366 | 39 |
| 164 RD (12 Army) | 9,930 | 78 | | | | 283 | 29 |

Sources: A. A. Gurov, "Boevye deistviia sovetskikh voisk na iugo-zapadnom napravlenii v nachal'nom periode voiny" [Combat actions of Soviet forces on the Southwestern Direction during the initial period of war], Voenno-istoricheskii zhurnal [Military-historical journal] 8 (August 1988): 33. Nachal'nyi period, 43–44. A. G. Khor'kov, Boevaia i mobilizatsionnaia gotovnost' prigranichnykh voennykh okrugov nakanune Velikoi Otechestvennoi voiny [Combat and mobilization readiness of the border military districts on the eve of the Great Patriotic War] (Moscow: VAGSh, 1989), 7. Figures in brackets are 1 June 1941 strengths from A. V. Vladimirsky, Na kievskom napravlenii [On the Kiev axis] (Moscow: Voenizdat, 1989), 22–23. All sources cite archival records. The discrepancies probably reflect conflicting reports.

Table 5.4. Comparison of the Strength of Soviet and German Tank and Motorized Divisions

| | Tank Divisions | | Motorized Divisions | |
|---|---|---|---|---|
| Composition | Red Army | German Army | Red Army | German Army |
| Personnel | 10,940 | 16,000 | 11,650 | 14,029 |
| Tanks | 375 | 135–209 | 275 | 0 |
| Armored cars | 95 | 25 | 49 | 37 |
| Motorcycles | 454 | 1,289 | 183 | 1,323 |
| Guns | 40 | 72 | 86 | 129 |
| Mortars | 18 | 30 | 12 | 42 |
| Tractors | 84 | 200 | 153 | 0 |
| Vehicles | 1,568 | 1,275 | 1,587 | 2,278 |

Source: *Nachal'nyi period*, 46.

Table 5.5. Location and Strength of Soviet Mechanized Corps in the Western Military Districts on 22 June 1941

| Military District | Number | Date Formed | Men | Strength | | | | | | | |
|---|---|---|---|---|---|---|---|---|---|---|---|
| | | | | Tanks | Armored Cars | Artillery | Mortars | Vehicles | Tractors | Motorcycles |
| Establishment | | | 36,080 | 1,031 | 268 | 172 | 186 | 5,165 | 352 | 1,678 |
| Leningrad | 1 | March 1940 | 31,439 | 1,037 | 239 | 148 | 146 | 4,730 | 246 | 467 |
| | 10 | March 1941 | 26,168 | 469 | 86 | 75 | 157 | 1,000 | 34 | 460 |
| Baltic Special | 3 | July 1940 | 31,975 | 651 | 220 | 186 | 181 | 3,897 | 308 | 457 |
| | 12 | March 1941 | 28,832 | 749 | 23 | 92 | 221 | 2,531 | 194 | 39 |
| Western Special | 6 | July 1940 | 32,382 | 1,131 | 242 | 162 | 187 | 4,779 | 294 | 1,042 |
| | 11 | March 1941 | 21,605 | 414 | 84 | 40 | 104 | 920 | 55 | 148 |
| | 13 | March 1941 | 17,809 | 282 | 34 | 132 | 117 | 982 | 103 | 246 |
| | 14 | March 1941 | 19,332 | 518 | 44 | 126 | 114 | 1,361 | 99 | 216 |
| | 17 | March 1941 | 16,578 | 63 | 38 | 12 | 104 | 607 | 40 | 26 |
| | 20 | March 1941 | 20,391 | 94 | 11 | 58 | 76 | 431 | 25 | 92 |
| Kiev Special | 4 | July 1940 | 28,098 | 979 | 175 | 134 | 152 | 2,854 | 274 | 1,050 |
| | 8 | July 1940 | 28,713 | 898 | 172 | 142 | 152 | 3,237 | 359 | 461 |
| | 9 | March 1941 | 26,833 | 298 | 73 | 101 | 118 | 1,067 | 133 | 181 |
| | 15 | March 1941 | 33,395 | 749 | 160 | 88 | 139 | 2,035 | 165 | 131 |
| | 16 | March 1941 | 26,920 | 482 | 118 | 72 | 137 | 1,777 | 193 | 91 |
| | 19 | March 1941 | 21,654 | 453 | 26 | 65 | 27 | 865 | 85 | 18 |
| | 22 | March 1941 | 24,087 | 712 | 82 | 122 | 178 | 1,226 | 114 | 47 |
| | 24 | March1941 | 21,556 | 222 | 16 | 0 | 0 | 229 | 69 | 5 |
| Odessa | 2 | June 1940 | 32,396 | 517 | 186 | 162 | 189 | 3,794 | 266 | 375 |
| | 18 | March 1941 | 26,879 | 282 | 6 | 83 | 30 | 1,334 | 58 | 157 |
| Total strength | | | 517,047 | 11,000 | 2,035 | 2,000 | 2,529 | 39,816 | 3,111 | 5,699 |

Source: *Nachal'nyi period*, 49–50.

Table 5.6. Tank Strength of Mechanized Corps in Western Military Districts

| Military District and MC | Total Tanks | | New Tanks | |
|---|---|---|---|---|
| | Quantity | Percent Fill | Quantity | Percent Fill |
| Leningrad | | | | |
| 1st | 1,037 | 100.1 | 0 | 0 |
| 10th | 469 | 45.5 | 0 | 0 |
| Baltic Special | | | | |
| 3d | 651 | 63.1 | 110 | 20.1 |
| 12th | 749 | 72.6 | 0 | 0 |
| Western Special | | | | |
| 6th | 1,131 | 109.7 | 452 | 82.7 |
| 11th | 414 | 40.2 | 20 | 3.6 |
| 13th | 282 | 27.4 | 0 | 0 |
| 14th | 518 | 50.2 | 0 | 0 |
| 17th | 63 | 6.1 | 0 | 0 |
| 20th | 94 | 9.1 | 7 | 1.2 |
| Kiev Special | | | | |
| 4th | 979 | 95.0 | 414 | 75.8 |
| 8th | 898 | 87.0 | 171 | 31.2 |
| 9th | 298 | 29.0 | 0 | 0 |
| 15th | 749 | 72.6 | 136 | 24.9 |
| 16th | 482 | 46.8 | 0 | 0 |
| 19th | 453 | 43.9 | 5 | 0.9 |
| 22d | 712 | 69.1 | 31 | 5.6 |
| 24th | 222 | 21.5 | 0 | 0 |
| Odessa | | | | |
| 2d | 517 | 50.1 | 60 | 10.9 |
| 18th | 282 | 27.4 | 0 | 0 |

Note: The figures for the Odessa Military District corps are as of 1 June 1941.
Source: *Nachal'nyi period*, 49–50; Ramanichev, 90–92, citing TsAMO, f. 38, op. 11353, d. 5, l. 139; op. 11360, d. 5, l. 13, 35; f. 15, op. 881454, d. 12; f. 10a, op. 2766, d. 107, l. 83–116.

Table 5.7. Disposition of Mechanized Corps on 22 June 1941

| Military District | Corps | Distance from the Border (kilometers) | Distance between Corps Brigades (kilometers) |
|---|---|---|---|
| Baltic Special | 12 | 80–120 | 50–70 |
| | 3 | 50–100 | 60–75 |
| Western Special | 6 | 70–90 | 10–15 |
| | 11 | 40–100 | 35–60 |
| | 13 | 35–60 | 40–50 |
| | 14 | 10–100 | 65–90 |
| | 17 | 150–220 | 60–100 |
| | 20 | 280–340 | 70–110 |
| Kiev Special | 4 | 50–80 | 10–15 |
| | 8 | 40–90 | 40–60 |
| | 9 | 200–250 | 50–60 |
| | 15 | 90–130 | 50–60 |
| | 16 | 30–70 | 70–140 |
| | 19 | 380–400 | 40–115 |
| | 22 | 20–190 | 140–180 |
| | 24 | 130–170 | 50–60 |

Source: *Nachal'nyi period*, 51.

Table 5.8. 15th Mechanized Corps Personnel Combat Strength, 22 June 1941 (percentages)

| Unit | Command | Junior Command | Enlisted |
|---|---|---|---|
| Corps headquarters | 50.0 | 44.5 | 78.0 |
| Separate signal battalion | 40.0 | 16.5 | 131.0 |
| Engineer battalion | 45.0 | 23.0 | 63.0 |
| Motorcycle regiment | 30.0 | 53.0 | 105.0 |
| 10th Tank Division | 87.0 | 75.0 | 91.0 |
| 37th Tank Division | 50.0 | 45.0 | 101.5 |
| 212th Motorized Division | 56.0 | 60.0 | 94.0 |

Source: *Sbornik boevykh dokumentov Velikoi Otechestvennoi voiny* [Collection of combat documents of the Great Patriotic War] 36 (Moscow: Voenizdat, 1958), 253.

Table 5.9. 15th Mechanized Corps Equipment Strength, 22 June 1941

| Type of Equipment | 10th Tank Division | 37th Tank Division | 212th Motorized Division |
|---|---|---|---|
| Tanks | | | |
| KV | 63 | 1 | 0 |
| T-34 | 37 | 32 | 0 |
| T-28 | 44 | 0 | 0 |
| BT-7 | 147 | 239 | 32 |
| T-26 | 27 | 13 | 5 |
| Armored cars | | | |
| BA-10 | 53 | 35 | 18 |
| BA-20 | 19 | 10 | 17 |
| Total | 318 tanks | 272 tanks | 37 tanks |
| | 72 armored cars | 45 armored cars | 35 armored cars |

Source: *SBDVOV* 36 (1958), 253.

Table 5.10. Combat Strength of 15th Mechanized Corps, 22 June through 12 July 1941

| Formation | 22 June 1940 | | 26 June 1940 | | 6 July 1941 | | 12 July 1941 | |
|---|---|---|---|---|---|---|---|---|
| | Tanks | Artillery | Tanks | Artillery | Tanks | Artillery | Tanks | Artiller |
| 10th Tank Division | 318 | | 39 | 36 | 20 | | 6 | 4 |
| 37th Tank Division | 285 | | 219 | 11 | 10 | | 3 | 1 |
| 212th Motorized Division | 37 | | 2 | 0 | 0 | | 0 | 1 |
| 8th Tank Division (attached) | 0 | | 65 | 0 | 0 | | 0 | 0 |
| 15th Mechanized Corps | 640 | | 325 | 0 | 30 | | 9 | 0 |

Source: *SBDVOV* 36 (1958), 253–269.

Table 5.11. 37th Tank Division Strength, 22 June through 15 July 1941

| | 22 June 1941 | 28 June 1941 | 15 July 1941 |
|---|---|---|---|
| Personnel | 10,900 (approx.) | 5,067 | 2,423 |
| Tanks | | | |
| KV | 1 | 0 | 0 |
| T-34 | 34 | 26 | 1 |
| BT-7 | 258 | 177 | 5 |
| T-26 | 22 | 8 | 0 |
| T-26 (flamethrower) | 1 | 0 | 0 |
| Artillery | | | |
| 37mm AA | 4 | 4 | 0 |
| 122mm Howitzer | 6 | 3 | 2 |
| 152mm Howitzer | 4 | 4 | 0 |
| 76mm AT | NA | 26 | 1 |
| 45mm AT | NA | 201 | 16 |

Source: *SBDVOV* 33, 216–231.

Table 5.12. 43d Tank Division Strength, 22 June 1941

|  | Establishment | On-Hand | Shortage |
|---|---|---|---|
| Personnel |  |  |  |
| Command | 1,253 | 711 | 542 |
| Junior command | 2,172 | 1,054 | 1,118 |
| Enlisted | 6,451 | 6,669 | — |
| Total | 9,876 | 8,434 | 1,442 |
| Tanks |  |  |  |
| KV | 63 | 5 | 58 |
| T-34 | 210 | 2 | 208 |
| T-26 | 74 | 230 | — |
| BT | 26 | 0 | 26 |
| Trucks and special vehicles | 1,500 | 571 | 929 |
| Tank trucks | 137 | 69 | 68 |
| Tractors | 83 | 15 | 68 |
| 152mm guns | 12 | 4 | 8 |
| 122mm guns | 12 | 12 | 0 |
| 76mm field guns | 4 | 4 | 0 |
| 37mm AA guns | 12 | 4 | 8 |

Source: *SBDVOV* 33 (1957), 233.

Table 5.13. Organization and Strength of Cavalry Divisions and Corps, 22 June 1941

|  | Cavalry Division | Cavalry Corps |
|---|---|---|
| Personnel | 9,240 | 19,430 |
| Horses | 7,940 | 16,020 |
| Light tanks | 64 | 128 |
| Armored cars | 18 | 36 |
| Guns: |  |  |
| Total | 68 | 136 |
| Field (76mm, 122mm) | 32 | 64 |
| Antitank | 16 | 32 |
| Antiaircraft | 20 | 40 |
| Mortars (50mm, 82mm) | 64 | 128 |
| Vehicles | 555 | 1,270 |
| Tractors | 21 | 42 |

Source: *Nachal'nyi period*, 53.

# CHAPTER 6

# Combat Readiness: Combat Support and Rear Service Forces

## ARTILLERY

On the eve of war, Red Army artillery consisted of force artillery and artillery of the Reserve of the High Command (RGK). The former, organized into regiments and battalions, was designated to support Red Army formations and was included in the establishment structure of fortified regions, rifle and airborne brigades, rifle, tank, mechanized, and cavalry divisions, and rifle, mechanized, cavalry, and airborne corps. The latter consisted of artillery formations, units and subunits under RGK control that were attached to or supported Red Army armies and corps in wartime. Overall, on 22 June 1941, the Soviet artillery park consisted of 117,600 guns and mortars of all calibers. Of this total, 37,500 guns and mortars were located in formations in the western border military districts.[1]

Most of the Red Army's artillery (92 percent) was found in 94 corps artillery regiments allocated to support armies, corps, and divisions (see Table 6.1 at the end of this chapter). On paper, the corps artillery regiments totaled 1,320 107 to 122mm guns and 2,220 152mm gun-howitzers organized into three types of regiments: mixed regiments of 24 107 to 122mm guns and 12 152mm gun-howitzers; regiments of 36 152mm gun-howitzers; and regiments of 24 122mm guns and 24 152mm gun-howitzers. RGK artillery, which constituted 8 percent of the total Soviet artillery force, consisted of large caliber gun and howitzer systems organized into 60 howitzer (27 48-gun 152mm and 33 24-gun 203mm), 14 gun regiments (48-gun 122mm and 152mm), 15 high-power (BM, *bol'shoi moshchnosti*) artillery battalions, 2 separate special-power (OM, *osoboi moshchnosti*) artillery batteries, and 12 separate mortar battalions.

Soviet artillery systems were of the most modern design and technologically equal to their German counterparts. The 76mm regimental, divisional, and mountain gun was assigned to regimental artillery batteries and divisional artillery regiments. Division and corps artillery regiments, as well as many RGK regiments, were equipped with 122mm and 152mm howitzers. Corps and RGK artillery regiments also had 107mm and 122mm guns. Higher caliber weapons, including 152mm and 210mm guns, 203mm and 305mm howitzers, and 280mm mortars, were found in RGK artillery regiments, battalions, and batteries. Other mortar systems included the light 50mm mortar, which was found within rifle companies and cavalry and airborne forces, 82mm rifle battalion mortars, and 120mm regimental mortars.

On the eve of war, Soviet weapons constructors created a "field reactive artillery" (rocket launcher) system, code-numbered the BM-13. However, development of the new system was slow, and by June 1941 only seven experimental vehicles with the system mounted on them existed; five of these were located at a research institute and the other two in a Voronezh factory. The Soviet government ordered serial production of the new "Katiushas," as they would later be named, on 21 June 1941.[2] The first Katiushas went into action in July 1941, too late to affect initial combat. The Germans, too, had developed their own equivalent to this weapon, a six-barrel 180mm rocket-propelled mortar system that was initially deployed with engineer forces and intended for the delivery of chemical munitions (Nebelwerfer).

In addition to underestimating the importance of rocket launcher systems, until the Finnish War, Soviet authorities largely ignored the combat capabilities and potential combat contributions that mortars could make to the outcome of battle. After the heavy fighting to overcome the vaunted Finnish "Mannerheim Defense Line," the Red Army embarked on a crash program to increase the production and fielding of mortars. Between 1 January 1939 and June 1941, the Red Army's mortar inventory increased from 3,200 to 56,900 weapons, and mortar units and subunits were added to virtually every combat formation and unit. Unfortunately, much of this effort focused on production of 50mm mortars (35,100 of the total 56,900), which were too light to have any appreciable impact in modern combat. Increased production of mortars also detracted from the production of the valuable 45mm and 76mm guns and antitank rifles.

Most of the RGK regiments assigned to reinforce armies were better equipped than their corps artillery counterparts. However, even they lacked up to 85 percent of required special tractor systems for movement, and on 22 June most of their vehicles required capital repairs. The major weakness of RGK artillery was the fact that only 8 percent of its regiments were retained in RGK reserve. In addition, RGK artillery in general lacked antitank artillery systems and antiaircraft formations and units.[3]

Perhaps the greatest weakness of Red Army artillery was its lack of mobility due to the severe shortage on the eve of war of transport vehicles and tractors. All rifle division artillery, except the howitzer regiment, was supposed to be horse-drawn, and the remaining artillery was supposed to be towed by slow-moving tractors provided by the civilian agricultural sector. Although Soviet industry had developed several specific model tractors for towing artillery, as was the case with other systems, production was slow and few units had them. In June 1941 combat formations had only 37.8 percent of their required tractors.

A similar picture prevailed in the logistical field. As was the case in mechanized forces, artillery formations and units lacked any repair, reconstruction, or evacuation capability. In the border military districts, half of the RGK artillery regiments had no such support.

Another major artillery deficiency was the Soviet failure to develop more modern and effective target acquisition and fire control systems. Although ground systems functioned adequately if manned by experienced personnel, air systems had been neglected. All corps were supposed to have correction (artillery adjustment) aircraft, but few actually possessed them. In May 1941 the NKO ordered creation of 15 aerostatic detachments to acquire targets and correct artillery fire, but only 3 had been created by the outbreak of war.

An extensive number of contemporary Soviet archival reports and after-action assessments noted several major deficiencies in artillery systems. Inspections conducted in spring 1941 indicated that regimental personnel, in particular junior and mid-range commanders, were poorly trained and unable to employ their artillery effectively in combat. Firing units experienced major difficulties in target acquisition and fire direction and were unable to coordinate their fire with that of supposedly cooperating units. The most serious deficiency found in gun artillery units was their inability to bring effective fire to bear on enemy tanks, which was one of the most critical tasks assigned to artillery units by prewar regulations. This may have been due, in part, to Soviet creation of and reliance on specialized antitank forces created on the eve of war.

A report prepared on 14 July 1941 by Lieutenant General M. A. Parserov, the Southwestern Front chief of artillery, exemplified the state of Red Army armaments on 22 June 1941 and typified similar reports from other *front* sectors: "Up to the beginning of war, the support of military operations, in particular, in forming units, was especially low. There were shortages in weapons systems, large-caliber and light machine guns, revolvers, pistols, submachine guns, 82mm mortars, etc." (See Table 6.2 for the details of Parserov's status report as of 22 June.)[4]

The report stated that newly formed formations, such as 2d Rifle and 5th Mechanized Corps, were especially short of rifles and mortars. Moreover, after mobilization was declared, "There were units on the territory of the military district that could not even be armed with ordinary rifles."[5] Among these units were the 15,000-man Red Army railroad corps, more than 45 construction battalions, regular formations from other military districts (206th, 227th, and 147th Rifle Divisions, which were short of weapons), 5 fortified regions of the second defense line (which had no weapons whatsoever), antidiversionary detachments, some mobilizing units, and mobilizing internal security forces. At the time he wrote the report, Parserov declared there were no reserve weapons stocks in the military district save 6,000 rifles and 450 Maksim machine guns, which needed repair. Parserov's accompanying report on the status of military district artillery weapons was similarly devastating (see Table 6.3).

Regarding rifle and artillery ammunition, on 22 June rifle and cavalry divisions, corps units, and RGK regiments had 1.5 combat loads each, and tank and motorized rifle divisions had 1.5–3.0 combat loads each. There was, however, a severe shortage of 37mm and 85mm antiaircraft ammunition and armor-piercing shells for tanks. The most serious problem regarded transport for ammunition resupply: "From the beginning of combat operations, the majority of units in the border sectors, lacking sufficient quantities of auto-transport for resupply of ammunition, were forced to leave more than half of their shot at their home station, and given the rapid development of combat operations, the artillery shells left by the units at home station were blown up or left to the enemy."[6]

The Soviets had long appreciated the function and importance of mechanized and tank forces in modern battle. Their degree of fixation on tank warfare, however, was not matched by their concern for developing an antitank capability. In the last analysis, it was German combat performance in the West in 1940 that finally generated heightened Soviet concern for antitank warfare.

Reflecting growing Soviet concern, in May 1941 the NKO began forming ten specialized antitank artillery brigades in the border military districts (see Table 6.1). Assigned generally on the basis of one brigade per forward rifle army, each brigade consisted of 120 76mm and 85mm antitank guns and 16 37mm antiaircraft guns organized into two subordinate regiments. The new brigades experienced the same sorts of problems as the mechanized corps with which they were to cooperate. By 22 June, largely due to industrial production problems, the brigades had only 30–78 percent of their required guns and few of the 85mm models. Like the mechanized corps and other artillery forces, they also had insufficient vehicular transport, tractors, and logistical support. On 13 June, four of ten brigades had between 4 and 46 of their required 189 tractors, and the remaining brigades had no tractors at all. At the same time, the brigades had only 18 percent (1,308) of their required 7,070 vehicles.[7] These realities stripped the brigades of necessary wartime mobility. Predictably, when war began they were quickly destroyed.

As was the case with tanks, which on the eve of war gravitated into mechanized forces to the detriment of rifle formations, the bulk of divisional and corps antitank guns were cannibalized to form the new antitank brigades. This left most Soviet forces deficient in antitank capability, and once war began, these forces had to make do with the cheaper and more easily produced, but markedly less effective, antitank rifles.

Thus, on the eve of the war, although numerically superior to German artillery, Soviet artillery was inferior in terms of its mobility, logistical support, target acquisition, communications, and fire control, and the Soviets had failed to keep up with the Germans in the fielding of rocket artillery and antitank weaponry. Soviet artillery was inferior, in particular, at the division level. Most important, in the Red Army artillery had not been molded into an efficient combined-arms team to the extent that it was in the German Army. It lacked adequate reconnaissance and cooperated poorly with infantry, mechanized, and air forces. These faults significantly reduced the impact of artillery in battle and more than compensated for the Soviet numerical advantage in artillery tubes.

## ENGINEERS

Red Army engineer forces, like the artillery, consisted of force engineers (and sappers), which served at and beneath army level, and RGK engineer forces, which were used to reinforce *fronts* and armies. Force engineers existed on the basis of one sapper company per rifle regiment, a two-company sapper battalion per rifle division, and a three-company engineer-sapper battalion with each rifle corps. A tank division had a motorized sapper battalion, and an army contained engineer battalions and separate specialized engineer companies. RGK engineer forces consisted of separate engineer and pontoon-bridge battalions.

On the eve of war, Soviet engineer forces were also in the midst of structural and technical reformation. From February through May 1941, the NKO formed 18 engineer and 16 pontoon-bridge regiments from existing RGK engineer battalions and companies (see Table 6.1). These 1,000-man regiments were supposed to generate 156 engineer regiments, battalions, and separate companies between the second and tenth day of mobilization. In reality, most of these regiments devoted their efforts to the construction of new fortified regions rather than support of operating forces. On 22 June, all 160 corps and division sapper battalions and 9 of 10 engineer regiments in the western border military districts were working on the construction of border defenses, along with 41 sapper battalions from internal military districts. This deprived all operating forces and many reserves of any engineer support when war began and, ultimately, reduced their combat readiness.[8] Moreover, when war began, the critical engineer-sapper forces were too close to the front lines and were swallowed up in initial combat.

When war began, the engineer mobilization system also failed. The few new units that were created lacked trained personnel and had only 50 percent of their required bridging and engineer equipment. As a result, such critical combat functions as mining, restoring damaged bridges, constructing new defensive lines in the depth, and supporting mechanized corps' counterattacks were simply not performed.

Numerous reports document the dangerously vulnerable position in which engineer forces found themselves early in the war and the difficulty operating forces had in securing engineer support thereafter. A report prepared shortly after 13 August 1941 by Major General Vorob'ev, chief of the Western Front's Engineer Directorate, detailed the problems faced by engineers within the *front* and is typical of similar reports from other *fronts:*

> First. From February to March 1941, all sapper battalions and engineer regiments of the Western Special Military District were involved in special work fortifying the state boundary. Engineer units, year in and year out, were drawn into defensive construction separated from their formations, without sufficient time for combat and, now and then, political training, and were reduced to work parties. Sappers, separated from their formations, were not trained in engineer support of combat or in cooperation with other types of forces.
>
> Second. At the moment of the beginning of combat operations, all engineer units were located in the border sector and suffered great combat losses in killed and wounded officers cadre and Red Army soldiers. Heavy engineer equipment (road machines, compressors, etc.) were destroyed by enemy artillery fire and aviation. . . . By 24.6.41, the 23d Engineer Regiment in the Sopotskin region was disorganized and scattered. The main subunits of the 10th Engineer Regiment were drawn into battle along the state borders, and the regimental command group with specialized subunits was with the 1st Rifle Corps at Vizna. According to information from soldiers of the chief of the construction administration that had arrived from the front, all rifle corps and rifle division sapper battalions, which were working along the border, were sucked into battle and suffered great losses, and separate subunits were absorbed into other types of forces.[9]

Vorob'ev stated that by 27 June only three sapper battalions and two pontoon-bridge battalions remained functional within the Western Front. These were used to erect barriers to the German advance on Orsha, Vitebsk, and the Dnepr River. The *front* drafted civilian labor to assist them, but their efforts were in vain, partly because the engineers had no transport means or mines and very few explosive materials. Thereafter, *front* created new engineer units, both too late and in insufficient quantities to halt the German advance.

## SIGNAL FORCES

Signal force suffered similar problems. In June 1941 signal forces consisted of force, army, and *front* regiments and subunits. Force signal forces were distributed on the basis of a signal platoon in each combat battalion, a signal company in each combat regiment, and signal battalions in each division and corps. Signal battalions assigned to regiments, divisions, and corps were responsible for communications within and between their parent organizations. In peacetime, each army headquarters was served by a separate signal battalion, which, upon mobilization, was to expand into a full regiment. Each military district (wartime *front*) was served by its own signal regiment, and other separate signal regiments were subordinate to the RGK. In wartime, the 799-man *front* signal regiment was to consist of a two-company radio battalion equipped with 10 radio stations and a telegraph-telephone (wire) battalion equipped with 57 telegraphs and 2 radio sets. The similarly organized army regiment was to have 684 men, 9 radio stations, and 45 telegraphs.[10]

The RGK prewar signal force, which consisted of 19 separate signal regiments (14 military district and 5 army), 25 separate signal battalions, 16 special-purpose radio battalions (for radio intercept), and 17 signal centers (one for the NKO and one for each military district), was, according to General Staff plans, supposed to produce a wartime signal force structure of 37 separate signal regiments, 98 separate line signal battalions, and 298 separate signal companies. In actuality, it produced only 17 regiments (48.6 percent short), 25 battalions (74.4 percent short), and 4 companies (98 percent short).

Signal forces were equipped with insufficient quantities of largely obsolete radios, and Soviet industry lagged severely in the production of all types of modern communications equipment. In June 1941 mobilized signal units were at 39 percent fill in RAT radios, 46 percent in army and airfield radios, 77 percent in regimental radios, 35 percent in telegraph sets, and had only 43 percent of their required telephone wire. Overall, *fronts* averaged 75 percent of their required radios, Army 24 percent, divisions 89 percent, and regiments 63 percent. This quantity, coupled with the general lack of experience on the part of commanders in using radios and radio procedures, made communications during the initial period of war a nightmare.

Given the shortage of radios and the discomfort on the part of commanders using them, Red Army forces relied heavily on wire communications. This, in turn, was quickly disrupted by German diversionary activity during the early hours of the war and, subsequently, by the rapid German ground advance. The NKO attempted to reduce the tendency of commanders to rely on wire. On 15 February 1941, it directed all commanders and staffs to "learn the art of controlling forces by radio."[11]

In general, mobilization failed, and forces went into combat with insufficient quantities of largely obsolete communications equipment. Compounding the equipment and mobilization problems, many communications personnel were only partially trained or totally untrained, and command personnel were largely inexperienced in the art of combat communications. This was a fatal flaw for forces attempting to wage mobile warfare. Numerous Soviet archival reports document the gruesome consequences.[12]

Even before the outbreak of war, warnings were being aired about the Red Army's communications difficulties. Less than an hour before the German attack, the chief of staff of the Baltic Special Military District, Lieutenant General P. S. Klenov, sent an unsettling message to the General Staff:

> Weak places in district communications that could cause a crisis are:
>
> 1. The weakness of *front* and army signal units in the number of personnel and the demands of their related missions.
>
> 2. The incomplete *front* and army communications centers.
>
> 3. The insufficient maturity of wire communications from the Panvezh and Dvinsk communications centers.
>
> 4. The absence of communications for providing rear area communications.
>
> 5. The weak provision of signal equipment to district and army signal units and the air forces.[13]

Very shortly, Klenov's fears were borne out. Four days later, Colonel Kurochkin, chief of the Northwestern Front's Signals Directorate, reported the grisly realities of *front* communications after four days of combat. In a report entitled "Communications Conditions since the Beginning of the Campaign," he wrote:

> Corps and division separate signal battalions, being in peacetime condition and lacking complete auto-transport, could not fully pick up emergency stores of wire communications materials and left them in warehouses at their home bases. The border battles took place with the divisions and corps struggling on a very wide front. . . .
>
> From the onset of war, fixed wire lines along the border were destroyed by enemy aviation and diversionary groups, and therefore the divisions and corps were forced to fill in that distance by field means. . . .
>
> On the second and third day of the war, a rather dynamic and bloody battle occurred, and as a result our units began to withdraw rapidly to rear defense lines. . . .
>
> This withdrawal was not of a planned nature. Almost every division was half encircled and independently made its own way to the Western Dvina River.
>
> Division and corps separate signal often took immediate part in battle with the enemy along with their headquarters.

In summary, losses occurred of almost all wire communications equipment and a considerable number of radios. A considerable number of
these battalions' personnel perished in battle.

On the second and third day of war, the primary means of communications at division and corps level was by radio or liaison officer. . . .

RADIO COMMUNICATIONS

1. From the first days of war, radio communications worked practically without interruption, but in the beginning of war, headquarters
employed these means reluctantly and unskillfully. . . .

WIRE COMMUNICATIONS

In the beginning of the campaign, *front* and army headquarters did
not have establishment means (aviation, vehicles, and motorcycles) for
mobile means of communications.

Chiefs of staff were often reluctant to appropriate these means from
combat units.[14]

Reports from other *front* sectors replicate this description of signal support and problems many times over.

AIR DEFENSE

The problem of air defense in modern war was a natural outgrowth of the
increased importance of air power and, in particular, bomber aviation. Despite
this fact, before 1940 Soviet military authorities generally underestimated
the importance of air defense in modern war. In spring 1940, however, the
German military vividly demonstrated what air power could achieve in their
blitzkrieg operations in the West. At that time, massive German bombing of
western cities, economic objectives, and communications hubs, skillful inte-
gration of air support with ground operations, terror bombing of civilian
population centers, and rapid German seizure of air superiority had a sobering effect on the Soviet military.

Soviet theorists closely analyzed the role of air power in German military
victories and wrote extensively about it in their military journals. They erro-
neously concluded, however, that air power was of use only against small and
weak states that lacked a large, well-developed economy and an extensive
military force: "They recognized such means [air power] as groundless in war
with a large state that possessed equal or even greater military-economic
potential, that was vigilant, and that had a highly combat-ready armed force."[15]

Consequently, in June 1941 they "had not created a reliable system for antiaircraft defense of forces and important national objectives."[16] An NKO order of 14 February 1941, "Concerning the Strengthening of the Country's Antiaircraft Defense," had created a new national air defense system (PVO-strany) under the Main PVO Directorate of the Red Army. They designated 13 special PVO zones that encompassed "threatened territory" in the western Soviet Union to a depth of 1,200 kilometers, whose borders corresponded with those of military districts, and which, in turn, were subdivided into PVO regions and points.[17]

Specially designated PVO formations, units, and subunits (corps, divisions, and brigades) defended elements of this territorial system, and others defended large population centers (Moscow, Leningrad, Kiev) and important objectives 400 to 600 kilometers from the western border (200 to 250 kilometers in the Caucasus) in conjunction with ground force air defense elements and Air Force and Navy forces. These combined forces were responsible for providing air defense to the state and for repelling enemy air attack. Military district commands were responsible for air defense within their districts through the commander of the PVO zone.

National air defense forces (PVO-strany) were equipped with fighter aircraft, antiaircraft guns and machine guns, searchlights, aerostatics balloons, and optical observation equipment. Gun systems included the 7.62mm mounted machine guns, model 1931, and the 12.7mm heavy machine gun, model 1938, developed by V. A. Degtiarev and G. S. Shpagin. Both systems were competitive with like German models.

Although force air defense was the responsibility of respective combined arms commanders through their artillery commanders, there were no special organs in the military districts to control air defense or to prepare and train wartime *front* or army air defense forces. Instead, the NKO granted responsibility for combat and specialized training of air defense units to the Main PVO Directorate of the Red Army. In accordance with a 31 January 1941 NKO decision, the Main PVO Directorate was to "control combat training and the employment of antiaircraft artillery, antiaircraft machine guns, antiaircraft searchlights, fighter aviation, aerostatic balloon obstacles, and VNOS [air defense warning system] units designated for the air defense of USSR territory."[18]

Although creation of the new system was viewed as a positive development, it failed to provide a unitary system for either the state as a whole or for specific potential wartime targets. Fighter aviation was subordinate to the military district Air Force commander, and fighter aviation regiments that were tasked with providing for their defense of Moscow, Leningrad, and Baku were operationally subordinate to PVO corps commanders. Antiaircraft artillery was responsible to two headquarters: to the Main PVO Directorate regarding combat and specialized training, and to the artillery commander regarding firing training and material and technical support.

These and other conflicting responsibilities hindered the development and support of an effective air defense system. In addition, severe personnel turbulence in PVO commands at all levels also damaged force readiness. For example, during 1940 and 1941, the Red Army PVO Directorate (after 27 December 1940, the Main PVO Directorate) had six different commanders. These included Major Generals of Artillery Ia. K. Poliakov and M. F. Korolev, Lieutenant General of Aviation E. S. Ptukhin, Colonel General G. M. Shtern, and from 14 June through 19 July 1941, Colonel General N. N. Voronov. In the realm of air defense, as elsewhere, the purges caused much of this turbulence, and the resulting turbulence reached down to cause chaos in lower ranks as well.

These organizational problems and the turbulence in command cadre adversely affected general and specific air defense planning, officer training, command and control of the system, and its ability to effect efficient wartime mobilization. Planning remained superficial: "The plans for the air defense of zones was not concrete. They reflected only the factual stationing of antiaircraft units and subunits, provided brief characteristics of defended objectives, and identified the most probable axes of probable enemy air raids. The plans did not reflect the means for command and control of forces."[19]

Attempts to accelerate the training of PVO specialists in May 1941 backfired and adversely affected command, staff, unit, and individual crew effectiveness. In particular, PVO formations, units, and subunits were generally incapable of operating at night. On the eve of war, there were no modern regulations or common procedures for air defense, and existing regulations were obsolete versions that had been prepared in the mid-1930s. Unified staff procedures were in the process of being worked out.[20]

Air defense communications, which were supposed to be based upon around-the-clock air communications provided by the People's Commissariat of Communications, had not yet been organized. The Western and Kiev Special Military Districts alone had 119 and 110 communications centers that were not connected to a unified system, and in the Leningrad Military District, communications between PVO, the air forces, and the Baltic Fleet were confused. Observation posts and radio communications within the VNOS system either did not exist, did not work, or the information provided by them was untimely because of the inordinate reliance on wire communications. The VNOS system within the border military districts consisted of 70 to 75 percent wire (telephone), 15 to 20 percent direct lines, and 20 to 25 percent radio communications. Moreover, most personnel had difficulty using radios. Therefore, notification of forces, objectives, and airfields about enemy air action required between 4.5 and 15 minutes. As a result, between 1 January and 10 June 1941, there was no effective response by the VNOS system to 84 percent of the 122 German reconnaissance flights over Soviet territory prior to the German invasion.[21]

Compounding these organizational and systemic problems, existing air defense weaponry (37mm and 25mm automatic guns, 85mm guns, and 12.7mm machine guns) was old and ineffective, and production of newer-model 45mm automatic guns and 100mm and 130mm guns was going very poorly. Stockage levels of ammunition for even the older guns were low, ranging from 13 to 75 percent of required stockage for three months of war.[22] Shortages of older model guns (7,190 37mm and 1,308 85mm) could only be remedied by mid-1942. Production of new 85mm antiaircraft guns in 1941 increased by 1.7 times over 1940 production. The new weapons were assigned primarily to PVO formations and units in the western military districts or major population centers such as Moscow and Leningrad. Another 480 85mm guns were allocated especially for antitank use.

Soviet ground air defense forces in June 1941 consisted of three PVO corps, two PVO divisions, six PVO brigades, 26 PVO brigade regions, two separate PVO regiments, and nine separate antiaircraft battalions, manned by 182,000 men and equipped with 3,329 85mm guns, 335 37mm guns, 649 12.7mm machine guns, 1,597 antiaircraft searchlights, 853 balloon obstacles, and 75 radio-location (radar) stations (with RUS-2 and RUS-1 radio-locators) (see Table 6.1).[23]

Within Red Army ground forces, each rifle division had one antiaircraft artillery battalion of 8 37mm and 4 76.2mm antiaircraft guns, and each regiment had an antiaircraft machine-gun company of 3 heavy machine guns and 8 automatic machine guns on mounts. The corps antiaircraft battalion had 12 76.2mm antiaircraft guns, 2 heavy caliber machine guns, and 3 automatic machine guns on mounts. Although these subunits required 4,900 37mm guns according to establishment, in June 1941 only 1,382 were on hand. Therefore, the majority of combat divisions had only 4 to 8 of these guns rather than the required 12.[24]

Actual antiaircraft coverage by these battalions was inadequate because a rifle corps deployed on a frontage of 10 kilometers could effectively engage only one target flying level at an altitude of 3,000 meters in the forward edge, two flying level in the depth of the defense, or 14 to 15 assault aircraft. As the corps' frontage increased, the effectiveness also decreased. Moreover, antiaircraft forces could not fire at all while ground forces were moving, and night fire was limited due to the shortage of searchlights. The distribution of air PVO formations and units on the eve of war is shown in Table 6.4.

The Red Army Air Force allocated a total of 40 fighter aviation regiments totaling (in establishment strength) 2,520 aircraft for the performance of air defense missions. This included the dedicated divisions and regiments listed above and other regiments subordinate to military district air forces. However, these regiments possessed only 60 percent of their required air crews and 83 percent of their aircraft and other equipment. About 91 percent of their aircraft were older I-16, I-15, and I-153 aircraft, and the remainder were new IaK-3s and MiG-3s. None of the aircraft had radar sights, the radios on the new planes did not meet expectations, and the pilots were reluctant to use them. Pilots were untrained in night operations, and there were not enough searchlights to support night operations. The searchlights themselves were also less capable than foreign models.

VNOS formations and units employed vision methods of aircraft detection and primitive means to determine the course and objectives of enemy aircraft. Even these methods of target acquisition were hindered by the shortage of binoculars at VNOS posts (which reached 74 percent). In June 1941, only six VNOS stations were equipped with new experimental RUS-2 radios, and the older RUS-1 radios went out of production in 1940. Although a series of PVO exercises were conducted by the Red Army Main PVO Directorate in 1941, the German invasion intervened before any real positive results were achieved. Thus, "in general, the combat training of pilots, antiaircraft troops, searchlight forces, and staff officers of the PVO regions and zones remained low, and that negatively influenced the repulse of the initial enemy air strikes."[25]

In June 1941 PVO forces defending rear area objectives on European territory of the Soviet Union formed two belts of PVO zones. The first belt, which consisted of the Northern, Northwestern, Western, Kiev, and Southern PVO zones, contained 579 antiaircraft artillery batteries, 50 percent of the total, and 17 fighter aviation regiments, 42.5 percent of the total number of aviation regiments allocated to defend large centers of the country.[26] Of the 17 regiments, 9 defended Leningrad, 4 defended Kiev, and 1 each defended Riga, Minsk, Odessa, and Krivoi Rog. Antiaircraft artillery formed point defenses around these potential enemy objectives and were at 86 to 97 percent strength. Eighty-two batteries defended along the northwestern direction [axis] (the Northern and Northwestern PVO zones), 69 along the western axis (Western PVO zone), and 73 along the southwestern axis (the Kiev and Southern PVO zones). The remaining 355 batteries were assigned to PVO divisions defending Kiev and L'vov and the PVO corps defending Leningrad.

The second PVO belt consisted of the Moscow, Orel, and Khar'kov PVO zones and contained 223 antiaircraft batteries (19 percent of the total). Of these, 137 (more than 61 percent) were employed in the defense of Moscow. In addition, 11 fighter aviation regiments (27.5 percent of the total) defended the capital. However, only 6 of these fighter regiments had necessary equipment, and the other 5 were in the process of formation.

Antiaircraft forces in the forward areas were placed on alert on 18 June as the indicators of impending hostilities mounted. On that day, Colonel

General Kuznetsov, commander of the Baltic Special Military District, issued a top secret order:

> With the aim of bringing the theater of military operations of the district to combat readiness, *I order:*
> 1. The chief of the PVO zone to bring all district air defenses to full combat readiness by 19 June, in order to:
>     a. organize around-the-clock service of all air observation posts, alert signal elements, and secure uninterrupted communications;
>     b. prepare all antiaircraft artillery and projector [searchlight] batteries by appointing around-the-clock duty personnel in the batteries, organizing regular communications with their posts, preparing them in an engineer sense, and providing them with ammunition;
>     c. organize cooperation between fighter aviation and antiaircraft artillery units; and
>     d. by 1 July complete construction of command points, beginning from battery commanders to commanders of brigade regions.
>         On 19.6.41 report the priority of coverage of large railroad and highway bridges, artillery warehouses, and important objectives against dive bombers.
>         By 21.6.41, together with local antiaircraft defense organs, organize: blackout of the cities of Riga, Kaunas, Vilnius, Dvinsk, Mitava, Libava, and Shauliai and antifire measures in them; medical assistance for victims; and determine locations that can be used as bomb shelters;
>     e. force all organized measures to the maximum and complete them not later than 1 July 1941.[27]

Similar orders were issued in all border military district commanders. In the Western and Kiev Special Military Districts, all antiaircraft batteries in the sector from Grodno to L'vov to a depth of from Minsk to Novograd-Volyn'skii occupied firing positions. However, many of Western Front's batteries were engaged in practice training in the rear and could not deploy. By 21 June, 60 duty antiaircraft batteries defended Moscow and 30 Leningrad. The remaining 50 percent of the batteries in the Moscow region remained in their camp at Kosterovo. VNOS forces in the border military districts also went on alert to a depth of 150 to 250 kilometers. Further east, other VNOS forces were to go on alert only in the event of war.

Despite all of these measures, according to one official assessment, "As a whole, at the beginning of war, the combat readiness of PVO forces was at a comparatively low level. Although by that time serious changes had occurred in the organization and structure of PVO forces to strengthen centralized control, the Soviet government had not succeeded in creating unified direction of the entire PVO system."[28]

The same critique catalogued many problems, including weak organizational structures, inadequate quantities of already obsolete weaponry, poor personnel and unit training, especially in night operations, shortages of communications equipment, disorganized command and control, absence of uniform regulations and procedures in PVO zones and regions, and numerous like problems in supporting PVO aviation. In short, the consequences of these problems during wartime demonstrated the perils of entering combat without adequate air defense.

## BORDER GUARDS AND NKVD FORCES

The principal border guards force on the eve of war were the 49 detachments stationed along and patrolling the borders of the Soviet Union. Each of these detachments consisted of four or five *komendaturas*. The *komendatura* contained four line border outposts *(zastav)*, three with 42 to 64 men and a reserve outpost of 42 men, a maneuver group of three to five outposts with 50 men each, and an NCO school with 70 to 100 men. The border guards detachment contained 1,400 to 2,000 men, 20 to 30 50mm mortars, 80 to 122 submachine guns, 48 to 60 Maksim heavy machine guns, 25 to 30 vehicles, 200 to 300 horses, and 120 to 160 dogs.[29]

Border guards were light security forces equipped to patrol the border, detain line-crossers, counter enemy reconnaissance and diversionary action, and serve as a trip wire for regular forces. In no circumstances were they equipped or trained to engage in combat with regular armed force combat formations. Another primary mission of NKVD and border guards troops in peacetime, which continued during war, was to man and provide security for the Soviet system of punitive labor camps (the GULags). In case of war, their instructions were to either move the prison laborors or exterminate them. All indications are that when NKVD forces were summoned to the front they did the latter.

The 171,900-man NKVD force with its many subordinate elements received priority attention in the years preceding the outbreak of war. In general terms, therefore, they were well suited to perform the missions assigned to them. With the rapid collapse of Red Army defenses, however, they were called upon to do more than their normal camp security and internal security missions required. In essence, they were often required to operate as combat formations. In addition, the high attrition rate among army forces forced the enlistment of many NKVD troops into regular army units (see chapter 8).

The suddenness of the German attack severely disrupted planned NKVD mobilization. A 1 August 1941 after-action report by Lieutenant Colonel Golovko, commander of the 22d NKVD Motorized Division stated:

> In accordance with the mobilization plan, the 22d NKVD Motorized Rifle Division was created, which consisted of the 1st, 3d, and 5th Motorized Rifle Regiments. However, since the 1st and 3d Regiments had already been drawn into combat operations in Lithuania, and it was already impossible to establish communications with them, and the situation required urgent readiness to meet the fascist regular army, I included in the 22d Motorized Rifle Division's composition the 83d Railroad Regiment, the 5th NKVD Motorized Rifle Regiment and 155th Escort Battalion and organized a Red Guards regiment from Riga workers' battalions. Thus, in fact, the 22d NKVD Division consisted of three regiments and a separate battalion.[30]

After 30 June, combat circumstances required the 22d Motorized Rifle Division to operate as an integral part of 8th Army's 10th Rifle Corps; however, it had no organic artillery, engineer, or logistical support. A review of the scanty number of available NKVD documents indicates that some formations experienced equipment shortages. For example, the combat journal of the 2d NKVD Division (railroad security), subordinate to the Northwestern Front, reported on 2 July 1941 that, although "weapons and ammunition were fully provided," the formation's 109th Regiment "lacked 250 sets of clothing and 900 food pots."[31]

A subsequent report from the same regiment indicated that on 30 July "the regiment consisted of three companies with 67 men, a reserve company of 52 men and other subunits with 280 men, and three heavy machine guns," for a total strength of 399 men.[32] Because of its weakness, it was integrated into the Red Army's 320th Rifle Regiment. In fact, while NKVD mobilization proceeded apace, most NKVD forces operating in the border belt of the western military districts were soon resubordinated to Red Army field commands. NKVD forces seemed well prepared to perform their wartime missions and the NKVD mobilization process seemed to function efficiently, but NKVD forces were not trained and equipped to fight as regular combat units. As a result they seem to have suffered heavy losses.

## REAR SERVICES

During peacetime, the Red Army maintained all rear service units and facilities in their combat force structure at drastically reduced manning and equipment levels. *Front* and army rear services did not exist. There were a few separate hospitals, repair facilities, and warehouses for the peacetime support of forces, and these were designed to provide the base for subsequent mobilization. The mobilization plan (MP-41) required divisions to mobilize in 3 days, armies to mobilize more than 100 rear service units within 7 days after mobilization began, and *fronts* to organize 400–500 like units within 15 days. National armed forces rear service administrations were to be fully mobilized within 30 days. Based on the experiences of World War I and subsequent smaller conflicts, Soviet military authorities planned for combat force reserve stocks to support 3 days of combat operations and contain 5 to 6 days of foodstuffs. A fixed and stable system of *front* warehouses and supply points was to contain 9 to 10 ammunition loads, 10 fills of fuel, and 30 days' provisions. These operational rear service elements lacked single command and were subordinate both to the Red Army Rear Services Directorate and the Commissariat of Defense.[33]

The mobilization plan included a plan for developing rear services further. It postulated creation of stockage levels sufficient to support *fronts* for three months of operations (and six months of foodstuffs). In the border military districts, however, a shortage of warehouse space reduced reserve supplies, and there was only a one-month supply of fuel and ammunition. On the other hand, 38 percent (340 of 887) of existing warehouses were located near operating forces in the western military districts, and most of these were near the border, where they were most vulnerable to enemy attack.

The central bases and warehouses of the Main Artillery Directorate held 20 percent of all reserve artillery shells and 9 percent of the mines, while in the western border military districts a great part of these supplies were maintained near the border. For example, 25 percent of all ammunition in the Western Theater of Military Operations, amounting to over 30 million shells and mines, was stored 50 to 200 kilometers from the border, where much of it fell into enemy hands shortly after war began.

There were both doctrinal and structural problems regarding the availability of ammunition to operating forces. In 1938, based on an analysis of ammunition consumption in previous conflicts, the Red Army established the norm for ammunition consumption at 5,000 to 6,000 rounds per tube during the course of a war. Based on new data obtained from analysis of Finnish War combat and combat at Khalkhin-Gol, in 1940 and 1941 the General Staff reduced this norm to an average of 1,000 rounds per tube. Depending upon industrial output, the Red Army planned to build up a two-month supply of ammunition in the western and southern border military districts, a three-month supply in the Trans-Baikal Military district, and a four-month supply in the Far East.[34] A two-month norm constituted 600 to 800 rounds per gun and 1,000 to 1,600 rounds per mortar.

Despite this careful planning, in June 1941 the ammunition supply was inadequate to meet the established norms. (See Table 6.5 for Red Army on-hand ammunition supplies on 22 June 1941.) In terms of specific weapons, there was enough ammunition for 1,700 rounds per 45mm antitank gun, more than 1,000 rounds per 76mm field gun, 700 to 800 rounds per 122mm and 152mm guns, and 453 rounds per 203mm howitzer. None of these quantities met the establishment requirements for a two-month supply. In absolute terms, as well, ammunition supplies in the western military districts were inadequate and met between 6 and 84 percent of their required fill (see Table 6.6).

On the eve of war, rear services elements in operating forces were at 25 to 30 percent of their wartime strength and were to reach full strength on the third day of mobilization. However, shortages in transport (from 50 to 80 percent of required vehicles) and lack of plans to distribute supplies in the event of war made mobilization of existing force rear services chaotic and ineffective.

Lack of required transport was a particularly vexing problem. If norms were to be met at all, field operating forces required more than 60 percent of the total ammunition supply. Much of this ammunition, however, was located in warehouses in the internal military districts and required transport over long distances to operating forces. In addition, about one third of the ammunition in the western military districts (the less vulnerable portion) was located up to 700 kilometers to the rear. This also needed to be transported forward. The problem was that the same shortage of vehicles and tractors that existed in combat units existed to an even greater extent in the rear services. In the end, this lack of transport paralyzed the resupply effort and deprived operating forces of ammunition when they most needed it.

Although rail transport carried about 90 percent of Soviet cargo in 1941 and road transport only 1.8 percent, because of its flexibility and accessibility to field forces, road transport by truck was most critical for the support of military operations. The Red Army vehicle park had increased sevenfold since 1937, in consonance with the motorization and mechanization program. During this accelerated period of production, Soviet industry produced 145,390 vehicles in 1940 and 124,176 in 1941, presumably over half of these (62,000) before June.[35] The total Soviet cargo truck park on 22 June numbered 700,000 vehicles, predominantly of the 1.5-ton GAZ-AA model. However, poor road conditions, shortages of spare parts, repair facilities, and tires, and the technological backwardness of drivers and mechanics took a heavy toll on these vehicles. Consequently, about 45 percent of these vehicles were inoperable, and stocks of tires met only 25 percent of demand.

During mobilization and wartime, the Red Army required 744,000 motor vehicles and 92,000 tractors, and on 22 June only 272,200 vehicles and 42,000 tractors were available. This amounted to 36 percent of establishment requirements, and only 193,200 of these vehicles were cargo trucks. In addition, more than 58 percent of the cargo trucks were older GAZ-AA models with low cargo capacities, a fact that in turn tended to increase their use and, hence, the frequency of breakdowns. Because of this and poor repair facilities, 23.1 percent of Red Army vehicles were inoperable on the eve of war (see Table 6.7).

Because of the truck and vehicle shortage, the Army planned to mobilize 240,000 vehicles from the economy, including 210,000 GAZ-AA and ZIS trucks. However, existing organized mobilization organs had only 90,000 vehicles, and mobilization authorities had to organize anew measures for requisitioning the remaining trucks from the civil economy. By 22 August 1941, the Red Army had mobilized a total of 206,000 vehicles, while at the same time it lost 271,400 in combat.[36]

Another major problem for the Soviet military, in general, was the formation of forces that could maintain the cargo capacity of roads during mobilization and wartime, given the poor condition of the roads and the anticipated heavy cargo traffic. The Red Army had mobilized a sizable number of road units during the Soviet-Finnish War, but most of these had been demobilized at war's end to rejoin the economy. Consequently, in peacetime, the Red Army maintained 8 training road-exploitation regiments and 35 reduced-establishment regimental headquarters in military districts and under General Staff control, and virtually no road construction forces (or auto-transport units) existed in armies, divisions, or regiments. During mobilization and wartime, the few existing units were to expand into a force of 49 regiments and 39 battalions over a period of five to eight days. Once again, however, civilian resources were inadequate to support such an expansion, and even had it occurred, the roads would have gone without servicing for at least the first week of war. Complicating the situation further, many of the road units were under NKVD control, and it is questionable whether they would have been available for Army use.[37]

An analogous situation existed regarding fuel stocks and resupply. Measures to conserve fuel in light of inadequate production hindered combat training, in particular for mobile forces in 1941. Although fuel and oil stocks almost reached required norms in June 1941, the same fuel storage patterns and transport problems that plagued ammunition supply also affected fuel supply. Moreover, unlike ammunition, 40 to 60 percent of the precious fuel was kept in warehouses in the Moscow, Orel, and Khar'kov Military Districts and at fuel production facilities. Efforts to move this fuel to more forward bases in 1941 came to naught. As a result, on 22 June 1941, operating forces in the Baltic, Western, and Kiev Special Military Districts had 6, 8, and 15 days of fuel supplies, respectively, rather than the required norm of two months.

The final important category of service support was foodstuffs necessary to feed the Red Army. Army expansion between 1937 and 1941 had placed a huge burden on Soviet agriculture, and mobilization would double this burden. In general terms, the economy could not support such requirements, and foodstuffs remained scarce and primitive by Western standards. According to one source, "from 1939, on-hand reserves of foodstuffs and forage turned out to be insufficient. . . . The army was provided with a three- to four-month supply of basic, traditional products (grain, flour, groats, macaroni, sugar, tea, and salt) and two months of meat products and tobacco."[38] A major problem remained the machine-processing of foodstuffs and its vehicular distribution to the forces. The same situation existed in the stockage of clothing and uniforms.[39]

Numerous combat reports describe rear area support difficulties during the early days of war, how rear service support organs were paralyzed by the German attack and the debilitating effect of this paralysis on unit combat readiness and performance:

As a whole, operational rear service organs were insufficiently prepared for a major war and were not mobilized in timely fashion. With hastily put together and incomplete transport, they could not fulfill the function of force resupply to full measure in the beginning of war, especially in conditions of withdrawal and encirclement. The echelonment and accumulation of material reserves did not correspond to transportation capabilities. Therefore, in the beginning of war, forces of the western *fronts* remained without necessary rear service support, and many warehouses were destroyed or seized by the enemy.[40]

# STATISTICAL DATA

Table 6.1. Red Army Artillery and Engineer Forces, 22 June 1941

| Formation | Force Artillery | RGK Artillery | Air Defense | Engineers |
|---|---|---|---|---|
| **Field forces** | | | | |
| **Northern Front** | | | | |
| 7th Army | | | 208th AABn | 184th SBn |
| 14th Army | | 104th GAR | | 31st SBn |
| 23d Army | 24th, 28th, 43d CAR; 573d GAR; 20th MBn | 101st HAR; 108th, 519th HPHAR | 27th, 241st AABn | 153d EngBn; 109th MotEngBn |
| Front | | 541st, 577th HAR | 2d PVOC (115th, 169th, 189th, 192d, 194th, 351st AAR) | 12th, 29th EngR 6thPBR |
| **Northwestern Front** | | | | |
| 8th Army | 9th ATB; 47th, 51st, 73d CAR | | 39th, 242d AABn | 25th EngR |
| 11th Army | 10th ATB; 270th, 448th, 615th CAR | 110th HPHAR; 429th HAR | 19th, 247th AABn | 38th EngBn |
| 27th Army | 613th, 614th CAR | | 103d, 111th AABn | |
| Front | | 402d HPHAR | 10th, 12th, 14th PVOB; 11th AABn | 4th, 30th PBR |
| **Western Front** | | | | |
| 3d Army | 7th ATB; 152d, 444th CAR | | 16th AABn | |
| 4th Army | 447th, 455th, 462d CAR | 120th HPHAR | 12th AABn | |
| 10th Army | 6th ATB; 130th, 156th, 262d, 315th CAR | 311th GAR; 124th, 375th HAR | 38th, 71st AABn | |
| Front | 8th ATB; 29th, 49th, 56th, 151st, 467th, 587th CAR; 24th MBn | 293d, 611th GAR; 360th HAR; 5th, 318th, 612th HPHAR; 32d SPABn | 4th, 7th PVOB; 86th AABn | 10th, 23d, 33d EngR; 34th, 35th PBR; 275th EngBn |
| **Southwestern Front** | | | | |
| 5th Army | 1st ATB; 21st, 231st, 264th, 460th CAR | | 23d, 243d AABn | 5th PBR |
| 6th Army | 3d ATB; 209th, 229th,441st, 445th CAR | 135th GAR | 17th, 307th AABn | 9th EngR |
| 12th Army | 4th ATB; 269th, 274th, 283d, 468th CAR | | 20th, 30th AABn | 37th EngR; 19th PBR |
| 26th Army | 2d ATB; 233d, 236th CAR | | 28th AABn | 17th PBR |
| Front | 5th ATB; 205th, 207th, 368th, 437th, 458th, 507th, 543d, 646th CAR | 305th, 555th GAR; 4th, 168th, 324th, 330th, 526th HPHAR; 331st, 376th, 529th, 538th, 589th HAR; 34th, 245th, 315th, 316th SPABn | 3d, 4th PVOD; 11th PVOB; 263d AABn | 45th EngR; 1st PBR |
| 9th Separate Army | | 320th GAR; 430th HPHAR;265th, 266th, 374th, 648th CAR; 317th SPABn | 26th, 268th AABn | 8th, 16th EngBn; 121st MotEngBn |

| ormation | Force Artillery | RGK Artillery | Air Defense | Engineers |
|---|---|---|---|---|
| avka reserves | | | | |
| 16th Army | 126th CAR | | 12th AABn | |
| 19th Army | 442d, 471st CAR | | | 111th MotEngR; 238th, 321st SBn |
| 20th Army | 438th CAR | 301st HAR; 537th HPHAR | | 60th PBR |
| 21st Army | 420th, 546th CAR | 387th HAR | | |
| 22d Army | 336th, 545th CAR | | | |
| 24th Army | 392d, 542d, 685th CAR | 524th HGAR | | |
| Stavka | 267th, 390th CAR | | | |
| ilitary districts and onoperating fronts | | | | |
| Moscow | 275th, 396th, 649th CAR | 403d, 590th HPHAR; 594th GAR; 40th, 226th, 228th, 23d SPABn | 1st PVOC (176th, 193d, 250th, 251st, 329th, 745th AAR | 28th EngR; 40th EngBn |
| Volga | | 637th CAR; 592d GAR | | |
| Orel | 364th, 488th, 643d, 644th CAR | 281st SPHAR; 399th HAR | 733d, 46th, 123d AABn | |
| Ural | | | | 22d EngR |
| Siberian | 11th MBn | 486th, 544th HPHAR | | 27th EngR |
| Khar'kov | 435th, 645th CAR | 191st HPHAR | | |
| North Caucasus | 394th, 596th CAR; 138th, 302d HAR; 440th HPHAR; 5th MBn | | | |
| Odessa | 268th, 272d, 377th CAR | 137th, 515th, 522d, 527th HPHAR | 296th, 391st AABn | 7th PBR; 8th EngR |
| Trans-Caucasus | 25th, 456th, 457th, 647th CAR | 116th, 337th, 547th HAR; 136th, 350th HPHAR | 3d PVOC (180th, 190th, 195th, 252d, 335th, 339th, 513th AAR); 31st AABn | 21st EngR |
| Central Asian | 123d, 450th CAR; 9th MBn | | 143d, 187th, 189th AABn | 20th EngR |
| Arkhangel'sk | | 310th GAR; 1st, 6th, HGABtry | | |
| Trans-Baikal | | | | |
| 17th Army | | 185th GAR | | 17th PBR |
| Mechanized Division | 13th MBn | 106th HPHAR; 216th, 413th HAR | 68th AABn | 31st EngR; 15th PBR; 39th SR |
| Far Eastern Front | | | | |
| 1st Army | 50th, 273d CAR | 165th HAR; 199th, 549th HPHAR | 115th, 129th AABn | 29th EngBn |
| 2d Army | 42d CAR | 114th, 550th HPHAR | | 2d HPBR; 36th PBR |
| 15th Army | 52d, 76th CAR | | 110th AABn | 3d HPBR; 11th, 16th PBR; 129th SBn |
| 25th Army | 282d, 548th CAR; 215th, 386th HAR | | 59th AABn | 32d EngR; 69th SBn |
| Mechanized Division | 187th CAR; 362d, 367th ABn; 21st, 22d MBn | 181st, 372d, 411th HAR | 70th AABn | 26th EngR; 60th SBn |

Note: For abbreviations, consult List of Abbreviations, p. xv.
Source: *Boevoi sostav Sovetskoi Armii*, 7–14.

Table 6.2. Southwestern Front Rifle-Mortar Weapons, 22 June 1941

|  | Planned for 1941 | On Hand on 22 June 1941 | Shortage |
|---|---|---|---|
| 7.62mm carbine | 140,434 | 66,228 | 74,206 |
| 7.62mm submachine gun | 61,207 | 15,780 | 45,427 |
| 7.62mm revolver-pistol | 245,931 | 165,205 | 80,726 |
| 7.62mm light machine gun | 28,336 | 21,334 | 7,002 |
| 7.62mm heavy machine gun | 2,330 | 956 | 1,375 |
| 12.7mm machine gun (AA) | 1,087 | 186 | 901 |
| 82mm mortar | 2,283 | 1,829 | 454 |
| 120mm mortar | 432 | 264 | 168 |

Source: *SBDVOV* 36 (1958), 93–100.

Table 6.3. Southwestern Front Artillery Weapons, 22 June 1941

|  | Required | On Hand (unserviceable) | Shortage |
|---|---|---|---|
| 45mm gun (AT) | 2,134 | 1,912 (62) | 222 |
| 76mm gun, 1927 model | 714 | 641 | 73 |
| 76mm gun, 1936 model |  | 797 (23) |  |
| 76mm gun, 1939 model | } 1,037 | 84 | } 1,301 |
| 76mm gun, 1902/03 model |  | 420 (66) |  |
| 76mm mountain gun | 192 | 200 |  |
| 122mm howitzer, 1910/30, 1909/37 model | 1,074 | 999 (46) | 75 |
| 122mm howitzer, 1938 model | 320 | 278 (102) | 42 |
| 122mm corps gun | 358 | 187 | 171 |
| 107mm gun | 0 | 213 (105) |  |
| 152mm howitzer, 1909/30 model | 357 | 310 (30) | 47 |
| 152mm howitzer, 1938 model | 492 | 236 | 256 |
| 152mm gun, 1910/30 model | 12 | 28 |  |
| 152mm gun-howitzer, 1937 model | 622 | 523 | 99 |
| 152mm gun-howitzer, 1910/34 model | 0 | 43 |  |
| 203mm howitzer | 192 | 192 |  |
| 280mm howitzer, BR-5 | 24 | 18 | 6 |
| 280mm howitzer, 1914/15 model | 0 | 6 |  |
| 37mm antiaircraft gun | 984 | 240 | 744 |
| 76mm antiaircraft gun | 796 | 599 (53) | 197 |
| 85mm antiaircraft gun | 600 | 542 | 58 |

Source: *SBDVOV* 36 (1958), 93–100.

Table 6.4. Distribution of Air PVO Forces, 22 June 1941

| Parent Force | Air Defense Force |
|---|---|
| Northern Front | 3d Fighter Aviation Division PVO |
|  | 54th Fighter Aviation Division PVO |
| Northwestern Front | 21st Fighter Aviation Regiment PVO |
| Western Front | 184th Fighter Aviation Regiment PVO |
| Southwestern Front | 36th Fighter Aviation Division PVO |
| 9th Separate Army | 131st Fighter Aviation Regiment PVO |
| Trans-Caucasus Military Distinct | 27th Fighter Aviation Division PVO |
|  | 71st Fighter Aviation Division PVO |
| Trans-Baikal Military District | 9th Fighter Aviation Regiment PVO |
| Far Eastern Front | 18th Fighter Aviation Regiment PVO |

Source: *Boevoi sostav Sovetskoi armii*, 7–12.

Table 6.5. Red Army Ammunition Supply, 22 June 1941

| | Total Rounds | | Rounds per Tube | |
|---|---|---|---|---|
| | Western Military District | Red Army | Western Military District | Red Army |
| Field artillery | 27,326,500 | 55,492,000 | 1,135 | 1,150 |
| Antiaircraft artillery | 2,838,900 | 6,101,600 | 588 | 710 |
| Mortars | 15,732,200 | 26,560,900 | 641 | 472 |
| Total | 36,585,400 | 88,154,500 | 697 | 788 |

Source: Ramanichev, 145–146, citing archival reference *TsAMO*, f. 81, op. 12076, d. 8, l. 98–101; d. 16, l. 3–12; op. 12074, d. 36, l. 6–7; op. 11624, d. 296, l. 9–77.

Table 6.6. Level of Supply of Artillery Ammunition in the Western Military Districts, 22 June 1941 (percentage of required)

| | Military District | | | | | |
|---|---|---|---|---|---|---|
| | Leningrad | Baltic | Western | Kiev | Odessa | Total |
| 45mm antitank | 48.5 | 30.9 | 48.9 | 29.1 | 59.2 | 37.7 |
| 76mm division gun | 74.7 | 24.7 | 42.1 | 25.2 | 57.6 | 33.4 |
| 122mm howitzer | 91.9 | 72.2 | 82.4 | 36.5 | 44.4 | 57.2 |
| 152mm howitzer | 100.3 | 73.0 | 66.6 | 45.1 | 94.9 | 61.1 |
| 152mm howitzer-gun | 60.2 | 67.1 | 81.0 | 39.0 | 57.4 | 55.5 |
| 37mm antiaircraft | 5.3 | 9.6 | 8.9 | 7.8 | 2.4 | 7.5 |
| 76mm antiaircraft | 159.6 | 90.4 | 83.5 | 66.8 | 50.8 | 84.4 |
| 50mm mortar | 19.8 | 31.6 | 36.1 | 16.5 | 31.5 | 24.0 |
| 82mm mortar | 57.5 | 38.3 | 53.1 | 29.0 | 64.2 | 40.7 |
| 120mm mortar | 8.2 | 6.2 | 8.2 | 4.8 | 13.1 | 6.6 |

Source: Ramanichev, 148–149, citing archival reference *Arkhiv GSh*, f. 10, op. 370. d. 30, l. 1–2.

Table 6.7. Distribution of Red Army Vehicles and Auto-Transport Units, 22 June 1941

| | | Number of Automobile Units | | |
|---|---|---|---|---|
| Military District | Number of Vehicles | Regiments | Battalions | Depots[*] |
| Western military districts | 149,300 | 9 | 6 | 8 |
| Internal and southern border military districts | 57,700 | 4 | 10 | 57 |
| Trans-Baikal Military District and Far Eastern Front | 63,600 | 6 | 21 | |
| Central warehouses | 1,600 | | | |
| Total | 272,200 | 19 | 37 | 65 |

[*]During mobilization, depots formed auto-tranport battalions comprising reservists and vehicles mobilized from the civilian economy.
Source: Ramanichev, 163–164, citing archival reference *TsAMO*, f. 41, op. 34880, d. 3, l. 1; f. 38, op. 11492, l. 44.

# CHAPTER 7

# Air Forces

Reflecting the extensive theoretical writings of the interwar years, the importance of Air Forces in modern war grew considerably. The Soviets were strongly influenced by Western theoretical writing on the nature of future war and the perceived increased importance of air power on its outcome. Albert Douhet's theories of the strategic use of air power against national economies and a nation's population were translated into Russian and studied intensely by Soviet military theorists. Soviet theorists of the 1930s who developed the twin concepts of "deep battle" and the "deep operation" were keenly aware of the vertical dimension of warfare and the fact that successful projection of ground military power was predicated on the achievement and maintenance of air superiority. Therefore, a wide range of interwar theorists, like M. N. Tukhachevsky and V. K. Triandafillov, included air power in their calculations, and Soviet writers like A. N. Lapchinsky, A. S. Algazin, and S. A. Mezhenikov wrote extensively on the role and function of air power in modern war.[1] Therefore, by June 1941 the Red Army Air Force had emerged with the ground forces and the fleet as one of the three Soviet service arms.

Based on sound theoretical foundations for the employment of air power, the Soviets moved rapidly in the late 1930s to create an industrial base capable of producing aircraft, a wide range of specific aircraft types, and a force structure for effective use of the aircraft in war. By 1940, 40 percent of the Soviet Union's military budget was allocated to the Air Force, and the number of aircraft factories rose by 75 percent. As a result, by June 1941 the Soviet aviation production base was one and a half times larger than Germany's. Between 1938 and 22 June 1941, the Soviet aviation industry doubled its output and produced 22,685 combat aircraft.[2]

While increasing aircraft production, Soviet aircraft design bureaus fielded an entirely new generation of aircraft, including the Iak-1, MiG-3, and LaGG-3 fighters, the Pe-2 dive bomber, and the Il-2 assault aircraft (shturmovik). Serial production of these new aircraft began in late 1940, when 96 planes were produced (20 MiG-3, 64 Iak-1, and 12 Pe-2). By 1 June 1941, another 2,653 new aircraft had come off the assembly line, but this represented only 48 percent of the plan.[3] These joined the already large air fleet of older model aircraft. Full production of new aircraft and the complete outfitting of the reformed Soviet Air Force force structure was to be completed by summer 1942.

As was the case with mechanized forces, Soviet study of war experience in the late 1930s, in particular of combat in the Spanish Civil War, at Khalkhin-Gol, and in Finland, prompted Soviet theorists to modify their views on the utility of strategic and operational air power. Clearly, developments in the field of air power permitted the Air Force to resolve larger operational-strategic missions. Foremost among these missions was the support of ground force operations and the achievement of air superiority. The Air Force was also expected to cover and protect one's own mobilization, disrupt enemy mobilization and deployment, and destroy enemy force concentrations and key political-administrative targets and military-economic centers. In theory, the Air Force could operate independently or in close concert with the ground forces and fleets.

The experience of Soviet pilots and aircraft during the Spanish Civil War underscored the urgency of the ensuing Soviet aviation reform program. Combat in Spain demonstrated vividly the weaknesses of Soviet aircraft in battle with their German foes. The I-16 and I-153 were outgunned and outmaneuvered even by German bombers. About 90 percent of Soviet fighters had only machine guns, whereas German aircraft had guns and cannons. It is no coincidence that the Soviet construction program for newer modern fighters began shortly after the end of that war.

During the Finnish War, the Soviets used their air power primarily in support of ground armies, which were attempting to penetrate heavily fortified defensive lines. Attacks on enemy aviation were not needed against the insignificant Finnish Air Force, with its 114 planes. Although the Germans in the West employed air power against strategic targets and in support of ground forces in devastatingly effective centralized fashion, the Soviet leadership did not react to those experiences. Instead, they decentralized their long-range bomber aviation and placed most of their air power at the disposal of *front* and army commanders. Under the new Air Force employment scheme, the air superiority mission was to be accomplished in air battles with enemy air formations rather than by the destruction of enemy airfields, which were considered to be too difficult to effectively engage and destroy. As June 1941 would indicate, this deprived the Soviet Air Force command from reacting to counter the sudden German attack and literally set them up for rapid defeat in detail.

In accordance with these doctrinal adjustments, in fall 1940 the NKO mandated creation of a larger fighter aviation force at the expense of bombers. In October 1940 the correlation of bomber to fighter aircraft was roughly 57 percent to 43 percent, and Red Army Air Force expansion plans reflected that ratio. Between October and November 1940, however, the commissar of defense instituted a new program that shifted priority in the formation of Air Force units from bomber to fighter aircraft. Under the November program, which was to be complete by 31 December 1941, the ratio was to shift to 60 to 40 in favor of fighters (see Table 7.1 at the end of this chapter). The program sought to increase the number of aviation regiments from 249 to 323 and the number of aircraft from 19,977 to 20,607. The NKO made similar changes in pilot training programs, which were designed to more than double the number of pilots and other flight personnel by 1 January 1942 (see Table 7.2).

By summer 1941, because of this shift in priorities and the fact that fighters were cheaper to produce, the ratio had reversed to 53 percent to 41 percent in favor of fighters. At the December 1940 Red Army commanders' conference in Moscow, the chief of the Red Army Main Air Force Directorate, Lieutenant General P. V. Rychagov, and the commander of the Baltic Special Military District Air Forces, Lieutenant General G. P. Kravchenko, addressed Air Force missions. Their speeches and other Soviet theoretical writings focused primarily on air support of offensive operations. Other missions received less or little attention. One assessment noted: "The extent to which aviation missions were worked out in practice by the beginning of war was insufficient. Many estimates of expected results of aviation operations were exaggerated and did not have a scientific basis. The level of cooperation with forces, in particular at the tactical level, was low. The situation was exacerbated by the absence of communications, command and control, and reciprocal information."[4]

In short, experience seemed to indicate that more emphasis had to be placed on the role of air support for ground forces, in particular, tactically. Therefore, in November 1940, after abolishing their mechanized corps a year before, the Soviet shelved their plans to field separate air armies of long-range bomber aviation, which were capable of conducting independent air operations. Instead, they fielded 5 aviation corps and 3 separate aviation divisions of long-range aviation and subordinated these to military district commanders for support of ground force operations. The remaining 61 bomber, fighter, and mixed aviation divisions also remained in a ground support role.

## STRUCTURE, EQUIPMENT, AND COMMAND
## AND CONTROL

On the eve of war, Soviet ground forces were supported by *front* and force aviation. The former, which was subordinated in peacetime to western border military district commanders, was organized into two basic groups, *front* and army. The *front* group comprised bomber, fighter, and, in some instances, mixed air divisions and separate air reconnaissance regiments immediately subordinate to military districts. Aviation subordinate to army consisted of one to two mixed aviation divisions and communications and reconnaissance squadrons. The mixed aviation divisions, which included three to five bomber, fighter, or assault aviation regiments, were to perform missions assigned by the army commander. Force aviation, which was subordinate to rifle and mechanized corps, consisted of separate aviation squadrons, each with reconnaissance, artillery-correction, and communications aircraft.

By June 1941 there were 32 aviation divisions in the western border military districts, including 5 bomber, 8 fighter (including 4 forming), and 19 mixed aviation divisions (see Table 1.4, p. 20).[5] Given this total, *front* aviation comprised 40.5 percent of the Red Army Air Force, and army aviation 43.7 percent.[6] In terms of aircraft, 53.4 percent of the Soviet aircraft fleet of 15,599 aircraft in the long-range aviation (DBA) and the military districts (excluding PVO, schools, and training installation aircraft) were fighters, 41.2 percent were bombers, 3.2 percent reconnaissance aircraft, and 0.2 percent ground assault models.[7] Eighty percent of these aircraft were of older design, like the I-15, I-1-15bis, and I-16 fighters, SB, TB-3, and DB-3 bombers, and R-5 reconnaissance aircraft. German intelligence during the Finnish War had correctly concluded that these older model Soviet aircraft had been "ineffectual against the minuscule Finnish Air Force."[8] When the newer Soviet aircraft finally entered the aircraft park in 1941, the multiplicity of types and models (20 types and 70 modified versions), together with the over 86 types of bombs, complicated organization of air formations, logistical support, and planned wartime employment of the aircraft.[9]

While industry geared up for more extensive serial production of newer aircraft models, the NKO struggled to train requisite cadre to man the planes and direct the growing number of required air formations and units. From 1939 to summer 1941, total Air Force personnel increased threefold to 476,000 men. During the same period, Air Force training schools increased from 32 to 111, including more than 60 pilot training facilities. On 25 February 1941, a decree of the Central Committee, "Concerning the Reorganization of the Red Army Aviation Forces," mandated the formation by summer 1942 of 106 new aviation regiments added to the 242 already in existence. By June 1941 the difficulty in instituting this new program was apparent, and only 19 of these new regiments had been formed.[10]

At the same time, the Soviets strove to increase their networks of airfields to accommodate the new aviation formations. Each new regiment of 63 aircraft required 3 airfields for normal operations. Given the planned creation of new regiments, this meant that, on 1 May 1941, the western military districts alone required 592 new airfields. Therefore, the Soviets formed 100 new airfield construction battalions numbering 25,000 men to hasten the construction effort and convert older airfields into more modern facilities. These new construction forces were to build 480 new airfields in the western military districts by 31 December 1941. This, in turn, required wholesale redeployment of aircraft to temporary airfields while construction of new airfields and renovation of the old proceeded. The resulting concentration of aircraft on existing fields made it difficult to conceal or disperse them and increased their vulnerability to enemy attack. This new construction program also fell short of its goals, only increasing the chaos in Air Force deployment on the eve of war.

On the eve of war, because of the haste of the rebasing program and its partial implementation, in many cases two regiments shared a single airfield, creating aircraft densities of up to 150 aircraft per single field and tremendous vulnerability to enemy attack. Many regiments were based at airfields too close to the border, even to within the range of enemy artillery. For example, the Western Front's 9th Mixed Aviation Division, with 358 aircraft (233 new), was deployed in airfields from 12 to 40 kilometers from the frontier. Often, because of confusion at the top levels, all available airfields were not used. The Western Special Military District commander only used a fraction of his 382 airfields.

The expansion of the Air Force and the airfield network also required reformation and expansion of the Air Force's rear service structure. The existing structure was suited to support the peacetime demands of the 1940 Air Force. In this structure each aviation unit had its own rear service organ, an "aviation park." Whenever a regiment redeployed, its "aviation park" also had to move, and, while the regiment and its park were making the time-consuming move, the unit was not combat ready.[11] In April 1941, the VVS instated a new "autonomous" system of rear service support by creating "regions of aviation basing" (RABs), each of which was associated with a specific aviation unit or formation. Each RAB consisted of two to three aviation bases, which, in turn, contained four to five airfield service battalions. The presumption was that each RAB could support its own plus two to three additional aviation divisions in its area of responsibility, and each airfield service battalion could support one aviation regiment. The entire system was geared to support the wholesale expansion of aviation formations and units. By 22 June 1941, only 8 of 54 planned RABs had been created, and the new ones were only partially formed. The 8 new RABs had only 28.1 percent of their required equipment.[12]

Needless to say, the Air Force command and control system functioned neither properly nor effectively. A system of command posts had not been created to tie the entire system together, and headquarters relied on static wire lines for most communications. This system lacked mobility and flexibility and could be disrupted by enemy diversionary actions, as the first few days of war would prove. As was the case throughout the force structure, trained communications specialists and communications equipment, in particular, radios, were in short supply. Radio communication was scarce and unreliable, and those who had radios often did not know how to use them properly.

## PERSONNEL AND UNIT TRAINING AND TACTICS

The drastic expansion of the Air Force force structure, the addition to the weapons inventory of complex new aircraft, and the growth of Air Force support infrastructure necessitated the training of thousands of new pilots, staff officers, and technical support personnel. The fact that development of personnel training facilities lagged behind other Air Force development programs caused a temporary reduction in the combat readiness of existing units, many of whose experienced cadre were assigned to help form the new units. In addition, the new weaponry being fielded required creation of entirely new training programs and programs to retrain existing officers and specialists on the new aircraft. In fact, overall force readiness would continue to suffer until the entire reform and reconstruction program and parallel training programs were in place by summer 1942. Compounding these systemic problems, the purges of high- and mid-level commanders that had begun in 1937 continued until the outbreak of war. As in the ground forces, this accelerated the promotion of less qualified officers into positions for which they were not qualified, and they themselves were replaced by less experienced officers.

Turbulence at the very top of the Air Force structure was characteristic of the post-purge period in the Red Army as a whole and did little to foster command and personnel stability in the lower ranks. As a result, Air Force formations and units were commanded by officers who lacked sufficient experience. The Air Force had four commanders during the four years preceding the outbreak of war. All four, Komandarm 1st Rank Ia. I. Alksnis, Colonel General A. D. Loktionov, and Lieutenant Generals Ia. V. Smushkevich and P. V. Rychagov, perished in NKVD camps as enemies of the people. In April 1941, Lieutenant General of Aviation P. F. Zhigarev was appointed to Air Force command and survived to experience the disaster of 22 June.[13]

To an even more devastating extent, the same debilitating effect of inexperience was felt at lower echelons of the air force:

A majority of flight crews lacked combat experience. The rapid growth of the VVS led to the advancement of a great number of young commanders at all levels of the VVS organizational structure. By June 1941 more than 91 percent of aviation formation commanders had commanded them for less than six months, 65 percent of the commanders at all levels had been in their duty positions for less than a year, and 43 percent for less than a year and a half. The young flight crews that had arrived in line units, particularly as a result of accelerated graduation from aviation schools, still required serious additional training.[14]

All of this reflected adversely on force readiness. For example, in winter 1940–1941 an NKO report recorded, "The Red Army Air Force's combat training was unsatisfactory. The flying-technical staff has poorly untilized the new equipment."[15] A March and April 1941 inspection by the Air Force Main Directorate of combat training conducted in the western military districts echoed the earlier observations. The inspectors noted that, in addition to poor flight training, pilots could not even carry out exercises with machine-gun fire against ground targets. Furthermore, unit combat readiness was low and maintenance was appalling.[16] During the winter period, for example, the average number of pilot flight hours ranged from a high of 18 hours for pilots in the Baltic Special Military District to 6 in the Kiev Special Military District.[17] Virtually no joint ground force and Air Force practical operations took place during the winter period in the military districts, and the Air Force Main Staff performed virtually no airfield communications exercises or command-staff exercises.

Subsequently, on 8 May 1941, the Main Military Council heard a report from Deputy Defense Commissar Meretskov and the chief of the Red Army Air Force's Main Directorate, Zhigarev, that summarized training deficiencies during the winter period. A resulting decree noted: "On the whole, combat training, although it has improved in comparison with 1940, still does not meet modern operational and combat demands and is characterized by the inability to fulfill the tasks set out in Defense Commissar's Order No. 30."[18]

Reflecting the stark accuracy of these reports and other subsequent reports, on 22 June 1941, 919 (12.9 percent) of aircraft in the western border military districts were nonoperational. Of 7,133 total aircraft, only 5,937 trained crews were available to man them. Even worse, although new aircraft numbered 14 percent of the fleet, there were only 208 crews capable of flying the new aircraft.[19]

Thus, in June 1941 the majority of Red Army Air Force officers and technical specialists were only partially trained and lacked experience. By June 1941 more than 91 percent of aviation formation commanders had commanded their formations less than six months, 65 percent of all officers had served in their positions for less than a year, and 43 percent had served for less than six months.[20] This had a particularly severe impact on pilots, whose graduation from flight school was often accelerated.

Complicating the deficiencies in training, the existence of a large number of obsolete aircraft hindered the development of modern air tactics. Older aircraft were slow and ponderous in their movements, and even the newer wooden LaGG-3, although sturdy, was sluggish and poorly maneuverable. According to one analyst, "The LaGG-3s low performance quickly produced a reputation for odds-on death in the minds of many Soviet fighter pilots. Its highly polished skinning (wood impregnated with plastic) suggested to these wary pilots, using the acronym 'LaGG,' that the new fighter was a *lakirovannyi garantirovannyi grob,* or a 'varnished guaranteed coffin.'"[21] The LaGG-3's counterpart, the German Messerschmitt Mf 109G, routinely outclassed the fighter in every respect.

Tactically, Soviet fighters flew in tight formations of three aircraft wings (*zveno*), which were far less flexible than the looser two to four aircraft formations of their opponents. In general, Soviet fighter tactics were, according to the assessment of one Soviet Air Force commander, "cautious and inflexible, limited largely to horizontal maneuver, and lacking in coordination with the land army."[22] Bomber tactics were little better in that they displayed a marked absence of caution given the old and slow nature of the aircraft:

From the opening moments, bombers had been thrown into battle in large numbers to slow the German advance, particularly at river crossings. . . . All of these bombers were slow, limited in range and payload, and extremely vulnerable to German interceptors and anti-aircraft units.

Soviet bombers typically flew in "wedge" and "line" configurations. . . . To reduce losses and maximize their defensive fire power, the bombers flew in tight formations. Despite these tactical adjustments, VVS bombers suffered high attrition during the summer of 1941.[23]

## READINESS FOR WAR

The Soviet Union adopted an ambitious and forced program to simultaneously expand, reform, and reconstruct the Red Army Air Force and to create an industrial and economic base to support the Air Force in the event of war. There is no doubt but that the program was needed. The only problem was that, while implementing the program, the Soviet Union also incurred a huge risk. In short, it had to win the race between reform and war. Failure to win the race would place the country's armed forces at a marked combat disadvantage. The government accepted the risk in the belief that it could avoid hostilities until at least the summer of 1942.

What that reform program did create was a force of over 15,000 aircraft in the DBA and military districts, which was organized into 5 long-range bomber aviation corps, 3 long-range bomber aviation divisions, and 61 fighter, bomber, and mixed aviation divisions backed up by a partially reformed logistical support structure. The long-range bomber aviation corps each consisted of 2 divisions. These and other divisions were considered the basic tactical formation in the Air Force and contained 3 to 4 and, sometimes, 5 to 6 regiments with a total of up to 350 aircraft. Fighter, bomber, and mixed regiments numbered from 4 to 5 squadrons of 12 to 15 aircraft each, except for heavy bomber regiments, which counted 40 aircraft. Each regiment had a command and control wing of 3 aircraft, for a total of 63 aircraft per regiment.[24] Fighter, bomber, and mixed aviation divisions and reconnaissance aviation regiments supported military districts as a whole (wartime *fronts*); however, normally army aviation consisted of 1 to 2 mixed aviation divisions and 2 aviation squadrons (signal and reconnaissance), which supported each forward army. The mixed aviation division, which included 3 to 5 bomber, fighter, or assault regiments, performed missions assigned by army commanders. Force aviation comprised separate communications, reconnaissance, and artillery correction aviation squadrons, assigned on the basis of one per corps.

For clear strategic reasons, in June 1941 the bulk of Soviet air power was concentrated in the western border military districts. However, of the 7,133 aircraft assigned to the five military districts, only 1,448 aircraft (20 percent) were newer models. (See Table 7.3 for precise aircraft distribution.) Of these aircraft, 2,481 were concentrated along the northwestern (Baltic) axis, 1,789 along the western (Minsk–Smolensk) axis, and 2,863 along the southwestern (Kiev) axis.

The majority of fighters in the fighter aircraft park (77 percent) were the older and obsolete models I-15, I-15bis, I-153, and I-16. Most (886) of the newer fighters were MiG-3 models, which lacked gun armament and were less maneuverable than their German counterparts at medium heights.[25] Bomber aviation divisions in the border military districts were equipped with primarily (94 percent) older model SB bomber aircraft, and the newer model Pe-2 were just beginning to arrive in the force. Assault aviation regiments had I-15bis, I-153, and R-5 aircraft, which were unsuited to perform in the assault role, and only a handful of the newer IL-2 assault craft.

Long-range bomber aviation fared little better. Nine long-range bomber aviation divisions, totaling 29 aviation regiments, were stationed in the European territory of the Soviet Union, in the Novgorod, Smolensk, Kursk, Zaparozh'e, and Skomorokha regions. Of the 1,339 aircraft assigned to these formations, around 16 percent were old TB-3 models, 24 percent were DB-3 with poor bomber characteristics, and 60 percent were D-3F (Il-4). A few new TB-7 (Pe-8) were assigned to these units on an experimental basis.[26] In addition to these forces in the western border military districts and long-range aviation, the Soviets had 1,445 aircraft, primarily fighters and bombers, available for use in the west from the Northern, Baltic, and Black Sea Fleets.

Thus, the total number of aircraft assigned to the western border military districts, long-range aviation, and the three fleets amounted to 9,917 aircraft. For a variety of reasons, however, not all of these aircraft could be used in combat operations. First, naval aviation was dedicated primarily to defense of naval interests, in particular, the defense of the fleets. They could cooperate with military district aviation only under special circumstances.

Second, and more important, many of the aircraft were not combat worthy. Of the 8,472 aircraft assigned to district Air Forces and long-range bomber aviation on 22 June, 1,090 (13 percent) were inoperable for various reasons.[27] Likewise, of the 7,133 aircraft subordinate to the western military districts, 919 (12.9 percent) were not combat ready.[28] An NKO directive assessing winter operations in 1940 and 1941 declared: "The combat preparation of the Red Army VVS is unsatisfactory. The mastery of the exploitation of new material support units by flight-technical personnel is weak."[29]

Third, only 5,937 trained flight crews were available to man the 7,133 aircraft in the western border military districts, and 1,196 planes remained without crews. Regarding the 8,472 aircraft of the western border military districts and long-range aviation, 6,385 crews were capable of flying during the day in average conditions, 1,285 could fly in difficult daytime conditions, 1,192 could fly in normal night conditions, and only 23 could fly in bad weather at night. Fourth, and finally, only 208 crews were trained to fly the new aircraft, that is, enough to put 14 percent of the planes into the air.[30] In fact, 15 of the 35 reequipped regiments had less than half of their required establishment strength in aircraft.

Strength comparisons between the Red Army and German Air Forces on 22 June 1941 cannot be made solely on the basis of absolute quantities of aircraft. If this were done, the ratio would have been 9,917 to 4,275, or 2.3:1 in the Soviets' favor, that is, absolute Soviet superiority. Considering the absent Soviet flight crews and inoperable aircraft, the ratio falls to 1.8:1, still a sizable Soviet advantage.

Other factors, however, significantly reduced the Soviet numerical advantage. Most important of these was the marked German superiority in aircraft quality and trained and experienced flight crews. In terms of aircraft performance characteristics and firepower, the German machines far outstripped the bulk of their Soviet counterparts. Moreover, the extensive experience received by German pilots and crews in earlier combat had a telling effect on the outcome of tactical air engagements. This German qualitative superiority was multiplied by organizational advantages. While Soviet air formations and units were distributed to military district (*front*), army, and force subordination and could not operate in concentrated fashion, the German air units were concentrated in air fleets that numbered up to 1,000 aircraft each. Hence, Soviet air operated in fragmented fashion, whereas the Germans brought the concentrated force of air power to bear in key sectors at the most critical times. Moreover, German air units had learned how to cooperate with one another and with ground forces in two years of previous combat. On the other hand, when required, they could operate effectively performing independent missions.

The NKO undertook measures in 1941 to increase the preparedness of air forces in the border military districts, but many of these measures were rendered irrelevant by official Soviet policies that sought to avoid provoking the Germans at the expense of combat readiness. From 1 January to 2 June, the NKO increased the number of aviation regiments in the region from 116 to 130 and the number of aircraft by up to 1,000. In addition, a portion of the air forces were placed on alert (duty status and ambush) in the border military districts, including 16 fighter wings in the Western Special Military District. Throughout the same period, however, the Germans were permitted to conduct frequent reconnaissance overflights to depths of up to 350 kilometers over Soviet territory without any Soviet counteraction. More than 150 such reconnaissance missions took place.[31]

On 19 June 1941, when indicators mounted that an attack was imminent, the NKO ordered military district commanders to camouflage airfields and disperse and conceal aircraft. The order was repeated on the night of 22 June. The last order arrived late, just as German aircraft were launching their strike.

Thus, in terms of long-range preparedness programs and short-term readiness measures, well-intentioned Soviet efforts totally aborted. Programs to reorganize and expand the Air Force, construct new airfields, create new basing and logistical support systems, and train new air crews were both ambitious and positive. They were not, however, timely. The Soviet assumption that peace would endure at least until 1942 was false, and the ensuing German attack occurred at the worst possible moment, when the Air Force was in the midst of turbulent change. In the short term, the paralysis in political direction left the Air Force especially vulnerable to surprise attack.

READINESS IN PRACTICE

Soviet field reports captured the seriousness of the initial devastation and the readiness state of the Air Force to cope with the German attack. Northwestern Front's first operational report, dated 2200 hours on 22 June, noted that enemy air attacks destroyed 56 Soviet planes in the air and 32 on the airfields themselves.[32] A companion report sent by *front* to the NKO raised the aircraft loss estimate to 100 planes, declared that the enemy had achieved air superiority, and lamented that "the lack of preparedness of the airfields is creating a serious situation for *front* air forces."[33] Within hours after the attack, repeated *front* reports complained about the absence of communications with air formations. The toll in lost aircraft mounted day by day to catastrophic proportions.

On 26 June the Northwestern Front commander, Colonel General Kuznetsov, assessed the toll: "The *front* air forces have suffered heavy losses [as a consequence] of the limited number of airfields. At the present time, they are not capable of effectively supporting and covering the ground forces and striking the enemy. 75 percent of the air crews are kept safe. Material losses are at 80 percent. Request you reinforce the *front* with three mixed aviation divisions. Fill up *front* Air Force units with, first of all, equipment and pilots."[34]

Deprived of adequate air support, the Northwestern Front continued to withdraw through the Baltic region under heavy German pressure. By 4 July the damage done to *front* air forces was vividly apparent from a status report sent from *front* headquarters to the General Staff that cited *front* air strength as follows: 6th Mixed Aviation Division, 69 aircraft; 7th Mixed Aviation Division, 26 aircraft (2 Il-16, 19 I-15bis, 2 I-153, and 3 SB); 8th Aviation Division, 29 aircraft (14 MiG-3, 8 I-153, 1 I-16, 6 I-15bis); and 57th Mixed Aviation Division, 29 aircraft (6 I-16, 18 I-153, 5 SB).[35] Within 12 days after the onset of hostilities, 153 aircraft survived out of an initial *front* air strength of 887 serviceable aircraft in the *front*'s mixed aviation divisions.

On 21 June 1942, Major General of Aviation D. F. Kondratiuk, then commander of 6th Air Army, prepared a retrospective account of air operations in the Northwestern Front during the initial days of war. In the report he detailed the strength of the *front*'s five mixed aviation divisions (4th, 6th, 7th, 8th, and 57th) and assessed the problems the divisions encountered. Kondratiuk's report began on a positive note: "The existing peacetime Red Army Air Force organization generally vindicated itself, in spite of some organizational inadequacies which appeared in war." Thereafter, Kondratiuk mentioned specific weaknesses. He noted the shortages of airfields and the fact that construction was under way on virtually all of the 21 constant and 49 operational fields. Despite efforts to camouflage aircraft, German overflights negated the effect of this work. He went on to highlight the following problems: the concentration of aircraft at existing airfields and the absence of airfields in the operational depths, which increased vulnerability to German attack; the proximity of airfields to the border and the poor aircraft dispersion and redeployment planning; the presence of older aircraft and equipment; the inability of pilots to operate at night and in poor weather; poor pilot training; faulty staff work and lack of cooperation between forces; poor radio and wire communications; utter lack of reconnaissance capability; incomplete basing reforms; and inadequate mobilization planning for logistical support. In conclusion, Kondratiuk wrote:

Soviet equipment (from top to bottom): T-26 light tank, T-28 medium tank, and T-35 heavy tank.

Soviet equipment, *continued* (from top to bottom): BT-7 tank, T-34 medium tank, and KV heavy tank.

Soviet equipment, *continued* (from top to bottom): 76mm divisional gun, 122mm howitzer, and 152mm gun-howitzer.

The year of war demonstrated that the Red Army air forces in some of its aspects, did not meet the requirements of war. In particular, four-squadron aviation regiments were unwieldy. A regiment based at two to three airfields lost operational control of its subunits, and the staff organizations did not provide combat command and control from two to three points.

The organization of peacetime aviation divisions generally vindicated itself in wartime. . . . It is necessary to mention that the frequent reorganization of aviation had a negative effect on the combat integrity of units.

The attack on the Soviet Union took place during a period of unit reorganization. The units had not yet been "knocked together." Many units were being retrained on new equipment, even within the limits of the district.

The absence of a precise plan for the employment of the air forces in the event of war led to the loss of a considerable number of aircraft and pilots.

Command and control by means of radio and concealed command and control had not been worked out.[36]

Western Front air forces suffered even heavier damage during the first hours and days of war. The Germans began hostilities with devastating attacks on the entire Western Special Military District airfield network, and German diversionary troops severed ground communications lines. With communications disrupted, loss reports came in exceedingly slowly, if at all, and high-level commanders could only imagine the carnage at airfields and in the skies. It was apparent, however, that the Germans had wrought havoc on Soviet airfields and had achieved total and overwhelming air superiority. In the wake of the disaster, *front* air commander I. I. Kopets committed suicide, thus avoiding the fate of *front* commander D. G. Pavlov, who was shot at Stalin's orders.

The first comprehensive assessment of Western Front air forces appeared on 31 December 1941. Written by the Western Front's Air Force commander, Lieutenant General of Aviation N. F. Naumenko, the report's first two sections contained a candid, if not grisly, assessment that highlighted the inadequacies of the air forces on the eve of war and described Air Force performance during the first eight days of war:

By April 1941 the combat readiness of Air Force units in the Western Special Military District can be characterized as follows: fighters—not combat capable (in the air they could not fire and conduct air combat); and bombers—limited capability (they could bomb little, fire little, and fly in formation little). The district had no reconnaissance aviation since the existing eight corps aviation squadrons received six P-series aircraft and were taking stock [inventory].

The 313th and 314th Reconnaissance Regiments had a full complement of young pilots but no equipment.

The 314th Reconnaissance Aviation Regiment began to receive IaK-2 and IaK-4 aircraft in April and by the beginning of the war had only six crews flying IaK-4.

The district had no assault aircraft at all. The 215th Assault Aviation Regiment, just then forming, had 12 I-15 by the beginning of the war and was preparing pilots for transition to the Il-2, which, at that time, the district did not have.[37]

Naumenko noted that all aviation divisions had older aircraft except the 9th Mixed Aviation Division, which was equipped with 262 new MiG-1 and MiG-3 planes. Even this formation had only 140 pilots qualified to fly the new aircraft, and during the training, which was ongoing when war broke out, there had been "a series of serious accidents." In addition, the 9th Mixed Aviation Division's 13th Aviation Regiment and the 11th Mixed Aviation Division's 15th Aviation Regiment had received 42 Pe-2 aircraft.[38] Thus, in Naumenko's words, "from the beginning of war the district was living through a period of rearmament with new equipment, and the interest in the older equipment noticeably fell. From the top to the bottom, all were preoccupied with rapid familiarization of the pilots with the new equipment."[39]

The commander repeated the lament of his counterparts in the other military districts about the critical aircraft-basing problems and the vulnerability of the bases to enemy attack. Likewise, he underscored the difficult logistical situation with the RAB system only partially implemented. Despite the extensive war games conducted in the military district in 1940 and 1941, Naumenko claimed that force command and staff groups "had insufficient experience," and "the subsequent course of events indicated that district Air Force headquarters were not sufficiently put together."[40]

Naumenko related in detail German actions the day before the war began and added: "As a result of German and Polish White Guard's diversionary action, from 2300 21.6.41, all wire communications of the Western Special Military District air forces headquarters with division headquarters and of division headquarters with their own regiments were disrupted and every airfield was left to itself. The Great Patriotic war began in such circumstances."[41]

He then tallied the consequences of the Air Force's lack of readiness. Citing an initial Western Front aircraft strength of 1,909 planes (which counts the long-range bomber aviation corps based at Smolensk), including 1,022 fighters and 887 bombers, Naumenko described the impact of the first eight days of combat:

Western Front Air Force units went to war on the morning of 22.6.41. That day was characterized by great losses suffered by *front* aviation inflicted by enemy air raids. . . .

On 22.6.41 at our airfields and in the air, the enemy destroyed 538 of our aircraft at a cost of 143 aircraft lost by the enemy. On the following day, the losses of the two sides were 125 and 124, respectively, and by the end of June, that is after eight days of war, our losses totaled 1,163 aircraft and enemy losses were 422.

By day's end on 30.6.41, *front* air forces numbered 124 fighters and 374 bombers for a total of 498 planes, combined into seven divisions.[42]

As was the case with ground forces, Soviet Air Forces were strongest in the Kiev Special Military District. Despite their greater strength, forces there also suffered from many of the same problems experienced in other front sectors. The most thorough assessment of the readiness of district air forces on the eve of war was contained in a report submitted on 21 August 1941 by Lieutenant General of Aviation F. A. Astakhov to the commander of the Red Army Air Force, Lieutenant General P. F. Zhigarev. The report provided Zhigarev with a detailed breakdown of the organization, strength, and readiness of Kiev Special Military district air forces on the eve of war and a survey of its combat operations once war began.

According to Astakhov, the district's 11 aviation divisions and 2 regiments (which included 1 attached long-range bomber division) was 1,166 fighters, 587 bombers, and 197 assault and 53 reconnaissance aircraft, for a total of 2,003 planes. Included in this number were 223 new MiG-3 and IaK fighters, 231 new Pe-2, IaK-2-4, and SU-2 bombers, and 31 new IaK-4 reconnaissance aircraft.[43] Of the total, 1,865 aircraft were ready for combat under normal daylight conditions, 595 for difficult daytime conditions, 361 for night combat, and 535 for combat at night and in bad weather. Most pilots of older aircraft were adequately trained for normal flying conditions but were less prepared to perform more complex missions. On the other hand, pilots for the new aircraft models had only rudimentary training and could not be certified as combat ready.

Astakhov's judgments on overall force combat readiness read as follows.

In general, Southwestern Front air forces were not sufficiently prepared for combat operations for the following reasons:

a. During the re-reequipping of Southwestern Front Air Forces with new weaponry, some of the old, well-formed aviation regiments (52d and 48th Short-range Bomber Aviation Regiments and others) did not have necessary quantities of new types of aircraft by the commencement of combat operations, and their older equipment was taken for new formations. As a result, before the beginning of war, these regiments turned out to be in a state of low combat readiness;

b. The flying personnel [pilots and crew] of all aviation regiments, which were reequipped with new equipment in the period immediately preceding war, did not possess new types of aircraft with rifle and bomber weaponry and, as a result, during the first days of the war the new equipment was not employed sufficiently effectively;

c. Some aviation regiments formed in 1940 (224th, 225th, and 138th Short-range Bomber Aviation Regiments and others) were filled with equipment to only 20 to 50 percent of their establishment norm, and as a result, their share in combat actions was insignificant;

d. Southwestern Front Air Force division and regimental commanders inadequately used the winter period of 1940–41 for the conduct of flight combat training while the airfields were blanketed with snow, and as a result, the vast majority of young pilots flew very little in winter and were not put into commission, and the period from May to June (the period of intense flight training) did not provide them with necessary training for combat actions;

e. Before the war, Southwestern Front Air Force units failed to resolve the problems of camouflaging airfields and their aircraft and organized antiaircraft defense of airfields in unsatisfactory fashion. This was explained not only by the absence of necessary camouflage materials and incomplete means for antiaircraft defense but also by the fact that commanders at all levels did not pay requisite attention to these questions;

f. The absence of necessary organization and precision in the actions of *front* Air Force flying and ground units when repelling enemy aviation raids on our airfields during the first three days of war confirmed that the combat readiness of Southwestern Front Air Force units was at a low level and that, during this crucial period of combat alert, the actions of Air Force flying and ground units did not conform to the demands of People's Commissariat of Defense Order No. 075 [alert orders].[44]

Because of these and other problems, in Astakhov's view, "the Southwestern Front's air forces, in general, were not prepared to repel the enemy surprise attack . . . on 2.6.41." As a result, from 22 through 24 June, the Germans destroyed 237 Soviet aircraft on the overly vulnerable airfields. Faulty equipment and poor training led to the loss of another 242 aircraft due to accidents during the period from 22 June through 10 August, which constituted 13 percent of total aircraft losses (1,861 planes) during the period.[45]

Like Soviet mechanized forces, the Red Army Air Force was an immense organization with tremendous combat potential. New weaponry was reaching the field in June 1941, which, when it was manned by trained personnel, would be a formidable opponent to the vaunted German Air Force. The many-faceted reform program, as a whole, was well thought out and suited to a first-class Air Force. Unfortunately for the Soviets, timing and circumstance turned the promises inherent in these military reforms into tragedy for thousands of pilots and crews.

## STATISTICAL DATA

Table 7.1. Red Army Air Force Expansion Plans, October to November 1940

| | October 1940 Plan | | November 1940 Plan | |
|---|---|---|---|---|
| Regiments | Regiments | Aircraft | Regiments | Aircraft |
| Heavy bomber | 6 | 306 | 6 | 306 |
| Long-range bomber | 49 | 3,675 | 36 | 2,196 |
| Close-range bomber | 84 | 6,552 | 102 | 6,222 |
| Assault | 11 | 858 | 15 | 945 |
| Mixed | 3 | 234 | 3 | 165 |
| Fighter | 96 | 8,352 | 161 | 10,773 |
| Total | 249 | 19,977 | 323 | 20,607 |

Source: A. A. Volkov, *Kriticheskii prolog* [Critical prologue] (Moscow: AVIAR, 1992), 40, citing TsGASA, f. 4044, op. 2, d. 169, l. 321–324, 351, 355.

Table 7.2. Projected Training of Flight Personnel, 1941

| | On Hand 20 October 1940 | Planned for 1 January 1942 | Percent Increase |
|---|---|---|---|
| Long-range bomber pilots | 1,975 | 10,000 | 506.3 |
| Short-range bomber pilots | 12,200 | 25,000 | 204.9 |
| Fighter pilots | 13,383 | 25,000 | 186.8 |
| Pilot-observers | 16,051 | 35,000 | 218.8 |
| Gunners and radiomen | 15,558 | 32,563 | 209.3 |
| Technicians and mechanics | 31,677 | 47,261 | 149.2 |
| Junior aviation specialists | 18,277 | 40,121 | 219.5 |
| Total | 109,121 | 214,945 | 196.0 |

Source: Volkov, *Kriticheskii prolog*, 40, citing TsGASA, f. 40442, op. 2, d. 169, l. 328–335.

Table 7.3. Distribution of Aircraft in the Western Military Districts, 22 June 1941

| Military Districts | Type of Aviation | | | | |
|---|---|---|---|---|---|
| | Bomber | Assault | Fighter | Reconnaissance | Total |
| Leningrad | 308 | 74 | 857 | 31 | 1,270 |
| Baltic Special | 425 | 93 | 621 | 72 | 1,211 |
| Western Special | 695 | 70 | 870 | 154 | 1,789 |
| Kiev Special | 516 | 80 | 1,238 | 79 | 1,913 |
| Odessa | 268 | 0 | 640 | 42 | 950 |
| Total aircraft | 2,212 | 317 | 4,226 | 378 | 7,133 |
| New model aircraft | 360 | 18 | 1,022 | 48 | 1,448 |
| (percent of total) | (31%) | (4.5%) | (59%) | (5.3%) | (100%) |

Source: *Nachal'nyi period*, 62, 64; Ramanichev, 116–118, citing *TsAMO*, f. 35, op. 107559, d. 5, l. 116–233; l. 4–82; d. 16, l. 276–319; op. 10756, d. 8, l. 216–271; d. 9, l. 159–216; op. 107562, d. 13, l. 171–258; op. 74313, d. 6, l. 274–379; op. 107567, d. 3, l 3–68; op. 107559, d. 5, l. 1.

CHAPTER 8

# Stavka and Strategic Reserves

## INITIAL RESERVES (JUNE TO 15 JULY 1941)

The partial mobilization that began several months before the outbreak of war and the full mobilization that followed produced tens of new armies and hundreds of new combat formations. Before 22 June and throughout the summer and fall of 1941, wave after wave of new armies appeared in the Soviet order of battle, and these armies in turn formed echelon after strategic echelon. These included a dizzying array of rifle divisions, whose unit designations, incredibly, reached well into the 400s, and over 100 cavalry divisions. By fall 1941, hundreds of tank and rifle brigades had joined the mobilized host. Although the Soviet mobilization process ultimately saved the Soviet state from destruction, it did so at an appalling cost in manpower and equipment losses. In fact, rather than preparing the Soviets to conduct war successfully, in 1941 the mobilization system enabled the Soviets to survive war, but only barely.

The mobilization system and the forces it produced were severely flawed, but those flaws must be appreciated within a broader context. As A. A. Svechin had predicted less than 20 years before, the Soviet Union would have difficulty mobilizing its "peasant rear" for war. Every facet of manpower and unit mobilization, and the necessary preparation of communications, military command and control, governmental organs, the industrial base, and the economy at large, proved immensely difficult. Stalin, the Stavka, and senior military organs prodded the ponderous Soviet governmental, military, and economic infrastructure into action, but, predictably, it responded glacially, despite the achievement of such prodigious feats as the partially successful transfer of elements of the industrial base eastward to relative safety. For every such feat that Soviet authorities bragged about after the war, there were striking examples that vividly underscored the Soviet state's inability to respond quickly and efficiently to the challenges of war.

Nevertheless, the very glacial nature of the Soviet response to war ultimately confounded their opponents. Once in motion, the Soviet mobilization proceeded inexorably forward and produced a military machine whose size was beyond German comprehension. Like many Soviet political and military leaders, the Germans, too, failed to understand the nature and com-

205

bat potential of the Soviet Union's "peasant rear." They would begin to do so around Smolensk in July and at Moscow in December, but they would not fully appreciate the fact until summer 1943. Ultimately, later in the war, the consequences of that misunderstanding would affect Germany's fate as much as it had affected Soviet fortunes earlier in the war.

Within this larger context, the Soviet mobilization system produced manpower that brought many existing formations near to full strength but failed to provide the equipment and support organs that new formations required to function effectively and survive in combat. Contrary to plan, the civilian economy failed to provide vehicular transport, tractors, and horses, and as a consequence, force logistical units could not move heavy weaponry or supply formations with critical fuel, ammunition, and other provisions. Formations mobilizing in internal military districts did so with transport means provided by the older, truncated 6,000-man division establishments, and because they also lacked necessary transport, they deployed to the front at reduced strength and without their full complement of weaponry and transport.

Of the first wave of mobilized reserves, the 6 armies, 14 rifle corps, and 42 divisions ordered forward on 13 May and 15 June, 14 remained at their point of origin, 19 were en route to designated concentration areas on 22 June, and only 9 (19th Army) had reached these areas when war broke out.[1] Although some of this movement was by rail, rail capacity was insufficient, and most formations had to move on foot and at night. Mobilization and transport difficulties fed these and other strategic reserves into the theater in piecemeal fashion. This, coupled with the rapid subsequent German advance, led to repeated defeats-in-detail of successive lines of defending Soviet strategic reserves.

The first armies to reinforce the border armies in combat were the reserve armies of the forward *fronts*. In the Western Front sector this involved 13th Army, which on 22 June had no combat forces assigned to it. During mobilization, however, Lieutenant General P. M. Filatov's army was to form initially from corps in the depths of the Western Special Military District (2d, 21st, and 44th). These corps, however, were sucked into combat around Minsk and either badly damaged or encircled and lost in the defense of the city. By 7 July, 13th Army was reconstituted, this time with 61st and 45th Rifle Corps from the Stavka reserve (originally, the Moscow and Orel Military Districts) and the remnants of 20th Mechanized Corps, which had fought its way eastward from Minsk. The new 61st Rifle Corps consisted of 53d, 172d, and 110th Rifle Divisions, and the 45th Rifle Corps contained the 132d, 148th, and 187th Rifle Divisions.[2] All of these divisions existed on 22 June 1941.

Two days later, Lieutenant General F. N. Remezov, who had replaced General P. M. Filatov in command, reported on 13th Army's condition. He stated that the army contained six rifle divisions, but only five divisions had completed concentration and the army headquarters was woefully incomplete:

The 13th Army has only 30 percent of its command personnel, and shortages include the following principal staff members:

Operational section, 6 men; encipherment section, 10 men; intelligence section, 7 men . . . ; rear service section, 24 men; engineer section, 3 men . . . ; signal section, 9 men; artillery section, 20 men. . . .

The signal battalion has not been formed.

Light and cargo vehicles are in very short supply.

There are no aircraft in the army, either for combat or for communications.

I request the army headquarters be filled out.[3]

Before it was fully regrouped, Remizov's army was caught up in the defense of Mogilev, and there it lost a large proportion of its initial forces, including the bulk of 61st Rifle Corps. Once again it reformed, this time from its remnants and those of 4th Army.

Numerous archival documents also underscore the lack of preparedness of the initial reserve armies, which the Stavka committed to combat along the Dnepr River line to reinforce the withdrawing forward armies. For example, a 9 July status report from Colonel M. A. Shalin, 16th Army chief of staff, declared, "The command group with supporting units, 32d Rifle Corps, as well as some units of 5th Mechanized Corps, are [still] at peacetime establishment strength."[4] Nevertheless, the army joined battle with the remnants of 5th Mechanized Corps, which had suffered a disastrous defeat near Lepel' only days before, two divisions of the rifle corps (46th and 152d), and separate 57th Tank Division from the Far East. By 20 July it had been joined by elements of the fresh 129th Rifle Division. The army's immediate mission was to defend the Smolensk axis, a task it was not equipped to perform.

A subsequent status report on 20 July noted, "Army units are still experiencing shortages of food and ammunition, especially for regimental and divisional (107mm) antiaircraft guns. A number of headquarters lack signal means, which, in turn, severely complicates the organization of command and control in combat. To this time, medical assistance is not going as well as it should."[5] The same day 129th Rifle Division's four committed battalions suffered 40 percent losses defending in the suburbs of Smolensk. Reinforced by 34th Rifle Corps, Lieutenant General M. F. Lukin's 16th Army defended at Smolensk until it was encircled and virtually destroyed in early August. A pathetic report prepared by Western Front on 23 July attested to the dilapidated state of 16th Army, noting, "During the course of 22.7, 16th Army units continued to conduct severe street battle to secure Smolensk. . . . In 34th RC, the trained and armed (almost without machine guns) 127th Rifle Division (up to 600 men) and 158th Rifle Division (about 100 men) went over to the offensive at 1200 22.7."[6]

Meanwhile, in early July, Soviet Lieutenant General I. S. Konev's 19th Army, with the six rifle divisions of 25th and 34th Rifle Corps, supported by elements of 23d Mechanized Corps (220th Motorized Division), then arriving from the Orel Military District, redeployed from the Kiev region, was fed into combat in the Vitebsk region in piecemeal fashion. Soon it was reinforced by remnants of withdrawing Soviet rifle divisions and 7th Mechanized Corps, which, with 5th Mechanized Corps, had been badly damaged in fighting near Lepel'.

A lengthier report prepared on 24 July by 19th Army chief of staff, Major General Rubtsov, covered army action between 9 and 24 July and indicated that the 220th Motorized Rifle Division was "hardly formed as a motorized rifle division and had no tanks and vehicles and was understrength in artillery." It then described army readiness:

> 1. Forces of 25th Rifle Corps were mobilized at the moment they took the field. 34th Rifle Corps forces were only in a state of reinforced combat readiness. The divisions were brought up to only 12,000 men, but were not fully mobilized.
> In the field the 12,000-man divisions experienced immense difficulties because of an absence of transport and were unable to maneuver. They could not pick up required quantities of ammunition, could not carry mortars, etc.
> 2. The artillery arrived late because the artillery had arrived in the Kiev region on the first trains and were the first to occupy firing positions in the former deployment region. For that reason, the artillery remained at the end of the loading queue, since they were located a great distance from the station. The artillery lost much time in moving to the railroad station.[7]

Further, the report admitted, "Army forces fought in units and groups, without artillery equipment. They did not fight poorly but were rapidly exhausted in battle and did not possess reserves . . . the absence of rear service units did not permit replenishment of ammunition. . . . Some regiments entered battle without their allotment of ammunition. They entered battle with one half to one quarter of their ammunition load and with small reserves of fuel."[8]

Speaking of command and control, Rubtsov noted that "forces employed radio especially poorly. Command and control by means of radio with the help of encipherment was torturous and they were not able to use radio signals." For these and other reasons command and control was difficult at best.[9] Furthermore, "In general, it is necessary to say that command and control was conducted under very great tension and spasmodically. I explain this by the fact that such command levels as 19th Army headquarters operated blindly. The absence of aviation and grounds reconnaissance means excluded the possibility of timely receipt of information about the enemy, and it follows that this had an adverse impact on combat measures."[10] Subsequently, 19th Army was caught up in the defense of Smolensk and largely destroyed. It too formed anew in early August along the Dnepr River east of Smolensk.

The Stavka committed another of its newly formed armies, the 20th from the Moscow Military District, to battle south of Vitebsk between 19th and 13th Armies. The army initially consisted of seven rifle divisions, most in 61st and 69th Rifle Corps, and 7th Mechanized Corps, which, with 5th Mechanized Corps, was to spearhead a Soviet armored thrust toward Lepel'. Immediately after its creation, 20th Army launched the attack, which failed after two bloody days of fighting. Subsequently, it lost 61st Rifle Corps to 13th Army.

A 27 July report by Lieutenant General P. A. Kurochkin, the 20th Army commander, described his army's readiness state between 1 to 25 July:

> The Army, failing to concentrate fully before the operation, was considerably understrength in personnel and material units. . . .
>
> a. . . . Army formations: 73d RD, 5th MC, 57th TD, 229th RD, 144th RD, and a TD arrived in the army at considerably reduced strength. . . . Army divisional strengths range from 4,000 to 6,500 men, and, to a considerable degree, those people were in rear service and supporting units. Forces conducting continuous combat number considerably less. During this period we have received 1,600 reinforcements, whereas we need 70,000 men and 9,000 horses. Attempts to fill out the army with soldiers and NCOs who have straggled from their units have had no effect since the majority of these are not armed and uniformed, and the army has no reserves of weapons and uniforms.
>
> b. Army signal units and formations have only 25 to 30 percent of their communications equipment and transport.
>
> c. The army has very few engineer and pontoon-bridge units. The strength of force sapper subunits amounts to 30 to 35 percent. Road bridging means are completely lacking.[11]

Kurochkin reported that on 26 July army tank strength was as follows: 17th Tank Division 29 tanks, 13th Tank Division 29 tanks, and 57th Tank Division 7 to 8 tanks; the artillery strength of 229th, 233d, 144th, 153d, and 73d Rifle Divisions and 5th Mechanized Corps was 28, 18, 30, 20, 47, and 34 guns, respectively. The army's artillery regiment had 98 artillery pieces and 120 antitank guns and was short 75 artillery tractors, around 500 kilometers of wire cable, and 100 vehicles.[12] Within the army, ammunition and fuel supplies were exceedingly low (0.5 to 1 combat load of ammunition and 1.5 refills of fuel). By 5 August the ultimate consequences of these problems were readily apparent. By this time, initial army unpreparedness and over 30 days of subsequent combat had reduced the army to a skeleton. The strength of 229th Rifle Division strength had fallen to 285 men, 17 machine guns, and 1 antitank gun, the 73d Rifle Division to 100 men and 4 to 5 machine guns, 144th Rifle Division to 440 men, and 153d Rifle Division to 750 men.[13]

A short 14 July report by Western Direction headquarters noted several problems with withdrawing and newly deploying divisions:

> As a consequence of the long withdrawal and prolonged difficult combat and also their hasty formation and the great losses of weapons, our forces are not stable. This is especially apparent during the attack. There have been instances when our units ran from enemy aviation and forward enemy tank detachments.
>
> The situation is complicated by the fact that the arrival of new formations is slowed and disorganized by the railroads. Rear service units arrive in the lead trains, and combat units linger long behind.
>
> As a result the *front* lacks reserves and is forced to commit quickly badly organized and trained units into the forward lines. Many divisions consist of differing units. Concerning tank formations, they do not possess equipment and, in essence, turn into technologically poorly equipped infantry.[14]

Another report, prepared by the Western Direction's Operational Department on 21 July, reflected on the problems associated with premature and disorderly formation and commitment of reserves:

> At the present time, the Western Front does not have reserves on hand to parry unexpected enemy penetrations and to develop success.
>
> According to the deployment plan, there were to have been two reserve armies, the 19th and 4th; however, the former concentrated southeast of Vitebsk at the time that the front extended along a line from Lepel' through Tolochin, that is, at a distance of 100 to 120 kilometers, and the 4th formed in the Propoisk region, with two divisions in the Novozybkov region, that is, at a distance of 40 kilometers from the front. Such a distance of the reserve armies from the *front* did not secure their concentration and formation, since, at the present offensive tempo (40 kilometers per day), the units were subjected to random and constant enemy air attacks. . . .

The units, not being ready, were forced to engage in battle piecemeal and without means of command and control and rear services (19th Army) and not fully formed and unarmed (4th Army), and during the course of the initial days, the *front* lost [its] reserves.[15]

The report then requested the wholesale reorganization and resubordination of *front* forces to include the abolition of 5th and 7th Mechanized Corps and the use of their remnants to form two new (presumably 100-series) tank division.

Western Direction headquarters prepared several reports that criticized the state of Western Front combat support for the initial wave of reserve armies committed to battle in early and mid-July. Many faults reflected problems that had plagued *front* formations since the onset of war, some were a product of faulty mobilization plans, and all were exacerbated by the spectacular German combat successes since 22 June.

On 28 July the temporary direction chief of communications reviewed the performance of high-level signal forces and systems:

In fact, the Western Front Radio Section was formed on 3.7.41. Valuable documents about Western Front radio communications from the beginning of war and up to 3.7.41 were not preserved, that is, documents of the Radio Bureau were partially destroyed or missing during the withdrawal of the headquarters from Minsk and Mogilev to Smolensk.

The establishment of the section is seven men, and five men are on hand: the chief, a deputy, and three inspectors. In practice, all available personnel are entirely occupied with operational communications as communications duty personnel and are fulfilling separate important missions in that realm (going out in separate groups with radio sets).

Consequently, systematic work with communications documents, besides radio data [call signs], is not being done to a proper degree.

During the course of 25 days, radio data were changed three times, on one occasion because of the suggestion that such data on 19th Army had fallen into enemy hands.[16]

Further, the report stated that communications did not exist with neighboring forces because of equipment shortages, and communications with Moscow were tentative at best. It concluded with an urgent request for the additional equipment necessary to establish proper communications with all armies. While indicating that section personnel had adequate training and a full range of missions, it complained about the poor training of individual radio operators and signal specialists and the general shortage of radios.

A later report by Captain Makarov, chief of the 4th Section of the Western Front's Signal Directorate, reviewed *front* communications since 22 June:

> The Signals Section of the Western Special Military District had inadequate mobile communications means from the moment the war began. The mobile signal company existing according to the mobilization plan had only personnel provided from the reserves, but lacked any equipment.
>
> From the first day of war right up to 1 July, in spite of my repeated requests for assistance to give me the capability to develop the work of my subordinate 4th Section and to fill up the mobile company with equipment, the former chief of communications, Grigor'ev, undertook no decisive measures, and the situation regarding this type of communications remained catastrophic.[17]

Makarov also listed necessary remedies and asked the Red Army Signals Directorate to provide vehicles, armored cars, and aircraft to correct the situation.

Air support also remained inadequate, particularly in light of the catastrophic losses suffered by the Soviets during the initial days of war. A brief report prepared on 31 December 1941 by Major General N. F. Naumenko, commander of Western Front air forces, reviewed the situation in July, starkly underscored the weakened condition of *front* air, and underscored recurring persistent problems that gave the Germans continued air superiority. Initially, in July, air units concentrated on support for forward armies (22d, 20th, 21st, 13th, 16th, and 19th), but after mid-month the bulk of support went to 16th, 19th, and 20th Armies then struggling in the Smolensk region. The Soviets devoted all of their efforts to counter-air missions and had no resources to strike enemy airfields. Most support was provided at army level.

By 22 July, army aviation consisted of five aviation divisions (13th and 46th Bomber and 11th, 23d, and 28th Mixed) and *front* aviation of two divisions (43d Fighter and 47th Bomber) and five separate regiments (1st, 3d, and 410th Bomber and 313th and 314th Recce) equipped with 389 aircraft (for details, see Table 8.1 at the end of this chapter). Thus, Western Front Air Force strength had fallen catastrophically from 1,789 aircraft on 22 June to fewer than 400 on 22 July. With this strength, *front* air forces could perform none of their missions satisfactorily. Most important, ground forces remained undefended against the devastating effects of German air attack.

Throughout June and July, the Stavka did not provide the Southwestern Direction with new reserve armies. In fact, it transferred 16th and 19th Armies, which had initially been in reserve along the Southwestern Direction, northward to deal with the most serious German threat. Despite this fact, many divisions mobilized in the south, and the Stavka sent other newly mobilized divisions to the region. On 25 July the Southwestern Direction command notified the Stavka as to how it planned to employ these fresh divisions and complained about the state of the new formations. The direction commander, Marshal of the Soviet Union S. M. Budenny, wrote, "Of the total number of 19 rifle and 5 cavalry divisions, only 4 rifle and 1 cavalry division have completed formation. The period of preparation of the remainder will stretch out into the second half of August, and, therefore, I request we temporarily postpone the question of their use."[18]

A follow-up report prepared on 31 July by Marshal Budenny and addressed directly to "Comrade Stalin, Headquarters, High Command of Southwestern Direction Forces," added details to his complaints and formed a stark picture similar to that which existed in other *front* sectors:

In accordance with Stavka Order No. 00495, 9 rifle divisions and 2 cavalry divisions formed in the Khar'kov Military District and 10 rifle divisions and 3 cavalry divisions formed in the Odessa Military District are being transferred to my command.

By 30.7.41, six rifle divisions and two cavalry divisions must be formed in the Khar'kov Military District. Today the situation is as follows:

1. In the Khar'kov Military District, we have succeeded with difficulty in forming two rifle divisions (223d and 254th), having collected for them equipment, weapons, and clothing directly from warehouses and wherever else it was possible to obtain it.

2. Four rifle divisions (289th, 301st, 284th, and 297th) and two cavalry divisions (34th and 37th) are not ready, in spite of the fact that the period of preparation has elapsed.

The arming of rifle divisions with submachine guns is incomplete.

The 289th Division has only 17 percent of its light machine guns.

The 284th Division completely lacks artillery.

Up to 30 July, the 297th Division completely lacked automatic weapons, and the latter were shipped from Moscow only on 27.7; the division has no artillery equipment or ammunition at all, and it is not known when or from where it will receive it.

3. Engineer equipment: The 289th Division has only 40 percent of its establishment [organizational] table requirements. For the 297th Division, it is being sent from Syzrani. The 301st and 284th Divisions do not have any notice as to when or from where the engineer equipment will be received.

4. A limited amount of communications gear was sent from Moscow on 27.7 and will arrive in the appointed location not earlier than 1.8.

5. Clothing: All divisions fully lack kit bags, towels, foot bindings, steel helmets, raincoats, mess tins (except the 301st Division, which is short 3,729 pieces), waist belts, and provision satchels.

6. All divisions are short from 16 to 25 field kitchens. Saddles are almost fully missing.

7. Sabers, automatic weapons, artillery, ammunition, engineer equipment, signal gear, cavalry trousers, soldiers blouses, steel helmets, raincoats, field kitchens, mess tins, and medical provisions are fully absent in cavalry divisions.

8. The formation of divisions in the Odessa Military District has also gone on unsatisfactorily. The 273d Division, whose period of preparation was determined to be by 1.8.41, today has no more than 45 percent of its personnel and completely no weapons, engineer gear, equipment, and clothing.

I consider it necessary to inform you that the period for formation established by the General Staff has turned out to be unrealistic, and the central supply administrations have done nothing to provide the forming divisions with equipment and gear called for by organization tables.

I request your intervention in the matter of material support and the arming of forming divisions in the Khar'kov and Odessa Military Districts. [19]

While Soviet ground force strength in the Southwestern Direction eroded without major reinforcements, air strength also steadily decreased to the extent that by 11 July it amounted to 20 percent of the *front*'s initial wartime strength (for details, see Table 8.2). By 29 July, subsequent reports showed a total Southwestern Front aircraft strength holding stable at 419 aircraft, of which 278 were operational.[20]

## SUBSEQUENT RESERVES (15 JULY TO AUGUST 1941)

By mid-July the Germans had done so much damage to forward deployed armies and those initially in reserve that Stavka and the Western Direction ordered creation and commitment of a new series of reserve armies to back up threadbare forward armies and help stem the German advance. Stavka order No. 003334, issued on 14 July, read:

1. Create a headquarters for a Front of Reserve Armies to control reserve armies in the second defensive belt. . . .

2. Include in the *front* composition:
   a. 29th Army consisting of five divisions, two corps artillery regiments and three antitank artillery regiments, one fighter aviation regiment, one bomber aviation regiment, and one squadron of Il-2;
   b. 30th Army consisting of five divisions, one corps artillery regiment, and two antiaircraft artillery regiments;
   c. 24th Army consisting of ten divisions, three gun, one howitzer, and three corps artillery regiments, and four antitank artillery regiments;
   d. 28th Army consisting of nine divisions, one gun, one howitzer, and four corps artillery regiments, and four antitank artillery regiments;
   e. 31st Army consisting of six divisions, one corps artillery regiment, and two antitank artillery regiments; and
   f. 32d Army consisting of seven divisions and one antitank artillery regiment.[21]

Almost immediately, it became apparent that neither the Stavka nor the Western Direction could raise the necessary forces to man the new armies in timely enough fashion to halt the German drive on Smolensk. Therefore, after a failed 19 July attempt by the General Staff order to cut down the size of each new army, the Stavka and Western Direction began forming simple operational groups to perform as stopgap armies. These groups, formed at the height of the Battle of Smolensk primarily to relieve the pressure on Soviet 16th and 20th Armies, which were encircled in the city, had small headquarters, light armor and artillery support, and no intermediate corps headquarters. In essence, they were mere collections of divisions reinforced by whatever fire support assets could be hastily assembled. For example, Group Kalinin, created on 22 July northeast of Smolensk and commanded by Lieutenant General S. A. Kalinin, consisted of the 166th, 91st, and 89th Rifle Divisions only.[22] Similar groups were created under the command of Lieutenant Generals I. I. Maslennikov, K. K. Rokossovsky, V. A. Khomenko, and V. Ia. Kachalov.[23]

In fact, most divisions and other formations in these and subsequently formed reserve armies were not combat ready. Up to 80 percent of the divisions were manned at a truncated peacetime establishment of 6,000 men. Only after full mobilization was declared did they receive new personnel and additional equipment. Even then, their personnel strength seldom exceeded 60 percent of required. The second wave of divisions mobilized between 22 June and 10 July were in scarcely better condition. Of the 38 divisions, 13 were hastily assembled from NKVD forces, the most readily available source of reliable, partially trained military manpower. A 29 June NKVD order originally called for creation by 17 July of 25 such divisions, beginning with 15 rifle divisions (from the 240–260 series) and five mountain rifle divisions:

> By decision of the government of the USSR, the NKVD of the USSR is charged with the formation of fifteen rifle divisions.
> In fulfillment of this decision, *I order:*
> 1. Lieutenant General I. I. Maslennikov is entrusted with direction of the formation of 15 rifle divisions of NKVD forces.
> 2. Create under Lieutenant General Maslennikov an operational group consisting of Colonel Miroshichenko, Brigade Commander I. S. Sheredeg, Brigade Commander M. N. Shishkarev, and Lieutenant Colonel S. I. Frolov.
> 3. Start forming the divisions immediately and deploy [them]:

| *243d Rifle Division* | | *250th Rifle Division* | | | *15th Mountain Rifle Division* | | | |
|---|---|---|---|---|---|---|---|---|
| 244th | " | " | 251st | " | " | 16th | " | " | " |
| 246th | " | " | 252d | " | " | 17th | " | " | " |
| 247th | " | " | 254th | " | " | 26th | " | " | " |
| 249th | " | " | 256th | " | " | 12th | " | " | " |

> 4. In the formation of the division listed above, assign from NKVD cadre 1,000 soldiers and noncommissioned officers and 500 command personnel to each division. For the remaining personnel, provide demands to the Red Army General Staff for call-up from the reserves of all categories of soldiers.
> 5. Complete the concentration of cadre from the NKVD at the formation points by 17.7.41.
> 6. Lieutenant General Maslennikov is responsible for approving the formation plan, for material technical support, and also for arranging the personnel.[24]

Although these divisions were better motivated than other Red Army formations, their NKVD cadre was relatively small and they suffered the same, or even worse, personnel and equipment shortages as other mobilized formations. Given the overall shortage of clothing, many lacked Red Army uniforms and went into battle in their NKVD garb.

The armies these divisions manned were pale reflections of the strong armies called for by Soviet prewar plans. For example, Lieutenant General I. I. Maslennikov's 29th Army, formed on 12 July 1941 from the headquarters of 30th Rifle Corps, consisted of three NKVD-based rifle divisions (256th, 252d, and 254th), the 245th Rifle Division, 69th Motorized Division, two corps artillery regiments (264th and 644th), three antitank artillery regiments (11st, 753d, and 759th), two aviation regiments, and a reconnaissance aviation squadron of Il-2 aircraft.[25] Major General V. A. Khomenko's 30th Army, formed the next day on the basis of 52d Rifle Corps headquarters, consisted of two Red Army rifle divisions (119th and 242d), two NKVD-based rifle divisions (243d and 251st), a single tank division (51st), one corps artillery regiment (43d), and two antitank regiments (533d and 758th).[26]

Of the 38 divisions mobilized by 10 July, 15 were people's militia divisions, formed largely by Party organizations in the Leningrad and Moscow Military Districts. These divisions consisted largely of volunteer or conscripted factory workers between 17 and 50 years of age who had only limited reserve military training. The first 3 divisions formed in the Leningrad Military District had a strength of 8,700 to 12,100 men, or 80 percent of required strength. The 12 initial Moscow people's militia rifle divisions counted between 7,500 and 15,000 men each and averaged about 10,000 men (for details, see Tables 8.3 and 8.4).

All of these divisions later received the numerical designations of divisions destroyed in earlier combat.[27] Although their personnel strength was adequate, because these divisions relied on local resources for their equipment, they were often deficient in weaponry and logistical support. Soviet 32d and 33d Armies of the Stavka reserve were manned almost exclusively with people's militia divisions. For example, 33d Army, fielded in late July, consisted of five militia divisions (1st, 5th, 9th, 17th, and 21st) and two antitank artillery regiments (876th and 878th). It possessed no organic tanks or field artillery to support its estimated 60,000 men.[28] The Stavka assigned the 4th and 6th People's Militia Divisions to 24th Army and the 2d, 7th, 8th, 13th, and 18th Divisions to 32d Army.

Combat reports from these armies eloquently speak to their condition. On 13 July General S. A. Kalinin, 24th Army commander, prepared a lengthy report on his army's defensive measures and combat composition. The army, which was concentrating around Viazma, included 166th Rifle Division with 4th People's Militia Division, 6th Motorized Engineer Battalion, 392d and 575th Artillery Regiments (20 guns) attached; 248th Rifle Division; 91st Rifle Division with 537th Motorized Engineer Battalion, and 524th and 32d (High Power) Artillery Regiments (still en route) attached; 53d Rifle Corps (133d, 178th, 107th Rifle and 6th People's Militia Divisions), with 275th, 264th, 685th Corps Artillery, 573d Gun Artillery, 509th, 700th, 701st Antitank Artillery, 303d, 544th, and 403d High Powered Artillery Regiments, 40th and 305th Gun Artillery Regiments and 43d Antiaircraft Artillery Regiments attached; and 26th Mechanized Corps, just then arriving.[29]

On 17 July, 24th Army composition decreased as some of its units were transferred elsewhere, and the army reorganized 26th Mechanized Corps into two new divisions, the 102d Tank and 103d Motorized, and shifted the corps' remaining command and staff personnel to other army formations and units.[30]

Companion reports clearly show the erosion of army strength as divisions were constantly reassigned to other threatened sectors. In light of this erosion in army strength, on 5 August the army received five new divisions, which had just been hastily formed in the Moscow and Orel Military Districts (269th, 279th, 280th, 298th, and 309th).[31] These divisions occupied defenses as soon as they exited the railroad cars and were far from full strength.

When it finally began assembling on 14 July, Lieutenant General V. Ia. Kachalov's 28th Army consisted of the following formations: 19th Rifle Division with one battery of the 488th Corps Artillery Regiment; 148th Rifle Division with three batteries of the 488th and 537th (High Power) Artillery Regiments; 217th Rifle Division; 33d Rifle Corps (145th, 120th, and 222d Rifle Divisions), supported by 364th Corps Artillery Regiment and several other artillery battalions; the 104th and 105th Tank Divisions (re-formed from mechanized corps remnants, specifically, from 27th Mechanized Corps' 9th and 53d Tank Divisions); and 89th Rifle Division.[32] Stavka and Western Direction ordered Kachalov and this force to launch a major attack from the south toward Smolensk into the teeth of Guderian's German Second Panzer Group. A disaster ensued as his force was encircled and destroyed in a major German counterthrust.

Before and during the ill-fated attack, Kachalov dispatched to the Western Direction headquarters two reports that vividly described shortcomings existing in his army. In a report dated 23 July, he admitted, "The order assigned to our units on 23.7 has not been fulfilled."[33] He attributed this to numerous training-related causes, including timidity on the part of all commanders, from squad level up, failure to organize and exploit fire support, poorly organized observation over the field of battle, and faulty cooperation between the various combat arms.

A week later Kachalov wrote an even more blistering report, beginning with the statement, "Combat experience shows that the extremely slow advance and destruction of the weakened enemy has occurred because of the weak leadership in battle on the part of all levels of command." Consequently, he added, "The Army Military Council demands every commander be with his forces, control his forces on the field of battle, intervene personally and demand movement when the advance has been stopped and when forces display insufficient vigor."[34] He detailed the command failures and singled out reconnaissance and the reluctance of commanders to get too close to combat. Within a week, Kachalov's force had been surrounded and largely destroyed and Kachalov himself was killed in battle.

Newly formed 29th Army escaped 28th Army's fate but itself suffered from many of the same problems. By 19 July General Maslennikov's army consisted of the NKVD-based 252d and 256th Rifle Divisions, each supported by 1 to 2 corps artillery regiments, and the 243d Rifle Division.[35] Soon after, 28th

Army conducted repeated attacks against German forces around Smolensk from the Demidov region northeast of the city, but in vain. In his assessment of the first three days of heavy battle, Maslennikov noted, "Not having reserves, the Military Council could not exploit the local successes of either the 252d or 243d Rifle Divisions, which had been weakened by long marches and unceasing three days of combat operations." He went on to complain, "In order to fulfill its assigned missions, the army must have howitzer artillery as well as explosives and sappers who are prepared to destroy enemy strong points; and, moreover, pontoon subunits and [river] crossing equipment. All of this the army lacks."[36]

A 12 August report by 29th Army's chief of artillery, Major General Kuteinikov, painted a bleak picture of the state of the Army's artillery when it originally mobilized and answered the question as to why artillery support was inadequate: "The artillery of 29th Army is woefully incomplete: there is no regimental artillery at all, a total of 50 percent of 45mm artillery, 33 percent of 122mm divisional howitzers, and we have just received 4 152mm howitzers (1938 model). Corps artillery totals 12 152mm gun-howitzers (1937 models). . . . Artillery personnel in army artillery units are especially young; the command personnel and staffs do not work [properly] and have received their first combat baptism in the past ten days."[37]

The report emphasized the inexperience and unskillful operation of artillery staffs, in particular, in target acquisition, counter-battery fire, artillery maneuver, cooperation with forces other than infantry, camouflage, and a host of other critical combat functions. However, the report ended optimistically, stating, "Army artillery and mortar units, on the whole lacking required training, are learning during the course of combat and to date have made considerable strides in mastering the equipment and the art of firing."[38]

On 14 July, Major General V. A. Khomenko's 30th Army was stronger than either 28th or 29th Armies. It consisted of the 119th and 242d Rifle Divisions, the NKVD-based 243d and 251st Rifle Divisions, 51st Tank Division, the 43d Corps Artillery Regiment, and the 533d and 758th Antitank Artillery Regiments.[39] Initially it was positioned in reserve covering the approaches to Rzhev.

Khomenko assessed his army's readiness in a 27 July report to the Western Direction Command. In it he catalogued many deficiencies, including the constant failure of staff and commanders to transmit orders properly, poor march discipline, chaotic fire coordination and support, inefficient and ineffective rear service operations, command and staff violations of the most basic combat staff procedures, and, finally, ineffective party organ support of combat commanders.[40]

In a lengthy subsequent report prepared on 5 August, Khomenko informed Western Front of the problems his command had experienced since mobilization. He detailed the disorganized process of assigning divisions to the army and the subsequent confused movement and assembly orders. Originally, four rifle divisions (119th, 242d, 243d, and 251st) and 51st Tank Division had been assigned to his army. Almost immediately, orders were changed and divisions were shuffled between forming armies. The three divisions ultimately assigned to his army (242d, 250th, and 251st) had to move to concentration areas on foot and, in his words, "were taken from their assembly points in the very midst of assembly, and, incomplete, they did not approach being 'knocked together' and went into battle unprepared for combat."[41]

To illustrate his point, Khomenko cited the case of the 251st Rifle Division, which was formed at the city of Kolomna. The division was sent to 30th Army on foot, understrength, and "totally lacking in cohesiveness." Before dispatch, the representative of the MVO [mobilization organ] reassured the division commander that all shortages would be made up at the concentration region. Khomenko described the arriving division's state:

1. The division was forced to arrive on foot, and it lacked a number of subunits (artillery, chemical company, etc.). It had no materiel support units, since the personnel of these subunits moved on three trains and arrived in the division's operational area only at the beginning of August. To date, some of them have still not arrived;

2. The division has not succeeded in forming and putting together rear service organs;

3. Party and Komsomol organizations have not been created in some units and subunits;

4. An overwhelming number of divisional personnel were mobilized from the reserves. The entire division has only about 400 cadre soldiers from the NKVD;

5. In the haste of formation, horses were improperly distributed. Artillery horses were left behind, and . . . for this reason, artillery horses were received as reinforcements only after the artillery regiment was loaded on trains;

6. Haste of formation led to subunit commanders not knowing their subordinates and subordinates not knowing their commanders, and, as a result, discipline in divisional units was poor;

These and a series of other instances, which related to the 251st Rifle Division, led to the fact that the division entered battle unprepared, badly executed the missions assigned to it, and suffered heavy losses.[42]

Khomenko added that the 250th Rifle Division was in a similar state and the 242d was only slightly more combat ready. In the same report, he listed all army deficiencies in detail. The army headquarters had only 40 percent of its required personnel, and by the time of the report, only 50 percent were present. The antiaircraft and aviation sections were missing altogether, the artillery section was woefully understrength, as were the intendants (road guide) service and key support organs, and rear services had only 3 of the 37 men required. Due in part to these deficiencies, in a period of under three weeks, army losses amounted to over 18,000 men out of its total strength of about 45,000 men.[43]

Khomenko's artillery numbered 24 37mm and 12 76mm antiaircraft guns and only 46 percent of its required antitank guns. The 250th and 251st Rifle Divisions had no howitzers at all. Severe shortages also existed in field guns and mortars, and ammunition of all types was short. Out of the three battalions of tanks (65) provided by 110th Tank Division for support of the operation, 24 remained, and another 10 serviceable tanks were at the disposal of the army.[44] In conclusion, Khomenko wrote:

1. 30th Army received its combat mission in the very period of its formation and assembly. In light of the fact that the army was formed from weakly trained reserves, the combat quality of the army when it received its combat mission was not at the proper level as confirmed by the outcome of combat operations.

2. Supply of the army with arms and combat equipment was unsatisfactory. The army had no air cover.

3. Provision of the army with all that was suitable and necessary on the part of higher-level supply organs occurred slowly and partially and was of insufficient quality.

4. The army suffered great losses in personnel and equipment. Require accelerated dispatch of reinforcements and a heightened tempo of army resupply.[45]

Khomenko could have been writing about all of the reserve armies because his detailed description suited them all. Within two months, most of the reserve armies that barely escaped the brutal battles around Smolensk, Demidov, and Elnia and along the Sozh River would be destroyed. In the fall it would take two more mobilized waves of these partially trained and poorly equipped reserve armies to finally halt the German thrust at the gates of Moscow.

## MECHANIZED RESERVES

Early in the war, German forces smashed Soviet mechanized forces in the western border military districts, depriving both hard-pressed Soviet infantry in the first strategic echelon and deploying second strategic echelon forces of critical armor support. To bolster sagging defenses, and in accordance with prewar defense plans, the Stavka moved second echelon mechanized forces forward and threw the first of these corps against German forces, which were then advancing toward the Dnepr River defense line. On 12 July, as German forces reached and breached the Dnepr, Soviet armored forces consisted of 5th and 7th Mechanized Corps (with 57th Tank Division), which had just unsuccessfully engaged German armored spearheads near Lepel' (west of Vitebsk), 25th Mechanized Corps, which was moving forward in support of 21st Army in the Rogachev sector, and the remnants of 20th Mechanized Corps, which were defending the city of Mogilev.

At this time Soviet armored strength in the entire Western Direction sector from Polotsk to Gomel' totaled 203 KVs, 676 T-34s, and 617 older light tanks. These 1,396 tanks numbered slightly more than the strength of one full-strength prewar mechanized corps and were clearly inadequate to provide armor support to deploying strategic reserves.[46]

To support these hastily fielded and largely unprepared new reserve armies, the Stavka converted tank divisions from mechanized corps in the internal military districts and from mechanized corps that had avoided destruction in the first several weeks of war into a new 100-series of tank divisions. Some of these, like the 101st, 102d, 104th, 105th, 108th, and 107th, were simply renumbered existing divisions (for example, the 52d and 56th from 26th Mechanized Corps, the 9th and 53d of 27th Mechanized Corps, 23d Mechanized Corps' 51st Tank Division, and the separate 69th Mechanized Division from the Far East).[47] Others, like the 111th and 112th, were formed in the Far East from local units and disbanded units of 30th Mechanized Corps. Still others were formed from reserve tank cadres and surviving elements of previously damaged mechanized corps.[48] Creation of the new tank divisions represented a stopgap measure to provide a modicum of armored support to hard-pressed rifle forces. The strength of these divisions was ad hoc. Tank divisions from the mechanized corps in the internal military districts had their own armor plus whatever armor the Stavka could provide from equipment reserves and recent production. Other divisions were manned with whatever local resources were available. For example, on 28 August, the 108th Tank Division had a strength of 62 tanks (5 KVs, 32 T-34s, and 25 T-40s).[49] Although in some instances these divisions had up to 150 tanks, by October virtually all had been destroyed or converted into smaller tank brigades. (For details of the conversion process, see Table 8.5).

Armor support of these reserve armies is best illustrated by a 21 July order from the Stavka to the Reserve Front, which ordered Generals Kalinin and Khomenko of 24th and 28th Armies to allocate 60 tanks from 110th and 102d Tank Divisions to support each rifle division.[50] The order specifically stated, "The tank division [104th] and tank battalions are employed in battle in close cooperation with infantry, artillery, and aviation, and do not permit any separation between tanks and infantry and under no circumstances throw tanks against an organized enemy defense."[51] This order indicated that the Stavka had abandoned any hope of using tank divisions en masse and instead acquiesced to the practice of parceling all existing armor out to support the hard-pressed rifle forces.

Because the main German effort was in the center along the Minsk-Smolensk-Moscow axis, this is where the bulk of Soviet strategic reserves were deployed. This meant that Soviet forces operating along the Southwestern Direction (Southwestern and Southern Fronts) had to make do with the armies and forces they possessed at the outbreak of war. In the meantime, individual divisions were mobilized and moved into the region, but entire reserve armies were not deployed to assist them until Kiev was threatened in August. During this period the two Soviet southernmost *fronts* struggled on with their existing armor formations. Unlike the situation farther north, the surviving Soviet mechanized corps remained in combat and exacted some toll on the advancing Germans. The cost to these corps was, however, substantial.

A report prepared on 15 July 1941 by Lieutenant General M. A. Purkaev, the Southwestern Front chief of staff, provided the Stavka with a vivid picture of the toll the fighting had taken on his *front*'s strength. Whereas rifle division strengths ranged from 100 to 11,000 men, and entire corps had sometimes dwindled to fewer than 1,000 men (15th Rifle Corps 2,614, 36th Rifle Corps 287, and 37th Rifle Corps 720 men), the once proud mechanized corps were in a parlous state (for details, see Table 8.6). The strongest remaining mechanized corps was the 16th, with over 87 tanks, but it had seen little action. The remaining mechanized corps averaged fewer than 50 tanks each, and their subordinate divisions around 20 tanks. The 15th Mechanized Corps, which had absorbed the brunt of initial fighting, had but 6 tanks remaining. A similar report during the same period from Southern Front, where no significant German armored forces were operating, showed slightly higher strength returns (see Table 8.7). There, the 2d and 18th Mechanized Corps numbered 468 and 297 tanks, respectively. Many of these forces, however, would soon be swallowed up in the disasters that would befall the Southwestern Front.

## SUPPORT FORCES

Reserve armies of the new Front of Reserve Armies and the re-formed tank divisions suffered from the same combat support deficiencies as the initial reserve armies. A wide variety of combat assessments document this lack of support. For example, a 19 July report by Lieutenant General I. A. Bogdanov, the *front* commander, indicated that an inspection of 24th Army artillery units demonstrated widespread deficiencies in the organization and conduct of artillery fires, in particular, improper employment of antitank artillery, poor support of infantry attacks, failure to use antiaircraft artillery in an antitank role, lax organization of artillery observation, and poor artillery reconnaissance.[52]

When subordinate armies failed to correct these shortcomings, on 21 July the *front* chief of artillery issued yet another order, which reinforced the original order and demanded corrective action be taken:

> The first clashes of *front* units with the enemy demonstrate that in spite of order No. 03/OP, the employment of antitank artillery observation, notification and the constant readiness of the guns to destroy enemy tanks by direct fire is organized poorly in forces.
>
> With impunity the enemy appears before the forward edge of our defense and also penetrates into its depth without being repulsed by required artillery fire. This is explained by the excessive carelessness and irresponsibility on the part of artillery chiefs in the organization of reconnaissance and observation and the absence of strong control by them over constant readiness of the antitank guns to engage in combat.[53]

Communications problems also plagued the Front of Reserve Armies as it had the Western Front. In a 29 July report, Major General Bulychev, *front* chief of signals, once again outlined those problems, beginning with the continuing equipment shortages:

> Unit and formation headquarters are poorly equipped with radio stations. The provision of radio stations to artillery units has been and continues to be especially weak. A number of artillery regiments have no radios at all. The majority of the small 1932 and 1933 model radio stations in rifle regiments are not standard. An absolute majority of division headquarters do not have the RSB radio stations, and the portable 5-AK-1 does not provide immediate communications for the division headquarters with army headquarters (corps-level headquarters have been disbanded). Radio stations for Air Force headquarters arrived on 27.7.41.[54]

Bulychev recommended a series of remedies for the problems. He was especially distressed over the lack of trained linguists capable of manning *front* radio intercept stations and translating the German message traffic: "Radio stations of *front* headquarters systematically conduct intercept work on enemy radio stations. All materials are then passed to the *front* encipherment and intelligence sections. A major deficiency is the lack of radiomen who have mastered the German language well and who, during the process of interception, can determine the degree of importance of intercepted material."[55]

As before, air support remained as inadequate for the Front of Reserve Armies as it had for Western Front. A short report, prepared on 28 July by Major General Pogrebov, commander of Front of Reserve Armies Air Forces, succinctly summed up the problems:

On the basis of brief war experience I consider that the Red Army Air Forces have suffered considerable losses in personnel and equipment and cannot provide full performance for the following reasons:

1. Weak training of flight and technical personnel arriving at the front with new technical equipment (Lagg-3, Mig-3, Pe-2, IL-2, Iak-1, etc.). Thus, for example, on the first day that the division of Colonel Zotov was under my subordination, 7 aircraft (2 Pe-2, 2 Il-2, and 2 Lagg and Mig-3) out of a total of 32 aircraft were put out of commission due to the aircraft crashing during takeoff and landing. Two Il-2 were crashed by the squadron commander and his deputy while taking off and landing.

Flight and technical personnel, including command personnel, poorly exploit the equipment on the ground and in the air.

2. Weak training of personnel in navigation, as a result of which "wandering" and forced landings occur outside of the airfield. Thus, for example, from 15 through 26.7.41, there were 16 instances of loss of orientation in 38th Fighter Aviation Division, as a result of which 9 aircraft were destroyed and 2 people were killed, and in Colonel Zotov's division, from 22 through 26.7.41, there were 4 instances of a loss of orientation and 1 destroyed aircraft. In Colonel Belov's division in the first day of flight during a combat exercise, 7 aircraft did not return to the airfield because of a loss of orientation.

3. The absence of a system to resupply Air Force units and formations. For example, the 31st Mixed Aviation Division (commander, Colonel Rudenko), the 12th Mixed Aviation Division (commander, Colonel Aladinsky), the 38th Fighter Aviation Division (commander, Major General of Aviation Evsev'ev), the division of Colonel Zotov, and the 10th Mixed Aviation Division (commander, Colonel Belov) arrived at the front with no rear services and at unequipped airfields. . . .

4. The absence of a system and flexibility in the restoration of Air Force units. . . .

5. Weak command and control of Air Force units due to the absence of communications means, like radios. . . .

Overall conditions demand that we undertake urgent measures to eliminate the reasons that weaken the combat power of our aviation and hinder the organization of victory over the enemy.[56]

Thus, all of the new reserve armies were but a pale reflection of the powerful army structures called for in prewar regulations and offensive and defensive military doctrine, and all lacked adequate combat and material support. Moreover, their quantity was in no way indicative of their strength. Prewar Soviet military theory had mandated the fielding of 200,000-man armies supported by 1,400 tanks and 2,700 guns and mortars. In June 1941 Soviet armies in the border military districts averaged 100,000 men, 400 to 700 tanks, and 1,200 to 1,300 guns. These newly mobilized armies consisted of between 50,000 and 60,000 men, fewer than 100 tanks, and about 200 guns. It would obviously require many of these armies for the Soviets to conduct a successful defense, much less an offensive. Fortunately for the Soviet Union, by December 1941 their mobilization system ultimately produced the requisite numbers of armies not only to repel but to drive back German forces.

## STATISTICAL DATA

Table 8.1. Western Front Combat Aircraft, 22 July 1941

|  | 20th Army | 21st Army | 22d Army | Front | Total |
|---|---|---|---|---|---|
| Fighters |  |  |  |  |  |
| I-153 | 15 | 6 | 0 | 20 | 41 |
| I-16 | 4 | 7 | 0 | 12 | 23 |
| MiG-3 | 12 | 11 | 0 | 0 | 23 |
| IaK-1 | 0 | 0 | 0 | 16 | 16 |
| Bombers |  |  |  |  |  |
| SB | 11 | 12 | 31 | 18 | 72 |
| AR-2 | 3 | 0 | 9 | 0 | 12 |
| Pe-2 | 0 | 10 | 0 | 50 | 60 |
| SU-2 | 0 | 57 | 0 | 0 | 57 |
| R-5, R-zet | 0 | 10 | 4 | 0 | 14 |
| TB-3 | 0 | 0 | 0 | 50 | 50 |
| Il-2 | 13 | 8 | 0 | 0 | 21 |
| Total | 58 | 121 | 44 | 166 | 389 |

Source: "Iz otcheta komanduiushchego voenno-vozdushnymi silami zapadnogo fronta ot 31 dekabria 1941 g. o boevykh deistviiakh voenno-vozdushnykh sil zapadnogo fronta za 1941 g." [From a 31 December 1941 assessment of the Western Front Air Force commander about Western Front Air Force combat operations during 1941], *SBDVOV* 37 (1959), 133–135.

Table 8.2. Southwestern Front Air Strength, 11 July 1941 (serviceable/unserviceable aircraft)

| | MiG-3 | I-153 | I-16 | I-156 | Pe-2 | SB | Su-2 | IaK-1 | IaK-2 | IaK-4 | Ar-2 | Il-2 | Total |
|---|---|---|---|---|---|---|---|---|---|---|---|---|---|
| 15th Mixed Aviation Division | 8/3 | 2/3 | 3/1 | 3/4 | | | | | | | | | 16/11 |
| 14th Mixed Aviation Division | | 6/6 | 6/8 | | | | | | | | | | 12/14 |
| 62d Mixed Aviation Division | | | | | 4/1 | 2/14 | 6/21 | | | | | | 12/36 |
| 17th Mixed Aviation Division | | 24/6 | | 6/0 | 0/4 | 3/2 | | 14/8 | | | | | 47/20 |
| 16th Mixed Aviation Division | 2/0 | 11/2 | 19/4 | | | 2/1 | | | | | | 10/10 | 44/17 |
| 36th Fighter Aviation Division | | 23/2 | 77/13 | | | | | | | | | | 100/15 |
| 19th Bomber Aviation Division | | | | | 2/1 | 3/6 | | | | 3/4 | 2/2 | | 10/13 |
| 315th Reconnaissance Regiment | | | | | | 3/1 | | | | | | | 3/1 |
| 316th Reconnaissance Regiment | | | | | | 1/0 | | | 2/2 | 2/1 | | | 5/3 |
| Total | 10/3 | 66/20 | 105/26 | 9/4 | 6/6 | 14/24 | 6/21 | 14/8 | 2/2 | 5/5 | 2/2 | 10/10 | 249/131 |

Source: "Svedeniia shtaba voenno-vozdushnykh sil Krasnoi Armii o boevom sostave chastei voenno-vozdushnykh sil iugo-zapadnogo fronta po sostoainiu na 11 iiulia 1941 g." [Information of the Red Army Air Force headquarters about the combat composition of Air Force units of the Southwestern Front on 11 July 1941], *SBDVOV* 38 (1959), 7–8.

Table 8.3. People's Militia Divisions Formed in the Leningrad Military District

| Guards | Strength | | |
|---|---|---|---|
| | Estimated | Actual | Shortage |
| 1st | 14,926 | 12,102 | 2,824 |
| 2d | 11,739 | 8,721 | 3,018 |
| 3d | 12,154 | 10,094 | 2,060 |
| 4th (later renumbered as 5th) | cadre only | 4,267 | |
| 1st | 10,815 | 10,538 | 277 |
| 2d | 10,836 | 11,489 | |
| 3d | | 10,334 | |
| 4th | 9,961 | 8,924 | 1,037 |

Source: A. D. Kolesnik, *Opolchenskie formirovaniia Rossiiskoi federatsii v gody Velikoi Otechestvennoi voiny* [People's Militia formations of the Russian Federation in the years of the Great Patriotic War] (Moscow: Nauka, 1988), 16–19.

Table 8.4. People's Militia Divisions Formed in the Moscow Military District

| | Original Number | Later Designation | Strength |
|---|---|---|---|
| Summer Formation | | | |
| Leninsky | 1st | 60th Rifle | 10,000 |
| Stalinsky | 2d | 2d Rifle | 8,385 |
| Kuibyshevsky | 4th | 110th Rifle | 11,755 |
| Frunzensky | 5th | 113th Rifle | 11,700 |
| Dzerzhinsky | 6th | 160th Rifle | 9,000 |
| Baumansky | 7th | 29th Rifle | 15,000 |
| Krasnopresnensky | 8th | 8th Rifle | 7,500 |
| Kirovsky | 9th | 139th Rifle | 10,500 |
| Rostokinsky | 13th | 140th Rifle | 8,010 |
| Moskvoretsky | 17th | 17th Rifle | 10,000 |
| Leningradsky | 18th | 18th Rifle | 10,000 |
| Kievsky | 21st | 173d Rifle | 7,660 |
| Fall Formation | | | |
| 3d Moscow Workers | | 130th Rifle | 9,753 |
| 4th Moscow Workers | | 155th Rifle | 7,260 |
| 5th Moscow Workers | | 158th Rifle | 7,291 |

Source: Kolesnik, 22.

Table 8.5. Distribution and Strength of Soviet Armored Forces, 22 June through October 1941

| Mechanized Corps | 22 June 1941 | | July to October 1941 | | | |
| | Division | Strength | July | August | September | October |
|---|---|---|---|---|---|---|
| 1st | 1st TD | | 1st TD | 1st TD | 123d TB | 123d TB |
| | 3d TD | | 3d TD | 3d TD | 3d TD | 3d TD |
| | 163d MD | | 163d MD | 163d RD | 163d RD | 163d RD |
| | | 163 (15) //1037 | | | | |
| 2d | 11th TD | | 11th TD | 11th TD | 132d TB | 132d TB |
| | 16th TD | | 16th TD | (Uman') | | |
| | 15th MD | | 15th MD | 15th RD | 15th RD | 15th RD |
| | | 489 (60) // 517 | | | | |
| 3d | 2d TD | | (Raseinai) | | | |
| | 5th TD | | (Minsk) | | | |
| | 84th MD | | 84th RD | 84th RD | 84th RD | 84th RD |
| | | 460 (109) // 651 | | | | |
| 4th | 8th TD | 325 (190) | 8th TD | 8th TD | 130th TB | 130th TB |
| | 32d TD | | 32d TD | (Uman') | 1st and 8th TB | 1st and 8th TB |
| | 81st MD | | 81st RD | 81st RD | 81st RD | 81st RD |
| | | 892 (414) // 979 | | | | |
| 5th | 13th TD | | 13th TD | (Smolensk) | | |
| | 17th TD | | 17th TD | (Smolensk) | 126th TB | (Viaz'ma) |
| | 109th MD | | 304th RD | 304th RD | 304th RD | 304th RD |
| | | 2602 (0)* // 350 (5 July) | | | | |
| 6th | 4th TD | | (Bialystok) | | | |
| | 7th TD | 368 (201) | (Bialystok) | | | |
| | 29th MD | | (Bialystok) | | | |
| | | 1021 (352)//1131 | | | | |
| 7th | 14th TD | | 14th TD | 14th TD | 27th and 28th TBs | (Viaz'ma) |
| | 18th TD | | 18th TD | 18th TD | 127th TB | (Viaz'ma) |
| | 1st MD | | 1st MD | 1st TD | 1st MRD | 1st MRD |
| | | 1036 (9) //350 (5 July) | | | | |
| 8th | 12th TD | | 12th TD | (Uman') | 129th TB | 129th TB |
| | 34th TD | | 34th TD | (Dubno) | 2d and 16th TBs | 2d and 16th TBs |
| | 7th MD | | 7th MD | 7th MD | (Kiev) | |
| | | 858 (171) //898 | | | | |
| 9th | 20th TD | 36 (0) | 20th TD | 20th TD | (Kiev) | |
| | 35th TD | 142 (0) | 35th TD | 35th TD | (Kiev) | |
| | 131st MD | 122 (0) | 131st RD | 131st RD | (Kiev) | |
| | | 285 (0) //298 | | | | |
| 10th | 21st TD | | 21st TD | 21st TD | 21st TD | 21st TD |
| | 24th TD | | 24th TD | 24th TD | 124th TB and 12th TR | 124th TB and 12th TR |
| | 198th MD | | 198th MD | 198th MD | 198th RD | 198th RD |
| | | 1343 (0) //469 | | | | |
| 11th | 29th TD | | (Bialystok) | | | |
| | 33d TD | | (Bialystok) | | | |
| | 204th MD | | (Bialystok) | | | |
| | | 237 (31) //414 | | | | |

*Includes 57th TD, 61st TD, and 82d MD.
Legend: —//—Strength according to recently released Russian articles // Strength according to *Nachal'nyi period.* For abbreviations, consult List of Abbreviations, p. xv. Place names in parentheses indicate where the unit was destroyed.

*Table 8.5 Continued*

| | 22 June 1941 | | July to October 1941 | | | |
|---|---|---|---|---|---|---|
| Mechanized Corps | Division | Strength | July | August | September | October |
| 12th | 23d TD | | 23d TD | (disbanded) | | |
| | 28th TD | | 28th TD | 28th TD | 28th TD | 241st RD |
| | 202d MD | | 202d MD | 202d RD | 202d RD | 202d RD |
| | | 933 (0) //749 | | | | |
| 13th | 25th TD | | (Bialystok) | | | |
| | 31st TD | | (Bialystok) | | | |
| | 208th MD | | (Bialystok) | | | |
| | | 294 (0)//282 | | | | |
| 14th | 22d TD | 235 (0) | (Bialystok) | | | |
| | 30th TD | | (Bialystok) | | | |
| | 205th MD | | (Bialystok) | | | |
| | | 520 (0)//518 | | | | |
| 15th | 10th TD | 318 (100) | 10th TD | 10th TD | 131st and 133d TBs | 131st and 133d TBs |
| | 37th TD | 285 (33) | 37th TD | (Uman') | 3d TB | 3d TB |
| | 212th MD | 37 (0) | 212th RD | 212th RD | 212th RD | 212th RD |
| | | 640 (133) //749 | | | | |
| 16th | 15th TD | | 15th TD | (Uman') | 4th TB | 4th TB |
| | 39th TD | | 39th TD | (Uman') | | |
| | 240th MD | | 240th MD | (Uman') | | |
| | | 608 (0) //482 | | | | |
| 17th | 27th TD | | (Minsk) | | | |
| | 36th TD | | (Minsk) | | | |
| | 209th MD | | (Minsk) | | | |
| | | 36 (0) //63 | | | | |
| 18th | 44th TD | | 44th TD | (Uman'); 44th TD, KharMD | | |
| | 47th TD | | 47th TD | (Uman'); 47th TD, SWF | 47th TD | 142d TB |
| | 218th MD | | 218th MD | 218th MD | 218th RD | 218th RD |
| | | 280 (0) //282 | | | | |
| 19th | 40th TD | 158 (0) | 40th TD | (Korosten'); 40th TD, NCMD | 45th and 47th TBs | 45th and 47th TBs |
| | 43d TD | 237 (7) | 43d TD | (Korosten'); 43d TD, KharMD | 10th TB | 10th TB |
| | 213d MD | 54 (0) | 213d MD | (Korosten') | | |
| | | 449 (7) //453 | | | | |
| 20th | 26th TD | | (Mogilev) | | | |
| | 38th TD | | (Mogilev) | | | |
| | 210th MD | | (Mogilev) | | | |
| | | 93 (0) //94 | | | | |
| 21st | 42d TD | | 42d TD | (disbanded) | 42d TB | (Briansk) |
| | 46th TD | | 46th TD | (disbanded) | 46th TB | 46th TB |
| | 185th MD | | 185th MD | 185th RD | 185th RD | 185th RD |
| | | 98 (0) | | | | |
| 22d | 19th TD | 163 (0) | 19th TD | 19th TD | (Kiev) | |
| | 41st TD | 425 (31) | 41st TD | 41st TD | (Kiev) | |
| | 215th MD | 94 (0) | 215th MD | 215th MD | (Kiev) | |
| | | 682 (31) //712 | | | | |

*Table 8.5 Continued*

| | 22 June 1941 | | July to October 1941 | | | |
|---|---|---|---|---|---|---|
| Mechanized Corps | Division | Strength | July | August | September | October |
| 23d | 48th TD | | 48th TD | 48th TD | 17th, 18th TBs | (Viaz'ma) |
| | 51st TD | | 110th TD | 110th TD | 141st and 142d TBs | (Briansk) 142d TB |
| | 220th MD | | 220th RD | 220th RD | 220th RD | 220th RD |
| | | 413 (21) | | | | |
| 24th | 45th TD | | 45th TD | (Uman') | | |
| | 49th TD | | 49th TD | (Uman') | | |
| | 216th MD | | 216th MD | (Uman') | | |
| | | 222 (0) //222 | | | | |
| 25th | 50th TD | | 50th TD | 50th TD | 150th TB | (Viaz'ma) |
| | 55th TD | | 55th TD | (Chernigov) | 8th and 14th Sep Tbns | 8th and 14th Sep TBns |
| | 219th MD | | 219th MD | (Chernigov) | | |
| | | 300 (20) | | | | |
| 26th | 52d TD | | 101st TD | 101st TD | 101st MRD | (Viaz'ma) |
| | 56th TD | | 102d TD | 102d TD | 144th TB (presumed) | (Viaz'ma) |
| | 103d MD | | 103d MD | 103d MD | 103d RD | (Viaz'ma) |
| | | 184 (0) | | | | |
| 27th | 9th TD | | 104th TD | 104th TD | 145th TB | (Viaz'ma) |
| | 53d TD | | 105th TD | 105th TD | 146th TB | (Viaz'ma) |
| | 221st MD | | (disbanded) | | | |
| | | 356 (0) | | | | |
| 28th | 6th TD | | 6th TD | 6th TD | 6th TD | 6th, 55th, and 56th TBs |
| | 54th TD | | 54th TD | 54th TD | 54th TD | 54th TB |
| | 236th MD | | 236th RD | 236th RD | 236th RD | 236th RD |
| | | 869 (0) | | | | |
| 30th | 58th TD | | 58th TD | 58th TD | 58th TD | 58th TB |
| | 60th TD | | 60th TD | 60th TD | 60th TD | 60th TD |
| | 239th MD | | 239th MD | 239th RD | 239th RD | 239th RD |
| | | 2969 (0)* | | | | |
| | 57th TD | | 57th TD | (Smolensk) | 128th TB | (Briansk) |
| | 59th TD | | 301st, 356th, 362d TBns | | | |
| | 61st TD | | 61st TD | 61st TD | 61st TD | 61st TD |
| | | | | 111th TD | 111th TD | 111th TD |
| | | | | 112th TD | 112th TD | 112th TD |
| | 69th MD | | 107th TD | 107th TD | 107th MRD | 107th MRD |
| | | | | 109th TD | 148th TB | (Viaz'ma) |
| | | | 108th TD | 108th TD | 108th TD | 108th TD |

*Includes 59th TD and 69th MD.

Sources: *Boevoi sostav sovetskoi armii*, vol. 1, and *Komandovanie korpusnogo i divizionnogo zvena Sovetskikh vooruzhennykh Sil perioda Velikoi Otechestvennoi voiny, 1941–1945* [Corps and divisional commanders of the Soviet Armed Forces during the Great Patriotic War, 1941–1945] (Moscow: Frunze Academy, 1964).

Table 8.6. Combat Strength of Southwestern Front Mechanized Forces, 15 July 1941

| Formation | Manpower | Tanks | Guns | Vehicles |
|---|---|---|---|---|
| 9th Mechanized Corps | 721 | 38 | 0 | 70 |
| 20th Tank Division | 5,633 | 1 | 8 | 260 |
| 35th Tank Division | 961 | 24 | 23 | 116 |
| 131st Mechanized Division | 4,283 | 12 | 27 | 349 |
| 19th Mechanized Corps | 315 | 0 | 0 | 40 |
| 40th Tank Division | 2,040 | 30 | 0 | 99 |
| 43d Tank Division | 2,625 | 52 | 17 | 342 |
| 22d Mechanized Corps | 1,122 | 0 | 1 | 79 |
| 19th Tank Division | 3,518 | 3 | 23 | 273 |
| 41st Tank Division | 4,826 | 28 | 32 | 407 |
| 215th Mechanized Division | 5,118 | 0 | 19 | 208 |
| 4th Mechanized Corps | 1,845 | 2 | 12 | 104 |
| 8th Tank Division | 1,306 | 29 | 11 | 137 |
| 32d Tank Division | 736 | 7 | 18 | 32 |
| 81st Mechanized Division | 3,287 | 13 | 33 | 344 |
| 15th Mechanized Corps | unknown | unknown | unknown | unknown |
| 10th Tank Division | 342 | 6 | 0 | 30 |
| 37th Tank Division | 0 | 0 | 0 | 0 |
| 212th Mechanized Division | 0 | 0 | 0 | 0 |
| 16th Mechanized Corps | unknown | unknown | unknown | unknown |
| 15th Tank Division | 2,066 | 87 | 35 | 162 |
| 39th Tank Division | unknown | unknown | unknown | unknown |
| 240th Mechanized Division | 9,847 | 13 | 41 | 381 |
| 24th Mechanized Corps | unknown | unknown | unknown | unknown |
| 44th Tank Division (18th Mechanized Corps) | 1,797 | 125 | 20 | 139 |

Source: "Svedeniia shtaba iugo-zapadnogo fronta o boevom i chislennom sostave soedinenii i otdel'nykh chastei fronta po sostoianiiu na 15.7.41 g." [Information from Southwestern Front headquarters about the combat and numerical strength of *front* formations and separate units on 15.7.41], *SBDVOV* 38 (1959), 35–36.

Table 8.7. Southern Front Armored Strength on 22 July 1941

| Formation | Tanks | Vehicles | Tractors |
|---|---|---|---|
| 2d Mechanized Corps | | | |
| 11th Tank Division | 181 (81 operational) | 1,070 | 71 |
| 16th Tank Division | 99 | 870 | 16 |
| 15th Mechanized Division | 188 (102 operational) | 0 | 122 |
| 18th Mechanized Corps | | | |
| 39th Tank Division | 198 (132 operational) | 465 | 43 |
| 47th Tank Division | 54 | 731 | 48 |
| 218th Mechanized Division | 45 | 741 | 91 |
| 2d Calvary Corps | | | |
| 5th Calvary Division | 45 | 148 | 13 |
| 9th Calvary Division | 56 | 188 | 20 |

Source: "Donesenie pomoshchnika komanduiushchego voiskami iuzhnogo fronta po avtobronetankovym voiskam ot 22 iiulia 1941 g. nachal'niku glavnogo avtobronetankovogo upravleniia Krasnoi Armii o nalichii material'noi chasti v bronetankovykh voiskakh fronta na 20 iiulia 1941 g." [A 22 July 1941 report by the assistant commander of the southern front for armored forces to the chief of the Red Army Armored Directorate about the presence of equipment in *front* armored forces on 20 July 1941], *SBDVOV* 38 (1959), 138.

# CHAPTER 9

# Red Army Intelligence on the Eve of War

Existing evidence on the state of Soviet intelligence on the eve of Operation Barbarossa provides an adequate basis for answering two fundamental questions: "What did the Red Army know about German offensive intentions?" and "When did they know it?" Less clear is the answer to a critical third question, "Why then did the Soviets not react?" A wealth of recently released documentary materials from Party, diplomatic, military, and NKVD archives makes it clear that Soviet intelligence organizations had ample warning of German hostile intentions at virtually every level. Even before the recent archival revelations, General A. M. Vasilevsky wrote in his postwar memoirs: "In June 1941 the General Staff had been continuously receiving alarming reports from operations departments of the western districts and armies. The Germans had completed the concentration of forces on our borders. In a number of places, they had started dismantling their own wire entanglements and making lanes in their minefields, clearly preparing ways of access to our positions. Large panzer groups had been brought up in the areas of departure; the roar of their engines was distinct at night."[1]

Hundreds of Soviet memoirs and many military studies have since supported the accuracy of Vasilevsky's view. One noted:

> Documents and facts bear witness to the fact that the political and military leadership of the Soviet Union, even before the beginning of war, possessed information about preparations for the attack of Nazi Germany on the USSR. The General Staff had sufficiently complete information about the strengthening of enemy forces along our western borders. The Soviet command received from various sources information about the possible enemy attack and the period of his offensive. Border guard forces, as well as military councils of the border military districts, informed the government and People's Commissariat of Defense about the frequent occasions when enemy aircraft and agents violated the state borders.[2]

## WARNING OF WAR

Soviet archival sources contain a host of diplomatic reports and information from NKVD and military intelligence (GRU) agents abroad attesting to the imminence of war. In his memoirs, Zhukov noted: "Winston Churchill sent Stalin a message at the end of April 1941, which read in part: 'I have information from a trusted agent that when the Germans thought they had got Yugoslavia in the net—that is to say, after March 20—they began to move three out of the five panzer divisions from Rumania to southern Poland. The moment they heard of the Serbian revolution, this movement was countermanded. Your Excellency will readily appreciate the significance of these facts.'"[3]

Zhukov then put his finger directly on why Stalin could not believe any such reports:

> Stalin received the message with suspicion. In 1940 rumors had circulated in the world press that the British and French armed forces were themselves preparing to invade the North Caucasus and bomb Baku, Grozny, and Maikop. Then there appeared documents confirming these rumors.
>
> In short, not only the anti-Soviet and anticommunist views and utterances that Churchill never bothered to conceal but also many concrete facts relating to diplomatic activity could have prejudiced Stalin against information from Western imperialistic sources.[4]

In fact, this suspicion on Stalin's part affected his reaction to Soviet intelligence materials as well. Stalin's fear of disinformation and his firm belief that he understood his fellow dictator, Hitler, consistently warped his judgment during the fateful period before the outbreak of war. The numerous diplomatic and agent reports included well-known, specific messages sent by the famous Richard Sorge (code-named Ramzaia) in Japan. These included a short 15 May transmission, "War will begin on 20–22 June . . . Ramzaia," and a subsequent message on 19 May, which read, "9 armies and 150 divisions will be concentrated against the Soviet Union . . . Ramzaia."[5] On 30 May 1941, Sorge dispatched the following telegram to the GRU:

> Berlin has informed Ott that the German offensive against the Soviet Union will begin in the second half of June. Ott is 95 percent sure that war will begin. Circumstantial evidence of this which I see at the present time is [as follows]:
>
> The technical department of the German Air Force in my city soon after received orders to return. Ott demanded that the VAT [military attaché] not send any sort of important communications through the USSR. The transport of rubber across the USSR is to be cut to a minimum.
>
> The reasons for the German attack are: the existing strength of the Red Army does not permit Germany the capability of widening the war

in Africa because Germany must hold a large army in Eastern Europe. In order to liquidate fully any danger from the USSR, the Red Army must be suppressed as soon as possible. So Ott declares.[6]

Recently released Party records include other samples of such warnings. Messages sent on 2 June, 19 June, and 21 June, from Party officials in Kishinev, Murmansk, and Rava-Russkaia in Ukraine, respectively, detailed Rumanian war preparations and increased German overflights and hostile air activity in the Soviet far north and in the southern Soviet Union.[7]

More germane to this study were the operations of Soviet military intelligence, the GRU, and military intelligence organizations throughout the entire chain of command and abroad, in particular, the military attachés in foreign embassies. Again the evidence seems conclusive that information about the impending German attack was extensive. A number of attaché reports stand out for their clarity and prescience. A 29 December report to the GRU from the Soviet military attaché in Berlin stated, "A source . . . reported that he knew from a highly informed military circle that Hitler gave an order about preparation for war with the USSR. War will be declared in March 1941."[8] Another attaché report sent to the GRU on 9 March 1941 from Belgrade, stated: "A source . . . reports information from a Court Minister: (1) The German General Staff has given up [the idea] of an attack on the British Isles and has established the immediate mission of seizing the Ukraine and Baku, which must be carried out in April–May of this year, and for which Hungary, Rumania, and Bulgaria are preparing. . . . (2) A reinforced transfer of forces is going on through Berlin and Hungary into Rumania.[9]

In March 1941, two more lengthy reports were sent to Stalin through NKVD channels from an agent code-named Korsikantsa in Berlin. Authenticated by the chief of the NKVD's 1st Directorate, both reports starkly laid out details of German offensive plans and indicated that the attack would occur in April or May. In part, the latter read:

The information reports that the chief of the General Staff of the Ground Forces, Colonel General Halder, counts on unconditional success and a lightning occupation by German forces of the Soviet Union, and first of all, Ukraine, where, in Halder's estimation, the successful operation will be facilitated by the good condition of the rail and road network. Halder considers the occupation of Baku and the oil fields to also be an easy mission, which the Germans can ostensibly restore rapidly after the destruction by military action. Halder considers that the Red Army will not be in any state to offer appropriate resistance to a lightning strike of German forces, and the Russians will not even succeed in destroying reserves.[10]

On 30 April a like report came through the same channels from GRU agent "Starshina," in Berlin:

> A source working in the German aviation headquarters reports . . .
> According to information received from a liaison officer, Gregor, be-tween the German Ministry of Foreign Affairs and the German aviation headquarters, the issue of Germany acting against the Soviet Union has been finally resolved, and its commencement can be expected from day to day. Ribbentrop, who to this time has not been a supporter of action against the Soviet Union, knowing the firm resolve of Hitler in the mat-ter, changed his position to advocate an attack on the Soviet Union.[11]

Starshina went on to report the details of Finnish, Rumanian, Hungar-ian, and Bulgarian collusion with Hitler and parroted German assessments of the likely ineffectiveness of the Soviet Air Force in combat. On the same day, a report from a GRU agent in Warsaw provided information about Ger-man troop movements in Poland and other offensive preparations, noting, in part, "From 10 through 20 April, German forces were moving continuously through Warsaw during the day and at night. Because of the unceasing flow of forces, all traffic on the streets of Warsaw has been halted. Trains loaded primarily with heavy artillery, trucks, and aircraft units are traveling along the railroad in an eastern direction. From mid-April a great number of military trucks and Red Cross vehicles have appeared on the streets of Warsaw."[12]

The flow of intelligence reports did not diminish in May. On 6 May Ad-miral N. G. Kuznetsov, people's commissar for the navy and commander of the Soviet fleet, passed a report to military intelligence from the Soviet naval attaché in Berlin: "Our naval attaché in Berlin, Captain 1st Rank Vorontsev, reports that . . . according to a German officer from Hitler's headquarters the Germans are preparing to invade the USSR on 14 May through Finland, the Baltic region, and Rumania. Simultaneously, powerful air raids are planned on Moscow and Leningrad, and airborne forces are to be landed at border centers." Kuznetsov, however, cast doubt on the information's validity and further reinforced Stalin's suspicions, adding, "I consider that this informa-tion is false and was specially sent through this channel so that the Germans could see how the USSR would react."[13]

Later in the month, on 28 May, the Red Army military attaché in Bucharest dispatched a lengthy message that assessed the impending German threat to the chief of the GRU:

> Generalizing, one can say that war against the USSR in general will not represent a problem from the military point of view. In two to three

months, German forces will stand at the Urals. The mechanized Russian Army has placed itself under the blow of the German offensive in the western part of the USSR, and there it will be routed in a short period, since, measured by its obsolete armored weapons and obsolete aircraft, the Red Army is not in a condition to stand against the advanced and numerically superior German weapons, which far surpass them. In close German circles, there is not one person at all who has the least doubt of a rapid victory over the USSR.[14]

After reviewing German attitudes further and commenting on other German offensive preparations, the attaché stated: "In conclusion, one can say that the noticeable 'lull,' the uncertainty over Hess and the silence of the press on that question, the intensified movements of the Germans, and the impudent behavior of the Rumanian press gives us the right to think about all the continuing preparations of the Germans for war with us."

As the date of Operation Barbarossa's execution neared, attaché traffic became even more insistent and precise. On 11 June Admiral Kuznetsov relayed a report from Bucharest:

I am reporting information received from our colleagues in Bucharest:
    1. From officer circles it is well known that the Rumanian Army and aviation have been given the order to be ready on 15 June for offensive operations.
    Judging by information from Bucharest, preparations for military action are proceeding very intensively. However, the Rumanians will not be ready in the appointed period. . . .
    2. The Rumanian military does not even want to fight against the Soviet Union. In truth the Rumanian people are inclined against any war.
    3. The movement of Rumanian–German forces to the north, and especially artillery, is continuing.[15]

Two days before the attack, the Red Army attaché in Sofia, Bulgaria, was even more precise about the threat: "The military clash is expected on 21 or 22 June, and 100 German divisions are located in Poland, 40 in Rumania, 6 in Finland, 10 in Hungary, and 7 in Slovakia. In all there are 60 motorized divisions. A courier who has flown in from Bucharest tells that mobilization in Rumania has been completed, and they expect war at any moment. Presently, 10,000 German forces are located in Bulgaria."[16]

The same day, Richard Sorge weighed in with a final prewar message to the GRU about German intentions and the potentially dangerous wartime attitude of Japan. He radioed from Tokyo on 20 June 1941:

The German ambassador in Tokyo, Ott, tells me that war between Germany and the USSR is inescapable. German military superiority also accords the possibility of destroying the last large European army because, to date, the strategic defensive position of the USSR is less combat capable then it was in the defense of Poland.

[A source] tells me that the Japanese General Staff has already discussed the position that it will take in the event of war.

The suggestions about Japanese-American negotiations and the internal struggle between Matsuoka, on the one hand, and Hiranuma, on the other, are at a standstill because all are awaiting resolution of the question of USSR and German relations.[17]

Lodged in the midst of this unnerving diplomatic intelligence traffic, on 19 June, Captain 2d Rank Zaitsev, a section chief at the People's Commissariat of Foreign Affairs responsible for monitoring attaché movements, notified his superiors that between 4 and 20 June all responsible figures from the naval attaché's staff in the German Embassy in Moscow had departed for Berlin. He added, "Thus, not one of those known by me in the apparatus of the attaché remains, and this is so unusual and strange that I consider it necessary to bring this to your attention."[18]

There is serious question, however, as to whether reports through diplomatic channels, GRU conduits, or NKVD or personal reports to Stalin were actually getting to People's Commissar of Defense Timoshenko or Chief of the General Staff Zhukov. In his memoirs, Zhukov claimed: "Did the Defense Commissariat and the General Staff know anything about the reports Stalin was getting through these channels? After the war, Marshal Timoshenko assured me that he, at any rate, had known nothing about them. And I, too, declare as the then chief of the General Staff, that I had no knowledge of them."[19]

This may well have been correct. The intelligence system presided over by Stalin was overly compartmentalized, and because of his own penchant for secrecy, the dictator probably did not share critical information with his always suspect subordinates. Nevertheless, when he wrote this, Zhukov was being more than a little disingenuous in separating himself from blame for the massive intelligence failure. Zhukov had at his disposal the bulk of Red Army intelligence collection means. As will be seen below, army organs had a vivid picture of German offensive preparations. The Zhukov proposal of 15 May for a preemptive attack on the concentrating Germans more than adequately attests to Zhukov's awareness of the real situation. What Zhukov should have said was that in the circumstances he was virtually powerless to do anything else but acquiesce in Stalin's judgment. In short, while intelligence collection concerning German military intentions was clearly more than adequate, interpretation by the High Command and political leadership was not.

The most frequent early indicator of German hostile intent was German intelligence collection, which accelerated as early as March 1940. After that date sporadic German reconnaissance aviation overflights became virtually routine. Early reports included a 17 March Western Special Military District report of violation of Soviet airspace by 32 German aircraft and subsequent reports from the Kiev and Baltic Special Military Districts on 4, 9, and 10 April about similar activity. From October 1939 until 22 June 1941, these incursions totaled more than 500 flights.[20] Military districts fully understood what was going on but were precluded from reacting on order of Stalin and the NKO. For example, shortly before the German attack, the Baltic Special Military District notified the NKO and General Staff that for 10 to 15 days German aircraft had conducted photographic reconnaissance over its positions to a depth of 100 kilometers.[21] On 19 July a flight of German aircraft penetrated to Proskurov in the Kiev Special Military District and even landed, but when challenged they refused to explain why they had done so.

The military district military councils notified the NKO of the violations and attempted to take remedial action. On 18 June 1940, for example, General Kirponos, the Kiev Special Military District commander, issued an order "On Prohibiting Air Flights," which required that "measures to force a landing should be initiated against aircraft appearing in a prohibited flight zone." On 16 July a subsequent order, "On Foreign Aircraft Violating the State Frontier," ordered "in any event should foreign aircraft attempt to violate the state frontier, effective measures are to be taken to eliminate the violation . . . so that no foreign aircraft can appear over our territory or escape with impunity."[22] Rather than ordering the military districts to shoot the aircraft down, on 29 March the people's commissar for internal affairs, probably on Stalin's instructions, issued a directive to the western border military districts that prohibited any counteraction. In part, it stated, "Do not open fire during any violation of the Soviet–German border by aircraft or air navigation devices, while limiting [yourselves] to drawing up a report about the violation of the state border." In April 1940 and March 1941, respectively, in obvious response to new command queries, the NKO ordered covering forces in the Western Special Military District and the Baltic Fleet to hold their fire against penetrating aircraft.[23]

NKVD channels raised similar complaints. On 7 April 1941, the Main Directorate of Border Forces reported to NKVD Central (Moscow) that German aircraft based in Rumania had been routinely flying over the Ukraine, and it asked permission to engage the aircraft. After the NKVD forwarded the request to the People's Commissariat for Foreign Affairs (NKID), on 10 April the latter replied, "It is necessary to formulate protests on the violation of the USSR border by German aircraft in accord with the existing rules, on the basis of the Convention Between the USSR and Germany on the Settlement of Border Conflicts and Incidents of 10 June 1940, and also to inform the NKID [so that] it can undertake appropriate measures through diplomatic channels."[24] Major General V. A. Khomenko, chief of Border Troops of the Ukrainian NKVD, bitterly noted on 4 April, "The presence of the order, as well as an order of the Red Army, reduces our role to passive observer and the declaration of claims that can provide no effective results."[25]

The Germans supplemented aerial reconnaissance with ground reconnaissance by normal embassy or consulate attaché personnel and Abwehr agents masquerading as refugees or smugglers. The former chief of Abwehr-1 Section (German intelligence) and supervisors of the famous Brandenburger Abwehr (diversionary) teams, Lieutenant General Hans Piekenbrock, reported at the Nuremberg Trials, "From August to September 1940, the Abwehr [received] a significant increase in intelligence assessments relating to the USSR. Undoubtedly, these assignments were linked to the preparation for war against Russia."[26] Most of these ground missions were designed to gain access to terrain and objectives in the tactical and operational depths (up to 200 kilometers). A recent Russian source cites archival documents that estimate the scale and growing intensity of German ground reconnaissance activity:

> Of the 232 agents apprehended by Soviet bodies in 1940, 119 were in the Minsk area, 87 in the Kiev region, and 26 in the Leningrad area. It must be pointed out that, although the total number of enemy agents apprehended on the western frontier in the first quarter of 1941 had increased by an average of more than fivefold in comparison with the corresponding period of the previous year, along the most important operational axes this increased by ten- to twelvefold. Reconnaissance was carried out in the entire sector of the forthcoming Nazi force offensive to a depth of 150 to 200 kilometers, and along the Leningrad, Minsk, and Moscow axes, it was carried out to 300 to 400 kilometers and more.
>
> By the summer of 1941, the activities of the Nazi intelligence services had noticeably increased. The agents were to be dropped in without radios and had an assignment of making their way back no later than 15 to 18 June, obviously so that their data could be effectively used by the commands.[27]

This reconnaissance work and intelligence collection achieved only mixed results. For example, on the eve of 22 June, the Germans had identified Soviet mechanized corps in the Kaunus and L'vov regions, probably because of the excellent agent network existing in those regions. In other sectors, however, German intelligence utterly missed the other new mechanized corps. Overall, on the eve of the invasion, the Germans developed a fairly accurate picture of Soviet forces in the western border military districts and actually overestimated their strength. However, they failed to detect the existence of most of the mechanized corps, and totally misassessing Soviet mobilization capability, they underestimated the overall strength of the Red Army by over 100 divisions (see Appendix D).

On the eve of and just after the German offensive, active reconnaissance and diversionary teams from German field commands replaced Abwehr agents in the Soviet rear area. Soviet formation and unit records are filled with accounts of the devastating work wrought by these forces, primarily against Soviet communications, supply lines, and logistical facilities.

Juxtaposed to these reports of German military intentions and heightened German military reconnaissance were Soviet assessments of German military capabilities. The most important of these were intelligence reports pertaining to German offensive preparations and the concentration of German forces opposite the Soviet Union's western borders. Again the documents speak for themselves. In early 1940 most Soviet reports reflected the German buildup in northern Europe and the Baltic region. However, after the German victory in the west in May and June 1940 and the Norwegian venture in summer, information on German attack preparations in the east mushroomed and continued to grow in volume and specificity until the very day Operation Barbarossa began.

In September 1940, Brigade Commander P. P. Evstigneev, Leningrad Military District chief of intelligence, reported the beginning of German concentration of forces in the north and that intensive road construction was under way in a closed zone along the Finnish–Soviet border. At the same time, Colonel S. V. Bokhin, chief of intelligence of the Western Special Military District, recorded growing German troop concentrations in eastern Poland, and the Brest Border Guards Detachment received information from refugees that new Wehrmacht units had arrived in the region.[28] Information reaching the ears of Soviet intelligence in December included news that between the 9th and 14th of that month, Field Marshal Walther von Brauchitsch, commander of German Army ground forces, had made a trip along the Polish-Soviet frontier, along with 30 senior officers, including Field Marshals W. List and W. Reichenau. His trip was followed by intensified engineer preparations of the region (communication, roads, airfields, and logistical facilities).[29]

These intelligence reports and those received from GRU agents abroad prompted a reaction by the Red Army intelligence leadership. On 20 March 1941, Major General F. I. Golikov, chief of the Red Army's Intelligence Directorate, submitted a detailed report to Stalin that quoted other intelligence information and assessed the nature and aim of the apparent German force regrouping. According to Zhukov, the report read:

Of the most probable military operations planned against the USSR, the following merits special attention:

Variant No. 3 according to information . . . relating to February 1941: "For the attack on the USSR," the message reads, "three army groups are being set up: the 1st group, under the command of General Field Marshal von Bock, will strike in the direction of Petrograd; the 2d group, under the command of General Field Marshal von Rundstedt, in the direction of Moscow; and the 3d group, under the command of General Field Marshal von Kleist, in the direction of Kiev. The tentative date for the beginning of the attack on the USSR is May 20." . . .

According to a message from our military attaché of March 14, a German major said: "We are changing our plan completely, We are going east, against the USSR. We will seize the USSR's grain, coal, and oil. Then we will be invincible and carry on with the war against England and America. . . ."

The beginning of military operations against the USSR may be expected between May 15 and June 15 1941.[30]

Despite this incredibly accurate assessment, in character with the times and Stalin's suspicious nature, Golikov added comments that negated the reports' worth and, in Zhukov's words, "misled Stalin." He concluded his report by stating:

1. On the basis of all of the aforesaid statements and possible variants of operations, this spring I consider that the most probable time operations will begin against the USSR is after the victory over England or the conclusion of an honourable peace treaty.

2. Rumors and documents to the effect that war against the USSR is inevitable this spring should be regarded as misinformation coming from the English or perhaps even the German intelligence service.[31]

Whether Golikov was sincere or simply pandering to Stalin's well-known preconceptions is unclear. What is clear, however, was the burgeoning number of intelligence reports that continued flowing in tallying up German force concentration in the east. In April those reports began to multiply.

On 1 May 1941, the Western Special Military District reported that the German troop buildup opposite its front had reached 28 to 29 infantry divisions, 7 to 8 panzer regiments, 3 to 4 motorized divisions, up to 3 cavalry divisions, and up to 5 combat engineer and 3 air regiments. Similar reports from the Kiev Special Military District prompted Golikov to compile a more comprehensive assessment, which in its entirety read:

SPECIAL REPORT NO. 660477, 5 MAY 1941

Concerning the grouping of German forces in the east and southeast on 5 May 1941:

The overall quantity of German forces against the USSR on 5 May has reached 103 to 107 divisions, including 6 divisions located in the Danzig and Poznan region. Of this number, there are 23 to 24 divisions in East Prussia, 29 divisions opposite the WSMD, 31 to 34 divisions opposite the KMD, 4 divisions in Pre-Carpathian Ukraine, and 10 to 11 divisions in Moldavia and Northern Dobrudga. (Some information received about the presence of 18 German divisions in Moldavia lacks required confirmation and must be verified.)

In the composition itself of forces concentrated against the USSR, pay attention to the reinforcement of tank forces from 9 divisions on 25 April to 12 divisions on 5 May; the motorized, including motorized cavalry, from 7 divisions on 25 April up to 8 divisions on 5 May; and mountain [divisions], from 2 divisions on 25 April to 5 divisions on 5 May.

All types of construction work is being carried out more intensively for preparing the theater of military operations. A second strategic railroad line is being constructed in the Protectorate of Slovakia and Rumania, especially leading from east to west.

Intensive construction is under way on warehouses for ammunition, fuel, and other sorts of military provisions.

The network of airfields and landing strips is being expanded.

In addition, along the entire border from the Baltic Sea to Hungary, the population is being evacuated from the frontier zone.

The Rumanian government gave out secret instructions concerning the evacuation of installations and valuables from Moldavia, and, in fact, that has already been carried out. The oil companies received orders about the construction of concrete walls around fuel reservoirs.

Training is being intensified for the air defense of cities, the construction of bomb shelters, and for experimental mobilization.

Intensified reconnaissance of our borders is being conducted by German officers.

There are reports from Vienna that officers are being called up who are familiar with Galicia and Poland.

Reserve groups of High Command officers are being created on Czech and Moldavian territory from forces freed from Yugoslavia at the same time that a grouping totaling 10 divisions, which was located there before the war with Yugoslavia, is being reestablished.

CONCLUSIONS

1. Over the course of two months, the quantity of German divisions in the frontier zone opposite the USSR has increased by 37 divisions (from 70 to 107). Of this number, tank divisions have increased from 6 to 12

divisions. With the Rumanian and Hungarian Armies, this constitutes around 130 divisions.

2. It is necessary to count on further reinforcement of German forces concentrated against the USSR at the expense of forces freed from Yugoslavia and their grouping in the Protectorate region [Slovakia] and on Rumanian territory.

3. The further reinforcement of German forces on Norwegian territory, the northern Norwegian grouping, is probable, which, in perspective, can be employed against the USSR across Finland and the sea.

4. At the present time, German forces available for action in the Near East amount to 40 divisions, of which 25 are in Greece and 15 are in Bulgaria. For the same aim, up to 2 parachute divisions are concentrated for probable use in Iraq.

> Chief of the Intelligence Directorate of
> the Red Army General Staff [Golikov][32]

The Golikov assessment no doubt prompted Chief of the General Staff Zhukov to advance his now notorious 15 May proposal for a preemptive attack on assembling German forces. Zhukov's recently unearthed proposal has fueled the fire of arguments that Stalin planned preemptive war against Hitler. The proposal, however, was probably only one of many made during 1941. It rests comfortably within the context of previous Soviet strategic planning, in particular, the experiences of the January war games, and it responds to the obligatory General Staff task of forecasting and contingency planning.

Entitled "A Report on the Plan of Strategic Deployment of the Armed Forces of the Soviet Union to the Chairman of the Council of People's Commissars on 15 May 1941" and cosigned by Timoshenko, Zhukov's report began by stating:

Considering that Germany, at this time, is mobilizing its forces and rear services, it has the capability of forestalling (preempting) our deployment and delivering a surprise blow. In order to avert such a situation, I consider it necessary on no account to give the initiative of action to the German command, to preempt the enemy deployment and to attack the German Army at the moment when it is in the process of deployment and has not yet succeeded in organizing the front and the cooperation of its forces.[33]

The report then postulated strategic objectives for the proposed operation, which was designed to defeat and destroy the estimated 100 German divisions assembling in eastern Poland.[34] Zhukov calculated that the Soviet attacking force of 152 divisions would be faced by roughly 100 German divisions.

Zhukov's report suggests the following conclusions. First, it confirms the accuracy of Golikov's 5 May intelligence assessment. Second, Soviet deployments on 15 May were insufficient to mount such an offensive. Between them, the Western and Southwestern Fronts counted about 102 divisions. Strategic second echelon and reserve forces were just then beginning their deployment forward and would arrive in the western border military districts in stages beween early June and July. By the time Zhukov's required correlation of forces would have been achieved (early July), German force strength would also have risen. It would have taken 60 days for Zhukov to achieve the necessary force correlation and by that time, given their successful prewar intelligence collection, the Germans would certainly have detected Soviet preparations and acted accordingly. Third, and most important, as documentary evidence clearly indicates, the Red Army was in no condition to launch such an ambitious offensive, and Stalin knew it. Finally, history itself has negated the importance of this sinister historical "What if?" The German 22 June attack rendered any postulated Soviet action utterly irrelevent.

Furthermore, despite the notoriety of the Zhukov proposal, there is no indication that Stalin ever saw it. Given Stalin's reaction to the existing intelligence information, it is doubtful whether he would have given it any thought if he had.

From mid-May through early June, German reconnaissance continued on both sides of the border, and much of the activity was detected by Soviet intelligence. On 2 June the Brest Border Guards Detachment reported German forces preparing pontoons, rafts, and boats along many sectors of the Western Bug River. The same day the Main Directorate of NKVD Border Guards Forces reported that "80–88 infantry divisions, 13–15 motorized divisions, 7 panzer divisions, and 65 artillery regiments and other units" had been concentrated near their western border (in April and May). Three days later the Directorate received information "that almost daily, 200 rail cars with ammunition, military supplies, and food were arriving in the Iassy, Botoshani, and other regions. All supplies were being concentrated along the railroad at temporary dumps under an awning." At the same time, the enemy was reinforcing artillery and machine guns along the entire frontier with "complete organization of telephone communications between the batteries and the command and observation posts."[35]

As the warm June days passed, the indications of an impending attack intensified. By 10 June German and Finnish forces along the Soviet–Finnish border were fully mobilized, and the civilian population had been moved into the rear area. On 17 June German vessels began leaving Soviet ports, and on the following day, reports began flooding in about the final movement of German forces into attack positions along the expanse of the frontier. Zhukov has recorded one version of Stalin's reaction to these reports:

On 13 June Timoshenko phoned Stalin in my presence and asked permission to alert the troops of the border military districts and to deploy
the first echelons according to the covering plans.

"We will think it over," Stalin replied.

The next day we visited Stalin and informed him of the general anxiety and the necessity for alerting the troops.

"You propose carrying out mobilization, alerting the troops, and moving them to the western borders? But that means war! Don't you understand that?"

Still, Stalin asked, "How many divisions do we have in the Baltic,
Western, Kiev, and Odessa Military Districts?"

We told him that by July 1 there would be 149 divisions and 1 separate rifle brigade in the 4 western military districts distributed as follows:

Baltic District—19 rifle, 4 tank, and 2 motorized divisions, and 1 separate brigade;

Western District—24 rifle, 12 tank, 6 motorized, and 2 cavalry divisions;

Kiev District—32 rifle, 16 tank, 8 motorized, and 3 cavalry divisions.

"Well, is that little?" said Stalin. "According to our information the
Germans do not have so many troops."

I informed him that according to intelligence, the German divisions
were manned and armed at wartime strength. The strength of a division
ranged from 14,000 to 16,000 men. Our divisions, even those of 8,000
men, were, in effect, only half as strong as the German divisions.

Stalin remarked, "You can't believe everything intelligence says. . . ."

During this conversation with Stalin, his secretary, A. N. Poskrebyshev,
came in and said N. S. Khrushchev was on the line from Kiev. We gath-
ered from his replies that the call concerned agriculture.

"Fine," said Stalin, and he smiled.

Evidently, Khrushchev had reported in glowing terms about the good
prospects for a bumper crop. . . .

We left the Kremlin with heavy hearts.[36]

Despite Stalin's optimism, the alarming reports from virtually every command level inexorably mounted. On 17 June, the 93d Border Guards Detachment reported that a man had shouted across the border, "The Germans
will be soon coming for you." On the same day, a deserter provided information that, at 0400 hours on the morning of 22 June, the Nazi troops would go
over to the offensive along the entire expanse of the Soviet–German border.[37]

A Baltic Special Military District top secret intelligence report of 18 June
from Colonel Safronov, chief of the Intelligence Section, "to army commanders and the commanders of corps, divisions, and brigades" reveals the extent

to which Soviet commands knew about German combat dispositions and offensive posture. In part, the lengthy report read:

On 17.6.41 opposite the Baltic Special Military District in the sector: from the left, Suwalki, Lusk, and Allenstein, and in the depth, Konigsberg, and Allenstein are identified: 2 army headquarters, 6 army corps headquarters, 12 infantry divisions, 5 motorized divisions, 1 armored division, 5 tank regiments, up to 9 separate tank battalions (totaling not less than a tank division), 6 to 7 cavalry regiments, 17 sapper battalions, and more than 500 aircraft.

The grouping and location of units (map 100,000):

In the Memel' region—headquarters, 291st Infantry Division, 401st and 610th Infantry Regiments, two battalions of the 337th Infantry Regiment, a training battalion of the 213th Infantry Regiment, 33d, 61st, and 63d Artillery Battalions, up to two tank battalions, a battalion of heavy machine guns, the 48th and 541st Sapper Battalions, 7th Naval Infantry Regiment, and an underwater swimming school;

In Mellneraggen (7804)—an antiaircraft artillery battalion;

In Bakhman (7610)—up to an artillery battalion; . . .

In Tilsit—headquarters, 7th Army Corps, 1st Infantry Division, 290th Infantry Division, 8th Motorized Division, 1st Cavalry Brigade; 43d, 45th, 216th, 213th, 94th, 501st, 502d, and 503d Infantry Regiments; headquarters, 469th Infantry Regiment, a battalion of a mountain rifle regiment, 202d, 204th, 227th, 206th and 209th Motorized Regiments, a battalion of the 272d Motorized Regiment, 1st and 2d Cavalry Regiments, 22d Heavy Artillery Regiment, 21st Light Artillery Regiment, 290th Artillery Regiment, 61st Artillery Regiment, an artillery battalion of 1st Cavalry Brigade, 212d Tank Battalion, 101st Tank Battalion, signal battalion, 7th Army Corps, 610th Separate Signal Battalion, 52d Pontoon-Bridge Battalion, and 552d and 557th Motorized Transport Battalions; . . .

In Gumbinnen—headquarters, 12th and 22d Army Corps (requires confirmation), 16th Infantry Division, a convoy division, 27th and 29th Infantry Regiments, 6th Mortar Regiment, 206th, 570th, 113th, and 32d Artillery Regiments, 4th Antitank Gun Regiment, 25th Tank Regiment, 206th Cavalry Regiment, 217th Reconnaissance Unit, 337th Guard [POW Security] Regiment, 46th, 10th, and 501st Infantry Battalions, 43d Reserve Battalion, and 16th Aviation Group (70 to 10 aircraft); . . .

In Konigsberg—headquarters, 18th Army, 8th Army Corps, 4th and 43d Infantry Divisions, 1st Air District, 210th, 217th, 110th, 21st, and 623d Infantry Regiments; 1st, 4th and 9th Artillery Regiments, 47th,

511th, and 536th Artillery Regiments (the last three require confirmation), and a tank regiment.[38]

If the detail found in the report is staggering, its accuracy is even more
so. Unfortunately, the report's accuracy and usefulness were also irrelevant.
On the basis of the summary, the Baltic Special Military District commander,
General Kuznetsov, ordered his 8th and 11th Armies' commanders to bring
the district's theater of military operations to combat readiness, but nothing
was done at higher command levels.

Lower-level commanders added their voices to the cries of warning. On
the evening of 18 June, Major General P. P. Bogaichuk, commander of the
125th Rifle Division, one of Kuznetsov's first echelon divisions, which was
stationed along the East Prussian border, sent more alarming intelligence
information to district headquarters:

> According to agent information and information from deserters, in recent
> days the Germans are concentrating up to seven divisions in the Tilsit region,
> not counting forces located in the Shilute region. Part of these forces have
> come up to the border. They have motor-mechanized divisions.
>
> On our side, measures of an antitank nature that guarantee against an
> attack by motor-mechanized units have not been undertaken, and it is
> sufficient for the Germans to launch one tank battalion for our defend-
> ing garrison to be taken unaware.
>
> Internal details and patrols can only warn units but cannot provide
> security.
>
> The sector of forward defensive positions lacks garrisons and cannot
> stop an attack by German forces, and border units cannot warn field forces
> in timely fashion.
>
> The sector of the division's forward defensive positions is located closer
> to the state border than to division units, and without preparatory mea-
> sures to gain time, they will be seized by the enemy before our forces can
> arrive there.[39]

The distraught division commander asked permission to increase his formations' combat readiness, but Kuznetsov could do no more than order
Bogaichuk "to complete work in the forward defensive positions," but "occupy
the forward defensive positions only in the event of enemy violation of the
border." While Kuznetsov required Bogaichuk to increase his division's combat readiness, he warned him "to pay special attention so that there will not
be a provocation and panic in our units. . . . Do all soundlessly, firmly, and
carefully. Each commander and political worker [must] soberly understand

the situation." Kuznetsov then ordered measures that were clearly beyond his instructions, ordering all divisions to:

4. Place minefields according to the army commander's plan where they must be placed according to the defense plan. Pay attention to full secrecy for the enemy and security for our units. Create obstacles and other antitank and anti-infantry impediments according to the army commander's plan and also the defense plan.

5. Army, corps, and division headquarters are at their CPs [command posts], which will provide antitank defense on the decision of the responsible commander.

6. Our forward deploying units must enter their covering region. Take into account the frequent instances of overflights by German aircraft.

7. Continue to replenish units urgently with ammunition and other types of supplies.

Urgently work on subunit cohesion on the march and in place. [40]

Shortly thereafter, the 8th Army commander, Major General P. P. Sobennikov, weighed in with his warnings to subordinate formations, writing in somewhat contradictory fashion: "(1) I once again affirm that units are not occupying combat installations in the sector of forward defensive positions. Units are holding behind the installations in combat readiness, while carrying out work to strengthen the defense. (2) Construct obstacles in such a manner that they are not noticeable from the border."[41]

Although the Baltic Special Military District took minimal precautionary actions, Admiral V. F. Tribets, commander of the Baltic Fleet, declared that "units of the Baltic Fleet have been brought to combat readiness as of 19.6.41 in accordance with Plan No. 2, the command post has been deployed, and patrol duty has been reinforced in the mouth of the Finnish Gulf and the Irben' Straits."[42]

Late on 20 June, the 11th Army chief of staff, Major General I. T. Shlemin, dispatched to district headquarters yet another unsettling intelligence report:

On the night of 20.6.41, a detained deserter from the 13th Company, 58th Infantry Regiment, 6th Infantry Division, revealed that his company was situated in Psherosl' (a company of 150mm heavy guns). In late May, 6th Infantry Division was transferred by train from Paris to the Suwalki region and unloaded 180 kilometers from Psherosl'.

In Suwalki, said the deserter, are a large number of forces and, at present, all forces are shifting from Suwalki to the border.

Infantry is located 5 kilometers from the border, artillery is in position, but the deserter did not see any large tank units.

The deserter revealed that the German troops did not dig foxholes near the border, having in mind transition to the offensive. In the deserter's words, military actions will begin in 8 to 10 days. For two months already, officers had persuaded [agitated] among the soldiers that the USSR was the main enemy of Germany. Fifty percent of the soldiers are against the war.[43]

The following day (21 June), at Kuznetsov's direction, the deputy chief of the district's air defense forces, Colonel Karlin, ordered, "Beginning from tonight until [receipt of] special instructions, observe light discipline in garrisons and places where forces are located. Provide transport with light-masking apparatuses. Organize firm control on the quality of light discipline. Pay special attention to the state of force camouflage and techniques for conducting aerial observation."[44]

While Kuznetsov was mandating these additional measures, further reports came in:

It was pointed out in the documents of the Baltic Special Military District on 21 June that "among the servicemen and civilian population of East Prussia, there is talk that the troops stationed in East Prussia have received orders to take up the initial position for the offensive." The documents also announced the completion of erection of pontoon bridges across the Neman River and that on 21 June, during exercises, a platoon commander, Lieutenant Schultz, explained to the soldiers that an offensive against the Soviet Union would commence at dawn on 22 June.[45]

The last Baltic Special Military District intelligence summary before the German assault, which was prepared at 2000 hours on 21 June, provided a detailed, stark, and frightening picture of German offensive posture. It stoically assessed German forces concentrated on the major axes into the district but made no overt judgment concerning German intent.[46] However, an accompanying operational summary to the chief of the General Staff, Zhukov, noted, "Units and formations of the Baltic Special Military District in their home stations are occupied with combat and political training, having moved separate units and subunits up to the state border for observation. At the same time, we are relocating separate formations to new regions."[47]

Shortly thereafter, Kuznetsov again exceeded his authority by ordering new preparatory measures. At 2135 hours his chief political officer, Riabchy, issued a directive: "Conditions require full combat readiness of units. With all means at your disposal, intensify explanations to personnel of the complicated international situation, which is fraught with all sorts of surprises. All actions of commanders, political workers, and Red Army soldiers must be oriented toward full accomplishment of missions and increasing the combat training of forces. Combat training must not cease for a moment."[48]

Less than an hour later, Major General Larionov, 8th Army chief of staff, issued the following instructions to army forces, "With the aim of rapidly bringing the theater of military operations to combat readiness, the 8th Army commander orders: 1. Quickly stockpile makeshift materials (rafts, barges, etc.) for constructing crossings over the Dubissa River).[49] Amid this increasingly frenetic message traffic, at 0345 hours on 22 June, a cryptic message that read, "From the German side there may be actions by small groups in violation of our border. Do not yield to provocations," arrived at district headquarters from 27th Army.[50]

Further south similar reports poured in. On 20 June the Western Special Military District received reports that "detachments of field troops with light machine guns have appeared on the borders." The same day, "near border markers Nos. 300 and 301, German soldiers drew 'USSR' on the sandy bank of the Western Bug [River] and then crossed out the letters, trampling them with their feet and threatening with their weapons our border troops serving there."[51]

## ON THE EVE OF BARBAROSSA

The General Staff did not remain totally oblivious to these warnings. Faced with Stalin's firm resistance to any measure that might seem provocative to the Germans, it undertook some actions on its own to improve readiness, but these paled in comparison to the threat. For example, on 19 June Zhukov and his staff associates prevailed on Timoshenko to issue an order requiring that airfields be camouflaged more thoroughly. These measures, however, were to be completed by 1 to 15 July.[52]

By late evening on 21 June, even the calm Zhukov was agitated over the intelligence information, and he pressed the issue with Stalin:

> On 21 June, in the evening, Lieutenant General Purkaev, Chief of Staff of the Kiev Military District, telephoned to inform me that a German sergeant-major had come to our frontier guards and said that German troops were moving to jumping-off areas and that the attack would begin in the morning of 22 June.
>
> I at once informed the Defense Commissar and Stalin of what Lieutenant General Purkaev had reported. Stalin said come to the Kremlin with the People's Commissar.
>
> Taking with me a draft of the directive for the troops, I went to the Kremlin, along with the Commissar and Lieutenant General Vatutin. On

the way we agreed that, at all costs, we must get permission to alert the troops.

Stalin was alone when he received us. He was plainly worried. "The German generals may have sent this turncoat to provoke a conflict," he said.

"No," Timoshenko replied, "We think he is telling the truth."

At that moment members of the Politburo came in.

"What are we to do?" Stalin replied.

No one answered.

"A directive must immediately be given to alert all troops in the border districts," Timoshenko said.

"Read it!" Stalin replied.

I read the draft directive. Stalin said: "It's too early to issue such a directive—perhaps the question can be settled peacefully. We must give a short directive stating that an attack may begin with provocative actions by the German forces. The troops of the border districts must not fall for any provocation and avoid complications."

Vatutin and I went into the next room and quickly drew up a draft of the directive to be sent by the People's Commissar.

Vatutin then returned to the office and asked for permission to read the directive.

Stalin listened to it and then read it over again and finally gave it to the People's Commissar to sign.[53]

[The directive read:]

ORDER OF THE PEOPLE'S COMMISSAR OF DEFENSE OF THE USSR NO. 1

To the Military Councils of the Leningrad, Baltic Special, Western Special, Kiev Special, and Odessa Military Districts, 22 June 1941; copy to the People's Commissar of the Navy:

1. During 22–23.6.41 a sudden German attack is possible on the fronts of the Leningrad, Baltic Special, Western Special, Kiev Special, and Odessa Military Districts. The German attack may begin with provocative actions.

2. The task of our forces is not to be incited by any provocative action that may cause serious complications. At the same time, the forces of the Leningrad, Baltic, Western, Kiev, and Odessa Military Districts are to be in full combat readiness to meet a possible strike by the Germans or their allies.

3. I order:

    a. During the early hours of 22.6.41, the firing posts in fortified areas on the state border are to be secretly manned;

b. Before dawn on 22.6.41 all aircraft, including army aviation, are to be dispersed among field airdromes and carefully camouflaged;

c. All units are to be placed on alert. Forces are to be kept dispersed and camouflaged;

d. Air defense is to be alerted without additional involvement of unit reservists. All preparations are to be made for blacking out cities and other targets;

e. No other measures are to be taken without further specific orders.

Timoshenko, Zhukov[54]

Vatutin took the directive to the General Staff, which then transmitted it to the military districts. Encipherment and transmission was completed at 0030 on the morning of 22 June 1941. The Western Special Military District received the directive at 0045 hours and sent it down to subordinate headquarters between 0225 and 0235 hours.[55] Deciphering the message accounted for the lapsed time. The following entry by the deputy chief of staff of the Western Front, Lieutenant General Malandin, in the combat journal of the Western Front for 22 June 1941 explains the sequence of events from the receipt of the message until the outbreak of hostilities:

Around 0100 in the night, a cipher communication was received from Moscow with an order about the rapid bringing of forces to combat readiness in the event of an expected attack by Germany in the morning.

At roughly 0200–0230 hours, an analogous order was prepared in cipher: to armies and FR [fortified region] units, ordering them to occupy quickly the fortified regions. Upon the signal "Storm," a "Red packet" was brought into action, which contained the plan for covering the state borders.

As it turned out, the cipher communications of the district headquarters were received by the army headquarters too late. 3d and 4th Armies succeeded in decoding the order and giving some sort of instructions, but 10th Army deciphered the warning already after military action had begun. . . .

At 0400 22.6, reports began to come into district headquarters continuously, chiefly through the PVO [air defense] system about the bombing.

At 0400 22.6, German units commenced artillery fire on our forces located on the border. At 0500 [they] assumed the offensive along the entire front.

Two squadrons of German aircraft bombed the city of Grodno.

At 0400 the city of Brest was subjected to bombardment.

Our IA [fighter aviation] engaged in combat in the Grodno region.

0425—Lida was subjected to bombing by two groups of aircraft (first of two aircraft, and the second of three).

0430—the city of Volkovysk was bombed by one aircraft.

At 0430 wire communications between 3d, 10th, and 4th Armies was disrupted.

According to PVO reports:

At 0400–0430, the company PVO post at Bel'sk was destroyed, and they suffered casualties.

0400–0430—the airfield at Borisovshchina (Volkovysk city) was bombed.

0637—one DO-17 bombed Lida and dropped five bombs from a great height. The bombs fell on the city.

In Lida a passenger train was destroyed.[56]


## JUDGMENTS ON SOVIET INTELLIGENCE IN JUNE 1941

The vast quantity of recently released archival intelligence materials validates the efficiency of Soviet prewar intelligence collection. More important, it proves beyond question that Soviet political and military leaders, as well as many figures lower down the chain of command, were well aware of German offensive preparations. Intelligence provided an adequate picture of the scope of those preparations, as well as strong indicators of German offensive intent. It is uncertain, however, to what degree political and military figures digested and accepted that intelligence.

Key contemporary military figures have weighed into the debate. The then chief of the General Staff, Zhukov, was somewhat reluctant to criticize Stalin in his memoirs and took a share of the blame on his shoulders: "During the time the dangerous military situation was ripening, we army leaders should probably have done more to convince Stalin that war with Germany was inevitable in the very near future and that the urgent measures provided for in the operational and mobilization plans should be implemented in all haste."[57] Zhukov did note the pandering to Stalin by his intelligence chief Golikov in the notable March report to Stalin by stating, "Unfortunately, even the reports we had were not always correctly interpreted, so as to provide the top leadership with a reliable and definite orientation."[58]

Vasilevsky commented more extensively on the failures of June 1941. He later noted, "The political and state leaders in the country saw war coming and exerted maximum efforts to delay the Soviet Union's entry into it." Vasilevsky concluded that, in trying to deter the outbreak of war, Stalin "overestimated the possibilities of diplomacy in resolving the issue." In essence, when faced with a decision of acting or not acting, "Stalin was unable to make that decision at the right time, and that remains his most serious political mistake."[59]

Vasilevsky also criticized the high-level intelligence assessments and national level assessments, which he claimed were often not coordinated with those of their military counterparts:

> What caused this experienced and far-sighted statesman to make such a gross error? Above all it was because Soviet intelligence agencies . . . failed to evaluate fully and objectively the information they were receiving on the war preparations of Nazi Germany and report it frankly to Stalin. . . . The isolation of the intelligence agency from the General Staff apparently played a part here. The head of intelligence, being also the deputy defense commissar, preferred to make his reports directly to Stalin without conferring with the chief of the General Staff. If Zhukov had been conversant with all the vital intelligence information . . . I am sure he could have made more precise conclusions from it and put them to Stalin in a more authoritative way.[60]

In this judgment, Vasilevsky echoes Timoshenko's criticism of Soviet intelligence when he took over as commissar of defense in May 1940:

> The organization of intelligence is one of the weakest sectors in the work of the Commissariat of Defense. There is no organization of intelligence and systematic receipt of information about foreign armies.
>
> The work of the Intelligence Directorate is not connected with the work of the General Staff. The Commissariat of Defense does not have a figure who provides the Red Army with information about the organization, condition, weaponry, and deployment readiness of foreign armies. At the moment of "reception," the Commissariat of Defense does not have at its disposal such intelligence information. The theater of military operations and its preparation are not studied.[61]

This disconnect between intelligence collection organs available to political authorities and those serving the Commissariat of Defense and the General Staff was a natural by-product of the period of the purges. During the purges the intelligence services, in particular the NKVD, accused the Red Army's leadership of treason for conspiring with foreign intelligence services. Thereafter, Stalin kept close control over intelligence collection, and military intelligence (the GRU) worked under close NKVD control. Therefore, the military had access to only that information available through field military channels (and probably not GRU information).

As Timoshenko pointed out, there were also glaring systemic problems in intelligence collection that endured after 1940 and impeded collection, despite the flood of reports cited above. Air surveillance, which in theory was considered the most important means for intelligence collection, was underdeveloped. In June 1941 the Red Army contained 10 reconnaissance aviation regiments and 2 separate squadrons totaling 387 aircraft, which comprised only 1 percent of the Red Army aircraft park.[62] Air crews were poorly trained and had only five hours of flying time. Accelerated training programs after 1 May did little to correct the problem and were irrelevant in light of political prohibitions on air activity associated with Stalin's fear of producing provocations.

Special intelligence gathering, which included all force reconnaissance measures, was responsible for determining the composition and disposition of enemy forces. However, "coordination of efforts in the organized conduct of *front-* and army-scale intelligence was not envisioned. The absence of a single organ capable of providing organized conduct of *front* intelligence gathering did not permit full subordination of the capabilities of special intelligence gathering in the interests of the concept of the offensive operation."[63] Here, too, organizations were poorly organized and equipped, and personnel manning them were poorly trained.

Despite these structural problems in intelligence collection and processing, the factual information generated by Soviet intelligence organs in 1941 provided a sufficient basis for accurately judging German offensive capabilities and hostile intent. Rather than citing "objective" reasons for the obvious Soviet intelligence failure, one must consider "subjective" reasons. Chief among these was Stalin's attitude and psychology, his domination and intimidation of all other High Command personalities and organs, and the nature of the Soviet system he embodied.

Key figures, such as Zhukov and Vasilevsky, who attempted to fathom Stalin's reasoning in those tense days before 22 June, attribute his inaction to political considerations, his overestimation of the power of diplomacy, his indecision, and his paranoia over the perceived role of disinformation. More recent critics have expanded this assessment to encompass the individual psychological dimension. As Stalin's biographer, D. A. Volkogonov, has noted:

It is perhaps easier to understand the drama of those last hours if we recall that an important feature of Stalin's psychological makeup was that of great cautiousness. Naturally in ordinary everyday affairs the question of audacity did not arise, but in major affairs he was extremely circumspect. . . .

His hyper-cautiousness in dealing with Hitler, however, was counterproductive, for Hitler outwitted him. Stalin's behavior was dictated not only by a realization of the consequences of a "premature war" but also by a deep inner insecurity. The USSR faced the capitalist world alone. Any false step could lead to irreparable results. Berlin took note of Stalin's obsessive avoidance of "provocations" and concluded that the USSR was weak. When Stalin ordered both the troops in the western sector and border units not to use weapons against German planes that violated the border, the Germans at once deduced that caution had become indecision.[64]

Among the many possible explanations for Stalin's behavior, it is reasonable to argue that Stalin understood the full range of intelligence indicators and the warnings of impending war and accepted what was about to occur, but in line with existing assumptions about how war would occur, he was unaware of the threat's acuteness and the scale of the impending German attack. This would explain the extensive partial Soviet mobilization and the prohibition on similar measures in the forward area. Another possible explanation is that Stalin well understood that war was inevitable but felt that it could be avoided until 1942, when the military reform program was to be complete. Active German deception, subsequent German spring operations in the Balkans, and the delay of Barbarossa until late June could have fostered this misperception. Although intensified indicators in June of impending action should have disabused Stalin of this misperception, once seized by procrastination, it would have been difficult for Stalin to alter his misperception.

Finally, there is Stalin's psychological profile, so lucidly described by Volkogonov. There is ample evidence from Stalin's earlier behavior (in particular, his institution of a "permanent" purge mentality) of his acute paranoia. This, juxtaposed against the common attribute of any tyrant's belief in his own infallibility, created a deadly combination of paranoia and blindness that gave rise to his seemingly "irrational" behavior in 1941. Far more important, Stalin personified the system he had created. His weaknesses and failures were inherently the Communist Party's weaknesses and failures. In turn, the Party embodied the nation and all of its institutions. When one failed, all failed. In this sense, Stalin's failure to heed intelligence warnings about impending war and the Red Army's unpreparedness for war in June 1941 were the fault of both the Party and the leader.

# Conclusions

Since the mid-1930s, the Soviet government had been keenly aware of the deteriorating security situation in Europe and Asia and the possibility of general war. Experience clearly indicated that if war broke out, given the ultimate political goals of the world's principal predatory powers, Nazi Germany and militaristic Japan, the Soviet state could well become a prime target. History, in the form of the Russian Civil War and Allied intervention, and ideological hatred manifested by the attitudes of Western nations to the new Bolshevik Soviet state during the time of its formation and by fascist states in the 1930s, only reinforced Soviet fears. In short, the paranoia of the Soviet regime was, to a large degree, understandable.

Their growing awareness of looming external threats and genuine belief in their own historical mission impelled the Soviets to increase their armed forces' size and attempt to improve its combat readiness. After 1935, the growth in Soviet military power was real, and the aims of their extensive rearmament program were unmistakable. The Soviet Union sought to become the leading military power in Europe, if not the world. Although the ultimate intent of Soviet military reform and rearmament programs can be debated, it is clear that military power, once created, tends to be employed. As if to underscore that historical principle, justifiably or not, the Soviet Union employed their military power in Poland and against Japan in 1939, against Finland the same year, against Rumania in 1940, and against the Baltic states shortly thereafter.

The fact that internal political developments within the Soviet Union, particularly the military purges, adversely affected the military expansion and reform programs and that Soviet foreign military ventures often ended with embarrassing near defeats altered neither the reality of Soviet military expansion nor the foreign perception, prevalent in some quarters, that the Soviet Union was becoming a global military menace. Moreover, Soviet military failures, coupled with dizzying German military successes, further fueled Soviet paranoia and the ongoing rearmament program.

The expansion of the Soviet armed forces accelerated in 1939 and 1940 and became positively frenetic in 1941. Soviet military writings of that time and archival materials make it clear, however, that by this time fear rather than hostile intent was the driving force. Soviet military assessments that

258

appeared in open and closed military journals, in particular, *Voennaia mysl'* (Military thought) and *Voenno-istoricheskii zhurnal* (Military-historical journal) were especially candid.[1] They demonstrated a clear Soviet appreciation of the superb German military performance, an acute understanding of the growing German military threat, and an unmistakable realization that the Soviet military in no way matched German military standards in terms of efficiency or effectiveness. Given this realization, it is no coincidence that many of the articles that appeared in these journals during 1940 and 1941 dealt with clearly defensive themes. In short, Soviet military theorists understood what could happen to the Soviet military and the Soviet state should war with Nazi Germany break out. Politicians, including Stalin, must have known as well. This understanding provided necessary context for all that occurred diplomatically and militarily in 1940 and 1941. At the least, it explains the magnitude of the ongoing Soviet military reform programs and the haste with which they were implemented. Unfortunately for the Soviet Union, this understanding of current threats and the wholesale rearmament program that followed did not adequately prepare the Soviet military for war.

By June 1941, according to every measurement, the Red Army was the largest and most complex fighting force in the world. Over 5 million men were under arms and more were mobilizing, it had more armies, corps, and divisions than all of its prospective opponents combined, its aircraft, tank, and artillery park was immense, it had the world's largest mechanized, cavalry, and airborne force, and although underestimated abroad, its mobilization potential was equally impressive. Moreover, ostensibly this entire force was undergoing thorough reform to improve its combat effectiveness. Outside observers such as Germany could scarcely ignore the ultimate consequences should Red Army reforms succeed.

However, the Soviet political and military leadership, as well as many perceptive military leaders abroad (in particular Germans), understood that the Soviet military colossus was severely flawed. The principal flaw was the nature of the Soviet Union itself. Its vast geographical expanse, its massive but diverse population, its underdeveloped economic and communications infrastructure, and its lagging technological base plagued Soviet political and military planners. In short, to some extent the Soviet Union's vast "peasant rear" negated the ruthless political efficiency of the Soviet state, and in the short term, crippled the state's ability to counter lightning war.

These realities became abundantly clear to both the Soviet leadership and their potential opponents during the wars of the late 1930s. The Soviets themselves recoiled from the over 250,000 military casualties they had suffered in Finland the year before.[2] They lamented the dismal performance of Soviet forces as they marched into eastern Poland in 1939. They understood the flaws that even the successful operation against the Japanese at Khalkhin-Gol had revealed. They knew the condition of their field forces and the state of their strategic reserves, the turbulence of command personnel, and the shortages of fully trained personnel, weaponry, communications equipment, vehicles, and logistical support. The haste with which they embarked on military reform underscored their realization that the Red Army was not ready for war. They also knew that the timetable for ongoing reform would not produce a combat-capable Red Army before summer 1942. Above all, they understood and feared the combat capabilities of the German Army and the political forces that drove the Germans inexorably toward further conquest. It was clear that sooner or later the Germans would move east. This understanding provided clear context for the seemingly irrational Soviet diplomatic and military activity from 1939 through summer 1941. It also explained the seemingly irrational response by Stalin and the Soviet political and military leadership to the clear indicators provided by intelligence in spring 1941 that war was imminent.

In short, the Soviet political and military leadership judged that the Red Army was not ready for war in June 1941 and acted accordingly. As subsequent events indicated, that judgment was correct. By 1 September 1941, after less than three months of war, the Red Army had lost over 2.8 million men, fully half of the Soviet Union's June 1941 peacetime army. By years' end, war had consumed almost 4.5 million men, nearly the entire strength of the 22 June 1941 Red Army.[3] This grizzly toll underscored the hard reality that the Red Army was woefully unprepared for war in 1941. In the end, the Soviet mobilization system, the Red Army's ability to educate itself during wartime, and the seemingly unlimited capacity of the Soviet soldier and nation to endure suffering saved the Soviet state and granted it final victory.

# Red Army Order of Battle, 22 June to 1 August 1941

| | Operating Armies | Stavka Reserves | Military Districts |
|---|---|---|---|
| June 1941 | Northern Front | | Moscow MD |
| | 7 Army | | 41 RC |
| | 54 RD | | 118 RD |
| | 71 RD | | 235 RD |
| | 168 RD | | |
| | 237 RD | | Orel MD |
| | 14 Army | | 30 RC |
| | 42 RC | | 19 RD |
| | 104 RD | | 149 RD |
| | 122 RD | | 217 RD |
| | 14 RD | | 33 RC |
| | 52 RD | | 89 RD |
| | 1 TD | | 120 RD |
| | 23 Army | | 145 RD |
| | 19 RC | | 222 RD |
| | 115 RD | | 23 MC |
| | 142 RD | | 48 TD |
| | 50 RC | | 51 TD |
| | 43 RD | | 220 MD |
| | 70 RD | | |
| | 123 RD | | Khar'kov MD |
| | 10 MC | | 2 AbnC |
| | 21 TD | | 2 AbnB |
| | 24 TD | | 3 AbnB |
| | 198 MD | | 4 AbnB |
| | | | 214 RD |
| | Front | | 18 ARMY (headquarters) |
| | 1 MC | | |
| | 3 TD | | |
| | 163 MD | | |
| | 177 RD | | Northern |
| | 191 RD | | Caucasus MD |
| | 8 RB | | 64 RC |
| | | | 165 RD |
| | Northwestern Front | | 175 RD |
| | 8 Army | | 28 MtnRD |
| | 10 RC | | 157 RD |
| | 10 RD | | |
| | 48 RD | | Odessa MD |
| | 90 RD | | 7 RC |

Note: For abbreviations, consult List of Abbreviations, p. xv.

| Operating Armies | Stavka Reserves | Military Districts |
| --- | --- | --- |
| 11 RC | | 116 RD |
| 11 RD | | 196 RD |
| 125 RD | | 206 RD |
| 12 MC | | 9 RC |
| 23 TD | | 106 RD |
| 28 TD | | 156 RD |
| 202 MD | | 32 CD |
| 11 Army | | 147 RD |
| 16 RC | | 3 AbnC |
| 5 RD | | 5 AbnB |
| 33 RD | | 6 AbnB |
| 188 RD | | 212 AbnB |
| 29 RC | | |
| 179 RD | | Trans-Caucasus MD |
| 181 RD | | 3 RC |
| 23 RD | | 4 RD |
| 126 RD | | 20 MtnRD |
| 128 RD | | 47 MtnRD |
| 3 MC | | 23 RC |
| 2 TD | | 136 RD |
| 5 TD | | 138 MtnRD |
| 84 MD | | 40 RC |
| 27 Army | | 9 MtnRD |
| 22 RC | | 31 RD |
| 180 RD | | 63 MtnRD |
| 183 RD | | 76 MtnRD |
| 24 RC | | 77 MtnRD |
| 181 RD | | 17 MtnCD |
| 183 RD | | 24 CD |
| 16 RD | | 28 MC |
| 67 RD | 24 Army | 6 TD |
| 3 RB | 52 RC | 54 TD |
| Front | 91 RD | 236 MD |
| 65 RC (Headquarters) | 119 RD | |
| 5 AbnC | 166 RD | |
| 9 AbnB | 53 RC | Central Asian MD |
| 10 AbnB | 107 RD | 58 RC |
| 201 AbnB | 133 RD | 68 RD |
| | 178 RD | 83 RD |
| Western Front | | 194 RD |
| 3 Army | 22 Army | 238 RD |
| 4 RC | 51 RC | 27 MC |
| 27 RD | 98 RD | 9 TD |
| 56 RD | 112 RD | 53 TD |
| 85 RD | 153 RD | 221 MD |
| 11 MC | 62 RC | 4 CC |
| 29 TD | 170 RD | 18 MtnCD |
| 33 TD | 174 RD | 20 MtnCD |
| 204 MD | 186 RD | 21 MtnCD |
| 4 Army | 21 Army | |
| 28 RC | 63 RC | Arkhangel'sk MD |
| 6 RD | 53 RD | 88 RD |
| 49 RD | 148 RD | 111 RD |

| Operating Armies | Stavka Reserves | Military Districts |
|---|---|---|
| 42 RD | 167 RD | |
| 75 RD | 66 RC | Trans-Baikal MD |
| 14 MC | 61 RD | 17 Army |
| 22 TD | 117 RD | 36 MRD |
| 30 TD | 154 RD | 57 MRD |
| 205 MD | 25 MC | 57 TD |
| 10 Army | 50 TD | 61 TD |
| 1 RC | 55 TD | 82 MD |
| 2 RD | 219 MD | 12 RC |
| 8 RD | 20 Army | 65 RD |
| 5 RC | 61 RC | 94 RD |
| 13 RD | 110 RD | 93 RD |
| 85 RD | 144 RD | 114 RD |
| 113 RD | 172 RD | |
| 6 MC | 69 RC | Far Eastern Front |
| 4 TD | 73 RD | 1 Army |
| 7 TD | 229 RD | 26 RC |
| 29 MD | 233 RD | 21 RD |
| 13 MC | 18 RD | 22 RD |
| 25 TD | 7 MC | 26 RD |
| 31 TD | 14 TD | 59 RC |
| 208 MD | 18 TD | 39 RD |
| 6 CC | 1 MD | 59 RD |
| 6 CD | | 1 RB |
| 36 CD | 20 RC | 4 RB |
| 155 RD | 137 RD | 5 RB |
| Front | 160 RD | 8 CD |
| 2 RC | 45 RC | 30 MC |
| 100 RD | 187 RD | 58 TD |
| 161 RD | 227 RD | 60 TD |
| 21 RC | 232 RD | 239 MD |
| 17 RD | 67 RC | 2 Army |
| 24 RD | 102 RD | 3 RD |
| 37 RD | 132 RD | 12 RD |
| 44 RC | 151 RD | 59 TD |
| 64 RD | 21 MC | 69 MD |
| 108 RD | 42 TD | 15 Army |
| 47 RC | 46 TD | 18 RC |
| 55 RD | 185 MD | 34 RD |
| 121 RD | | 202 AbnB |
| 143 RD | | 25 Army |
| 50 RD | | 39 RC |
| 4 AbnC | | 32 RD |
| 7 AbnB | | 40 RD |
| 8 AbnB | | 92 RD |
| 214 AbnB | | 105 RD |
| 17 MC | | Front |
| 27 TD | | Sp.RC |
| 36 TD | | 79 RD |
| 209 MD | | 101 MtnRD |
| 20 MC | | 35 RD |
| 26 TD | | 66 RD |

| Operating Armies | Stavka Reserves | Military Districts |
|---|---|---|
| 38 TD | | 78 RD |
| 210 MD | | |
| 13 Army (Headquarters) | | |
| Southwestern Front | | |
| 5 Army | 16 Army | |
| 15 RC | 32 RC | |
| 45 RD | 46 RD | |
| 62 RD | 152 RD | |
| 27 RC | 5 MC | |
| 87 RD | 13 TD | |
| 124 RD | 17 TD | |
| 135 RD | 109 MD | |
| 9 MC | 19 Army | |
| 20 TD | 25 RC | |
| 35 TD | 127 RD | |
| 131 MD | 134 RD | |
| 22 MC | 162 RD | |
| 19 TD | 34 RC | |
| 41 TD | 129 RD | |
| 215 MD | 158 RD | |
| 6 Army | 171 RD | |
| 6 RC | 38 RD | |
| 41 RD | 26 MC | |
| 97 RD | 52 TD | |
| 159 RD | 56 TD | |
| 37 RC | 103 MD | |
| 80 RD | | |
| 139 RD | | |
| 141 RD | | |
| 4 MC | | |
| 8 TD | | |
| 32 TD | | |
| 81 MD | | |
| 15 MC | | |
| 10 TD | | |
| 37 TD | | |
| 212 MD | | |
| 5 CC | | |
| 3 CD | | |
| 14 CD | | |
| 12 Army | | |
| 13 RC | | |
| 44 RD | | |
| 58 RD | | |
| 192 MtnRD | | |
| 17 RC | | |
| 60 RD | | |
| 96 MtnRD | | |
| 164 RD | | |
| 16 MC | | |
| 15 TD | | |
| 39 TD | | |
| 240 MD | | |

| Operating Armies | Stavka Reserves | Military Districts |
|---|---|---|
| 26 Army | | |
| 8 RC | | |
| 99 RD | | |
| 173 RD | | |
| 72 MtnRD | | |
| 8 MC | | |
| 12 TD | | |
| 34 TD | | |
| 7 MD | | |
| Front | | |
| 31 RC | | |
| 193 RD | | |
| 195 RD | | |
| 200 RD | | |
| 36 RC | | |
| 140 RD | | |
| 146 RD | | |
| 228 RD | | |
| 49 RC | | |
| 190 RD | | |
| 197 RD | | |
| 199 RD | | |
| 55 RC | | |
| 130 RD | | |
| 169 RD | | |
| 189 RD | | |
| 1 AbnC | | |
| 1 AbnB | | |
| 204 AbnB | | |
| 211 AbnB | | |
| 19 MC | | |
| 40 TD | | |
| 43 TD | | |
| 213 MD | | |
| 24 MC | | |
| 45 TD | | |
| 49 TD | | |
| 216 MD | | |
| 9 Separate Army | | |
| 14 RC | | |
| 25 RD | | |
| 51 RD | | |
| 35 RC | | |
| 95 RD | | |
| 176 RD | | |
| 48 RC | | |
| 30 MtnRD | | |
| 74 RD | | |
| 150 RD | | |
| 2 MC | | |
| 11 TD | | |
| 16 TD | | |

| | Operating Armies | Stavka Reserves | Military Districts |
|---|---|---|---|
| | 15 MD | | |
| | 18 MC | | |
| | 44 TD | | |
| | 47 TD | | |
| | 218 MD | | |
| | 2 CC | | |
| | 5 CD | | |
| | 9 CD | | |
| July 1941 | Northern Front | 248 RD (24 A) (NKVD) | Moscow |
| | 1 MilRD | 244 RD (31 A) (NKVD) | 242 RD (NKVD) (30 A) |
| | 2 MilRD | 246 RD (31 A) (NKVD) | 243 RD (NKVD) (29 A) |
| | 3 MilRD | 247 RD (31 A) (NKVD) | 245 RD (NKVD) (34 A) |
| | 4 MilRD | 249 RD (31 A) (NKVD) | 250 RD (NKVD) (30 A) |
| | | 272 RD (NF) | 251 RD (NKVD) (30 A) |
| | | | 252 RD (NKVD) (29 A) |
| | Southwestern Front | | 254 RD (NKVD) (11 A) |
| | 227 RD (SWDir) | | 256 RD (NKVD) (22 A) |
| | | | 257 RD (34 A) |
| | Southern Front | | 259 RD (34 A) |
| | 30 CD (18 A) | | 262 RD (34 A) |
| | | | 265 RD (NF) |
| | | | 268 RD (8 A) |
| | | | 1 MilRD (33 A) |
| | | | 2 MilRD (32 A) |
| | | | 5 MilRD (33 A) |
| | | | 6 MilRD (24 A) |
| | | | 7 MilRD (32 A) |
| | | | 8 MilRD (32 A) |
| | | | 9 MilRD (33 A) |
| | | | 13 MilRD (32 A) |
| | | | 17 MilRD (33 A) |
| | | | 18 MilRD (32 A) |
| | | | 21 MilRD (33 A) |
| | | | 45 CD |
| | | | 55 CD |
| | | | Orel |
| | | | 33 CD (disbanded in late July) |
| | | | Ural |
| | | | 311 RD |
| | | | 313 RD |
| | | | Siberian |
| | | | 49 CD |
| | | | Khar'kov |
| | | | 253 RD (NKVD) (SF) |
| | | | 264 RD (SWF) |
| | | | 48 CD (SF) |
| | | | Odessa |
| | | | 26 CD (6 A) |
| | | | 28 CD (6 A) |
| | | | North Caucasus |
| | | | 43 CD (Cav. Gp., CF) |
| | | | 47 CD (Cav. Gp., CF) |

| | Operating Armies | Stavka Reserves | Military Districts |
|---|---|---|---|
| | | | 50 CD (29 A) |
| | | | 52 CD (13 A) |
| | | | 53 CD (29 A) |
| | | | Central Asia |
| | | | 18 MtCD |
| | | | 20 MtCD |
| | | | 21 MtCD (13 A) |
| | | | 44 CD |
| | | | Leningrad |
| | | | 281 RD (NF) |
| | | | 25 CD (34 A) |
| August 1941 | Northern Front | | Moscow |
| | 268 RD (8 A) | | 211 RD (43 A) |
| | 265 RD (NF) | | 260 RD (50 A) |
| | 272 RD (NF) | | 266 RD (21 A) |
| | 281 RD (NF) | | 269 RD (3 A) |
| | | | 279 RD (50 A) |
| | 2 MilRD (Kingisepp Gp.) | | 280 RD (3 A) |
| | 3 MilRD (7 A) | | 282 RD (3 A) |
| | 4 MilRD (Kingisepp Gp.) | | 285 RD (52 A) |
| | 1 Gds MilRD (NF) | | 288 RD (52 A) |
| | 2 Gds MilRD (NF) | | 290 RD (50 A) |
| | 3 Gds MilRD (NF) | | 291 RD (23 A) |
| | 4 Gds MilRD (NF) | | 292 RD (52 A) |
| | | | 298 RD (13 A) |
| | Northwestern Front | | 305 RD (NWF) |
| | 254 RD (11 A) | | 307 RD (13 A) |
| | 1 MilRD (Novgorod Gp.) | | 27 CD |
| | 41 CD (NWF) | | 45 CD |
| | | | 55 CD |
| | Western Front | | |
| | 256 RD (22 A) | | |
| | 243 RD (29 A) | | Volga |
| | 252 RD (29 A) | | 46 CD |
| | 242 RD (30 A) | | |
| | 250 RD (30 A) | | Orel |
| | 251 RD (30 A) | | 258 RD (50 A) |
| | 50 CD (29 A) | | 267 RD (52 A) |
| | 53 CD (29 A) | | 271 RD (51 A) |
| | 101 TD (52 TD) (Iartsevo Gp.) | | 276 RD (51 A) |
| | 104 TD (9 TD) (28 A) | | 277 RD (21 A) |
| | 107 TD (51 TD) (Iartsevo Gp.) | | 278 RD (50 A) |
| | | | 283 RD (3 A) |
| | Reserve Front | | 287 RD (BF) |
| | 244 RD (31 A) | | 294 RD (RVGK) |
| | 245 RD (34 A) | | 299 RD (50 A) |
| | 246 RD (31 A) | | 303 RD (24 A) |
| | 247 RD (34 A) | | 309 RD (24 A) |
| | 248 RD (24 A) | | 4 CD |
| | 249 RD (31 A) | | 29 CD |
| | 257 RD (34 A) | | 31 CD |
| | 259 RD (34 A) | | |
| | 262 RD (34 A) | | |

| Operating Armies | Stavka Reserves | Military Districts |
|---|---|---|
| | | Ural |
| 1 MilRD (33 A) | | 311 RD (48 A) |
| 2 MilRD (32 A) | | 313 RD (RVGK) |
| 4 MilRD (24 A) | | |
| 5 MilRD (33 A) | | Siberian |
| 6 MilRD (24 A) | | 49 CD |
| 7 MilRD (32 A) | | |
| 8 MilRD (32 A) | | Khar'kov |
| 9 MilRD (33 A) | | 284 RD (37 A) |
| 13 MilRD (32 A) | | 293 RD (40 A) |
| 17 MilRD (33 A) | | 295 RD (40 A) |
| 18 MilRD (32 A) | | 297 RD (38 A) |
| 21 MilRD (33 A) | | 300 RD (38 A) |
| 25 CD (34 A) | | 34 CD |
| 54 CD (34 A) | | 37 CD |
| 102 TD (56 TD) (24 A) | | |
| 105 TD (53 TD) (43 A) | | North Caucasus |
| 108 TD (RF) | | 302 MtRD |
| 110 TD (31 A) | | 35 CD |
| 106 MD (24 A) | | 38 CD |
| | | 40 CD |
| | | 42 CD |
| Central Front | | 56 CD |
| 21 MtCD (13 A) | | |
| 32 CD (Cav.Gp., CF) | | Trans-Caucasus |
| 43 CD (Cav.Gp., CF) | | 236 RD (47 A) |
| 47 CD (Cav.Gp., CF) | | 317 RD (TCF) |
| 52 CD (13 A) | | |
| 109 TD (CF) | | Central Asia |
| | | 310 RD (NWF) |
| Southwestern Front | | 312 RD (52 A) |
| 227 RD (SWF) | | 314 RD (52 A) |
| 264 RD (SWF) | | 316 RD (52 A) |
| 289 RD (26 A) | | 18 CD |
| 301 RD (SWF) | | 20 CD |
| 304 RD (38 A) | | 39 MtCD |
| 19 CD (SWF) | | 44 MtCD |
| | | |
| Southern Front | | Arkhangel'sk |
| 223 RD (SF) | | 263 RD (KF) |
| 226 RD (6 A) | | 286 RD (RVGK) |
| 230 RD (6 A) | | |
| 253 RD (SF) | | Trans-Baikal |
| 255 RD (6 A) | | 51 CD |
| 261 RD (SF) | | |
| 270 RD (12 A) | | |
| 273 RD (6 A) | | |
| 274 RD (12 A) | | |
| 275 RD (6 A) | | |
| 296 RD (9 A) | | |
| 1 CD (Odessa) (Coastal A) | | |
| 26 CD (OMD) | | |
| 28 CD (OMD) | | |
| 30 CD (OMD) | | |
| 48 CD (SF) | | |

Summary of Red Army Order of Battle

| | Divisions | | | | | Rifle Brigades |
| | Rifle | Tank | Mechanized | Cavalry | Total | |
| --- | --- | --- | --- | --- | --- | --- |
| June 1941 | 198 | 61 | 31 | 13 | 303 | 5 |
| July 1941 | | | | | | |
|   Divisions added | 38° | | | 18 | | |
|   Total | 236 | 61 | 31 | 31 | 359 | 2 |
| 1 August 1941 | | | | | | |
|   Formations added | 99 | 8 | 1 | 36 | 144 | |
|   Strength | 288 | 51 | 18 | 44 | 401 | |
|   Formations lost, disbanded, or converted | | | | | 46°° | |

°15 militia.
°°41 rifle, tank, and mechanized divisions, including 6 mechanized divisions converted into rifle divisions, and 5 cavalry divisions.

*Sources*

*Boevoi sostav Sovetskoi armii, Chast' 1 (iun'–dekabr' 1941 goda)* [Combat composition of the Soviet Army, Part 1 (June–December 1941]. Prepared by the *Voenno-nauchnoe Upravlenie General'nogo Shtaba* [Military-scientific Directorate of the General Staff] (Moscow: VAGSh, 1963). Classified secret. Later declassified.

*Truppen-Ubersicht und Kriegsgliederungen Rote Armee, Stand August 1944* [Troop-List and Order of Battle of the Red Army in August 1944], FHO 1c [Foreign Armies East], Unterlagen Ost, Merkblatt geh. 11/6 Pruf-NR: 0157, in NAM (National Archives Microfilm), T-78, Roll 459. Used for verification purposes.

# Red Army 1941 Defense Plans

*People's Commissariat of Defense Planning Directive, 14 May 1941*

TOP SECRET: SPECIAL IMPORTANCE. Copy No. 2[1]
People's Commissar of
Defense of the USSR, 14 May 1941. No. 503920/ss/os

To the Commander of Baltic Special Military District Forces (Map 1: 1,000,000)

With the aim of covering the mobilization, concentration, and deployment of Baltic Special Military forces, by 30 May 1941, *you* personally, with the chief of staff and chief of the Operational Directorate of the district staff, will work out (a) a detailed plan for the defense of the state borders of the Latvian SSR from Palanga to excl. [exclusive of] Kapchiamiestis and a plan for the anti-amphibious defense of the Baltic Sea coast southward from the Matsalu Gulf and of the Islands of Dago and Ezel'; and b) a detailed plan for antiaircraft defense.

I. DEFENSIVE MISSIONS

1. Do not permit violation of district territory, by either an air or land enemy.

2. Firmly cover the mobilization, concentration, and deployment of district forces by obstinate defense of fortifications along the line of the frontier.

3. Together with the Baltic Fleet, do not permit the landing of enemy coastal assaults by defense of the coast and the islands of Dago and Ezel'.

4. Secure continuous operations of the railroads and the concentration of district forces by antiaircraft defense and air operations.

5. Determine in timely fashion the nature of the concentration and grouping of enemy forces by all types of district intelligence means.

6. Seize air superiority by active air operations and destroy and disrupt the concentration and deployment of enemy forces by powerful strikes against primary railroad junctions, bridges, staging yards, and force groupings.

7. Do not permit the dropping and landing on district territory of enemy air assaults and diversionary groups.

8. From the first day of mobilization, transfer to the commander of the Leningrad Military District [LMD] the defense of the Estonian coast from the Gulf of Narva to the Gulf of Matsalu and of Vormsi Island. Simultaneously, transfer the 65th Rifle Corps with the 16th and 11th Rifle Divisions and the 4th Aviation Division to the Leningrad Military District. The Leningrad Military District commander is responsible for working out a covering plan for that defensive sector.

II. ORGANIZE DEFENSE OF THE STATE BORDERS, WHILE GUIDED BY THE
FOLLOWING PRINCIPAL INSTRUCTIONS

1. Establish as the basis of the defense a stubborn defense of existing fortified regions and field fortifications along the line of the frontiers with the use of all forces and capabilities for its subsequent development.

The defense must be of an active nature. Quickly liquidate any enemy attempts to penetrate the defense by counterattacks with corps and Army reserves.

2. Devote special attention to antitank defense. In the event large enemy motor-mechanized units penetrate the defensive front, carry out the struggle with them and the liquidation of the penetration by means of the direct instructions of the district commander and, first and foremost, use antitank artillery brigades, mechanized corps, and aviation for that purpose. The mission of the antitank brigades is to engage enemy tanks from prepared positions with powerful artillery fire and, cooperating with aviation, hold them until the approach and counterattacks of our mechanized corps. The mission of the mechanized corps is to deploy under cover of the antitank brigades and, together with aviation, to inflict final defeat on enemy mechanized units by powerful flank and concentrated strikes and to liquidate the penetration.

3. Consider the following axes as especially crucial: (a) Memel', Tel'shiai; (b) Til'zit, Shiauliai; (c) Gumbinen, Kaunas; and (d) Suvalki, Olita.

4. In favorable conditions, all defending district and Army forces and reserves [must] be ready on the instructions of the High Command to inflict decisive blows.

III. TO THE RIGHT IS THE LENINGRAD MILITARY DISTRICT WITH THE PRINCIPAL
MISSION OF DEFENDING LENINGRAD

The reassigned 65th Rifle Corps is to organize a defense from the Gulf of Narva to the Gulf of Matsalu. The corps headquarters is at Tiuri.

The boundary with the LMD is Ostashkov (excl.), Vyru Island (excl.), Vil'iandi (excl.), and Ezel' and Dago Islands (incl.).

To the left is the Western Special Military District. From the third day of mobilization, its headquarters is at Baranovichi. Its right flank 3d Army is to organize a defense along the front Kapchiamiestis, Shchuchin. The headquarters of the Army is at Grodno.

The boundary with the WSMD is Polotsk (excl.), Oshmiany (excl.), Druskeniki (excl.), Marggrabova (excl.), Lettsen (excl.).

IV. HAVE [CREATE] THREE COVERING REGIONS TO FULFILL [YOUR] ASSIGNED
MISSIONS

COVERING REGION NO. 1—27th Army
Composition: 27th Army headquarters; 67th Rifle Division; 183d Rifle Division; 3d Separate Rifle Brigade; coastal defenses along the coast and Ezel' and Dago Islands; and border guards units.

The chief of the region is the 27th Army commander.

The Army headquarters is in Riga.

The left boundary is Mazheikiai, Palanga (excl.).

Missions:

a. Prevent landings by enemy amphibious assaults on the coast and on the islands by defense of the coast from the Gulf of Matsalu to Palanga (excl.) and Ezel' and Dago Islands. On Ezel' Island pay special attention to defense of the Gulf of Tagalakht.

b. Deny entry of the enemy fleet into the Gulf of Riga through the Irben', Soela-viain, and Sur-viain Straits and entry into the Gulf of Finland by the coastal defense of Ezel' and Dago Islands in cooperation with the Baltic Fleet, aviation, and the coastal defense of the Vindava coast and the Hanko peninsula.

c. Defense of the base in Liepaia.

d. Be prepared to provide assistance to personnel in the defensive garrison of Ezel' and Dago Islands.

Covering Region No. 2—8th Army

Composition: 8th Army headquarters; 10th and 11th Rifle Corps headquarters; 10th, 125th, 48th, and 90th Rifle Divisions; 12th Mechanized Corps headquarters; 25th and 28th Tank Divisions; 202d Motorized Division; 9th Antitank Brigade; garrisons of the Tel'shiai and Shiauliai Fortified Regions; 7th Mixed Aviation Division; and border units.

Have the 12th Mechanized Corps and 9th Antitank Brigade in the Uzhventis, Lyduvinai, and Kel'me region.

The chief of the region is the 8th Army commander. The Army headquarters is in Shiauliai.

The left boundary is Daugavpils, Panevezh (excl.), Seredzhius (excl.), Iurbarkas (Iurburg), and Insterburg.

Missions: Firmly cover the axes from Memel' to Kretinga and Tel'shiai and from Til'zit to Taurage and Shiauliai by defense of the field fortifications along the line of the state borders and the existing Tel'shiai and Shiauliai Fortified Regions.

Covering Region No. 3—11th Army

Composition: 11th Army headquarters; 16th and 24th Rifle Corps headquarters; 5th, 38th, 188th, 128th, 23d, 126th, 179th, and 184th Rifle Divisions; 3d Mechanized Corps headquarters; 2d and 5th Tank Divisions; 84th Motorized Division; 10th Antitank Artillery Brigade; 110th and 429th Howitzer Artillery Regiments (RGK); garrisons of the Kovno and Olita Fortified Regions; 8th Mixed Aviation Division; and border guards units.

Move the first mobilization echelon of the 126th Rifle Division to the Kazla Ruda Station region not later than the third day of mobilization and the 23d Rifle Division to the Kaunas region not later than the fourth day.

Have the 3d Mechanized Corps in the Kazla Ruda, Prenai, and Kaunas region.

Have the 29th Rifle Corps, consisting of the 179th and 184th Rifle Divisions, in the Vilnius and Orany regions.

The chief of the region is the 11th Army commander. The Army headquarters is in Kaunas.

Mission: Firmly cover the Kaunas and Olita axes by defense of field fortifications of the Kovno and Olita Fortified Regions along the front Iurburg (Iurbarkas) and Kapchiamiestis (excl.).

V. HAVE AT THE IMMEDIATE DISPOSAL OF THE DISTRICT COMMAND

22d Rifle Corps, consisting of the 180th and 182d Rifle Divisions and the 181st Rifle Division, in stationing points for their subsequent transfer in accordance with the deployment plan.

6th and 57th Mixed Aviation Divisions and the 5th Airborne Corps in the Daugavpils region.

VI. AVIATION MISSIONS

1. Destroy enemy aviation by consecutive strikes by combat aviation on established bases and airfields and also by combat operations in the air and gain air superiority from the initial days of the war.

2. Firmly protect the mobilization and concentration of district forces and the normal operation of railroads by fighter aviation in close cooperaion with all district air defense (PVO) systems and deny passage of enemy aviation across district territory into the depths of the country.

3. In cooperation with ground forces, destroy the advancing enemy and do not permit his large motor-mechanized force to penetrate the district defensive front.

4. Together with naval aviation and the Baltic Fleet, destroy the enemy naval fleet and transport in the Baltic Sea and prevent enemy amphibious landings of Ezel' and Dago Islands and on the coasts within the limits of the district.

5. Break up and disrupt the concentration of enemy forces by strikes on the rail centers of Konigsberg, Marienburg, Marienwerder, Deutsch Eylau, Allenstein, and Insterburg and on the railroad bridges across the Vistula River in the Danzig and Bydgosh sector, and also on enemy groupings.

6. Demolish the port of Memel'.

VII. IN ACCORDANCE WITH THE INSTRUCTIONS OF THE COMMANDER OF THE BALTIC SPECIAL MILITARY DISTRICT

1. Prepare rear [defensive] lines: (a) on the front Darbenai, Kulinai, Riga, Shilazh, Ulinas, Skaudvile, Raseiniai, and Seredzhius, Kazla Ruda, Pil'vishkiai, Moripole, Simnas, Lake Dysise, and Druskeniki (excl.); and (b) Barta River, Kalvariia Tel'shiai, Lussen, Dubisa, and Etlei along the eastern bank of the Neman River.

2. Provide for the delivery of counterattacks by mechanized corps and aviation in cooperation with reserve rifle forces and antitank brigades.

3. Reconnoiter and designate rear lines to the entire depth up to the old border with Latvia, Lithuania, and Poland within the limits of the Baltic Special Military District and cutoff positions along the Western Dvina River.

4. By 30 May 1941, accept the Sebezh Fortified Region from the Western Special Military District and work out a plan for bringing it to full combat readiness.

5. In the event of a forced withdrawal, work out a plan for the creation of antitank obstacles to the entire depth and a plan for mining bridges, railroad centers, and points of possible enemy concentration (forces, headquarters, hospitals, etc.).

6. In the plan for antiaircraft defense, provide for force air defense and territorial air defense in the Northwestern Air Defense (PVO) zone and, in particular, work out in detail:

    a. The organization of VNOS [air defense warning] service—rapid notification of aviation airfields, in the first place fighter, both from company and with line VNOS posts; and the notification of air defense points and objectives and command and control of brigade regions and zones.

    b. The use and actions of fighter aviation, having determined the regions for the destruction of enemy aviation for individual aviation units.

    c. The protection by antiaircraft artillery and fighter aviation of permanent air defense points and objectives, transshipment regions, and force concentration regions.

    d. Communications problems and the command and control of air defense means.

    7. Work out: the alert of forces and the allocation of detachments to support border guards forces; and a plan for the security and defense of important industrial enterprises, installations, and objectives.

    8. In the event of a forced withdrawal, work out a plan in accordance with special instructions for the evacuation of mills, factories, banks, and other economic enterprises, governmental installations, warehouses for military and state property, reservists, means of transport, and other.

VIII. INSTRUCTIONS REGARDING THE REAR

    Up to the 15th day of mobilization, the following expenditures are allowed:

    a. for ground covering forces: ammunition, 3 combat loads; fuel for combat vehicles, 5 refuelings; and transport, 8 refuelings;

    b. for the Air Force: fighters, 15 sorties; short-range bombers, 10 sorties; long-range bombers, 7 sorties; and reconnaissance, 10 sorties; and

    c. for all covering forces, 15 days of rations.

    Carry out the support of covering forces with all types of supplies and the repair and rehabilitation of vehicles at the expense of reserves and the district repair base.

    Execute the evacuation of ill and wounded personnel and horses within the limits of the district using, in the first place, the fixed network of clinics.

IX. GENERAL INSTRUCTIONS

    1. Permit the first overflight or crossing of the state border only with the special permission of the High Command.

    2. The covering plan must consist of the following documents:

    a. Notes on the planned actions of covering forces with an attached map of the decision and force grouping up to regiment and separate unit, inclusive.

    b. An order of battle list.

    c. A table of the arrival and concentration of covering units to the border.

    d. A plan for the employment of air forces with an attached map of the basing and operational use.

    e. An air defense plan with a map of the dispositions of VNOS and active PVO means.

    f. A plan for engineer support with calculations and a map.

    g.  A plan for the communications system with calculations and a map.

    h.  A plan for the organization of rear service and material support of ground and air forces with an attached map of the ground and aviation rear service support system.

    i.  A plan for medical and veterinary evacuation.

    j.  Instructions on alert notification of units and the allocation of support detachments to border guards units.

    k.  A list of objectives and structures protected by field forces and NKVD forces.

    l.  Implementing documents (directives, orders, and commands).

3.  The covering plan will be put into effect upon receipt of an enciphered telegram signed by me, a member of the Main Military Council, and the chief of the Red Army General Staff with the following contents: "Begin fulfilling the 1941 covering plan."

4.  Those permitted to work out the covering plan are:

    a.  In the district headquarters:

      In its entirety—the force commander, the member of the Military Council, the district chief of staff, and the chief of the district headquarter's operations section.

      In the Air Force portion of the plan—the commander of Baltic Special Military District air forces.

      In the rear service portion—the district assistant chief of staff for rear services.

      In the military reports portion—the chief of district military reports.

      In the communications portion—the chief of district communications.

      Other branch and service chiefs are permitted only to fulfill personal tasks in accordance with their speciality and without reporting the covering plan to them.

    b.  In Army headquarters: the Army commander, the member of the Army Military Council, the Army chief of staff, and the chief of the Army staff operations section.

5.  Prepare the covering plan in two copies; present one for approval through the chief of the General Staff and keep the second copy, sealed under the signature of the district Military Council, in the personal safe of the district chief of staff.

6.  Maintain the covering plans for each covering region, which have been prepared by the armies and approved by the district Military Council and sealed under the signature of the district Military Council, in the personal safe of the corresponding chief of the covering region.

7.  Secure implementing documents, which have been prepared for force formations, in packets sealed under the signature of the Army Military Council with the formation's mobilization plan.

8.  Reveal files and packets with covering [plan] documents upon receipt of written or telegraphic orders: in armies, from the district Military Council; and in formations, from the Army Military Council.

9.  All documents on the covering plan will be written in hand or typed on a typewriter personally by commanders and those permitted to work on it.

Enclosures: one copy of a map of Baltic Special Military District covering forces on a 1:1,000,000 scale map (only with copy No. 1).

USSR People's Commissar of Defense, Marshal of the Soviet Union S. Timoshenko
Chief of the Red Army General Staff, Army General G. Zhukov
Authenticated by: Deputy Chief of the Red Army General Staff Operational Group, Major General [A.] Vasilevsky

## Baltic Special Military District Covering Plan, 2 June 1941

TOP SECRET: SPECIAL IMPORTANCE. Copy No. 1[2]
'I Approve': People's Commissar of Defense of the USSR, Marshal of the Soviet Union S. Timoshenko, " " June 1941

Plan for Covering the Territory of the Baltic Special Military District During the Period of Mobilization, Concentration, and Deployment of District Forces (Map 1:500,000 scale)

I. CONSIDERATIONS ABOUT ENEMY CAPABILITIES

As a theater of military operations, the territory of East Prussia is well prepared for defensive and offensive operations. The presence of the Baltic Sea secures German conduct of combined operations of ground and naval forces and the landing of large-scale amphibious assaults.

The physical characteristics and size of East Prussia permits the large-scale employment all types of forces. With an overall capacity of up to 300 trains per day, of which up to 200 can be employed for operational deployments, by the twelfth day of mobilization the railroad net can already support the concentration of 40 reinforced infantry divisions, and the developed network of dirt roads and the presence of autobahns permits the transfer of motorized and mechanized forces, the quantity of which can be used against the Baltic Special Military District has been determined to be up to six tank and two to three motorized divisions. The enemy can also employ sea transport through the ports of Memel', Konigsberg, and others.

The airfield network in East Prussia (up to fifteen airfields and a large number of landing strips) permits the deployment of up to 20–24 aviation squadrons.

The most probable operational axes for the enemy will be (a) Til'zit, Shiauliai, and Riga (or Shiauliai and Daugavpils) with a secondary axis to Memel' and Tel'shiai or Memel' and Shiauliai for subsequent operations, or to Pskov in the Leningrad Military District rear, or joint operations with the Kaunas grouping; (b) Gumbinen, Kaunas, and Vilnius, with a subsequent attack on Minsk; (c) Suvalki, Alitus, and Lida (or Grodno) to influence the right wing and rear of the Western Front; and (d) a local attack from Suvalki through Kalvariia to Kaunas.

Probable regions for landing amphibious assaults are (a) the islands of Hiuma (Dago) and Saarema (Ezel'); and (b) the coastal sector from Cape Kolkasrag to Palanga at the points Ventpils, Pavilosta, and Liepaia.

One must count on operations by enemy naval forces to force the Irben' Straits to secure the Gulf of Riga and the Soela-viain and the Mukhu-viain Straits to secure Dago and Ezel' Islands.

II. COVERING MISSIONS

1. Do not permit violation of Baltic Special Military District territory by either enemy land or naval forces.

2. Repel the enemy offensive by stubborn defense along the line of the frontier in the positions of existing fortified regions, and protect mobilization, concentration, and deployment of district forces.

3. Prevent the landing of enemy amphibious assaults by defense of the coast and Dago and Ezel' Islands together with the Baltic Fleet, liquidate enemy air assaults by the actions of maneuver groups and aviation, and do not permit penetration by naval forces into the Irben' Straits and the mouth of the Finnish Gulf.

4. Protect the continuous operation of railroads, the concentration of forces, and the work of warehouses by antiaircraft defense and air operations.

5. Gain air superiority and destroy and retard concentration and deployment of enemy forces by strikes against railroad junctions, bridges, staging yards, and force groupings.

6. In cooperation with border guard forces, liquidate bandit and diversionary groups and prevent the dropping and landing of enemy air assault forces on district territory.

7. Organize the protection of important objectives and the restoration of destruction that may be caused by enemy aviation.

8. Determine in timely fashion by all types of reconnaissance the nature of concentration and the grouping of enemy forces, and, first and foremost, its motor-mechanized units and the axes of their attacks.

III. THE ORGANIZATION OF COVER

Subject to cover from intrusion from ground, naval, and air assault: (a) Dago, Ezel', and Mukhu Islands; (b) the Baltic coast from Cape Kolkasrag to Palanga; and (c) the ground border of the USSR from East Prussia and Suvalki *oblast'* from Palanga to Kapchiamistis.

Cover the most important objectives of the rail net, large population points, military warehouses, the most important river crossings, airfields, force unloading and concentration regions, command posts, and communications nodes by an air defense system and Air Force actions.

IV. THE ORDER FOR COVERING THE BORDER SECTOR (COVERING MAPS AND ORDERS OF BATTLE AT ENCLOSURE NOS. 1, 2, AND 3 [NOT INCLUDED])

Organize Army covering regions (RP) to cover the district border (coastal) sector.

COVERING REGION NO. 1—27th Army

Include in the region: Dago and Ezel' Islands, the coastal sector of the Gulf of Riga from the Gulf of Matsalulakht, the Soela-viain, Sur-viain, and Irben' Straits, the coastal sector of the Baltic Sea from Cape Kolkasrag to Palanga (excl.) in the boundaries: on the right, Vyru, Vil'iandi (excl.), Gulf of Matsalulakht, and the Khari-Kurk Straits; on the left, Ielgava (excl.), Mazheikiai, and Palanga (excl.); and to the rear, Lake Vyrts'iarv, Valga, Valmiera (excl.), Riga (excl.), and Ielgava.

The chief of RP 1 is the 27th Army commander. The Army headquarters is in Riga. Order of battle is in Enclosure No. 2.

Covering missions:

a. Prevent the landing of enemy amphibious and air assaults by defense of the coast from the Gulf of Matsalulakht to Palanga (excl.) and the Dago and Ezel' Islands.

b. In cooperation with the naval fleet and aviation prevent penetration of the enemy fleet into the Gulfs of Riga and Finland. To achieve this, prepare the fires of the 3d Separate Rifle Brigade and the 67th Rifle Division to reinforce the fire of Baltic Fleet naval batteries, which are defending the Irben', Soela-viain, and Sur-viain Straits and the entrance to the Gulf of Finland.

c. Defend the Libau naval base.

Participation of the Baltic Fleet in the defense of RP 1 has been determined by the plan of cooperation worked out by the 27th Army staff. Baltic Special Military District aviation will participate in repelling the enemy in accordance with the plan of the Air Force commander at the request of the 27th Army commander.

RP 1 is subdivided into three covering sectors (UP) and one observation sector (UN).

COVERING SECTOR 1. The sector chief is the 3d Separate Rifle Brigade commander. The headquarters is in Kuressare. The Dago, Ezel', and Mukhu Islands and the Khari-Kurk and Irben' Straits are being defended. The sector comprises the 3d Separate Rifle Brigade, "BOVRA" artillery, forces, and means, and the 10th Border Guards Detachment.

Sector missions:

a. Prevent enemy amphibious and air assaults on the islands.

b. Allocate not less than three artillery batteries to reinforce coastal naval batteries in the defense of the Irben' Straits and organize cooperation with Baltic Special Military District naval forces and aviation to repel enemy attempts to penetrate into the Gulf of Riga.

c. By coastal artillery fire, cooperate with Baltic Fleet operations and Leningrad Military District forces in prohibiting the forcing of the mouth of the Gulf of Finland.

COVERING SECTOR 2. The sector chief is the 114th Rifle Regiment commander. The headquarters is in Ventspils (Vindava). The sector's territory is the Baltic Sea coast from Cape Kolkasrag to the sea Gulf of Labrags. The boundaries are: to the left, Kuldiga and the Gulf of Labrags; to the rear, Val'demarpils and Renda. The sector comprises the 114th Rifle Regiment, the 1st Battalion, 242d Howitzer Artillery Regiment, and coastal defense units of the 12th Border Guards Detachment's 1st and 2d *Komendatura*.

Missions:

a. Prevent the landing of enemy amphibious assaults on the coast and, in the event of landings, destroy them; pay special attention of points favorable for landings—Mazirbe, Ovishi, and Ventspils.

b. Prevent enemy penetration into the Irben' Straits by coastal defense fire, reinforced by field artillery fire in cooperation with UP 1, the Baltic Fleet, and aviation.

c. Do not permit air assault landings, and pay special attention to the Kuldiga region.

COVERING SECTOR 3. The sector chief is the 67th Rifle Division commander. The sector headquarters is in Aizpute. The sector's territory is the Baltic Sea coast from the Gulf of Labrags to Palanga (excl.). The rear boundary is from Renda to Skrunda to Barstichiai. The sector consists of the 67th Rifle Division minus the 114th Rifle Regiment and the 1/242d Howitzer Artillery Regiment, the 12th Border Guards Detachment minus its 1st and 2d *Komendatura,* the coastal defense, and all forces and means of the Libau naval base.

Missions:

a. While defending the coast, pay particular attention to the repulsion of enemy assaults at points which are favorable for landings—Pavilosta and Liepaia.

b. Allocate one rifle battalion to defend the naval base in Liepaia (Libau).

c. Prepare maneuver of the 18th Railroad Battery and a battalion of field artillery to reinforce the fire of coastal batteries in the defense of the Irben' Straits.

d. Have a maneuver reserve of not less than two battalions along the Libava axis at the disposal of the chief of UP 3.

e. Conduct observation and reconnaissance of the coast with your forces and reconnaissance at sea, on the instructions of the chief of the Libau base.

OBSERVATION SECTOR 4. The coast of the Gulf of Riga from the Gulf of Matsalulakht to Cape Kolkasrag is the second defense line of UP 1, and it is observed by aviation, outposts of the 8th Border Guard's 5th *Komendatura,* and units and ships of the Baltic Fleet's base at the mouth of the Dvina River. In the event of the penetration of separate small diversionary groups or landings by enemy air assaults, destroy them by mobile maneuver groups, which are to be formed at the direction of 27th Army headquarters from personnel of the Riga Infantry School and units of the Riga city garrison.

COVERING REGION 2—8th Army

Defense of the state border along the front from Palanga to the Neman River. Boundaries: on the right, Ielgava, Mazheikiai (excl.), and Palanga; on the left, Dotnuva, Sredniki, and the Neman River to Iurburg and Insterburg; in the rear, Ielgava, Sheduva, and Dotnuva.

The chief of the RP is the 8th Army commander. The RP headquarters is in Bubiai (15 kilometers southwest of Shiauliai). Combat composition is in Enclosure No. 2.

Missions:

a. Firmly cover the Memel', Tel'shiai and Til'zit, Taurage, and Shiauliai axes by defensive field fortifications along the line of the state border and the existing Tel'shiai and Shiauliai Fortified Regions.

b. Prepare for a counterattack by 12th Mechanized Corps, 9th Antitank Artillery Brigade, and four rifle divisions along the axes: Shiauliai, Memel'; Shiauliai, Til'zit; and Shiauliai, Sredniki, Pil'vishkiai. Conduct the counterattack in cooperation with *front* aviation.

c. Set about preparing Army rear lines from the first days of war: Darbenai, Miniia River, Zharenai, Varniai, Krazhiai, Lidoviany, and Dubissa River; Barta River, Barstichiai, Tel'shiai, Shiauliai, Shushve River, and Nevezhis River.

In the first place, rapidly outfit operational antitank regions along these lines in accordance with the map at Enclosure No. 4; and to prepare the antitank regions and rear lines use construction battalions, drawn during the first days of the war from the sectors of newly constructed fortified regions.

RP 2 consists of two covering sectors.

COVERING SECTOR 1. The sector chief is the 10th Rifle Corps commander. The sector headquarters is in Varniai. The sector boundaries are: on the left, Krazhiai (excl.), Upinas (excl.), and Sartyniki; and to the rear, Barstichiai, Tverai, and Kalgipchenai.

The sector consists of the 10th Rifle Corps headquarters with subordinate units, the 10th and 90th Rifle Divisions, the 47th and 73d Corps Artillery Regiments, and the 115th Border Guards Detachment.

Covering missions:

a. Organize the sector's defense based upon the permanent fortifications of the Tel'shiai Fortified Region, having selected forward defensive positions in the sector and having adapted the fortified region for defense.

b. Develop obstacles in front of the forward edge and in the depth of the defense sector; have especially dense obstacles along the Kretinga, Endreiavas, Varniai, Vainutas, and Paiuris axes.

c. Erect a system of powerful obstacles in the Paiuris Antitank Region based on the calculation of solidly retaining that region, even if fully encircled; mass artillery fire, having created a group of five to six artillery battalions on the Paiuris, Vaipulas, and Sartyniki axis; organize flanking artillery fire on the approaches to Kretinga, Endreiavas, and Paiuris; and open fire from maximum range.

d. Have not less than a regiment in reserve in the Baisiai region. Mobilize one regiment of the 183d Rifle Division in good order in time for it to reach the Tel'shiai region by the end of M-2.

COVERING SECTOR 2. The sector chief is the 11th Rifle Corps commander. The covering UP headquarters is in Skaudvile. The rear boundary is Kaltinenai, Nemokchiai, Rossieny, and Blagoslovenstvo.

The sector consists of 11th Rifle Corps headquarters with subordinate corps units, the 125th and 48th Rifle Divisions, the 51st Corps Artillery Regiment, the 402d Howitzer Artillery Regiment, and the 1st and 2d *Komendatura* of the 106th Border Guards Detachment.

Missions:

a. Organize the defense of the sector based on the permanent fortifications of the Shiauliai Fortified Region and the forward defensive positions by forward units; prevent an enemy penetration on Shiauliai or along the Neman River to the east.

b. Finish outfitting and fortify a defensive belt in the border sector; especially firmly fortify and create a strong antitank defense along the Til'zit, Shiauliai road.

c. Mass artillery fire on the Taurage axis and unite command and control on the Paiuris, Saltyniki, and Taurage, Til'zit axes in the hands of the Army chief of artillery.

d. Have two rifle regiments in the corps commander's reserve on the Taurage axis.

Occupy positions in the entire Army sector from the first day. To do this, before the arrival of the 48th Rifle Division, occupy its sector with one regiment of the 202d Motorized Division, reinforced with tanks and artillery. Transfer the 48th Rifle Division to the border at the disposal of the 8th Army commander, for which the 414th and 445th Autotransport Battalions are attached to the Army.

Transfer the 402d Howitzer Artillery Regiment (*RGKA*) by rail. The unloading region is Vidukle. While it is fully assembling, it is envisioned to transfer the 47th and 73d Corps Artillery Regiments by rail from [their] camps. The unloading region of the 47th Corps Artillery Regiment is Tel'shiai and the 73d is Vidukle.

COVERING REGION 3—11th Army

Defense of the border from the Neman River to Kapchiamiestis. Boundaries are: on the right, Dotnuva (excl.), Sredniki, Neman River to Iurburg, and Insterburg (excl.); on the left, Oshmiany (excl.), Druskeniki (excl.), Troiburg, and Lettsen (excl.); in the rear, Iunava and Orany.

The chief of RP 3 is the 11th Army commander. The headquarters is in Kaunas. Missions:

a. Organize a defense of field fortifications along the line of the state border and the existing Kovno and Olita Fortified Regions and firmly cover the Gumbinen, Kaunas and Kaunas, Suvalki, and Alitus axes.

b. In the event of an incursion by a large enemy force, prepare a counterstroke with the forces of the 3d Mechanized Corps, the 10th Antitank Artillery Brigade, and four to five rifle divisions and aviation in the direction of Shiauliai, from Kaunas to Mariampol' and Simno, and to the south along the right bank of the Neman River to destroy the penetrating enemy and, in particular, his motor-mechanized formations.

Prepare a counterstroke by 3d Mechanized Corps, four to five rifle divisions, and the 10th Antitank Artillery Brigade from the Kazla Ruda forest region along the axis. . . .

c. From the first days of war continue the fortification of rear lines and antitank regions with construction battalions:

1. The northern, western, and southern edges of Kazla Ruda forest.
2. Prepare an especially firm and deep obstacle belt south of Kazla Ruda forest and Lake Zhuvinty.
3. Prepare for stubborn defense a bridgehead on the left bank of the Neman River along the line Sredniki, Viliuse, Iura Station, and Darsunishkis. To do so, quickly begin to erect permanent powerful fortifications in the Veivery and Girniki regions, while preparing antitank obstacles to the west of these points. Prepare crossings over the Neman River in the region of this bridgehead west and east of Kaunas.
4. Along the eastern bank of the Neman River along the front Sredniki, Merkine (see map at Enclosure No. 4).

Until the arrival of 29th Rifle Corps headquarters, RP 3 will consist of three covering sectors. When 29th Rifle Corps headquarters arrives in the Simno region, RPs 2 and 3 will be subordinate to it.

COVERING SECTOR 1. The sector chief is the 16th Rifle Corps commander. The headquarters is at Iura. The sector boundaries are: on the right, Bel'verzhishki, Mariampol', and Vizhainy; on the left, Blagoslovenstvo, Pil'vishkiai, and Mariampol'.

The sector consists of: 16th Rifle Corps headquarters with subordinate corps units; the 5th, 33d, and 188th Rifle Divisions; the 270th and 448th Corps Artillery Regiments and 40th Howitzer Artillery Regiments (RGK); and the 107th Border Guards Detachment's 3d and 4th Komendatura.

Missions:

a. Organize a defense along the front of the existing sector of the Kovno Fortified Region, having concentrated the main strength along the front Naumietis, Vyshtynets and while firmly holding on to the Shaki region.

b. Mass artillery fire in the direction of Shirvind and prepare concentrated fire of not fewer than 150 guns on the front Gudvaitshen, Pilliupenen and extensively exploit flanking approaches favorable for tanks.

c. Develop obstacles along the front Naumietis, Pilliupenen, while extensively exploiting swampy terrain.

d. Create a rear position along the front Pil'vishkiai, Vil'kovishkis, and Liudvinov, having envisioned maneuver of the antitank artillery brigade to that position.

e. Have a reserve of up to one regiment in every division: hold the 188th Rifle Division's reserve behind the left flank in order to be able to cooperate with UP 2.

COVERING SECTOR 2. The sector chief is the 126th Rifle Division commander. The sector headquarters is in Kalvariia. The boundaries are: on the left, Piateronis Station, Simno (excl.), and Pun'sk; in the rear, Mariampol' and Simno.

The sector consists of the 126th Rifle Division, the 429th Howitzer Artillery Regiment (RGKA), and the 107th Border Guards Detachment's 2d Komendatura.

Before the arrival of the 126th Rifle Division, from the first day, occupy the sector with one regiment of the 84th Motorized Division reinforced with tanks and artillery from the 84th Motorized Division.

Missions:

a. Organize a defense along the front of the existing Olita Fortified Region and prevent enemy incursion from the Suvalki region in the direction of Mariampol' and Kaunas.

b. Prepare the sector to repel atttacks by large masses of enemy tanks, having created antitank obstacles extensively exploiting the swampy terrain.

c. Have the main mass of artillery in the right flank sector and in the center.

COVERING SECTOR 3. The sector chief is the 128th Rifle Division commander. The sector headquarters is in Bogdany. The rear boundary is Simno and Druskeniki.

The sector consists of the 128th Rifle Division and the 107th Border Guards Detachment's 3d and 4th Komendatura.

Missions:

a. Organize a defense along the front of the existing Olita Fortified Region and protect the Olita axis.

b. While exploiting the lake-filled terrain, create a solid system of antitank defenses; devote special attention to the Kaletnik, Loz'dzee, Alitus, the Seiny, Loz'dzee, and the Seiny, Alitus axes.

IV. RESERVES FOR REINFORCING COVER OF THE BORDER SECTOR

To reinforce cover along the Memel', Tel'shiai, and the Til'zit, Shiauliai axes, from the first day, place [the following] concentrated formations at the disposal of the 8th Army commander: 12th Mechanized Corps headquarters and units in the Kel'me region; 23d Tank Division in the Upina and Uzhventis region; 28th Tank Division in the Shiauliai region; 202d Motorized Division in the Vaiguva, Krazhiai, and Kel'me region; 9th Antitank Artillery Brigade in the Uzhventis, Varniai, and Krazhiai region; and 7th Mixed Aviation Division.

As they arrive by rail and concentrate at the disposal of the 8th Army commander, [the following] are forthcoming: 22d Rifle Corps headquarters and units in the Bei [illegible] region; 183d Rifle Division in the Tel'shiaia region; and 181st Rifle Division in the Lidoviany and Tsitoviany region.

The aforementioned units will be concentrated from the eighth through the thirteenth day of mobilization. On the thirteenth day, the 438th Separate Antiaircraft Artillery Division will arrive in the Shiauliai region.

To reinforce cover on the Gumbinen, Kaunas, Suvalki, Kaunas, and Suvalki, Alitus axes, from the first day [the following formations], which have concentrated on the march according to this plan, will be at the disposal of the 11th Army commander: 3d Mechanized Corps headquarters and units in the Ionava region; 2d [Tank Division] in the Keidany, Labunovo, and Okmeniai region; 5th [Tank Division] in the Sheta, Lukshta, and Meshkuchiai region; 84th Motorized Division in the Gaizhiunai, Pravienishkis Station, and Smil'chiai region; 10th Antitank Artillery Brigade in the Kazla Ruda, Dombrava, and Povemon' region; and 8th Mixed Aviation Division.

The first mobilization echelon will be concentrating by rail on the second through the fourth day of mobilization [to include]: 126th Rifle Division in Kazla Ruda; and 23d Rifle Division in the Kaunas region and to enter into the Kazla Ruda region.

As mobilization is completed, [the following] will concentrate (marching according to the 11th Army plan) at the disposal of the 11th Army commander: 179th Rifle Division in the Lake Dus' and Lake Paserniki region; 184th Rifle Division in the Gudels, Zhuvinty, Mashch'ki, Lake Dus', and Palynia region; 29th Rifle Corps headquarters and units in the Simno region; and by rail: 24th Rifle Corps headquarters and units in the Preny region; and 182d Rifle Division in the Butrimonis, Alitus, and Slobodkiai region.

Missions of these formations:

a. Destruction of enemy motor-mechanized formations that are penetrating and percolating into the Army zone. In cooperation with aviation, the artillery brigades that are supporting the antitank regions will meet the tanks with fire, while disrupting the attack and retarding it until the approach of the mechanized corps. While deploying under the protection of antitank regions and the fire of the artillery brigades, in cooperation with aviation, the mechanized corps will destroy the enemy mechanized units by flank and concentric attacks.

b. Struggle with and destruction of air assaults that have landed in the rear.

c. Preparation and outfitting of antitank regions and rear lines.

Army commanders will employ the mechanized corps only with the approval of the *front* commander.

In the event of an incursion by a large enemy force, both mechanized corps, the antitank artillery brigades, and the rifle divisions from Army reserve will be employed in accordance with the decision of the *front* commander. Command and control of the counterstroke can be united on any axis under the direction of the commander.

The most probable maneuver of 12th Mechanized Corps is along the [following] axes: from the north to Sredniki and Pil'vishkiai and in the direction of Shiauliai and Ionava, [and] 3d Mechanized Corps along the Keidany, Rosseiny, Skaudvile or Keidany, Sredniki axes.

To facilitate this maneuver, the 11th Army commander will have pontoon bridges in the Vil'ki and Rumshishkis region and will be supported by a floating bridge at

Sredniki. Have no less than three crossings for tanks across the Viliia River in the Skerei, Ionava, and Kazliava sector.

The *front* reserve consists of the 180th Rifle Division and 5th Airborne Corps, which are to be employed for participation in the counterstroke to be organized by the *front* commander in accordance with the situation.

V.  COMMAND AND CONTROL

1. Crossings of the border by ground forces and overflights of it by aircraft will occur only with the special permission of the High Command.

2. The order of reports about enemy incursions. In the event of a surprise incursion by large enemy forces or overflights of the border by his aviation formations, notification will occur in the following manner:

    a. Having received information [about] crossings (overflights) of the border from commanders of border troops, NKVD forces or, from their own reconnaissance units (observation posts), commanders of the border region divisions will quickly personally inform (report), in the first place, to the commander of district forces or the district chief of staff and then to Army commander and corps commander, while taking measures to repel the attack.

    b. Indicate in the report where, when, and with what force the enemy crossed (flew over) the border and in which direction he spread.

    c. Transmit the report by telegraph, NKS, radio, VNOS communications (telegraph, telephone, or radio), or by a delegate sent by aircraft or vehicle. For receipt beyond any regular channel [wire], the division commander will report by telegraph (telephone) station the password *"slon"* [elephant]. Upon receipt of that password, the channel must be quickly left [opened] to Riga, and all conversation regardless of its nature must cease. A special messenger will be sent by aircraft to Riga and by auto to the next highest headquarters (that which sends its delegate). To verify its authenticity, at the end of the report, communicate the password [reply] *"snariad"* [shell].

Upon receipt of the report, corps and division commanders who have eleven AK and RSB radio stations will quickly duplicate it by radio in open text on the radio frequency of the district headquarters. The report must be preceded by the password, *"slon,"* and at the end will be the reply, *"snariad."*

3. Reconnaissance during the covering period. The aim of reconaissance is, from the first day of the war, to reveal enemy intentions, his grouping, and his preparation period for going over to the offensive. Pay particular attention to the concentration of motor-mechanized formations and the establishment of aviation groups.

Reconnaissance missions:

    a. Discover the direction of the main stream of railroad transport from the line of the Vistula River and determine the most important of them and the intensity of transport.

    b. Ascertain and determine the basing of enemy ground and naval aviation and also the growth in its strength.

c. Establish the main enemy groupings, their strength, composition, and direction of movement to the east from the line Labiau, Insterburg, and Darkemen.
d. Establish the presence of motor-mechanized formations, their grouping, direction of movement, and the period of their arrival at the border.
e. Establish the river crossing points across the Neman River for enemy forces, and the period, strength, and direction of movement.
f. Ascertain and continuously observe enemy groupings on the Memel', Insterburg–Til'zit, Gumbinen, and Suvalki axes. Establish their strength, composition, and period of arrival at the border.
g. Ascertain the distribution and regrouping of large enemy headquarters.
h. Ascertain the execution of work on outfitting fortified regions, strengthening lines, and creating obstacles along the border.
i. Determine the basing and location of enemy naval forces in East Prussian ports.
j. In timely fashion, reveal enemy preparations for amphibious operations and the beginning of movement of transports from bases.

4. Communications of the district headquarters with RPs, the Baltic Fleet, force unloading regions, unit mobilization points, warehouses, shop and other facilities. Establish and maintain communications with air forces and air defense (PVO) by wire, radio, and aircraft in accordance with the communications plan at Enclosure No. 5. The organization of communications is according to the special plan at Enclosure No. 5.

5. Mobilization of the first headquarters echelon. The district headquarters will mobilize according to the plan. Six hours after the beginning of the war or the announcement of mobilization, the headquarters operational echelon will deploy to the location of the Northwestern Front headquarters, in the forest 8 kilometers north of Panevezh. The composition of the headquarters' first echelon, calculated on the departure and the assembly and notification orders of the headquarters commanders is at Enclosure Nos. 6, 7, and 8.

VI. THE ORDER FOR COVERING DISTRICT TERRITORY AGAINST ENEMY AIR ATTACK

From the first day, the enemy will direct the strength of his Air Force toward disrupting the mobilization and concentration of our forces. The objectives of his aviation can include:

1. The railroad network (nodes, bridges, railroad defiles, and loading and unloading regions).
2. Military warehouses and storehouses of all types of supplies.
3. Our aviation both in the air and on the ground.
4. Large population points.
5. Regions of our force groupings and movement along dirt roads, and concentration regions; these must be especially considered.

Simultaneously, one must expect enemy Air Force operations to protect [his] ground and air operations. The landing of air assaults is likely.

Employ [the following] for the struggle with enemy aviation: the district air defense (PVO) system, air forces, and all types of deception-camouflage. Organize mobile detachments in all units and employ rear service units, installations, and reserve regiments at the disposal of Army commanders for the struggle with air assaults and for destruction of the landings on the ground.

A. Antiaircraft defense (see the plan at Enclosure No. 9). Missions of district air defense (PVO):

1. Protect large railroad centers, inhabited centers, bridges, and warehouses with the air defense system.

2. Protect force—unloadings, concentration, movement, communications centers, etc.

3. Timely notification about the appearance of enemy aircraft.

B. Measures for camouflage and for combating fires:

1. Complete all force movements at night, while implementing measures to conceal movement and deployment and to delude the enemy.

2. Black-out all population points and railroad objectives.

3. Create fire crews both in forces and in all enterprises, railroad stations, population points, airfields, etc.

C. Strengthen security, which was organized in peacetime, for railroads, bridges, dirt roads, and warehouses; in the RPs' sectors on the orders of their chiefs and in garrisons and warehouses by the orders of their chiefs; and strengthen security on the railroads and dirt roads at the expense of NKVD forces, reserve regiments, and local rifle forces, in accordance with the list at Enclosure No. 10.

The destruction caused by enemy aviation will be restored by NKT and UShOSDORA forces in accordance with information in Enclosure No. 11. Dirt roads in the Army and force rear area will be restored on the orders of formation commanders.

VIII.  USE OF AIR FORCES

Air Force missions during the covering period:

1. Destroy enemy aviation and gain air superiority in the first days of war by successive strikes of combat aviation, in cooperation with the air forces of the High Command and neighboring districts, on established bases and by combat operations.

2. Firmly protect mobilization and concentration of forces and normal rail by fighter aviation in cooperation with air defense systems and do not permit flights by enemy aviation into the depth of the country.

3. In cooperation with ground forces, destroy the attacking enemy and prevent penetration by his large motor-mechanized units.

4. Together with naval aviation and the Black Sea Fleet, destroy the enemy Navy and transports, having prohibited the landing of amphibious assaults on Dago and Ezel' Islands and the coast of the Baltic Sea.

5. Disrupt and delay concentration of forces by strikes against the Konigsberg, Marienberg, Eylau, Allenstein, and Insterburg railroad centers and against railroad bridges across the Vistula River in the Danzig, Bydgosh sector, as well as against force groupings.

6. Destroy the port of Memel'.

7. Prevent the landing of air assaults.

8. [Deliver] massive strikes on enemy ground forces.

The order of fulfilling missions, the allocated forces, means, and the plan of Air Force operations is at Enclosure No. 12.

From the first day, allocate the 21st Fighter Aviation Regiment to reinforce air defenses in operational subordination to the commander of the 10th Air Defense (PVO) Brigade.

During fulfillment of the principal missions in the interests of the district as a whole, the Air Force commander is accountable for their fulfillment by aviation assigned to the RP. The operational plan for air forces is at Enclosure No. 13.

VIII.  ENGINEER SUPPORT

The missions of engineer support:

1. Complete the outfitting and construction of an obstacle system in the sector of field fortifications along the border and, having provided that capability, occupy defensive positions with units of the covering regions (RP) along the line constructed by the fortified regions and halt the enemy tanks.

2. Complete the outfitting and adapt for defense the belt of existing permanent fortifications of the Tel'shiai, Shiauliai, Kovno, and Olita Fortified Regions as the principal defensive positions.

3. Complete the outfitting, reinforce, and construct antitank regions in accordance with the map at Enclosure No. 4.

4. Create rear Army and *front* lines [positions].

5. In the event of a forced withdrawal, organize continuous obstacles with destroyed roads, bridges, railroad nets, and communications networks and by destroyed objectives of importance to the enemy in the sector from the state borders up to the line Venta River, Shiauliai, Nevezhis River, and Neman River.

6. Repair and restore roads that have been destroyed by enemy aviation in the force and Army sectors.

7. Create and maintain crossings over the Neman River and the floating bridge at Sredniki, the pontoon [bridges] at Vil'ki and Rumshishkes, the permanent [bridges] at Kaunas, Preny, Alitus, and Merkine, and across the Western Dvina at Riga, Krustpils, and Daugavpils.

From the beginning of war, employ the sapper [combat engineer] and construction battalions of the UNS [Directorate for People's Construction] for the work:

1. From the first day of war, the sapper battalions of Baltic Special Military District formations are directed at the disposition of the Army headquarters [staffs] to the regions and sectors that are designated to be covered by their respective formations; they are not to return to the location of their winter quarters.

2. From the first day of war, sapper battalions not from Baltic Special Military District forces are subordinated to the chiefs of the covering regions (RP), and they will be employed, together with infantry, for work on constructing obstacles, their defense, and for outfitting the principal defensive positions, and, on the order of the Red Army General Staff, they shall leave Baltic Special Military District forces.

3. From the first day of war, construction battalions of the UNS are assigned at the disposition of the Army commanders to the first Army rear line [position], where they will set about completing the outfitting of antitank regions and creating rear

lines. The chiefs of Army engineer forces organize and plan the work according to the Army commanders' plan.

The district engineer directorate supports the work with materials, equipment, and tools in a scale depending on deliveries from the center [government]. Plan No. 4.

IX. MATERIAL-TECHNICAL SUPPORT OF COVERING IS ACCOMPLISHED ACCORDING TO THE PLAN AT ENCLOSURE NO. 14

Medical [sanitary] and veterinary evacuation will take place according to the plan at Enclosure No. 14.

The evacuation of families of command cadres from the border sector and the property of combat units is according to the plan at Enclosure No. 14.

Provision with topographical maps in wartime is at Enclosure No. 15. Map reserves will be delivered to units and formations in the course of the month of June.

[Enclosures not included.]

Commander of Baltic Special Military District forces, Colonel General Kuznetsov
Member of the Baltic Special Military District Military Council Corps, Commissar Dibrova
Chief of Staff of the Baltic Special Military District, Lieutenant General Klenov

No. 0030, 2 June 1941. Prepared by Major General Trukhin in two copies: Copy No. 1 in twenty-five pages to the General Staff; Copy No. 2 in the district headquarters.

*Notes*

1. From "Konets global'noi lzhi: Operativnye plany zapadnykh prigranichnykh voennykh okrugov 1941 goda svidetel'stvuiut: SSSR ne gotovilsia k napadeniiu na Germaniiu" [The end of a global lie: The operational plans of the western border military districts in 1941 bear witness: The USSR did not prepare for an attack on Germany], *VIZh* 2 (March–April 1996): 5–8, citing from archival reference *TsAMO*, f. 16A, op. 2951, d. 227, ll. 33–47. Geographical placenames are transliterated directly from the original Russian.

2. From "Konets global'noi lzhi: Operativnye plany zapadnykh prigranichnykh voennykh okrugov 1941 goda svidetel'stvuiut: SSSR ne gotovilsia k napadeniiu na Germaniiu" [The end of a global lie: The operational plans of the western border military districts in 1941 bear witness: The USSR did not prepare for an attack on Germany], *VIZh* 2 (March–April 1996): 9–15, citing from archival reference *TsAMO*, f. 16, op. 2951, d. 242, ll. 1–35. The complete plans for the Western and Southwestern Military Districts, respectively, are found in "Konets global'noi lzhi" [The end of a global lie] in *VIZh* 3 (May–June 1996): 5–17, and 4 (July–August 1996): 3–17.

# An Opponent's View:
# German Intelligence Assessments
# on the Eve of War

During the planning period for Operation Barbarossa, German intelligence over-estimated the strength of Soviet ground forces in the border military districts but underassessed the active strength of the Red Army as a whole. In addition, it failed to detect the altered size and composition of the Soviet's new mechanized force.[1] Curiously enough, when German planning for the invasion of the Soviet Union commenced in summer 1940, the Germans had a fairly accurate view of Soviet forces, but it became increasingly inaccurate as the Germans apparently failed to detect Soviet General Staff mobilization measures implemented throughout the ensuing year (or, as the Soviets referred to it, the stage of "creeping up to war") (see Table C1).

In August 1940 the Germans estimated Soviet military strength at 151 infantry divisions, 32 cavalry divisions, and 38 mechanized brigades, at a time when actual Soviet ground force strength was 152 rifle divisions, 26 cavalry divisions, and 9 newly forming mechanized corps (each with 2 tank and 1 motorized rifle division).[4] The Germans estimated that 96 infantry divisions, 23 cavalry divisions, and 28 mechanized brigades could be used against them in the West. Although German estimates of Soviet regular infantry and cavalry forces were close to accurate, the Germans began a long-lasting process of underestimating Soviet armored strength. Against this force the Germans postulated their own attack force of 147 divisions (24 panzer, 1 cavalry, 12 motorized infantry, and 110 infantry), a force that would remain stable throughout subsequent planning.

An October German General Staff Operation's Division estimate raised total Soviet strength in the West to about 170 divisions of all types, including about 70 in Ukraine, 60 in Belorussia, 30 in the Baltic region, and the remainder in reserve. At a 3 February 1941 planning conference, Chief of the General Staff Franz Halder mentioned a Soviet strength of 100 infantry divisions, 25 cavalry divisions, and 30 mechanized brigades that could oppose the German invasion.[5]

The final German assessment of Soviet strength, prepared in early June 1941, estimated a Soviet force of 170 infantry divisions, 33⅓ cavalry divisions, and 46 motorized and armored brigades (the latter equivalent to 15 mobile divisions). At this time, the Red Army strength numbered 196 rifle divisions, 13 cavalry divisions, 61 tank divisions (58 with mechanized corps and three separate), and 31 motorized divisions (29 with mechanized corps and 2 separate). Of this total, the Germans assessed Soviet strength in the border military districts at 118 infantry divisions, 20 cavalry divisions, and 40 mobile brigades (a total of about 150 divisions), whereas actual Soviet strength was 171 divisions of all types. German intelligence estimated there were another 32⅓ divisions in the remainder of European Russia, when in fact about 100 existed.

Table C1. The Accuracy of German Intelligence Estimates, 1940–1941

| | German Estimate | Soviet Strength |
|---|---|---|
| **August 1940** | | |
| Armies | | 20 |
| Infantry divisions | 151 | 174 (3 motorized) |
| Cavalry divisions | 32 | 26 |
| Mechanized brigades | 38 | 8 (corps) (26 divisions) |
| **15 January 1941** | | |
| Armies | 20 | 20 |
| Rifle corps | 30 | 50 |
| Rifle divisions | 150 (15 motorized) | 179 |
| Cavalry corps | 9 | 6 |
| Cavalry divisions | 32 | 25 |
| Motor-mechanized corps | 6 | 9 (20 divisions) |
| Motorized brigades | 36 | 0 |
| **11 June 1941** | | |
| Armies | 20 | 20 |
| Rifle corps | 40 | 62 |
| Rifle divisions | 175 (15 motorized) | 198 (+ 3 brigades) |
| Cavalry corps | 9 | 4 |
| Cavalry divisions | $33^{1/3}$ | 13 |
| Tank or mechanized corps | 3 | 29 |
| Tank divisions | 7 | 61 |
| Mechanized brigades | 43 | 31 (divisions) |
| Parachute brigades | 7 | 15 (in 5 corps) |
| Mobilization divisions | 200 | 518 division equivalents by 31 December 1941 |
| Total mobilizable personnel | 6.2 million men out of a 11–12 million man manpower reserve.[2] | 7.85 million man total initial mobilization; ultimately, 29,574,900 were mobilized.[3] |

German estimates of Soviet air power vary greatly, indicating some German confusion over actual Soviet air strength. Sources place that strength between 8,000 and 14,000 aircraft, with about 6,000 in the western Soviet Union.[6] The latter, which included 1,500 modern aircraft, consisted of the following types: 800 obsolete close reconnaissance planes; 2,000 fighters, including 250 to 300 modern types; 1,800 bombers, including about 800 modern types; 700 fighter-bombers, including Shturmoviks and obsolete planes; and 700 naval aircraft of primarily obsolete design.

These figures underscore two major faults in German assessments of existing Soviet military strength. First, the Germans did not adequately keep track of the scale of the Soviet prewar mobilization efforts. Although this was true of military districts along the borders, it was even more pronounced in the internal military districts, where mobilization could be better concealed. Second, the Germans had a poor appreciation of Soviet force restructuring efforts, in particular, the restructuring associated with the Soviet mechanization program. As late as 22 June, German intelligence continued to count older Soviet tank brigades and cavalry divisions without realizing that most of these had re-formed into tank and mechanized divisions of the new mechanized corps. By 22 June the Germans had identified 1 mechanized corps each in the Baltic, Western, and Kiev Special Military Districts out of the 16 that were actually in these regions. Nor did the Germans detect the large antitank brigades formed in the border military districts, which were designated to cooperate with the new mechanized corps. It is true, however, that German operational and tactical proficiency more than compensated for these intelligence failures during the initial period of war. In the long term, however, the pattern of German intelligence failures persisted, with disastrous consequences for German forces.

The Germans also appreciated the problems the Soviets had experienced during the Finnish War and the ensuing force reforms, although they failed to anticipate the total scope of those reforms. They tended to discount the effectiveness of the reform program and believed that, in light of the continuing purges, Soviet military leadership would not be capable of handling large forces in mobile warfare. Still, they accepted the fact that the strength of the Soviet armed forces lay in their numbers, the large equipment stocks, the courage and tenacity of the Soviet soldier, and the vastness and relative backwardness of the Soviet theater of military operations.

Far more serious than these problems, however, was the German failure to appreciate the size and efficiency of the Soviet mobilization system in terms of the sheer quantity of forces it was capable of producing. German intelligence estimates tended to count only what it could see, that is, active forces that were maintained in peacetime at various manning levels. They did not, however, detect or closely examine Soviet mobilization or "spin-off" divisions, which had seemingly insignificant numbers of cadre and equipment complements in peacetime. This was perhaps understandable given the German assumption that Operation Barbarossa would be over within about four months, before the Soviets could generate significant new combat-ready forces. The German High Command reasoned that any new Soviet formations could be dealt with in successive stages throughout the duration of the operation. History proved that this assumption and its associated reasoning were fatally flawed.

## Notes

1. For details, see David M. Glantz, *Soviet Military Intelligence in War* (London: Frank Cass, 1990), 43–48.

2. OKH GenStdH, *Die Kriegswehrmacht der Union der Sozialistischen Sowjetrepubliken (UdSSR), Stand: 1.1.1941, Teil I: text; H3/1692; Teil II: Anlagenband; H3/637.*

3. Krivosheev, *Grif*, 139. This figure is for the Red Army. Total mobilization for all forces was 34,476,700 men and women.

4. See German estimates of Soviet strength in "The German Campaign in Russia, Planning and Operations (1940–1941)," *DA Pamphlet No. 20-261a* (Washington, DC.: Department of the Army, March 1955), 7.

5. Ibid., 30.

6. *Die Kriegswehrmacht* places air strength at 12,000 to 14,000, whereas *DA Pamphlet No. 20-261a*, 42, estimates Soviet air strength at 8,000 aircraft.

# Correlation of Forces on the German–Soviet Front, 22 June 1941

One of the most controversial questions associated with Operation Barbarossa, and with Soviet combat performance in the operation, has been the balance of forces of the contending sides. Many have used the correlation, with other factors, to explain subsequent Soviet performance and the ultimate outcome of the operation. Existing records now enable the historian to reconstruct fairly accurately what that balance was and better assess how that correlation contributed to Soviet defeat.

Soviet open-source histories have consistently overemphasized German strength and played down their own. By the mid-1960s, these sources claimed German armed forces strength in June 1941 amounted to 8,500,000 men, including around 6,000,000 men in the ground forces, 1,700,000 in the air forces, and the remainder in the Navy and specialized formations (like SS). According to these sources, the ground forces consisted of 214 divisions (including 169 infantry, 21 panzer, 14 motorized, and 10 others) and 7 brigades, supported by 11,000 tanks and assault guns, around 78,000 guns and mortars, and 11,000 aircraft.[1]

Of this total, the Germans were said to have committed 152 divisions to combat in the East, including 19 panzer and 14 motorized divisions and 2 separate brigades, for a total ground force of 3,300,000 men. Added to this force were 1,200,000 men of the Air Force and 100,000 from the Navy, for a total of 77 percent of German operating forces. The same Soviet source placed German satellite strength at 29 divisions (16 Finnish and 13 Rumanian) and 16 brigades (3 Finnish, 9 Rumanian, and 4 Hungarian) totaling 900,000 men. This produced a grand total of 5,500,000 men (4,600,000 German) and 181 divisions and 18 brigades, supported by 2,800 tanks and assault guns, 48,000 guns and mortars, and 4,950 aircraft (up to 1,000 of which were Finnish and Rumanian).[2]

The same source placed Soviet strength on 22 June at "4,207,000 men," plus those mobilized in the first half of 1941, which later sources listed as 793,000 men, for a total of 5,000,000.[3] This included 2,900,000 men in the western military districts, organized into 170 divisions and 2 brigades, supported by 1,800 heavy and medium tanks (including 1,475 new models), 34,695 guns and mortars, and 1,540 new model aircraft (plus many obsolete aircraft).

According to this source, the correlation of forces in the East was as follows:

|  | Red Army | Axis | Correlation |
|---|---|---|---|
| Divisions or division equivalents (2 brigades equals 1 division) | 171 | 190 | 1 : 1.1 |
| Personnel | 2,900,000 | 5,500,000 | 1 : 1.9 |
| Tank and assault guns | 1,800 | 2,800 | 1 : 1.6 |
| Guns and mortars | 34,695 | 48,000 | 1 : 1.4 |
| Aircraft | 1,540 | 4,950 | 1 : 3.2 |

By the late 1980s, Soviet open sources listed the strength of German and satellite forces committed against the Soviet Union as 5,500,000 men, organized into 190 divisions (including 19 tank and 14 motorized) and supported by 4,300 tanks and assault guns, 47,200 guns and mortars, and 4,980 combat aircraft (83 percent of the Wehrmacht).[4] The same source places Soviet overall armed forces strength at 5,373,000 men, including 4,553,000 in the ground forces and PVO, 476,000 in the Air Force, and 344,000 in the Navy, supported by 1,861 new model tanks, 67,000 guns and mortars, and 2,700 new model aircraft. Soviet forces in the western military districts, which numbered 2,680,000 men, 1,475 new model tanks, 37,500 guns and mortars, and 1,540 new model aircraft, were organized into 170 divisions (103 rifle, 40 tank, 20 motorized, and 7 cavalry) and 2 brigades.[5] The correlation of forces was as follows:

|  | Red Army | Axis | Correlation |
| --- | --- | --- | --- |
| Divisions | 171 | 190 | 1 : 1.1 |
| Personnel | 2,680,000 | 5,500,000 | 1 : 2.1 |
| Tanks and assault guns | 1,475 | 4,300 | 1 : 2.9 |
| Guns and mortars | 37,500 | 47,200 | 1 : 1.3 |
| Aircraft | 1,540 | 4,980 | 1 : 3.2 |

In 1991, Soviet assessments of the correlation once again changed. An authoritative and detailed article by M. I. Mel'tiukhov, which was based on archival sources, placed overall Soviet armed forces strength at 5,373,000 men, 23,140 tanks, 104,114 guns and mortars, and 18,570 aircraft, with 303 ground force divisions and 16 airborne and 3 rifle brigades.[6] Of this number, 2,780,000 men (including Air Force, PVO forces, and NKVD border troops), organized into 177 division equivalents, were deployed in the western border military districts, supported by 10,394 tanks (including 1,325 new models), 43,872 guns and mortars, and 8,154 aircraft (including 1,540 new models). Mel'tiukhov uses German archival sources to place German strength on 15 June 1941 at 8,229,000 overall, including 3,960,000 in the Field Army, 1,240,000 in the Reserve Army, 1,545,000 in the Luftwaffe, 160,000 in the SS, 404,000 in the Navy, and 920,000 in all types of specialized support organizations. These forces were organized into 208 divisions, 1 combat group, 3 motorized and tank brigades, and 2 infantry regiments and contained 5,694 tanks and assault guns, 88,251 guns and mortars, and 6,413 aircraft. Of this total, Germany planned to commit 4,600,000 men (3,300,000 ground force and SS, 1,200,000 Air Force, and 100,000 Navy), organized into 155 division equivalents, 3,998 tanks and assault guns, 43,407 guns and mortars, and 3,904 aircraft, to combat in the East. In actuality, it committed 127 divisions, amounting to 4,029,250 men, 3,648 tanks and assault guns, 35,791 guns and mortars, and 3,904 aircraft.

Based on foreign archival materials, Mel'tiukhov assesses the strength of Germany's satellite armed forces, which were committed in the East as follows: Finland, 302,600 men (17.5 divisions), 86 tanks, 2,047 guns and mortars, and 307 aircraft; Rumania, 358,140 men (17.5 divisions), 60 tanks, 3,255 guns and mortars, and 423 aircraft; Hungary, 44,000 men (2 divisions), 116 tanks, 200 guns and mortars, and 100 aircraft; total, 704,740 men (37 divisions), 262 tanks, 5,502 guns and mortars, and 937 aircraft.

Therefore, according to Mel'tiukhov, the combined strength of German and satellite forces committed in the East was 4,733,990 men (161 divisions), 3,899 tanks and assault guns, 41,293 guns and mortars, and 4,841 aircraft. The resulting correlation of forces is as follows:

|  | Red Army | Axis | Correlation |
|---|---|---|---|
| Divisions | 174 | 164 | 1.1 : 1 |
| Personnel | 2,780,000 | 4,733,990 | 1 : 1.7 |
| Tanks and assault guns | 10,394 | 3,899 | 2.6 : 1 |
| Guns and mortars | 43,872 | 41,293 | 1.1 : 1 |
| Aircraft | 9,576 | 4,841 | 2.0 : 1 |

Formerly classified Soviet sources place the total strength of the German armed forces and those of her satellites at 7,254,000 men, 6,677 tanks and assault guns, 77,800 guns and mortars, and 10,100 combat aircraft. Of this total, 5,500,000 men, 3,582 tanks and assault guns, 41,763 guns and mortars, and 4,275 aircraft (in 191.5 divisions) were committed against the Soviet Union. The same source states that the Soviet armed forces numbered 5,373,000 men, 18,680 tanks, 91,400 guns and mortars, and 15,599 aircraft. Of this number, 2,901,000 men, 11,000 tanks, 21,556 guns and mortars, and 9,917 aircraft were deployed in the western border military districts.[7] This source adds the numbers of older Soviet tanks and aircraft, which earlier sources would not admit to, increases the amount of artillery in the Red Army (from 67,000 to 91,400 tubes), and raises the total manpower deployed in the western military districts (from 2,680,000 to 2,901,000). Although these figures for Soviet strength are likely correct, the German figures require confirmation. The resulting correlation of forces is as follows:

|  | Red Army | Axis | Correlation |
|---|---|---|---|
| Divisions | 171 | 191.5 | 1 : 1.1 |
| Personnel | 2,901,000 | 5,500,000 | 1 : 1.9 |
| Tanks and assault guns | 11,000 | 3,582 | 3 : 1 |
| Guns and mortars | 21,556 | 41,763 | 1 : 1.9 |
| Aircraft | 9,917 | 4,275 | 2.3 : 1 |

German sources show German armed forces (Wehrmacht) strength on 22 June 1941 to have been 7,234,000 men. Of this number, 3,800,000 were in the Field Army (Feldheer), 1,200,000 in the Replacement Army (Erzatsheer), 1,680,000 in the Luftwaffe, 404,000 in the Navy, and 150,000 in the Waffen-SS.[8] Army and SS ground forces initially committed to combat in the East numbered 3,050,000 (with 67,000 in Finland). Initial Luftwaffe strength was about 700,000 men. The total of 3,750,000 men were supported by 3,350 tanks, 7,000 guns, and almost 3,000 aircraft.[9] Of 210 German divisions, 145 were to be committed in the East.

The Mel'tiukhov figures appear to be the most accurate regarding Soviet forces and those of Germany's allies. German personnel strength (with 700,000 Luftwaffe) should be 3,750,000 men organized into 135 divisions (including strategic reserves and nine security divisions), supported by 3,350 tanks and assault guns, 7,184 guns and mortars, and 2,000 aircraft. With committed allied strength (most Finnish force and half of the Rumanians), the Axis grand total rises to about 4,200,000 men, 3,612 tanks and assault guns, 7,686 guns and mortars, and 2,937 aircraft. Considering Mel'tiukhov, classified Soviet data, additional German data, and immediate strategic reserves,[10] the resulting correlation would be as follows:

| | Red Army | Axis | Correlation |
|---|---|---|---|
| Divisions | 174 | 164 | 1.1 : 1 |
| Personnel | 2,780,000 | 4,733,990 | 1 : 1.7 |
| with strategic reserves | 3,700,000 | 4,733,990 | 1 : 1.3 |
| Tanks and assault guns | 11,000 | 3,612 | 3 : 1 |
| Guns and mortars | 43,872 | 12,686 | 3.5 : 1 |
| Aircraft | 9,917 | 2,937 | 3.4 : 1 |

Soviet strategic reserves include about 1 million of the almost 2 million men mobilized on or shortly after 22 June, most of which found their way into new reserve armies committed to combat in July and August (series 21st thorough 43d Armies). The Axis had no equivalent to these reserves.

## Notes

1. P. N. Pospelov, ed., *Velikaia Otechestvennaia voina Sovetskogo soiuza 1941–1945* [The Great Patriotic War of the Soviet Union] (Moscow: Voenizdat, 1967), 33.

2. Ibid.

3. Ibid., 52. For the increase by June 1941, see P. N. Pospelov, *Great Patriotic War of the Soviet Union 1941–1945* (Moscow: Progress, 1970), 44–45.

4. M. M. Kir'ian, ed., *Velikaia Otechestvennaia voina 1941–1945.* [The Great Patriotic War 1941–1945] (Moscow: Politicheskaia literatura, 1988), 10.

5. Ibid., 11.

6. M. I. Mel'tiukhov, "22 iiunia 1941 g.: Tsifry svidetel'stvuiut" [22 June 1941: Numbers bear witness], *Istoriia SSSR* [History of the USSR] 3 (March 1991): 16–27. Mel'tiukhov provides figures for each sector and for each weapons system as well.

7. *Nachal'nyi period Velikoi Otechestvennoi voiny* [Initial period of the Great Patriotic War] (Moscow: Voroshilov Academy of the General Staff, 1989), 97. Western Military District forces also had 14,962 50mm mortars.

8. B. Mueller-Hillebrand, *Das Heer 1933–1945* [The Armed Forces 1933–1945], vol. 2 (Frankfurt, 1956), 102.

9. OKH/GenStdH, *Barbarossa Band II, Anl. 123, 125; H22/353.*

10. For German equipment strength during Barbarossa, see "The German Campaign in Russia: Planning and Operations (1940–1942)," *Department of the Army Pamphlet No. 20-261a* (Washington, D.C.: Department of the Army, March 1955), 10–41.

## Introduction

1. Viktor Suvorov, *Icebreaker: Who Started the Second World War?* (London: Hammish-Hamilton; 1990). Translated from the Russian title *Ledokol* by Thomas B. Beattie.

2. Viktor Suvorov, *Den'-M* [M-day] (Moscow: Vse dlia Vas," 1994).

3. G. A. Bordiugova and V. A. Nevezhin, *Gotovil li Stalin nastupatel'nuiu voinu protiv Gitlera?* [Did Stalin prepare an offensive war against Hitler?] (Moscow: AIRO-XX, 1995).

4. David M. Glantz, ed., *The Initial Period of War on the Eastern Front: 22 June–August 1941* (London: Frank Cass, 1993).

## 1. Red Army Forces

1. *Nachal'nyi period Velikoi Otechestvennoi voiny* [The initial period of the Great Patriotic War] (Moscow: Voroshilov Academy of the General Staff, 1989), 43. Classified "For the use of those serving." Hereafter cited as *Nachal'nyi period*. Unclassified accounts of Red Army expansion between 1937 and 1941 and Army structural reforms on the eve of war are found in I. Kh. Bagramian, *Istoriia voin i voennogo iskusstva* [A history of wars and military art] (Moscow: Voenizdat, 1970); V. A. Anfilov, *Proval blitskriga* [The failure of blitzkrieg] (Moscow: Nauka, 1974).

2. *Nachal'nyi period*, 39–43.

3. Ibid., 97. See also G. F. Krivosheev, "Nakanune" [On the eve], *Voenno-istoricheskii zhurnal* 6 (June 1991): 42. M. I. Mel'tiukhov, "22 iiunia 1941 g." [22 June 1941], *Istoriia SSSR* 3 (March 1991): 18, places Soviet armed forces strength on 22 June at 5,373,000. In a more recent work, *Grif sekretnosti sniat* [Secret classification removed] (Moscow: Voenizdat, 1993), Krivosheev places Red Army and fleet strength at 4,826,907 men, plus 74,945 serving in the Commissariat of Defense. Hereafter cited as *Grif sekretnosti*.

4. For an explanation of Soviet prewar readiness states, see Robert Savushkin, "In the Tracks of a Tragedy: On the 50th Anniversary of the Start of the Great Patriotic War," *Journal of Soviet Military Studies* 4, 2 (June 1991): 240–242.

5. *Boevoi sostav Sovetskoi armii, chast' 1 (iun'–dekabr' 1941 goda)* [Combat composition of the Soviet Army, part 1 (June–December 1941)] (Moscow: Voroshilov Academy of the General Staff, 1963), 7–14. Prepared by the General Staff Military-Scientific Directorate and classified secret. Now declassified. Soviet wartime *fronts* were roughly equivalent to Western Army groups. Hereafter cited as *Boevoi sostav*.

6. In peacetime, these reserves were under High Command control, meaning the senior political leadership (Stalin), the NKO, and the General Staff. In wartime, a High Command headquarters (Stavka) would emerge, consisting of key political and military figures. This Stavka would exercise strategic control over the war effort, form strategic reserves, and allocate these reserves to field operating forces.

7. *Nachal'nyi period*, 58.

8. Ibid., 64.

9. *Vnutrennie voiska v gody mirnogo sotsialisticheskogo stroitel'stva, 1922–1941 gg.* [The internal forces in the years of peaceful socialist construction, 1922–1941] (Moscow: Iuridicheskaia Literatura, 1977), 507–508.

10. N. Ramanichev, "The Red Army, 1940–1941: Myths and Realities," 106. This draft manuscript (title tentative) is being translated and prepared for future publication. It is particularly strong on the condition of the average Soviet soldier and provides keen interpretation of the context in which the Red Army developed during the period preceding the war.

11. This figure of 5.3 million includes forces called up during the prewar mobilization. According to Krivosheev, "Nakanune," 43, the Soviet Union mobilized more than 10 million men during the first eight months of war, of which more than 3 million were immediately dispatched to the front. In *Grif sekretnosti*, 139, Krivosheev places total Soviet wartime mobilization at 29,574,900 men (including some multiple enlistments). Details on the mobilization process are found in *Nachal'nyi period*, 29–44, and in A. G. Khor'kov, *Boevaia i mobilizatsionnaia gotovnost' prigranichnykh voennykh okrugov nakanune Velikoi Otechestvennoi voiny* [Combat and mobilization readiness of the border military districts on the eve of the Great Patriotic War] (Moscow: Voroshilov Academy of the General Staff, 1985). Classified secret, but now declassified.

12. For month-by-month additions to and deletions from the Red Army force structure, see *Boevoi sostav*.

13. See for example, "Iz opisaniia boevykh deistvii 22 motostrelkovoi divizii voisk NKVD v Pribaltike s 22 iiunia po 12 iiulia 1941 g." [From the description of combat actions of the NKVD 22d Motorized Division in the Baltic region from 22 June through 12 July 1941], in *Vnutrennie voiska v Velikoi Otechestvennoi voine 1941–1945 gg.: Dokumenty i materialy* [Internal troops in the Great Patriotic War 1941–1945: Documents and materials] (Moscow: Iuridicheskaia Literatura, 1975), 37–42. This lengthy volume sketches the actions of many NKVD formations and units and provides an excellent portrait of the extensive NKVD wartime structure.

## 2. Command and Control and Command Personnel

1. Details on command and control are found in *Nachal'nyi period, Velikoi Otechestverroi voiny* [The initial period of the Great Patriotic War] (Moscow: Voroshilov Academy of the General Staff, 1989), 90–91.

2. For details, see articles and documents published in the journal *Izvestiia TsK KPSS* [News of the Central Committee of the Communist Party of the Soviet Union], a short-lived journal published under the auspices of Party First Secretary M. S. Gorbachev as a vehicle for glasnost. Between 1988 and its demise in 1991, the journal

published a series of unprecedented documents on the crimes of the Party and Stalin. It ceased publication when the Soviet Union fell in 1991. Unfortunately, no Russian publication has since matched its candor or historical value. For these purge details, see *Izvestiia TsK KPSS* 4 (April 1989): 43.

3. O. F. Suvenirov, "Vsearmeiskaia tragediia" [An all-Army tragedy], *Voenno-istoricheskii zhurnal* 3 (March 1989): 39.

4. Ibid., 40.

5. Ibid.

6. "Trial of Red Army Commanders," *USSR (Combat—Army)*, G-2 Report No. 866-6320 (Washington, D.C.: Military Intelligence Division, War Department, 12 June 1937). Classified secret. For complete attaché reports on the Soviet purges, see David M. Glantz, "Observing the Soviets: U.S. Army Attaches in Eastern Europe During the 1930s," *Journal of Military History* 55, 2 (April 1991): 153–184. Hereafter cited as *VIZh*.

7. Suvenirov, "Vsearmeiskaia tragediia," 40.

8. "Treason Trials, Red Army," *USSR (Combat—Army)*, G-2 Report No. 875-6320 (Washington, D.C.: Military Intelligence Division, War Department, 17 June 1937). Classified secret.

9. Suvenirov, "Vsearmeiskaia tragediia," 45.

10. Ibid.

11. Ibid., 42.

12. Ibid., 41.

13. N. Ramanichev, "The Red Army, 1940–1941: Myths and Realities," Unpublished manuscript, 177–178.

14. A. A. Maslov, "General'skaia zhertva Pribaltiki" [General officers victims of the Baltic], *Journal of Soviet Military Studies* 9, 1 (March 1996): 194–197.

15. Ramanichev, "Red Army," 176, citing *RGVA*, f. 33987, op. 3, d. 152, l. 151, and A. T. Ukolov and V. I. Ivkin, "O masshtabakh repressii" [About the scale of repression], *VIZh* 1 (January 1993): 56.

16. Ukolov and Ivkin, "O masshtabakh," 59. The same article states that between 1921 and 1 February 1954 the courts found 3,777,380 persons guilty of counterrevolutionary crimes. This does not include those who died in the famines or were killed or transported to the GULag as the result of collectivization or, later, presumed or proven collaboration with the Germans during the war. For an extensive list of those purged, see the series, "Pogibli v gody bezzakoniia" [Perished in the years of lawlessness], *VIZh*, 2, 3, 5, 6, 7, 8, 9, 10, 11, 12 (February–December 1993).

17. "Treason Trials."

18. "Numbers of Officers Removed from the Red Army," *Soviet Russia (Combat—Army)*, G-2 Report No. 6300 (Washington, D.C.: Military Intelligence Division, War Department, 10 August 1938).

19. Suvenirov, "Vsearmeiskaia tragediia," 44.

20. Ibid., 43.

21. Ibid., 45.

22. Ibid., 42, quoting from the letter in *Druzhba narodov* [Friend of the people] 3 (March 1988): 234.

23. Ibid., 45.

24. Ibid., 46.

25. "Estimate of the Military Situation," G-2 Report Number 10 (Washington, D.C.: Military Intelligence Division, War Department, January 31, 1940). Classified secret.

26. Ramanichev, "Red Army," 199.

27. Ibid., 179, quoting from archival citations, *RGVA*, f. 31983, op. 3, d. 152, l. 152; f. 4, op. 14, d. 2371, l. 37; and f. 33987, op. 3, d. 1280, l. 37.

28. Ibid., 180, citing archival reference *RGVA*, f. 4, op. 19, d. 91, l. 15.

29. "O nakoplenii nachal'stvuiushchego sostava i popolnenii im Raboche-Krest'ianskoi Krasnoi Armii" [Concerning the accumulation of command personnel and their replenishment in the Workers' and Peasants' Red Army], *Izvestiia TsK KPPS* 1 (January 1990): 177–178.

30. Ibid., 178.

31. Ibid., 179.

32. Ibid.

33. "O rabote za 1939 god: Iz otcheta nachal'nika Upravleniia po nachal' stvuiushchemu sostavu RKKA Narkomata Oborony SSSR E. A. Shchadenko, 5 maia 1940 g." [About work during 1939: From the assessment of the chief of the Red Army Cadres' Directorate of the USSR's People's Commissariat of Defense, E. A. Shchadenko, 5 May 1940], *Izvestiia TsK KPSS* 1 (January 1990): 186.

34. Shchadenko provides data on all catagories of dismissals from services, as well as those cleared of charges in each year. Ibid., 188–189.

35. Ibid., 191.

36. "Akt o Prieme Narkomata Oborony Soiuza SSR tov. Timoshenko S. K. ot tov. Voroshilova K. E." [Act of reception of the USSR People's Commissarist of Defense to Comrade Timoshenko, S. K., from Comrade Voroshilov, K. E.], *Izvestiia TsK KPSS* 1 (January 1990): 193.

37. Ibid., 198.

38. Ibid.

39. Ibid.

40. Ibid., 199.

41. Ibid.

42. For further details, see Ramanichev, "Red Army," 182. A detailed analysis of the work and output of all military academies and schools is found in F. B. Komal, "Voennye kadry nakanune voiny" [Military cadre on the eve of war] , *VIZh* 2 (February 1990): 21–28.

43. Komal, "Vooennye kadry," 22.

44. Ibid., 28.

45. Ramanichev, "Red Army," 224–225.

46. V. Anfilov, "Semen Konstantinovich Timoshenko," in H. Shukman, ed., *Stalin's Generals* (London: Weidenfeld and Nicolson, 1993), 253. Hereafter cited as *Stalin's Generals*.

47. B. M. Shaposhnikov, *Vospominaniia i voenno-nauchnye trudy* [Recollections and scientific works] (Moscow: Voenizdat, 1974), 16. From the foreword, written by A. M. Vasilevsky and M. V. Zakharov.

48. S. M. Shtemenko, *The Soviet General Staff at War, 1941–1945,* vol. 1 (Moscow: Progress, 1985), 210.

49. Among many biographies, see G. Jukes, "Alexander Mikhailovich Vasilevsky," in *Stalin's Generals,* 275–285.

50. R. Woff, "Alexsi Innokentievich Antonov," in *Stalin's Generals,* 14.

51. I. Vakurov, "General-polkovnik M. P. Kirponos" [Colonel General M. P. Kirponos], *VIZh* 1 (January 1977): 125–128.

52. G. Zhukov, *Reminiscences and Reflections,* vol. 1 (Moscow: Progress, 1985), 225.

53. "Dmitri Grigor'evich Pavlov," *VIZh* 2 (February 1990): 54.

54. "General-polkovnik F. I. Kuznetsov," *VIZh* 9 (September 1968): 124–126.

55. "Mikhail Fedorovich Lukin," *VIZh* 8 (August 1989): 44–45.

56. P. A. Kurochkin, "70 let v armeiskom stroiu" [10 years in Army service], *VIZh* 2 (February 1988): 36.

57. Ibid.

58. Shtemenko, *General Staff,* 24–25.

59. C. Andreev, "Andrei Andreevich Vlasov," in *Stalin's Generals,* 301–311.

## 3. The Soviet Soldier

1. V. E. Korol', "The Price of Victory: Myths and Reality," *Journal of Soviet Military Studies* 9, 2 (June 1996): 422. Hereafter cited as *JSMS.*

2. Petro G. Grigorenko, *Memoirs* (New York: Norton, 1982), 109–110.

3. Ibid., 110.

4. Ibid.

5. Ibid.

6. A. Samsonov, "Eto nenasytnoe chudovishche—voina" [This insatiable monster—war], in *LG Dos'e Prilozhenie k Literaturnoi gazete* [The LG dossier: Supplement to the *Literary Gazette*] (June 1990): 19.

7. F. D. Sverdlov, "What's New About a Well-known Raid: A Selection from a Supressed Memoir," *JSMS* 9, 1 (March 1996): 861–871. Contains excerpts from Konenenko's diary.

8. Korol', "Price of Victory," 422–423.

9. S. A. Il'enkov, "Concerning the Registration of Soviet Armed Forces' Wartime Irrevocable Losses, 1941–1945," *JSMS* 9, 2 (June 1996): 441.

10. Korol', "Price of Victory," 423.

11. F. W. von Mellenthin, *Panzer Battles* (Norman: University of Oklahoma Press, 1956), 292–296.

12. David M. Glantz, ed., *The 1984 Art of War Symposum: From the Don to the Dnepr: Soviet Offensive Operations—December 1942–August 1943: A Transcript of Proceedings* (Carlisle, Pa.: U.S. Army War College Center for Land Warfare, 1984), 431.

13. A. G. Khor'kov, *Boevaia i mobilizatsionnaia gotovnost' prigranichnykh voennykh okrugov nakanune Velikoi Otechestvennoi voiny* [Combat and mobilization readiness of the border military districts on the eve of the Great Patriotic War] (Moscow: Voroshilov Academy of the General Staff, 1985), 53.

14. Ibid.

15. Ibid., 54–55.

16. A. G. Khor'kov, *Analiz boevoi gotovnosti voisk zapadnykh prigranichnykh voennykh okrugov nakanune Velikoi Otechestvennoi voiny* [An analysis of the combat readiness of forces in the western border military districts on the eve of war] (Moscow: Voroshilov Academy of the General Staff, 1985), 47–48.

17. Ibid., 50.

18. A. A. Volkov, *Kriticheskii prolog: Nezavershennye frontovye nastupatel'nye operatsii pervykh kampanii Velikoi Otechestvennoi voiny* [Critical prologue: Incompleted front offensive operations of the initial campaigns of the Great Patriotic War] (Moscow: Aviar, 1992), 43–44.

19. Ibid., 44.

20. Ibid.

21. Ibid.

22. Ibid.

23. Ibid., 44–45.

24. N. Ramanichev, "The Red Army, 1940–1941: Myths and Realities," Unpublished manuscript, 153.

25. For the most detailed examination in this regard, see ibid., 173–225.

26. Roger R. Reese, *Stalin's Reluctant Soldiers: A Social History of the Red Army, 1925–1941* (Lawrence: University Press of Kansas, 1996).

27. Ibid., 5.

28. Ibid., 9.

29. Ibid., 12.

30. Ibid., 15.

31. Ibid., 187.

32. Ibid., 202.

33. Ibid., 203.

34. Ibid., 207.

35. Grigorenko, *Memoirs,* 34.

36. Ibid., 111.

37. Ibid., 133.

38. For a superb analysis of the mind-set of party members and their reaction to the purges, see Georgi Arbatov, *The System: An Insider's Life in Soviet Politics* (New York: Random House, 1992): 13–17.

39. Ibid., 23.

40. Ibid., 24, 30.

41. Vladimir Voinovich, *The Life and Extraordinary Adventures of Private Ivan Chonkin,* trans. Richard Lourie (New York: Farrar, Straus and Giroux, 1977), 125.

42. L. Tarrasuk, "Views of a Red Army Soldier," in David M. Glantz, ed., *1985 Art of War Symposium: From the Vistula to the Oder: Soviet Offensive Operations— October 1944–March 1945* (Carlisle, Pa.: Center for Land Warfare, U.S. Army War College, 1986), 54–55. Tarassuk served in Hungary with the 53d Rifle Division.

43. Ibid., 55.

44. Ibid.

45. Ibid., 59.

## 4. Strategic Deployment Planning and Mobilization

1. A. A. Svechin, *Strategy* (Minneapolis: East View Press, 1992). Translation of A. A. Svechin, *Strategiia* [Strategy] (Moscow: Voenizdat, 1927), with introductory essays by A. A. Kokoshin, V. V. Larionov, V. N. Lobov, and Jacob W. Kipp.

2. *Nachal'nyi period Velikoi Otechestvennoi voiny* [The initial period of the Great Patriotic War] (Moscow: Voroshilov Academy of the General Staff, 1989), 29. For a survey of Soviet strategy during this period, see David M. Glantz, *The Military Strategy of the Soviet Union* (London: Frank Cass, 1992), 55–103.

3. M. V. Zakharov, *General'nyi shtab v predvoennye gody* [The General Staff in the prewar years] (Moscow: Voenizdat, 1989), 111–116.

4. Ibid., 125.

5. Ibid., 126–127.

6. Ibid., 129–130. The first variant involved an enemy attack north of the Pripiat Marshes along the Minsk–Smolensk axis; the second, an enemy thrust into economically vital Ukraine. Shaposhnikov and the General Staff considered the former more decisive and, hence, more likely. In this variant the German–Polish main attack would be in the north, and Polish forces would launch a secondary attack in the south. In the latter, a German–Polish force would strike into Ukraine, while a secondary attack would occur in the north. Preparation times for either variant would require 20–30 days and would presume full mobilization. A Japanese threat of 27–33 divisions remained constant.

7. Ibid., 163–171. A more detailed view of Soviet deployments during the crisis appears in A. Antosiak, "Osvobozhdenie zapadnoi Ukrainy i zapadnoi Belorussii" [The liberation of western Ukraine and western Belorussia], *Voenno-istoricheskii zhurnal* 9 (September 1989): 51–60; and formerly classified U.S. Army attaché reports, including "Military Operations—General–Soviet Invasion of Poland," *USSR (Combat-Army)*, G-2 Report No. 1598-6900 (Washington, D.C.: Military Intelligence Division, War Department, October 25, 1939).

8. For an excellent discussion of the state of Soviet fortified regions, see N. Ramanichev, "The Red Army, 1940–1941: Myths and Realities," Unpublished manuscript, 82–83.

9. M. Moiseev, "Smena rukovodstva Narkomata Oborony SSSR v sviazi s urokami sovetsko-finliandskoi voiny 1939–1940 gg." [Replacement of the leadership of the USSR People's Commissariat of Defense in connection with the lessons of the Soviet-Finnish War of 1939–1940], *Izvestiia TsK KPSS* 1 (January 1990): 211.

10. For example, the Soviets redeployed the 44th Rifle Division from the Kiev Military District to Finland to operate in central Karelia. The division was virtually destroyed by Finnish forces on the road to Suomussalmi. A recent Soviet critique of the operation stated: "Before the combat operations, neither the division command personnel nor the soldiers were familiar with the particular features of the forest–lake terrain of the Finnish theater of military operations or enemy tactics. Moreover, there were insufficient skis in the division and ski training in the division was only begun on the eve of 1940. Regimental personnel could basically move only on the roads. The deep snow was a serious impediment to movement and any sort of maneuver. . . .

"Subsequently, all blame for negligence was placed on the division commander. However, one must note that the absence of required experience on the part of the 44th Rifle Division commander was made possible by the overall policy regarding the RKKA conducted at the end of the 1930s: as a result of the repression against command personnel, people were rapidly promoted and appointed to command duties who did not fully correspond to the post and did not have necessary knowledge and experience.

"In that regard, the promotion of the commander and chief of staff of 44th Rifle Division were entirely typical. Thus, the personnel records of the 44th Division commander, Aleksei Ivanovich Vinogradov, mention that he was a major in 1936, from June of the following year he commanded the 143d Rifle Regiment, in February 1938 he received early promotion to the rank of colonel, and in March he was assigned to the RKKA Cadre Directorate. A. I. Vinogradov was appointed to command 44th Rifle Division in January 1939, and was then awarded with the next rank of Kombrig [brigade commander].

"The 44th Rifle Division chief of staff, Onufry Ioskovich Volkov, was appointed to that post on 26 December 1938. He had been awarded the rank of captain on 30 December 1935, and having completed three courses at the Frunze Academy of the RKKA, by 31 July 1939 he had already become a colonel.

"The majority of 44th Rifle Division personnel were poorly educated and trained for military action. The majority had been conscripted into the Red Army on the eve of war. Thus, of the 3,229 Red Army men in the 25th Rifle Regiment, only 900 were cadre, that is, less than 30 percent of the personnel."

For details of the division's actions, see O. A. Dudorova, "Neizvestnye stranitsy 'zimnei voiny'" [Little-known pages of "the winter war"], *VIZh* 9 (September 1991): 12–23, which includes entries from the division's war diary. According to Dudorova, between 1 and 7 January 1940, the division suffered 1,001 killed, 1,430 wounded, 82 frozen, and 2,243 missing and lost most of its equipment. For a frank account of the war, see N. I. Baryshnikov, "Sovetsko-finliandskaia voina 1939–1940 gg." [The Soviet-Finnish War of 1939–1940], *Novaia i noveishaia istoriia* [New and recent history] 4 (March 1989): 28–41.

11. Ibid., 213.

12. "Akt o prieme Narkomata Oborony Soiuza SSR. tov. Timoshenko S. K. ot tov. Voroshilova K. E." [Act of reception of the USSR People's Commissariat of Defense to Comrade Timoshenko, S. K., from Comrade Voroshilov, K. E.], *Izvestiia TsK KPSS* 1 (January 1990): 194.

13. Later, in August 1940, when Stalin appointed K. A. Meretskov as chief of the General Staff, Vatutin became first deputy chief, Malandin became chief of the Operations Directorate, and Vasilevsky was his first deputy. Initial orders reforming the rifle division structure and creating the new mechanized corps can be found in V. A. Anfilov, "Krasnaia Armiia: Za god do fashistskoi agressii" [The Red Army: During the year before the fascist aggression], *VIZh* 4 (July–August 1996): 18–23.

14. Zakharov, *General'nyi shtab,* 213–214. Of this total, the plan assumed Germany and her alllies could commit 233 divisions, 10,550 tanks, up to 18,000 guns, and 13,900 aircraft against the Soviet Union. Overall German armed forces strength in wartime was placed at 8 million men, 240–243 divisions, 9,000–10,000 tanks, 20,000 guns, and 13,900 aircraft.

15. Ibid., 215.

16. *Nachal'nyi period*, 30.

17. Zakharov, *General'nyi shtab*, 218. The new total threat was increased to 280–290 divisions, 11,750 tanks, 30,000 guns, and 18,000 aircraft.

18. Ibid.

19. *Nachal'nyi period*, 31.

20. D. Volkogonov, *Triumf i tragediia: I. V. Stalin. politicheskii portret* [Triumph and Tragedy: I. V. Stalin, a political portrait], vol. 2 (Moscow: Novosti, 1989), 133.

21. *Nachal'nyi period*, 31.

22. Zakharov, *General'nyi shtab*, 219.

23. Volkogonov, *Triumf*, 135.

24. Complete transcripts of the conference are now available, as are the scenarios for the war games. For details, see Glantz, *Military Strategy*, 81–86.

25. *Nachal'nyi period*, 32.

26. For the contents of the Zhukov proposal and an analysis of its contents, see Glantz, *Military Strategy*, 87–90.

27. Ibid., 32–33. See also A. G. Khor'kov, *Boevaia mobilizatsionnaia gotovnost' prigranichnykh voennykh okrugov nakanune Velikoi Otechestvennoi voiny* [Combat and mobilization readiness of border military districts on the eve of the Great Patriotic War] (Moscow: Voroshilov Academy of the General Staff, 1985), 17, which states that the directives were sent to the Leningrad, Western Special, and Kiev Special Military Districts on 5 May, the Odessa Military District on 6 May, and the Baltic Special Military District on 14 May.

28. For details on the required and actual contents of these defense plans, see *Nachal'nyi period*, 33–37, and Khor'kov, *Boevaia*, 17–26. For how these directives and orders translated into action at the Army level, see A. V. Vladimirsky, *Na kievskom napravlenii* [On the Kiev axis] (Moscow: Voenizdat, 1989), 42–49, which describes planning by Kiev Special Military District's 5th Army.

29. *Nachal'nyi period*, 32.

30. Ibid., 38.

31. I. B. Pavlovsky, *Sukhoputnye voiska SSSR* [The ground forces of the USSR] (Moscow: Voenizdat, 1985), 65–68.

32. For example, the 82d Rifle Division, which fought in July and August 1939 at Khalkhin-Gol, was still essentially a territorial division, and at first its reservists performed poorly. See G. Zhukov, *Reminiscences and Reflections*, vol. 1 (Moscow: Progress, 1985), 204.

33. Pavlovsky, *Sukhoputnye voiska*, 66.

34. S. A. Tiushkevich, ed., *Sovetskie vooruzhennye sily* [The Soviet armed forces] (Moscow: Voenizdat, 1978), 236.

35. *Nastavlenie po mobilizatsionnoi rabote voiskovykh chastei, upravlenii i uchrezhdenii Krasnoi Armii* [Instruction on the mobilization work of the force units, directorates, and establishments of the Red Army] (Moscow: Voenizdat, 1940), 5. Classified secret, now declassified.

36. *Nachal'nyi period*, 38.

37. Khor'kov, *Boevaia*, 34.

38. Ibid., quoting from archival reference TsAMO, f. 138, op. 2181, d. 30, l. 373.

39. *Nachal'nyi period,* 38.

40. Khor'kov, *Boevaia,* 36.

41. Ibid., 35. See ibid. also for all details of the mobilization process and for a superb assessment of how the process worked in the western military districts in June 1941. Khor'kov also completely surveys material stockage and distribution in the region.

42. *Nachal'nyi period,* 39.

43. Ibid., 97.

44. Ibid., 41.

45. Ibid.

46. Ibid.

47. A. G. Khor'kov, "Nekotorye voprosy strategicheskogo razvertyvaniia Sovetskikh Vooruzhennykh Sil v nachale Velikoi Otechestvennoi voiny" [Some questions concerning the strategic deployment of the Soviet armed forces in the beginning of the Great Patriotic War], *VIZh* 1 (January 1986): 11.

48. Ibid.; Zakharov, *General'nyi shtab,* 259; and *Nachal'nyi period,* 93.

49. *Nachal'nyi period,* 93, quoting from archive reference *TsAMO,* f. 16, op. 29500, d. 406, l. 104–119.

50. Ibid., 91.

51. "Prikaz voiskam Pribaltiiskogo osobogo voennogo okruga no. 0052 ot 15 iiulia 1941 g. po obespecheniiu boevoi gotovnosti voisk okruga" [Baltic Special Military District Order No. 0052, dated 15 June 1941, about securing combat readiness of district forces], *Sbornik boevykh dokumentov Velikoi Otechestvennoi voiny* [Collection of Combat documents of the Great Patriotic War] issue 34 (Moscow: Voenizdat, 1958), 8. Hereafter cited as *SBDVOV.*

52. "Direktiva voennogo soveta Pribaltiiskogo osobogo voennogo okruga No. 00224 ot 15 iiulia 1941 g. o poriadke opoveshcheniia voisk okruga v sluchae narusheniia granitsy krupnymi silami protivnika" [Directive No. 00224 of the Baltic Special Military District Military Council, dated 15 July 1941, about the notification sequence of district forces in the event of violation of the border by large enemy forces], *SBDVOV,* issue 34, 12–13.

53. "Prikaz komanduiushchego Pribaltiiskim osobym voennym okrugom No. 00229 ot 18 iiunia 1941 g. upravleniiui voiskam okruga o provedenii meropriatii s tsel'iu bystreishego privedeniia v boevuiu gotovnost' teatra voennykh deistvii okruga" [Order No. 00229 of the Baltic Special Military District commander, dated 18 June 1941, to district force directorates about the conduct of measures aimed at rapidly bringing the district's theater of military opertions to combat readiness], *SBDVOV,* issue 34, 21–24.

54. *Nachal'nyi period,* 89. For even greater detail, see Khor'kov, *Boevaia.*

55. *Nachal'nyi period,* 96. See chapter 6.

56. *Nachal'nyi period,* 96.

## 5. Combat Readiness: Ground Combat Forces

1. M. Zakharov, "Predislovie" [Foreword], *Voprosy strategii i operativnogo iskusstva v sovetskikh voennykh trudakh (1917–1940 gg.)* [Questions of strategy and

operational art in Soviet military works (1917–1940)] (Moscow: Voenizdat, 1965), 23. Zakharov accurately captures the impressions and fears of many Soviet military commentators who assessed recent German combat performance in Soviet military journals.

2. *Nachal'nyi period Velikoi Otechestvennoi voiny* [The initial period of the Great Patriotic War] (Moscow: Voroshilov Academy of the General Staff, 1989), 42–43. Details on rifle force structure are found in many sources, including Iu. P. Babich and A. G. Baier, *Razvitie vooruzheniia i organizatsii sovetskikh sukhoputnykh voisk v gody Velikoi Otechestvennoi voiny* [The development of Soviet ground force weaponry and organization during the Great Patriotic War] (Moscow: Frunze Academy, 1990), 31–38.

3. *Nachal'nyi period*, 44, citing *Operatsii Sovetskykh Vooruzhennykh Sil v Velikoi Otechestvennoi voine 1941–1945 gg.* [Operations of the Soviet armed forces in the Great Patriotic War 1941–1945], vol. 1 (Moscow: Voenizdat, 1958), 79.

4. The Reserve of the High Command (RGK) became the Reserve of the Supreme High Command (RVGK) in August 1941.

5. *Nachal'nyi period*, 44–45; A. G. Khor'kov, *Boevaia i mobilizatsionnaia gotovnost' prigranichaykh voennykh okrugov nakanune Velikoi Otechnestvennoi voiny* [Combat and moblization readiness on the eve of the Great Patriotic War] (Moscow: Voroshilov Academy of the General Staff, 1985), 34–67.

6. *Nachal'nyi period*, 45.

7. "Prikaz voiskam Pribaltiiskogo osobogo voennogo okruga No. 0052 ot 15 iiunia 1941 g. po obespecheniiu boevoi gotovnosti voisk okruga" [Baltic Military District Forces Order No. 0052, dated 15 June 1941, about securing combat readiness of district forces], in *Sbornik boevykh dokumentov Velikoi Otechestvennoi voiny* [Collection of combat documents of the Great Patriotic War], issue 34 (Moscow: Voenizdat, 1958), 7–8. Prepared by the Military-Scientific Directorate of the General Staff. Numbered and classified secret. Original report classified *"sov. sekretno, osoboi vazhnosti"* (top secret, special importance). Hereafter cited as *SBDVOV*. All subsequent documents in this and companion issues were similarly classified.

8. "Donesenie shtaba Pribaltiiskogo osobogo voennogo okruga ot 22 iiunia 1941 g. General'nomu Shtabu Krasnoi Armii o nedostatkakh v organizatsii sviazi v okruge" [A report on 22 June from the Baltic Military District staff to the Red Army General Staff concerning deficiencies in the organization of district communications], *SBDVOV*, issue 34, 34.

9. "Donesenie komanduiushchego voiskami severo-zapadnogo fronta ot 22 iiunia 1941 g. narodnomu komissaru oborony o proryve krupnykh tankovykh i motorizovannykh sil protivnika na Druskeniki i meropriiatiiakh komandovaniia fronta po organizatsii razgroma til'zitskoi gruppirovki protivnika" [A report of 22 June 1941 from the commander of Northwestern Front forces to the people's commissar of defense concerning the penetration by large enemy tank and motorized forces at Druskeniki and measures undertaken by the *front* command to organize the destruction of the enemy Til'sit grouping], *SBDVOV*, issue 34, 36.

10. "Donesenie nachal'nika artilleriiskogo upravleniia severo-zapadnogo fronta ot 23 iiunia 1941 g. zamestiteliu narodnogo komissara oborony SSSR ob ostrom nedostatke boepripasov v resul'tate pervogo dnia boevykh deistvii voisk fronta" [A

report on 23 June 1941 by the chief of the Artillery Directorate of the Northwestern Front to the people's commissar of defense of the USSR concerning the acute shortage of ammunition as a result of the first day's battle of *front* forces], *SBDVOV*, issue 34, 48.

11. "Doklad nachal'nika upravleniia sviazi severo-zapadnogo fronta nachal'niku upravleniia sviazi Krasnoi Armii ot 26 iiulia 1941 g. o sostoianii i ispol'zovanii voisk sviazi fronta v nachal'nyi period voiny" [A report on 26 July 1941 from the chief of the Northwestern Front Communications Directorate to the chief of the Red Army Communications Directorate concerning the status and use of *front* signal forces during the initial period of war], *SBDVOV*, issue 34, 187–188.

12. "Doklad nachal'nika artillerii 8-i armii nachal'niku General'nogo Shtaba Krasnoi Armii i nachal'niku artillerii severnogo fronta ot 26 avgusta 1941 g. o boevoi deiatel'nosti artillerii armii za period s 22 iiunia po 20 avgusta 1941 g." [A report of 26 August 1941 by the 8th Army chief of artillery to the Red Army chief of staff and the Northern Front chief of artillery about the combat activities of Army artillery for the period 22 June to 20 August 1941], *SBDVOV*, issue 34, 230–231.

13. "Prikaz nachal'nika shtaba 27-i armii no. 1 ot 7 iiulia 1941 g. ob ustranenii nedostatkov v rabote lichnogo sostava polevogo upravleniia armii" [27th Army Chief of Staff Order No. 1 of 7 July 1941 about the elimination of deficiencies in the work of Army field directorate personnel], *SBDVOV*, issue 34, 276–277.

14. "Direktiva voennogo soveta zapadnogo fronta ot 23 iiunia 1941 g. voennym sovetam armii i komandiram korpusov o navedenii poriadka v obespechenii voisk" [A directive of 23 June 1941 from the Western Front Military Council to Army Military Councils and corps commanders about restoring order in force protection], *SBDVOV*, issue 35 (Moscow: Voenzdat, 1958), 34–35.

15. "Donesenie komanduiushchego voiskami 3-i armii ot 23 iiunia 1941 g. komanduiushchemu voiskami fronta ob otsutstvii v voiskakh armii transporta, goriuchego i vooruzheniia" [A 23 June 1941 report by the 3d Army commander to the *front* commander about the absence in Army forces of transport, fuel, and weaponry], *SBDVOV*, issue 35, 137.

16. "Boevoe donesenie komandira 2-go strel'kovogo korpusa no. 1 ot 25 iiunia 1941 g. shtabu zapadnogo fronta o khode otmobilizovaniia chastei korpusa" [Combat report no. 1 of the 2d Rifle Corps commander, dated 25 June 1941, to the Western Front staff concerning the course of mobilization of corps units], *SBDVOV*, issue 35, 183–184.

17. "Boevoe donesenie komandira 2-go strelkovogo korpusa no. 2 ot 28 iiunia 1941 g. komanduiushchemu voiskami zapadnogo fronta o boevykh deistviiakh korpusa" [Combat report no. 2 of the 2d Rifle Corps commander, dated 28 June 1941, to the commander of Western Front forces concerning corps combat operations], *SBDVOV*, issue 35, 184–185.

18. "Operativnaia svodka shtaba iugo-zapadnogo fronta no. 9 k 20 chasam 26 iiunia 1941 o boevykh deistviiakh voisk fronta" [Operational summary no. 9 of the Southwestern Front staff, prepared at 2000, 26 June 1941, about combat operations of *front* forces], *SBDVOV*, issue 36 (Moscow: Voenizdat, 1958), 28–29.

19. "Direktiva voennogo soveta iugo-zapadnogo fronta no. 00207 ot 29 iiunia 1941 g. komanduiushchemu voiskami 6-i armii ob ustranenii nedostatkov v boevykh

deistviiakh soedinenii armii" [Military Council of the Southwestern Front directive no. 00207 of 29 June 1941 to the 6th Army commander concerning the elimination of deficiencies in the combat operations of Army formations], *SBDVOV*, issue 36, 49–50.

20. "Doklad nachal'nika artillerii iugo-zapadnogo fronta nachal'niku glavnogo artilleriiskogo upravleniia Krasnoi Armii ot 14 iiulia 1941 g. ob obespechennosti chastei iugo-zapadnym frontom artilleriiskim i strelkovo-minometnym vooruzheniem po sostoianiiu na 10 iiulia 1941 goda" [A 14 July 1941 report of the Southwestern Front chief of artillery to the chief of the Red Army's Main Artillery Directorate about the provisioning of Southwestern Front artillery and rifle-mortar units with weaponry based on conditions on 10 July 1941], *SBDVOV*, issue 36, 93–100.

21. A. V. Vladimirsky, *Na kievskom napravlenii* [On the Kiev axis] (Moscow: Voenizdat, 1989), 30.

22. Ibid., 32–33.

23. Formed on an experimental basis beginning in 1932, the tank corps had begun their history as mechanized corps and were renamed "tank" in 1938. A special commission (the Kulik Commission) formed by Stalin in 1939 to study the experiences of the Spanish Civil War recommended abolishing the corps and replacing it with smaller armored formations that could cooperate better with infantry. As a result, in November 1939 the commission ordered the abolition of the tank corps and their replacement by separate tank brigades and combined arms motorized divisions. The conversion process was slow, and a tank corps participated in the Finnish War (the 10th). All tank corps finally disappeared by early 1940. By 1 March 1940, the Soviet force structure contained 39 light and heavy tank brigades, 3 RVK (Reserve of the High Command) motorized armored brigades, 31 tank regiments, and 100 tank battalions serving in rifle and cavalry divisions, for a total tank park of 20,000 tanks. Plans were also under way for formation of 15 motorized rifle divisions.

24. "Akt o priem narkomata oborony soiuza SSR tov. Timoshenko S. K. ot tov. Voroshilova K. E." [Act of reception of the USSR People's Commissariat of Defense to Comrade Timoshenko, S. K., from Comrade Voroshilov, K. E.], *Izvestiia TsK KPSS* 1 (January 1990): 201. Dated 8 May 1940.

25. During the first stage of this process, about 25 tank brigades were to be retained to provide tank support to infantry, but during the second stage (in 1941), all existing tank brigades and battalions were disbanded to provide material for the new mechanized corps. This left virtually no armor in rifle and cavalry divisions and corps in June 1941. Of the 37,895 tanks required by mechanized, rifle, cavalry, and airborne formation establishments in June 1941, only 23,100 old model tanks were on hand, and 18,700 of these were combat ready. In addition, 3,600 of the tanks were T-37, T-38, and T-40 models, which were equipped with only machine guns. See N. Ramanichev, "The Red Army, 1940–1941: Myths and Realities," Unpublished manuscript, 92, quoting archival materials in *TsAMO*, f. 38, op. 11353, d. 909, l. 2–18, l. 924, and l. 135–138.

26. Among many sources on the composition of the mechanized corps, see *Nachal'nyi period*, 45–47; *Stroitel'stvo i boevoe primenenie sovetskikh tankovykh voisk v gody Velikoi Otechestvennoi voiny* [The formation and combat use of Soviet tank forces during the Great Patriotic War] (Moscow: Voenizdat, 1979), 44.

27. *Nachal'nyi period.*, 46.

28. Ibid., 47.

29. Truck fill included 66 percent of required GAZ-AA and 31 percent of ZIS-4 trucks, and 27 percent of their fuel trucks.

30. Ibid. Later during the war, Rokossovsky would rise to *front* command.

31. For details on Soviet and German tanks, see Steven J. Zaloga and James Grandsen, *Operation Barbarossa* (London: Arms and Armor Press, 1985); and Steven J. Zaloga, Jim Kinnear, and Peter Sarson, *KV-1 & 2 Heavy Tanks, 1941–1945* (London: Osprey, 1995).

32. "Doklad komandira 12-go mekhanizirovannogo korpusa ot 27 iiunia 1941 g. komanduiushchemy voiskami severo-zapadnogo fronta o nedostatkakh v ispol'zovanii korpusa" [A 27 June 1941 report of the 12th Mechanized Corps commander to the Northwestern Front commander about shortcomings in the employment of the corps], *SBDVOV*, issue 34, 322–323. Shestapalov was wounded in action on 27 June and died in a hospital on 6 August 1941.

33. Ibid., 322.

34. Ibid., 323.

35. "Boevoe donesenie komandira 21-go mekhanizirvannogo korpusa no. 3 ot 29 iiunia 1941 g. o resul'tatakh boevykh deistvii korpusa" [Combat report no. 3, dated 29 June 1941, of the 21st Mechanized Corps commander concerning the results of corps' combat operations], *SBDVOV*, issue 33, 30–31. During the war, Leliushenko would rise to command the famous 4th Guards Tank Army.

36. "Donesenie pomoshchnika komanduiushchego severo-zapadnym frontom ot 11 iiulia 1941 g. o sostoianii mekhanizirovannykh korpusov" [An 11 July 1941 report by the deputy commander of the Northwestern Front about the condition of mechanized corps], *SBDVOV*, issue 33, 12.

37. Ibid.

38. "Pis'mo nachal'nika avtobronetankovogo upravleniia severo-zapadnogo fronta ot 11 iiulia 1941 g. o sostoianii mekhanizirovannykh korpusov i prichinakh bol'shikh poter'" [A letter of 11 July 1941 from the chief of the Northwestern Front Armored Directorate about the condition of mechanized corps and the reasons for their great losses], *SBDVOV*, issue 33, 14–16. Major General Kurkin was the commander of 3d Mechanized Corps. Poluboiarov would become the commander of 4th Guards Tank Corps and would serve with that corps through the Battle of Berlin.

39. Ibid., 16.

40. "Doklad komandira 21-go mekhanizirovannogo korpusa komanduiushchemu 27-i armii o sostoianii korpusa na 23 iiulia 1941 g." [A report by the commander of 21st Mechanized Corps to the commander of 27th Army concerning the corp's condition on 23 July 1941], *SBDVOV*, issue 33, 40–41.

41. Ibid., 41.

42. "Spravka komandira 12-go mekhanizirovannogo korpusa ot 29 iiulia 1941 g. o nedostatkakh v ispol'zovanii korpusa i upravlenii im" [Information from the 12th Mechanized Corps commander on 29 July 1941 about deficiencies in corps employment and command and control], *SBDVOV*, issue 33, 42–43.

43. "Otchet komandira 1-go mekhanizirovannogo korpusa ot 2 avgusta 1941 g. nachal'niku shtaba severo-zapadnogo fronta o boevykh deistviiakh 1-go mekhani-

zirovannogo korpusa za period s 22 iiunia po 24 iiulia 1941 g." [An assessment by the commander of 1st Mechanized Corps on 2 August 1941 to the chief of staff of the Northwestern Front about the combat operations of 1st Mechanized Corps during the period from 22 June through 24 July 1941], *SBDVOV*, issue 34, 324.

44. "Rasporiazhenie komandira 1-go mekhanizirovannogo korpusa ot 1 avgusta 1941 g. ob ustranenii nedostatkov v organizatsii upravleniia boem soedinenii i chastei korpusa" [An instruction from the 1st Mechanized Corps' commander of 1 August 1941 concerning the elimination of deficiencies in the organization of the command and control in combat of corps' formations and units], *SBDVOV*, issue 33, 44–45.

45. "Doklad komandira 7-i tankovoi divizii 6-go mekhanizirovannogo korpusa ot 28 iiulia 1941 g. o primenenii i kharakter deistvii mekhanizirovannykh soedinenii s 22 iiunia po 20 iiulia 1941 g." [A 28 July 1941 report by the commander of 6th Mechanized Corps' 7th Tank Division about the use and nature of operations of the mechanized formations from 22 June through 20 July 1941], *SBDVOV*, issue 33, 117–118.

46. "Boevoe rasporiazhenie komanduiushchego voiskami zapadnogo fronta ot 23 iiunia 1941 g. komanduiushchemu voiskami 10-i armii o navedenii poriadka v upravlenii voiskami armii" [A 23 June 1941 military directive of the commander of Western Front forces to the commander of 10th Army forces about the institution of order in the command and control of Army forces], *SBDVOV*, issue 35, 30.

47. "Boevoe donesenie shtaba zapadnogo fronta no. 008 k 16 chasam 45 minutam 25 iiunia 1941 g. o polozhenii soedinenii i chastei fronta" [Combat report of Western Front headquarters no. 008, dated 1645 25 June 1941, concerning the situation of *front* formations and units], *SBDVOV*, issue 35, 45.

48. "Operativnaia svodka shtaba zapadnogo fronta no. 7 k 22 chasam 25 iiunia 1941 g. o boevykh deistviiakh voisk fronta" [Operational summary of Western Front headquarters no. 7, dated 0722 hours 25 June 1941, about the combat actions of *front* forces], *SBDVOV*, issue 35, 45.

49. "Operativnaia svodka shtaba zapadnogo fronta no. 8 k 20 chasam 27 iiunia 1941 g. o boevykh deistviiakh voisk fronta" [Operational summary of Western Front headquarters no. 8, dated 2000 hours 27 June 1941 about combat operations of *front* forces], *SBDVOV*, issue 35, 50.

50. Ibid.

51. "Donesenie nachal'nika avtobronetankovogo upravleniia zapadnogo fronta nachal'niku glavnogo avtobronetankovogo upravleniia Krasnoi Armii o sostoianii avtobronetankovykh voisk fronta na 29 iiunia 1941 g." [A report of the chief of the Western Front Armored Directorate to the chief of the Red Army Armored Directorate about the condition of *front* armored forces on 29 June 1941], *SBDVOV*, issue 35, 65.

52. "Donesenie nachal'nika avtobronetankovogo upravleniia zapadnogo fronta nachal'niku glavnogo avtobronetankovogo upravleniia Krasnoi Armii ot 1 iiulia 1941 g. o sostoianii avtobronetankovykh voisk fronta" [A report from the chief of the Western Front Armored Directorate to the chief of the Red Army Armored Directorate on 1 July 1941 concerning the condition of *front* armored forces], *SBDVOV*, issue 35, 83–84.

53. "Doklad nachal'nika avtobronetankovogo upravleniia zapadnogo fronta zamestiteliu narodnogo komissara oborony Soiuza SSR ot 5 avgusta 1941 g. o boevykh

312    Stumbling Colossus

deistviiakh mekhanizirovannykh korpusov s 22 iiunia po 27 iiunia 1941 g." [A 5 August 1941 report by the chief of the Western Front's Armored Directorate to the deputy people's commissar of defense of the USSR about mechanized corps combat operations from 22 June to 27 June 1941], *SBDVOV*, issue 33, 73–77.

54. Ibid., 73.

55. Ibid., 75–76.

56. V. P. Krikunov, "Kuda delis' tanki?" [What happened to the tanks?], *VIZh* 11 (November 1988): 31.

57. "Prikaz komanduiushchego 20-i armiei no. 7 ot 8 iiulia 1941 g. o nedostatkakh, vyiavlennykh v 5-m i 7-m mekhanizirovannykh korpusakh v khode dvukhdnevnykh boev" [Order no. 7 of the 20th Army commander, dated 8 July 1941, about the shortcomings revealed in 5th and 7th Mechanized Corps during the two-day battle], *SBDVOV*, issue 33, 86. Kurochkin served throughout the war in Army command and after the war became an important military historian and theorist.

58. "Prikaz 7-mu mekhanizirovannomu korpusu no. 7" [Order no. 7 to 7th Mechanized Corps], *SBDVOV*, issue 33, 104.

59. Ibid.

60. Krikunov, 33–35, quoting from "Doklad komandira 7-i tankovoi divizii 6-go mekhanizirovannogo korpusa o sostoianii i deistviiakh 7 TD" [A report of the 7th Tank Division commander about the condition and operations of 7th TD]. The 7th Tank Division had been virtually destroyed in fighting south of Grodno during the first week of war.

61. "Boevoe donesenie komandira 37-i tankovoi divizii ot 28 iiunia 1941 g. o resul'tatakh boevykh deistvii divizii" [A combat report of 28 June 1941 of the 37th Tank Division commander about the results of division combat operations], *SBDVOV*, issue 33, 174–175.

62. "Opisanie komandirom 8-go mekhanizirovannogo korpusa boevykh deistvii korpusa s 22 po 29 iiulia 1941 g." [A description by the commander of 8th Mechanized Corps of corps combat operations from 22 through 29 June 1941], *SBDVOV*, issue 33, 164. Riabyshev survived the initial period of war and later commanded armies and rifle corps to war's end.

63. Ibid., 168–170.

64. "Kratkoe opisanie boevykh deistvii 15-go mekhanizirovannogo korpusa v period s 22.6.41 po 12.7.41 g." [A short description of 15th Mechanized Corps combat operations during the period from 22.6.41 through 12.7.41], *SBDVOV*, issue 36, 253.

65. Ibid., 253–254.

66. "Doklad nachal'nika avtobronetankovogo upravleniia iugo-zapadnogo fronta voennomu sovetu fronta ot 30 iiunia 1941 g. o sostoianii mekhanizirovannykh korpusov i ob otvode ikh dlia vosstanovleniia material'noi chasti" [A report of the chief of the Southwestern Front Armored Directorate to the *front* Military Council on 30 June 1941 about the condition of the mechanized corps and about their withdrawal for the restoration of equipment], *SBDVOV*, issue 33, 129.

67. "Doklad nachal'nika avtobronetankovogo upravleniia iugo-zapadnogo fronta voennomu sovetu fronta o sostoianii mekhanizirovannykh korpusov na 1 iiulia 1941 g." [A report by the chief of the Southwestern Front's Armored Directorate to the

*front* Military Council concerning the condition of mechanized corps on 1 July 1941],
*SBDVOV*, issue 33, 131.

68. Ibid.

69. "Doklad nachal'nika avtobronetankovogo upravleniia iugo-zapadnogo fronta nachal'niku glavnogo avtobronetankovogo upravleniia ot 3 iiulia 1941 g. o prichinakh bol'shikh poter' v mekhanizirovannykh korpusakh i predlozheniia po uluchsheniiu ikh ispol'zovaniia" [A 3 July 1941 report of the chief of the Southwestern Front's Armored Directorate to the chief of the Main Armored Directorate about the reasons for great mechanized corps losses and proposals to improve their employment], *SBDVOV*, issue 33, 132–133.

70. "Direktiva komanduiushchego iugo-zapadnom frontom ob uluchshenii organizatsii i rukovodstva boem mekhanizirovannykh korpusov" [A directive of the Southwestern Front commander about improving the organization and control of mechanized corps in battle], *SBDVOV*, issue 33, 134.

71. "Spravka nachal'nika avtobronetankovogo upravleniia iugo-zapadnogo fronta komanduiushchemu voiskami fronta o sostoianii avtobronetankovykh voisk na 17 iiulia 1941 g." [Information from the chief of the Southwestern Front Armored Directorate to the commander of *front* forces about the condition of armored forces on 17 July 1941], *SBDVOV*, issue 36, 102–103. The total tank strength cited in the report does not match total strength by type. The same report assessed armored strength on 17 July as follows: 8th MC, 57 (including 28 KV and T-34); 15th MC, 10 (1 T-34); 4th MC, 100 (10 KV and 49 T-34); 16th MC, 73; 9th MC, 38; 19th MC, 77 (31 T-34); 22d MC, 40; 24th MC, 100. Morgunov noted that during the entire period Soviet industry provided the *front* with 4 new KV and 34 T-34 tanks.

72. Ibid., 103.

73. Ibid., 105.

74. "Doklad pomoshchnika komanduiushchego voiskami iugo-zapadnogo fronta po tankovym voiskam zamestiteliu narodnogo komissara oborony Soiuza SSR ot 5 avgusta 1941 g. o nedostatkakh v upravlenii boevymi deistviiami mekhanizirovannykh korpusov" [A 5 August report of the assistant commander of the Southwestern Front for Armored Forces to the deputy people's commissar for defense of the USSR about the deficiencies in command and control of mechanized corps combat operations], *SBDVOV*, issue 33, 135–139. Vol'sky would later become a mechanized corps commander at Stalingrad and commander of 5th Guards Tank Army late in 1944.

75. Ibid., 135.

76. "Doklad komandira 41-i tankovoi divizii pomoshchniku komandiushchego iugo-zapadnym frontom po tankovym voiskam ot 25 iiulia 1941 g. o boevykh deistviiakh 41-i tankovoi divizii s 22 iiunia po 11 iiulia 1941" [A 25 July report of the 41st Tank Division commander to the assistant commander of the Southwestern Front about 41st Tank Division combat operations from 22 June through 11 July 1941], *SBDVOV*, issue 33, 176–179.

77. "Doklad komandira 32-i tankovoi divizii nachal'niku avtobronetankovogo upravleniia iugo-zapadnogo fronta o boevykh deistviiakh divizii za period s 22 iiunia po 14 iiulia 1941 g." [A report of the 32d Tank Division commander to the chief of

the Southwestern Front Armored Directorate about division combat operations from 22 June through 14 July 1941] *SBDVOV*, issue 33, 180–188.

78. "Doklad komandira 10-i tankovoi divizii zamestiteliu narodnogo komissara oborony Soiuza SSR ot 2 avgusta 1941 g. o boevykh deistviiakh divizii v period s 22 iiunia po 1 avgusta 1941 g." [A 2 August 1941 report of the 10th Tank Division commander to the deputy people's commissar of defense of the USSR about division combat operations from 22 June through 1 August 1941], *SBDVOV*, issue 33, 192–213.

79. "Doklad komandira 37-i tankovoi divizii nachal'niku avtobronetankovogo upravleniia iugo-zapadnogo fronta o boevykh deistviiakh divizii v period s 22 iiunia po 10 iiulia 1941 g. i ee sostoianii na 15 iiulia 1941 g." [A report of the commander of the 37th Tank Division to the chief of the Southwestern Front Armored Directorate about the division's combat operations during the period from 22 June through 10 July 1941 and its condition as of 15 July 1941], *SBDVOV*, issue 33, 216.

80. Ibid.

81. Ibid., 217.

82. "Doklad komandira 43-i tankovoi divizii komanduiushchemu voiskami iugo-zapadnogo fronta o boevykh deistviiakh divizii za period s 22 iiunia po 10 avgusta 1941 g." [A report by the commander of 43d Tank Division to the commander of Southwestern Front forces on division combat operations for the period from 22 June through 10 August 1941], *SBDVOV*, issue 33, 233.

83. Ibid., 234.

84. Ibid.

85. "Doklad komanduiushchego voiskami iugo-zapadnogo fronta nachal'niku general'nogo shtaba Krasnoi Armii ot 7 iiulia 1941 g. o polozhenii mekhanizirovannykh korpusov fronta" [A report on 7 July 1941 by the commander of Southwestern Front forces to the chief of the Red Army General Staff about the situation of *front* mechanized corps], *SBDVOV*, issue 36, 81–82.

86. "Operativnaia svodka shtaba 5-i armii no. 024 k 11 chasam 8 iiulia 1941 g. o resul'tatakh otkhoda voisk armii na liniiu korostenskogo ukreplennogo raiona" [5th Army headquarters operational report no. 024, dated 1100 hours 8 July 1941, about the results of the withdrawal of Army forces to the line of the Korosten' fortified region], *SBDVOV*, issue 36, 161–162.

87. Based on 1985 and 1986 interviews with former Lieutenant Helmut Ritgen, who served in 6th Panzer Division's reconnaissance battalion during battles for Raseiniai. The interview took place at the U.S. Army War College during symposia that addressed the conduct of operations on the German Eastern Front.

88. This information is based on interviews with numerous German veterans at four Art of War Symposia conducted in 1984, 1985, and 1986 at the U.S. Army War College, Carlisle, Pennsylvania.

89. "Opisanie komandirom 8-go mekhanizirovannogo korpusa boevykh deistvii korpusa s 22 po 29 iiunia 1941 g." [An account by the commander of 8th Mechanized Corps of corps combat operations from 22 through 29 June 1941], *SBDVOV*, issue 33, 164–170.

90. Details on cavalry force organization and combat readiness in June 1941 are found in *Nachal'nyi period,* 52–53; and Babich and Baier, *Razvitie vooruzheniia,* 61.

91. See *SBDVOV*, issue 35, for details on 36th Cavalry Division's early destruction.

92. Airborne force organization, readiness, and combat performance are found in *Nachal'nyi period,* 53–54, and David M. Glantz, *A History of Soviet Airborne Forces* (London: Frank Cass, 1994), 38–56.

93. Glantz, *Airborne Forces,* 43.

94. "Boevoe rasporiazhenie komanduiushchego voiskami zapadnogo fronta ot 28 iiunia 1941 g. komandiru 4-go vozdushnodesantnogo korpusa i komanduiushchemu voenno-vozdushnymi silami fronta na desantirovanie 214-i vozdushnodesantnoi brigady v raion Slutsk" [Combat instructions of the Western Front commander, dated 28 June 1941, to the commander of 4th Airborne Corps and the commander of *front* air forces concerning the air landing of the 214th Airborne Brigade in the Slutsk region], *SBDVOV,* issue 35, 56.

95. "Chastnyi prikaz komanduiushchego voiskami zapadnogo fronta no. 012 ot 29 iiunia 1941 g. komandiru 4-go vozdushnodesantnogo korpusa na vydvizhenie 214-i vozdushnodesantnoi brigady na glusskoe napravlenie i na perekhod k oborone ostal'nymi voiskami korpusa" [Personal order no. 012 of the Western Front commander, dated 29 June 1941, to the commander of 4th Airborne Corps on the movement of the 214th Airborne Brigade along the Glutsk axis and on the transition of the corps' remaining forces to the defense], *SBDVOV,* issue 35, 63.

96. For a description of the composition and deployment of fortified regions, see A. G. Khor'kov, "Ukreplennye raiony na zapadnom granitsakh SSSR" [Fortified regions on the western borders of the USSR], *VIZh* 12 (December 1987): 47–54.

97. Ibid., 45; *Boevoi sostav Sovetskoi armii* [Combat composition of the Soviet Army], part 1 (Moscow: Military-Scientific Directorate of the General Staff, 1963), 7–12.

98. Ramanichev, "Red Army," 82–83, quoting from *TsAMO,* f. 15a, op. 2245, d. 83, l. 36. Ramanichev adds that in 1940 the Army received only 81,118 of the planned production of 100,000 submachine guns and 368,934 of 711,000 planned rifle production by Soviet industry.

## 6. Combat Readiness: Combat Support and Rear Service Forces

1. N. Ramanichev, "The Red Army: Myths and Realities," Unpublished manuscript, 96, citing archival reference *TsAMO,* f. 13, op. 11624, d. 296, l. 9–37; f. 81, op. 12074, d. 8, l. 125–126; f. 157, op. 222, d. 18. The recent book by A. A. Volkov, *Kriticheskii prolog: Nezavershennye frontovye nastupatel'nye operatsii pervykh kampanii Velikoi Otechestvennoi voiny* [Critical prologue: Incomplete *front* offensive operations of the first campaigns of the Great Patriotic War] (Moscow: AVIAR, 1992), 24, cites archival data to place artillery strength on 22 June 1941 at 115,900 tubes.

2. P. A. Degtiarev and P. P. Popov, *"Katiushi" na pole boia* [Katiushas on the field of battle] (Moscow: Voenizdat, 1991), 4–6.

3. *Nachal'nyi period Velikoi Otechestvennoi voiny* [Initial period of the Great Patriotic War] (Moscow: Voroshilov Academy of the General Staff, 1989), 54–55. See also numerous specific reports in *Sbornik boevykh dokumentov Velikoi Otechestvennoi voiny* [Collection of combat documents of the Great Patriotic War], issues 34–36 (Moscow: Voenizdat, 1958). Hereafter cited as *SBDVOV.*

4. "Doklad nachal'nika artillerii iugo-zapadnogo fronta nachal'niku glavnogo artilleriiskogo upravleniia Krasnoi Armii ot 14 iiulia 1941 g. ob obespechennosti chastei fronta artilleriiskim i strelkovo-minometnym vooruzheniem po sostoianiiu na 10 iiulia 1941 g." [A 14 July report of the chief of the Southwestern Front Artillery to the chief of the Red Army Artillery Directorate about the provision of *front* units with artillery and rifle-mortar weapons as of 10 July 1941], *SBDVOV*, issue 36, 93–100.

5. Ibid., 94.

6. Ibid., 99.

7. Ibid., 54–55. For the experience of one of these brigades, see K. S. Moskalenko, *Na iugo-zapadnom napravlenii* [On the southwestern direction] (Moscow: Nauka, 1969), 17–30. Moskalenko commanded the 1st Antitank Brigade of Southwestern Front and later in the war rose to command of 38th and 40th Armies.

8. *Nachal'nyi period*, 55–56.

9. "Kratkii otchet nachal'nika inzhenernogo upravleniia zapadnogo fronta nachal'niku glavnogo voenno-inzhenernogo upravleniia Krasnoi Armii o rabote inzhenernykh chastei fronta za period s 22 iiunia po 13 avgusta 1941 g." [A short assessment by the chief of the Western Front's Engineer Directorate to the chief of the Red Army Engineer Directorate about the work of *front* engineer units during the period from 22 June through 13 July 1941], *SBDVOV*, issue 35, 123–124.

10. Ibid., 56–57.

11. Ramanichev, "Red Army," 209, citing archival reference *TsAMO*, f. 32, op. 11309, d. 15, l. 16.

12. For example, see "Kratkii otchet nachal'nika upravleniia sviazi iugo-zapadnogo fronta nachal'niku upravleniia sviazi Krasnoi Armii ot 27 iiulia 1941 g. o rabote sviazi iugo-zapadnogo fronta s 22 iiunia po 26 iiulia 1941 g." [A short report on 27 July 1941 by the chief of the Southwestern Front's Signals Directorate to the chief of the Red Army's Signal Directorate about communications work in the Southwestern Front from 22 June 1941 through 26 July 1941], *SBDVOV*, issue 36, 106–109.

13. "Donesenie shtaba Pribaltiiskogo osobogo voennogo okruga ot 22 iiunia 1941 g. general'nomu shtabu Krasnoi Armii o nedostatkakh v organizatsii sviazi v okruge" [A 22 June report of the Baltic Special Military District headquarters to the Red Army General Staff about deficiencies in the organization of district communications], *SBDVOV*, issue 34, 34.

14. "Doklad nachal'nika upravleniia sviazi severo-zapadnogo fronta nachal'niku upravleniia sviazi Krasnoi Armii ot 26 iiulia 1941 g. o sostoianii i izpol'zovanii voisk sviazi fronta v nachal'nyi period voiny" [A 26 July report of the chief of the Northwestern Front Signals Directorate to the chief of the Red Army Signals Directorate about the condition and use of *front* signal forces in the initial period of war], *SBDVOV*, issue 34, 187–190.

15. *Nachal'nyi period*, 81.

16. Ibid.

17. The 13 zones were: Northern, Northwestern, Western, Kiev, Southern, North Caucasus, Trans-Caucasus, Central Asian, Trans-Baikal, Far Eastern, Moscow, Orel, and Khar'kov. All bore the names of their parent military districts, except the Southern (Odessa Military District). See also A. Koldunov, "Organizatsiia i vedenie protivovozdushnoi oborony po opytu nachal'nogo perioda Velikoi Otechestvennoi

voiny" [The organization and conduct of antiaircraft defense based on the experience of the initial period of the Great Patriotic War], *VIZh* 4 (April 1984): 12–19.

18. Ibid., 82.

19. Ibid., 83.

20. For details, see N. Svetlishin, "Primenenie voisk protivovozdushnoi oborony v letne–osennei kampanii 1941 goda" [The employment of antiaircraft defense forces during the summer–fall campaign of 1941], *VIZh* 3 (March 1968): 26–39. Training problems are covered in V. Medin, "Slovo v boiu bylo delom" [Words in battle were the issue], *Protivovozdushnaia oborona* [Antiaircraft defense] 11 (November 1991): 76–77.

21. Svetlishin, "Primenenie," 84. For documentary evidence of the German overflights and the text of a 10 June 1941 NKO order on the matter, see L. G. Ivashov, "Ot 'Iunkersa' 1941 k 'Tsessna' 1987-go" [From the Junkers of 1941 to the Cessna of 1987], *VIZh* 6 (June 1990): 43–46.

22. Ammunition stocks were broken down as follows: 37mm, 23 percent; 76.2mm, 75 percent; and 85mm, 13 percent.

23. *Boevoi sostav Sovetskoi armii* [Combat composition of the Soviet Army], part 1 (Moscow: Military-Scientific Directorate of the General Staff, 1963), 7–12; *Nachal'nyi period,* 88.

24. Ramanichev, "Red Army," 125, citing archival reference *TsAMO,* f. 81, op. 11627, d. 296, l. 5.

25. *Nachal'nyi period,* 86.

26. Ibid.

27. "Prikaz komanduiushchego Pribaltiiskim osobym voennym okrugom no. 00229 ot 18 iiunia 1941 g. upravleniiu i voiskam okruga o provedenii meropriiatii s tsel'iu bystreishego privedeniia v boevuiu gotovnost' teatra voennykh deistvii okruga" [Order of Baltic Special Military District commander no. 00229, dated 18 June 1941, to the district directorate and forces about the conduct of measures with the aim of rapidly bringing the theater of military operations of the district to combat readiness], *SBDVOV,* issue 34, 21–22.

28. Ibid., 88.

29. Ramanichev, 102–103, citing archival reference *Tsentral'nyi arkhiv pogranichnoi voisk,* f. 16, op. 226, ed.khr., 264, l. 70–81. Hereafter cited as *TsPV.*

30. "Iz opisaniia boevykh deistvii 22 motostrel'kovoi divizii voisk NKVD v Pribaltike s 22 iiunia po 13 iiulia 1941 g." [From a description of 22d NKVD Motorized Rifle Division operations in the Baltic region from 22 June through 13 July 1941], in *Vnutrennie voiska v Velikoi Otechestvennoi voine 1941–1945 gg.* [Internal forces in the Great Patriotic War 1941–1945] (Moscow: Iuridicheskaia Literatura, 1975), 39. Hereafter cited as *Internal forces.*

31. "Iz zhurnala boevykh deistvii 2 divizii voisk NKVD s 1 po 10 iiulia 1941 g." [From the journal of 2d NKVD Division combat operations from 1 through 10 July 1941], in *Internal forces,* 43.

32. "Iz opisaniia boevykh deistvii garnizonov i podrazdelenii 109 polka voisk NKVD po okhrane zheleznodorozhnykh sooruzhenii pri otkhode s territorii Estonii s 7 iiulia po 29 avgusta 1941 g." [From a description of the combat actions of 109th NKVD Regiment garrisons and subunits in the defense of railroad installations during

the withdrawal from Estonian territory from 7 July through 10 August 1941], in *Internal forces*, 46.

33. Ibid., 88–90. See also A. G. Khor'kov, *Boevaia i mobilizatsionnaia gotovnost' prigranichnykh voennykh okrugov nakanune Velikoi Otechestvennoi voiny* [Combat and mobilization readiness of border military districts on the eve of the Great Patriotic War] (Moscow: Voroshilov Academy of the General Staff, 1985).

34. Ramanichev, "Red Army," 146, citing archival reference *TsAMO*, f. 13, op. 137145, d. 26, l. 70–71.

35. *Narodnoe khoziastvo SSSR v Velikoi Otechestvennoi voine, 1941–1945* [The economy of the USSR during the Great Patriotic War, 1941–1945] (Moscow: IIT's Goskomstata SSSR, 1993), 55. Hereafter cited as *USSR Economy*.

36. B. Sokolov, "Lend-Lease in Soviet Military Efforts, 1941–1945," *Journal of Slavic Military Studies* 7, 3 (September 1994): 571, quoting from *Tyl Sovetskoi armii v Velikoi Otechestvennoi voine, 1941–1945 gg.* [The rear services of the Soviet Army during the Great Patriotic War, 1941–1945] (Moscow: Voennaia Akademiia Tyl i Transporta, 1963), 46.

37. See Ramanichev, "Red Army," 150–151, for further details.

38. Ibid, 152–154.

39. See ibid., 153–157, 166–167, for complete details on the clothing situation and other aspects of combat support (medical, etc.).

40. Ibid., 90.


## 7. Air Forces

1. See, for example, A. I. Lapchinsky, *Vozdushnaia armiia* [The air Army] (Moscow: Voenizdat, 1939); and S. A. Mezhenikov, *Osnovnye voprosy primeneniia VVS* [Principal questions of the use of the Air Force] (Moscow: Voenizdat, 1926). Both advocated operational-strategic missions for air power.

2. *Nachal'nyi period Velikoi Otechestvennoi voiny* [Initial period of the Great Patriotic War] (Moscow: Voroshilov Academy of the General Staff, 1989), 57.

3. 1941 production included 1,946 MiG-3, LaGG-3, and Iak-1, 458 Pe-2, and 249 Il-2. Of these, some 700 remained at factory airfields on 22 June 1941. N. Ramanichev, "The Red Army: Myths and Realities," Unpublished manuscript, 113–114, citing archival materials in *TsAMO*, f. 35, op. 107559, d. 5, l. 116–154.

4. Ibid., 61.

5. A. G. Khor'kov, *Boevaia i mobilizatsionnai gotovnost' prigranichnykh voennykh okrugov nakanune Velikoi Otechestvennoi voiny* [Combat and mobilization readiness of border military districts on the eve of the Great Patriotic War] (Moscow: Voroshilov Academy of the General Staff, 1985), 9, agrees on the total, but counts 22 mixed, 8 fighter, and 4 bomber, whereas Ramanichev, "Red Army," cites 32 divisions, which included 22 mixed, 6 fighter, and 6 bomber.

6. Ramanichev, "Red Army," 108. Force aviation made up 2.3 percent and long-range aviation 13.5 percent.

7. *Nachal'nyi period*, 58.

8. Von Hardesty, *Red Phoenix: The Rise of Soviet Air Power, 1941–1945* (Washington, D.C.: Smithsonian Institution Press, 1982), 17.

9. Ibid., 58–59.

10. For more extensive discussion of Air Force expansion programs, see A. A. Volkov, *Kriticheskii prolog* [Critical prologue] (Moscow: AVIAR, 1992), 40–47.

11. For example, during the Soviet-Finnish War, the redeployment of 23 aviation regiments into the theater of operations required two months. See *Nachal'nyi period*, 60.

12. Ibid.

13. Ramanichev, "Red Army," 119.

14. *Nachal'nyi period*, 61.

15. Ibid., 118.

16. Ramanichev, "Red Army," 216.

17. Volkov, *Kriticheskii*, 45. Actual average pilot hours were as follows: Baltic Special Military District 18, Western Special Military District 9, Kiev Special Military District 6, and Odessa Military District 11.

18. Ibid., 217, quoting from archival document *TsAMO*, f. 2, op. 11569, d. 326, p. 15.

19. Ibid., 119.

20. *Nachal'nyi period*, 61.

21. Hardesty, *Red Phoenix*, 23.

22. Ibid., 26, from a report by I. V. Timokhovich.

23. Ibid.

24. Iu. P. Babich and A. G. Baier, *Razvitie vooruzheniia i organizatsii sovetskikh sukhoputnykh voisk v gody Velikoi Otechestvenoi voiny* [Development of the weaponry and organization of Soviet ground forces during the Great Patriotic War] (Moscow: Voenizdat, 1990), 67.

25. V. S. Shumikhin, *Sovetskaia voennaia aviatsiia 1917–1941 gg.* [Soviet military aviation 1917–1941] (Moscow: Nauka, 1986), 238.

26. *Nachal'nyi period*, 62, citing archival matierls in *TsAMO*, f. 35, op. 107559, d. 5, l. 169.

27. Ibid., 63.

28. Ibid., 64.

29. Ramanichev, "Red Army," 118, citing archival materials in *TsAMO*, f. 35, op. 11304, d. 13, l. 68.

30. *Nachal'nyi period*, 63.

31. Ibid., 64.

32. "Operativnaia svodka shtaba severo-zapadnogo fronta no. 1 k 22 chasam 22 iiunia 1941 g. o khode boevykh deistvii voisk fronta za istekshii den'" [Operational summary no. 1 of the Northwestern Front headquarters, dated 2200 22 June 1941 about the course of combat operations of *front* forces on the past day], *Sbornik boevykh dokumentov Velikoi Otechestvennoi voiny* [Collection of combat documents of the Great Patriotic War], issue 34 (Moscow: Voenizdat, 1958), 43.

33. "Donesenie komanduiushchego severo-zapadnym frontom ot 22 iiunia 1941 g. narodnomu komissaru oborony SSSR ob obstanovke na 22 chasa 22 iiunia 1941 g." [A 22 June 1941 report by the Northwestern Front commander to the USSR people's commissar of defense about conditions at 2200 hours 22 June 1941], *SBDVOV*, issue 34, 44.

34. "Donesenie komanduiushchego voiskami severo-zapadnogo fronta ot 26 iiunia 1941 g. narodnomu komissaru oborony SSSR ob obstanovke na fronte k 20 chasam 35 minutam 26 iiunia 1941 g." [A 26 June 1941 report of the Northwestern Front commander to the USSR people's commissar of defense about conditions at the front at 2035 hours 26 June 1941], SBDVOV, issue 34, 67.

35. "Donesenie shtaba severo-zapadnogo fronta ot 4 iiulia 1941 g. general'nomu shtabu Krasnoi Armii o boevom i chislennom sostave voisk fronta na 4 iiulia 1941 g." [A 4 July 1941 report by the Northwestern Front staff to the Red Army General Staff about the combat and numerical strength of front forces on 4 July 1941], SBDVOV, issue 34, 119.

36. "Iz godovogo otcheta shtaba 6-i vozdushnoi armii ot 21 iiulia 1942 g. 'O boevoi deiatel'nosti voenno-vozdushnykh sil severo-zapadnogo fronta za period s 22.6.41 g. po 1.7.42 g.'" [From the annual report of the 6th Air Army headquarters of 21 July 1942 "About the combat activities of the Northwestern Front Air Forces for the period from 22.6.41 through 1.7.42"], SBDVOV, issue 43, 179–183.

37. "Iz otcheta komanduiushchego voenno-vozdushnymi voiskami zapadnogo fronta za 1941 g. o sostoianii voenno-vozdushnykh sil fronta i boevykh deistviiakh za vosem' dnei voiny" [From a report by the Western Front Air Force commander for 1941 about the condition of front air forces and [their] combat operations during the first eight days of war], SBDVOV, issue 35, 127.

38. Ibid.

39. Ibid., 128.

40. Ibid., 129.

41. Ibid., 130.

42. Ibid., 131. Naumenko exaggerates German losses but is generally accurate concerning his own losses.

43. "Doklad komanduiushchego voenno-vozdushnymi silami iugo-zapadnogo fronta komanduiushchemu voenno-vozdushnymi silami Krasnoi Armii ot 21 avgusta 1941 g. o boevykh deistviiakh voenno-vozdushnykh sil fronta za period s 22 iiunia po 10 avgusta 1941 g." [Report of the Southwestern Front Air Force commander dated 21 August 1941 to the commander of Red Army Air Forces about the combat operations of front air forces from 22 June 1941 through 10 August 1941], SBDVOV, issue 36, 109.

44. Ibid., 116.

45. Ibid., 120.

## 8. Stavka and Strategic Reserves

1. Nachal'nyi period Velikoi Otechestvennoi voiny [Initial period of the Great Patriotic War] (Moscow: Military-Scientific Directorate of the General Staff, 1989), 90–96.

2. "Prikaz komanduiushchego voiskami 13-i armii no. 08 ot 7 iiulia 1941 g. o sostave i zadache voisk armii" [13th Army commander order no. 08, dated 7 July 1941, about the composition and mission of Army forces], Sbornik boevykh dokumentov Velikoi Otechestvennoi voiny [Collection of combat documents of the Great Patriotic War], issue 37 (Moscow: Voenizdat, 1959), 190. Hereafter cited as SBDVOV.

3. "Doklad komanduiushchego voiskami 13-i armii komanduiushchemu

zapadnym frontom o sostoianii armii na 9 iiulia 1941 g." [A report of the 13th Army commander to the Western Front commander about the condition of the Army on 9 July 1941], *SBDVOV*, issue 37, 192.

4. "Donesenie shtaba 16-i armii ot 9 iiulia 1941 g. shtabu zapadnogo fronta o boevom sostave armii" [A 9 July report of the 16th Army staff to the Western Front staff concerning the Army's combat composition], *SBDVOV*, issue 37 (Moscow: Voenizdat, 1959), 203.

5. "Boevoe donesenie shtaba 16-i armii no. 18/OP ot 20 iiulia 1941 g. shtabu zapadnogo fronta o polozhenii voisk armii" [16th Army combat report no. 18/OP, dated 20 July 1941, to Western Front headquarters about the situation of Army forces], *SBDVOV*, issue 37, 207.

6. "Operativnaia svodka shtaba zapadnogo fronta no. 55 k 20 chasam 23 iiulia 1941 g. o boevykh deistviiakh voisk fronta" [Western Front operational summary no. 55, dated 2000 hours 23 July 1941, about the combat operations of *front* forces], *SBDVOV*, issue 37, 102.

7. "Spravka shtaba 19-i armii ot 24 iiulia 1941 g. o deistviiakh voisk armii s 9 po 24 iiulia 1941 g." [Information from the 19th Army staff on 24 July 1941 about combat actions of Army forces from 9 through 24 July 1941], *SBDVOV*, issue 37, 226.

8. Ibid., 226–227.

9. Ibid., 227.

10. Ibid., 228.

11. "Doklad voennogo soveta 20-i armii ot 27 iiulia 1941 g. glavnokoman-duiushchemu voiskami zapadnogo napravleniia o sostoianii, obespechennosti armii i priniatom reshenii" [A 27 July report of 20th Army Military Council to the Western Direction high commander about the condition and provision of the Army and the decision made], *SBDVOV*, issue 37, 266.

12. Ibid.

13. See "Donesenie voennogo soveta 20-i armii ot 4 avgusta 1941 g. glavnoko-manduiushchemu voisk zapadnogo napravleniia o sostoianii voisk 20-i i 16-i armii" [A report of 4 August 1941 by the 20th Army Military Council to the Western Direction high commander about the condition of 20th and 16th Army forces], *SBDVOV*, issue 37, 271–272; "Donesenie komanduiushchego voiskami 20-i armii ot 5 avgusta 1941 g. glavnokomanduiushchemu zapadnym napravleniem o khode perepravy voisk armii za r. Dnepr" [A 5 August 1941 report by the 20th Army commander to the Western Direction high commander concerning the state of 20th Army forces crossing the Dnepr River], *SBDVOV*, issue 37, 272–273.

14. "Doklad voennogo soveta zapadnogo napravleniia ot 14 iiulia 1941 g. stavke verkhovnogo komandovaniia ob obstanovka na zapadnom fronte na 14 iiulia 1941 g." [A 14 July 1941 report by the Western Direction Military Council to the Stavka of the High Command about conditions on the Western Front on 14 July 1941], *SBDVOV*, issue 37, 30–31.

15. "Doklad nachal'nika operativnogo otdela shtaba glavnogo komandovaniia zapadnogo napravleniia ot 21 iiulia 1941 g. nachal'niku shtaba o sozdanii rezervov" [A 21 July 1941 report of the chief of the Western Direction's Operational Department to the chief of staff about the creation of reserves], *SBDVOV*, issue 37, 44.

16. "Doklad o sostoianii radiosviazi glavkoma zapadnogo napravleniia s armiiami

i gruppami po sostoianiiu na 28.7.1941 g." [A report about the radio communications of the Western Direction High Command with armies and groups according to its state on 28.7.1941], *SBDVOV,* issue 37, 58.

17. "Doklad nachal'nika 4-go otdela upravleniia sviazi zapadnogo fronta ot 14 avgusta 1941 g. zamestiteliu nachal'nika glavnogo upravleniia sviazi Krasnoi Armii o sostoianii i rabote podvizhnykh sredstv sviazi zapadnogo fronta za period boevykh deistvii s 22 iiunia po 14 avgusta 1941 g." [A 14 August 1941 report of the 4th Section chief of the Western Front's Signals Directorate to the deputy chief of the Red Army's Signals Directorate about the condition and work of Western Front's mobile communications means from 22 June through 14 August 1941], *SBDVOV,* issue 37, 131.

18. "Doklad glavnokomanduiushchego voiskami iugo-zapadnogo napravleniia ot 25 iiulia 1941 g. stavke verkhovnogo komandovaniia o plane izpol'zovaniia formiruemykh divizii" [A 25 July 1941 report by the high commander of Southwestern Direction forces to the Stavka of the High Command about the plan for employing the formed divisions], *SBDVOV,* issue 38, 18.

19. "Doklad glavnokomanduiushchego voiskami iugo-zapadnogo napravleniia ot 31 iiulia 1941 g. stavke verkhovnogo komandovaniia o nizkoi obespechennosti vooruzheniem i imushchestvom formiruemykh soedinenii" [A 31 July 1941 report by the Southwestern Direction high commander to the Stavka of the High Command about the low level of provision of arms and equipment to forming formations], *SBDVOV,* issue 39, 20–21.

20. "Svedeniia shtaba voenno-vozdushnykh sil Krasnoi Armii o boevom sostave chastei voenno-vozdushnykh sil iugo-zapadnogo fronta po sostoianiiu na 29 iiulia 1941 g." [Information of the Red Army Air Force headquarters about the combat composition of Southwestern Front Air Force units on 29 July 1941], *SBDVOV,* issue 39, 10–12.

21. "Prikaz stavki verkhovnogo komandovaniia no. 00334 ot 14 iiulia 1941 g. o formirovanii shtaba fronta rezervnykh armii, vkliuchenii v ego sostav 29, 30, 24, 28, 31 i 32-i armii i ikh zadachakh" [Stavka order no. 00334, dated 14 July 1941, about the formation of a headquarters of a Front of Reserve Armies, including 29th, 30th, 24th, 28th, 31st, and 32d Armies, and their missions], *SBDVOV,* issue 37, 13.

22. "Prikaz glavnokomanduiushchego voiskami zapadnogo napravleniia no. 0080 ot 22 iiulia 1941 g. na organizatsiiu gruppy Kalinina" [Order no. 0080 of the high commander of the Western Direction, dated 22 July 1941, on the organization of Group Kalinin], *SBDVOV,* issue 37, 47.

23. For example, according to a General Staff directive mandating formation of the groups, their composition was as follows: Group Maslennikov, 252d, 256th, and 243d Rifle Divisions; Group Khomenko, 242d, 251st, and 250th Rifle Divisions; Group Kalinin, 53d Rifle Corps with 91st and 166th Rifle Divisions; and Group Kachalov, 149th and 145th Rifle Divisions and 104th Tank Division. See "Direktiva general'nogo shtaba Krasnoi Armii ot 21 iiulia 1941 g. komanduiushchemu voiskami fronta rezervnykh armii o zadachakh grupp Maslennikova, Khomenko, Kalinina, i Kachalova v operatsii po okruzheniiu i razgromu smolenskoi gruppirovki protivnika" [Red Army General Staff Directive, dated 21 July 1941, to the commander of the

Front of Reserve Armies about the missions of Groups Maslennikov, Khomenko, Kalinin, and Kachalov in the operation to encircle and destroy the enemy Smolensk group], *SBDVOV*, issue 37, 18–19.

24. "Prikaz NKVD SSSR o formirovanii narkomatom piatnadtsati strelkovykh divizii dlia peredachi v deistvuiushchuiu armiiu" [Order of the NKVD of the USSR about the formation by the People's Commissariat of 15 rifle divisions for reassignment to the operating Army], in *Vnutrennie voiska v Velikoi Otechestvennoi voine 1941–1945 gg.* [Internal forces in the Great Patriotic War 1941–1945] (Moscow: Iuridicheskaia Literatura, 1975), 544.

25. "Prikaz stavka verkhovnogo komandovaniia no. 00293 ot 23 iiulia 1941 g. o sformirovanii 29-i armii i ee zadachakh" [Order of the Stavki of the High Command no. 00293, dated 23 July 1941, about the formation of 29th Army and its missions], *SBDVOV*, issue 37, 11–12.

26. "Prikaz stavka verkhovnogo komandovaniia no. 00305 ot 13 iiulia 1941 g. o sformirovanii 30-i armii i ee zadachakh" [Order of the Stavki of the High Command no. 00305, dated 13 July 1941, about the formation of 30th Army and its missions], *SBDVOV*, issue 37, 12–13. 30th Army consisted of 119th, 242d, 243d, and 251st Rifle Divisions, the latter two NKVD-based, 51st Tank Division, 43d Artillery Regiment, and the 533d and 758th Antitank Artillery Regiments.

27. A. D. Kolesnik, *Opolchenskie formirovaniia Rossiiskoi Federatsii v gody Velikoi Otechestvennoi voiny* [People's militia formations of the Russian Federation in the Great Patriotic War] (Moscow: Nauka, 1988), 15–56, covers the formation of militia formations throughout the Russian Federation. Documents in *SBDVOV* attest to the study's accuracy.

28. *Boevoi sostav Sovetskoi armii* [Combat composition of the Soviet Army] (Moscow: Military-Scientific Directorate of the General Staff, 1963), 32.

29. "Boevoi prikaz komanduiushchsego voiskami 24-i armii no. 03/OP ot 13 iiulia 1941 g. na oboronu" [24th Army commander's combat order no. 03/OP, dated 13 July 1941, about the defense], *SBDVOV*, issue 37, 313–314.

30. "Boevoi prikaz komanduiushchego voiskami 24-i armii no. 05/OP ot 17 iiulia 1941 g. o perepodchinenii i peregruppirovke voisk armii" [24th Army commander's combat order no. 05/OP, dated 17 July 1941, about the resubordination and regrouping of Army forces], *SBDVOV*, issue 37, 316.

31. "Boevoi prikaz komanduiushchego voiskami 24-i armii no. 09/OP ot 5 avgusta 1941 g. o sosredotochenii pribyvaiiushchikh v sostav armii divizii" [24th Army commander's combat order no. 09/OP, dated 5 August 1941, about the concentration of arriving Army divisions], *SBDVOV*, issue 37, 332–333.

32. "Direktiva komanduiushchego voiskami 28-i armii ot 14 iiulia 1941 g. ob organizatsii oborony voiskami armii" [28th Army commander's directive of 14 July 1941 about the organization of Army defenses], *SBDVOV*, issue 37, 341–342.

33. "Boevoe rasporiazhenie shtaba 28-i armii no. 037 ot 23 iiulia 1941 g. ob ustranenii nedostatkov v boevykh deistviiakh voisk" [28th Army staff's combat order no. 037, dated 23 July 1941, about the elimination of shortcomings in force combat operations], *SBDVOV*, issue 37, 349.

34. "Prikaz voennogo soveta 28-i armii no. 059/OP ot 30 iiulia 1941 g. voiskam operativnoi gruppy armii ob ustranenii nedostatok v boevykh deistviiakh" [28th Army

Military Council order no. 059/OP, dated 30 July 1941, to forces of the army operational group about the elimination of shortcomings in combat operations], *SBDVOV*, issue 37, 354.

35. "Boevoi prikaz komanduiushchego voiskami 29-i armii no. 02 ot 19 iiulia 1941 g. na sosredotochenie v raione Toropets" [29th Army commander's combat order no. 02, dated 19 July 1941, on concentrating in the Toropets region], *SBDVOV*, issue 37, 362–363.

36. "Doklad voennogo soveta 29-i armii ot 1 avgusta 1941 g. glavnokoman-duiushchemu zapadnym napravleniem o resul'tatakh trekhdnevnykh boev voisk armii" [Report of the 29th Army Military Council, dated 1 August 1941, to the high commander of the Western Direction about the results of the Army's three days of combat], *SDBVOV*, issue 37, 369–370.

37. "Doklad nachal'nika artillerii 29-i armii ot 12 avgusta 1941 g. nachal'niku artillerii zapadnogo fronta o boevom primenenii artillerii armii v period s 27 iiulia po 11 avgusta 1941 g." [A 12 August 1941 report of the 29th Army chief of artillery to the chief of Western Front artillery concerning the combat use of Army artillery during the period from 27 July through 11 August 1941], *SBDVOV*, issue 37, 376.

38. Ibid.

39. "Boevoi prikaz komanduiushchego voiskami 30-i armii no. 02 ot 14 iiulia 1941 g. na oboronu rubezha Selizharovo, Olenino, Vasil'evo" [30th Army combat order no. 02, dated 14 July 1941, on defense of the line Selizharovo, Olenino, and Vasil'evo], *SBDVOV*, issue 37, 381.

40. "Prikaz komanduiushchego voiskami 30-i armii no. 15 ot 27 iiulia 1941 g. ob izzhitii nedostatkov v boevykh deistviiakh voisk armii" [Order no. 15 of the 30th Army commander, dated 27 July 1941, concerning the elimination of deficiencies in Army forces' combat operations], *SBDVOV*, issue 37, 386–387.

41. "Doklad voennogo soveta 30-i armii ot 5 avgusta 1941 g. voennomu sovetu zapadnogo fronta ob ukomplektovannosti, snabzhenii i boesposobnosti voisk armii" [A 5 August 1941 report of the 30th Army Military Council to the Western Front Military Council about the completeness, supply status, and combat readiness of Army forces], *SBDVOV*, issue 37, 395–406.

42. Ibid., 395.

43. Specific Army losses were 242d Rifle Division 3,504 men, 250th Rifle Division 5,775 men, 251st Rifle Division 4,018 men, and 107th Tank Division 4,133 men, for a total of 18,431 men, or 40 percent of their original strength. By 1 August regiments numbered from 379 to 1,195 men. During that period the Army received 2,830 replacements.

44. Ibid., 398.

45. Ibid., 405.

46. "Vkleika no. 2 k 'Sbornik boevykh dokumentov'" [Insert no. 2 to "Collection of combat documents"], *SBDVOV*, issue 37, 88.

47. For this transformation of division numerals, see "Operativnaia svodka shtab zapadnogo fronta no. 50 ot 21 iiulia 1941 g. o boevykh deistviiakh voisk fronta" [Operational summary no. 50 of the Western Front staff, dated 21 July 1941, about combat operations of *front* forces], *SBDVOV*, issue 37, 99, and sequential reports in the same document series from the Reserve Front, such as "Operativnaia svodka shtab

fronta reservnykh armii no. 9 k 20 chasam 16 iiulia 1941 g. o polozhenii voisk fronta" [Operational summary no. 9, dated 2000 hours 16 July 1941, about the situation of *front* forces], *SBDVOV*, issue 37, 141–142, and "Boevoi prikaz komanduiushchego voiskami 24-i armii no. 05/OP ot 17 iiulia 1941 g. o perepodchinenii i peregruppirovke voisk armii" [Combat order no. 5/OP of the 24th Army commander, dated 17 July 1941, about the resubordination and regrouping of Army forces], *SBDVOV*, issue 37, 316. The only exception to this pattern was 26th Mechanized Corps' 103d Motorized Division, which remained a motorized division.

48. One of the few existing open-sources explanations of the origins of the 100-series tank divisions is found in O. A. Losik, *Stroitel'stvo i boevoe primenenie sovetskikh tankovykh voisk v gody Velikoi Otechestvennoi voiny* [The formation and combat use of Soviet tank forces during the Great Patriotic War] (Moscow: Voenizdat, 1979), 46. Losik states, "At this time [mid-July 1941] 10 tank divisions were formed from mechanized corps located in the internal military districts." Archival materials clearly support Losik's claim.

49. "Donesenie komandira 108-i tankovoi divizii komanduiushchemu voiskami brianskim frontom ot 17 sentiabria 1941 g o boevykh deistviiakh divizii v period s 28 avgusta po 4 sentiabria 1941 g." [A 17 September 1941 report by the 108th Tank Division commander to the Briansk Front commander about division combat operations during the period from 28 August 1941 through 4 September 1941], *SBDVOV*, issue 33, 121–125.

50. "Direktiva general'nogo shtaba no. 00455 ot 21 iiulia 1941 g. komanduiushchemu voiskami fronta rezervnykh armii ob usilenii tankami strelkovykh divizii grupp Khomenko, Kalinina i Kachalova" [General Staff directive no. 00455, dated 21 July 1941, to the commander of the Front of Reserve Armies about strengthening the rifle divisions of Groups Khomenko, Kalinin, and Kachalov with tanks], *SBDVOV*, issue 37, 18.

51. Ibid.

52. "Prikaz komanduiushchego voiskami fronta rezervnykh armii no. 3/OP ot 19 iiulia 1941 g. ob ustranenii nedostatkov v organizatsii sistemy protivotankovogo artilleriiskogo ognia" [Order no. 3/OP of the commander of the Front of Reserve Armies, dated 19 July 1941, about the elimination of shortcomings in the organization of a system of antitank artillery fire], *SBDVOV*, issue 37, 146–148.

53. "Prikaz nachal'nika artillerii fronta rezervnykh armii no. 2/OP ot 21 iiulia 1941 g. ob ustranenii nedostatkov v organizatsii sistemy protivotankovogo artilleriiskogo ognia" [Order no. 2/OP of the chief of artillery of the Front of Reserve Armies, dated 21 July 1941, about the elimination of shortcomings in the organization of a system of antitank artillery fire], *SBDVOV*, issue 37, 155–156.

54. "Doklad nachal'nika sviazi fronta rezervnykh armii ot 29 iiulia 1941 g. nachal'niku upravleniia sviazi Krasnoi Armii o sostoianii i rabote radiosviazi fronta" [A 29 July 1941 report by the Front of Reserve Armies' chief of signals to the chief of the Red Army Signals Directorate about the condition and work of *front* radio communications], *SBDVOV*, issue 37, 162–163.

55. Ibid., 164.

56. "Doklad komanduiushchego voenno-vozdushnymi silami fronta rezervnykh armii ot 28 iiulia 1941 g. zamestiteliu narodnogo komissara oborony soiuza SSR o

merakh povysheniia boesposobnosti voenno-vozdushnykh sil" [A 28 July report of
the commander of the Front of Reserve Armies Air Forces to the deputy people's
commissar of defense of the USSR about measures to increase the combat readiness
of the air forces], *SBDVOV*, issue 37, 161–162.

## 9. Red Army Intelligence on the Eve of War

1. A. M. Vasilevsky, *A Lifelong Cause* (Moscow: Progress, 1976), 82.
2. Iu. G. Perechnev, "O nekotorykh problemakh podgotovki strany i vooruzhennykh sil k otrazheniiu fashistskoi agressii" [Concerning some problems of preparing
the country and armed forces to repel fascist aggression], *VIZh* 4 (April 1988): 49.
3. G. K. Zhukov, *Reminiscences and Reflections*, vol. 1 (Moscow: Progress, 1985),
267–268.
4. Ibid., 268.
5. V. D. Danilov, "Sovetskoe glavnoe komandovanie v preddverii Velikoi
Otechestvennnoi voiny" [The Soviet High Command on the threshold of the Great
Patriotic War], *Novaia i noveishaia istoriia* [New and recent history] 6 (June 1988):
18, which contains these reports and the GRU reports that passed them on to Stalin.
6. I. Z. Evgen'ev, "Voennye razvedchiki dokladyvali . . ." [Military intelligence
officers reported], *VIZh* 2 (February 1992): 41. The telegram was received by the
GRU's 9th Section at 1745 on 1 June.
7. See "Telegramma iz Kishineva, 2 iiunia 1941 g." [Telegram from Kishinev, 2
June 1941]; "Telegramma iz Murmanska, 19 iiunia 1941 g." [Telegram from Murmansk,
19 June 1941]; "Informatsiia Glavnogo upravleniia politicheskoi propagandy Krasnoi
Armii Tsentral'nomu Komitetu VKP (b) o posadke germanskikh samoletov v raione
goroda Rava-Russkaia" [Information of the Main Political Propaganda Directorate of
the Red Army about the landing of German aircraft in the Rava-Russkaia region],
*Izvestiia TsK KPSS* 5 (May 1990): 206–211.
8. Evgen'ev, "Voennye razvedchiki," 36. Quoting a report received by the GRU's
9th Section at 1900 29 December 1940.
9. Ibid., 37. Quoting a report received by the GRU's 6th Section at 1400 10
March 1941.
10. Ibid. Both reports were addressed to Stalin, Molotov, Voroshilov, and Beria.
11. Ibid., 38.
12. Ibid.
13. Ibid., 39–40. Cited as Report no. 48582 and addressed directly to Stalin.
14. Ibid., 40. The telegraphic report was received by the GRU's 9th Department
at 0300 29 May 1941.
15. I. Z. Evgen'ev, "Voennye razvedchiki dokladyvali . . ." [Military intelligence
officers reported], *VIZh* 3 (March 1992): 41–42.
16. Ibid., 42. The telegram was received by the GRU's 9th Section at 1500 20
June.
17. Ibid. This report was received by the GRU's 9th Section at 1705 21 June.
Matsuoka was Japanese foreign minister, and Hiranuma was a representative of the
Japanese cabinet.
18. Ibid., 41–42.

19. Zhukov, *Reminiscences,* vol. 1, 274.

20. A. G. Khor'kov, "Nakanune groznykh sobytii" [On the eve of ominous events], *VIZh* 5 (May 1988): 42. See also *Nachal'nyi period Velikoi Otechestvennoi voiny* [Initial period of the Great Patriotic War] (Moscow: Voroshilov Academy of the General Staff, 1989), 23–24, for German ground and air reconnaissance measures.

21. Ibid., Khor'kov, "Nakanune," 42–43.

22. Ibid.

23. Ibid., 44.

24. Ibid.

25. Ibid.

26. Ibid., 45. Quoting from the transcripts of the Nuremberg Trials.

27. Ibid.

28. Ibid., 46.

29. Ibid.

30. Zhukov, *Reminiscences,* vol. 1, 273.

31. Ibid.

32. Evgen'ev "Voennye razvedchiki" (February 1992), 39.

33. V. Karpov, "Zhukov," *Kommunist vooruzhennykh sil* [Communist of the armed forces] 5 (May 1990): 67.

34. According to Zhukov's proposal, the first (initial) Soviet strategic objective was to destroy German forces assembled south of Brest and Demblin and, within 30 days, to advance to a line extending from north of Ostrolenka, south along the Narew River, through Lowicz, Lodz, Kreuzberg, and Oppeln to Olomouc. Subsequently, Soviet forces were to attack north or northwest from the Katowice region to destroy German forces in the center and northwest wing of the front and seize the remainder of former Poland and East Prussia. The immediate mission of Soviet forces during the first phase was to break up German forces east of the Vistula River and around Krakow, to advance to the Narew River, and to secure Katowice. Specific missions to carry out this task were: (a) strike the main blow by Southwestern Front forces toward Krakow and Katowice to cut Germany off from her southern allies; (b) deliver a secondary attack by the left wing of the Western Front toward Warsaw and Demblin to fix the Warsaw grouping and secure Warsaw, and also to cooperate with the Southwestern Front in destroying the Lublin group; and (c) conduct an active defense against Finland, East Prussia, Hungary, and Rumania and be prepared to attack Rumania, if favorable conditions arise.

35. Khor'kov, "Nakanune," 47.

36. Zhukov, *Reminiscences,* vol. 1, 275–276.

37. Khor'kov, "Nakanune," 47.

38. "Razvedyvatel'naia svodka shtaba Pribaltiiskogo voennogo okruga ot 18 iiunia 1941 g. o gruppirovke voisk protivnika protiv voisk okruga na 17 iiunia 1941 g." [Intelligence summary of the Baltic Special Military District Headquarters of 18 June 1941 about the grouping about enemy forces opposite district forces on 17 June 1941], *SBDVOV,* issue 34, 18–20. For a similar report from the Western Special Military District, dated 21 June, see *SBDVOV,* issue 35, 13–14.

39. "Pervye dni voiny v dokumentakh" [The first days of war in documents], *VIZh* 5 (May 1989): 47. The document, "Donesenie komandira 125-i strelkovoi divizii

komanduiushchemu Pribaltiiskim osobym voennym okrugom, 18 iiunia 1941 g. 20 ch 10 min" [A report by the commander of the 125th Rifle Division to the commander of the Baltic Special Military District, 18 June 1941, 2010 hours], is from *TsAMO*, f. 344, op. 5564, d. 10, ll. 3–4.

40. Ibid., 47–48; document entitled "Direktiva shtaba pribaltiiskogo osobogo voennogo okruga, 19 iiunia 1941 g." [Directive of the Baltic Special Military District headquarters, 19 June 1941], archival citation *TsAMO*, f. 344, op. 5564, d. 1, ll. 34–35.

41. Ibid., 48; document entitled "Rasporiazhenie komanduiushchego voiskami 8-i armii pribaltiiskogo osobogo voennogo okruga komandiram 10-go i 11-ogo strelkovykh korpusov, 20 iiunia 1941 g." [Instruction of the commander of the Baltic Special Military District's 8th Army to the commanders of 10th and 11th Rifle Corps, 20 June 1941], archival citation *TsAMO*, f. 344, op. 5564, d. 10, l. 36.

42. Ibid.; document entitled "Donesenie komanduiushchego krasnoznamennym baltiiskim flotom komanduiushchim leningradskim i pribaltiiskim osobymi voennymi okrugami, nachal'niku pogranvoisk 20 iiunia 1941 g." [Report of the commander of the Red Banner Baltic Fleet to the commanders of the Leningrad and Baltic Special Military Districts and the chief of Border Forces 20 June 1941], archival citation *TsAMO*, f. 221, op. 1304, d. 2, l. 59.

43. Ibid., 48; document entitled "Donesenie shtaba 11-i armii nachal'niku shtaba pribaltiiskogo osobogo voennogo okruga, 20 iiunia 1941 g. 23 ch 46 min" [Report of the chief of staff of Baltic Special Military District's 11th Army 20 June 1941 2346 hours], archival citation *TsAMO*, f. 221, op. 1394, d. 2, l. 76; annotated "Reported to Moscow, Comrade Korenevsky, 21.6.41 g."

44. Ibid., 49; document entitled "Rasporiazhenie shtaba pribaltiiskogo osobogo voennogo okruga komanduiushchim voiskami 8–i, 11–i, i 27-i armii" [Instruction of the Baltic Special Military District headquarters to the commanders of 8th, 11th, and 27th Army forces], archival citation *TsAMO*, f. 344, op. 5564, d. 1, l. 62.

45. Khor'kov, "Nakanune," 47–48.

46. "Razvedyvatel'naia svodka shtaba pribaltiiskogo osobogo voennogo okruga no. 02 ot 22 iiunia 1941 g. o gruppirovke voisk protivnika k 20 chasam 21 iiunia 1941 g." [Intelligence summary no. 02 of the Baltic Special Military District headquarters, dated 22 June 1941, about the grouping of enemy forces at 2000 hours on 21 June 1941], *Sbornik boevykh dokumentov Velikoi Otechestvennoi voiny* [Collection of Combat Documents of the Great Patriotic War], issue 34 (Moscow: Voenizdat, 1958), 28–30.

47. "Operativnaia svodka shtaba pribaltiiskogo osobogo voennogo okruga no. 01 ot 21 iiulia 1941 g. o gruppirovke voisk okruga k 22 chasam 21 iiunia 1941 g." [Operational summary no. 01 of the Baltic Special Military District headquarters, dated 21 July 1941, about the grouping of district forces at 2200 hours on 21 June 1941], *SBDVOV*, issue 34, 31–32.

48. "Pervye dni voiny," 51; document entitled "Direktiva upravleniia polit-propagandy pribaltiiskogo osobogo voennogo okruga 21 iiunia 1941 g. 21 ch 35 min" [Directive of the Baltic Special Military District Political-Propaganda Directorate 21 June 1941 2135 hours], archival citation *TsAMO*, f. 344, op. 5564, d. 1, l. 47.

49. Ibid.; document entitled "Prikaz komanduiushchego voiskami 8-i armii pribaltiiskogo osobogo voennogo okruga komandiru 11-go strelkovogo korpusa" [Order

of the 8th Army commander of the Baltic Special Military District to the commander of 11th Rifle Corps], archival citation *TsAMO*, f. 344, op. 5564, d. 10, l. 53.

50. Ibid.; document entitled "Prikaz shtaba 27-i armii pribaltiiskogo osobogo voennogo okruga 22 iiunia 1941 g. 3 ch 45 min" [Order of 27th Army headquarters of the Baltic Special Military District 22 June 1941 0345 hours], archival citation *TsAMO*, f. 325, op. 4579, d. 1, l. 43.

51. Khor'kov, "Nakanune," 47.

52. Ibid., 43, contains the full order.

53. Zhukov, *Reminiscences*, vol. 1, 277–278.

54. "Direktiva narodnogo komissara oborony S. K. Timoshenko i nachal'nika general'nogo shtaba G. K. Zhukova komanduiushchim prigranichnykh okrugov o privedeniii v boevuiu gotovnost' voisk v sviazi s vozdushnym napadeniem fashistskoi Germanii 21 iiunia 1941 g." [Directive of People's Commissar of Defense S. K. Timoshenko and Chief of the General Staff G. K. Zhukov to the commanders of the border districts about the bringing to combat readiness of forces in connection with the possible attack of fascist Germany], in *Vnutrennie voiska v Velikoi Otechestvennoi voine 1941–1945 gg.* [Internal forces in the Great Patriotic War, 1941–1945] (Moscow: Iuridicheskaia Literatura, 1975), 32. This closely corresponds with the copy in Zhukov, *Reminiscences*, vol. 1, 278.

55. "Pervye dni," 44.

56. "Iz zhurnala boevykh deistvii voisk zapadnogo fronta 22 iiunia 1941 g." [From the journal of combat operations of Western Front forces, 22 June 1941], in "Pervye dni," 45–46. Full text is in *SBDVOV*, issue 35, 7–10.

57. Zhukov, *Reminiscences*, vol. 1. 271–272.

58. Ibid., 272.

59. Vasilevsky, *Lifelong Cause*, 84.

60. Ibid., 84–85.

61. "Akt o prieme" [Act of reception], *Izvestiia TsK KPSS* 1 (January 1990): 203.

62. For further details on reconnaissance on the eve of war, see A. A. Volkov, *Kriticheskii prolog: Nezavershennye frontovye nastupatel'nye operatsii pervykh kampanii Velikoi Otechestvennoi voiny* [Critical prologue: Incompleted *front* offensive operations of the first campaigns of the Great Patriotic War] (Moscow: AVIAR, 1992), 48–52. This scarce but superb work was prepared under the auspices of the Geopolitical and Security Section of the Russian Federation's Academy of Natural Sciences.

63. Ibid., 50.

64. D. Volkogonov, *Triumf i tragediia* [Triumph and tragedy] (Moscow: Novosti, 1989), 401.

## Conclusions

1. Among these candid critiques, see A. Konenenko, "Germano-pol'skaia voina 1939 g." [The German–Polish War 1939], *VIZh* 11 (November 1940): 49–67; A. Konenenko, "Boi vo Flandrii (mai 1940 g.)" [The battle in Flanders (May 1940)], *VIZh* 3 (March 1941): 3–25; L. Desiatov, "Operatsiia v Norvegii (aprel'–iiun' 1940 g.)" [Operations in Norway (April–June 1940)], *VIZh* 4 (April 1940): 3–12; I. Ratner,

"Proryv na Maase (Na uchastke Divan-Sedan, mai 1940 g.)" [Penetration on the Maas (in the Divan-Sedan sector, May 1940)], *VIZh* 5 (May 1940): 3–22; A. Konenenko, "Kratkii obzor voennykh deistvii na Zapade" [A short survey of military operations in the West], *Voennaia mysl'* [Military thought] 7 (July 1940): 3–12; K. I. Khorseev, "VVS v germano-pol'skoi voine" [Air forces in the German–Polish War], *Voennaia mysl'* 7 (July 1940): 28–44; B. S. Belianovsky, "Deistviia tankovykh i motorizovannykh voisk v Pol'she, Bel'gii i Frantsii" [Tank and motorized force operations in Poland, Belgium, and France], *Voennaia mysl'* 8 (August 1940): 39–58, and many others.

2. According to G. F. Krivosheev, *Grif sekretnosti sniat* [Seal of classification removed] (Moscow: Voenizdat, 1993), 93–100, during the Soviet-Finnish War the Soviet armed forces lost 333,084 men, including 84,394 dead and missing. Initially, the Soviets fielded a force of 550,757 men, but this strength rose by war's end to 760,578 men. Thus, the total committed force was about 1 million. The 30 percent overall casualties were staggering.

3. Krivosheev, *Grif*, 143.

# Bibliographical Essay and
# Selective Bibliography

## Secondary Sources

Although a vast primary and secondary literature exists about the Soviet-German war, in general, the thoroughness and accuracy of this work has suffered from the inaccessibility of Soviet military accounts and, until recently, the utter lack of Soviet archival materials. As a result, since war's end most accounts of the war have included only German perception and detail. The opposing Red Army and the Soviet soldier have remained a virtually featureless and colorless mass, devoid of collective or individual personality. This is true, in particular, regarding descriptions of the Red Army on the eve of war, a subject postwar Soviet historians have avoided entirely. By default, German sources have provided the only credible description of the 1941 Red Army. Furthermore, for many of the same reasons, German perspectives on and interpretations of the war as a whole have also prevailed. Understandably, and with few exceptions, Western scholars and the reading public have treated existing Soviet or Soviet-based accounts of the war with suspicion and incredulity. In essence, although the German Army lost the war, it won the initial stages of the historical struggle with relative ease.

### THE GERMAN SCHOOL

The German school of historiography emerged dominant during the immediate post-war years. Its creation and growth was a perfectly natural phenomenon because most available sources on the war were German in origin and perspective. The first group of German-based source materials was produced by U.S. governmental agencies, which, as the victors, reaped the archival spoils of war. These agencies had the practical mission of analyzing the character of the war and the armies that fought in it, in particular the Red Army, so that the U.S. military could better understand and deal with future Soviet military threats. In subsequent postwar decades, these initial official accounts were first supplemented by an impressive array of German memoir materials prepared by a generation of former German senior commanders, who were now unemployed and eager to share their unique wartime perspectives with the new enemies of their most bitter wartime rival, the Soviet Union. Later, a growing number of historians wrote scholarly accounts of the war based initially upon official U.S. governmental materials and German memoir literature and, later, on newly released German archival records. In time, this mass of German sources swelled with the addition of the memoirs of private soldiers and a steady stream of published German wartime unit histories. Although much of this material was written in German, Western historians were generally better equipped to master this language and more intellectually inclined to exploit these sources and accept these interpretations than was the case with similar Russian source materials.

From the very outset, three imposing barriers inhibited the utility of Soviet (Russian) sources. The first two, Western historians' unfamiliarity with Soviet historical works and their general inability to read Russian, were basically mechanical in nature and would erode over time as more Western historians learned the Russian language. The third barrier, a deep-rooted and often justified distrust of Soviet historical credibility, was fundamental and more difficult to overcome because the content of most readily available Soviet historical works was significantly and blatantly ideological. A more credible Soviet school of historiography would emerge only after Western historians were able to tap into a broader and more credible base of Soviet works and when they were able to test the veracity of Soviet sources against German archival accounts. The clearly limited value of Soviet works produced in the decade immediately following the end of the war also discredited the positive efforts the Soviets made during the late 1950s and 1960s to improve the quality and accuracy of their historical accounts. In fact, despite the efforts of a few superb Western historians to replace Soviet bombast with hard fact, the credibility of the Soviet school would not improve until the 1980s, when significant amounts of Soviet archival materials finally began to be released to the public.

Secondary materials that, by virtue of the nature of their source material, fall into the German school of historiography include several series of "official" studies and histories prepared and published by national military historical organizations, primarily in the United States and Germany; personal memoirs; and other standard historical surveys of individual operations and the war in general.

The first official U.S. studies on the Soviet-German war appeared in the Department of the Army Pamphlet series, which was prepared and published during the late 1940s and early 1950s as a product of the extensive U.S. government effort to debrief former German military commanders and to analyze the nature of combat on the German Eastern Front. The series included only a fraction of the material collected by the U.S. European Command in its postwar analysis and debriefing program. These pamphlets received wide dissemination and, even today, have been reprinted by the U.S. Army's Center for Military History for modern reading audiences. Although these pamphlets made valuable initial contributions to a better Western understanding of the war, their accuracy was suspect because their authors, all of whom had been wartime German commanders and staff officers, wrote them largely from memory and without access to German archival materials. Thus, in addition to their natural German bias, they contained numerous errors in fact.

In the 1960s the U.S. Army's Office of the Chief of Military History (CMH) began preparing substantive studies of the Soviet-German war to supplement an extensive ongoing series of publications on the U.S. Army's role in the war. CMH commissioned three volumes, which were to cover the war chronologically, but the first volume on 1941 never appeared. More recently, in the 1980s, the German Military History Office (Freiberg) also began preparing an extensive series of official works on the Second World War. One volume of this new series covers the circumstances of 1941.

The second major genre of German secondary sources was the postwar memoirs by or biographies of prestigious German wartime military leaders, the most famous of which appeared in the late 1940s and 1950s. These volumes established the motifs for the German school, appearing at a time when it was both necessary and sensible to disassociate oneself from Hitler or Hitler's policies. Among the most notable memoirs are works by Walter Warlimont (OKW), Erich von Manstein (LVI Panzer Corps, Eleventh Army, and Army Groups Don and South), Heinz Guderian (Panzer Group 2 and Second Panzer Army), and F. W. Mellenthin (11th Panzer Division and XLVIII Panzer Corps), all of whom provided their perspective on the Red Army and the Soviet soldier.

All of these authors wrote their memoirs on the basis of their memory or their personal notes or records. Interpretation aside, this absence of archival sources often left the accuracy of their work seriously flawed. Fascinating as they were, these popular memoirs and biographies described war against a faceless enemy, an armed host that possessed neither concrete form nor precise features. In short, other than sensing the size and power of their foe and the ferocity and inhumanity of combat, they knew not what they fought. Nevertheless, these authors shaped lasting stereotypes of the Red Army and the Soviet soldier. Although a subsequent generation of talented Western professional military historians has left a legacy of superb works, by virtue of their source materials, their work remains firmly imbedded in the German school. Try as they did to reconstruct the Soviet face of war, they failed in the effort because much of their primary material remained, of necessity, German.

Beginning in the early 1960s, an increasing number of reputable trained historians began producing accounts of war and operations on the German Eastern Front. These works were more thorough than those of their predecessors, but they were based primarily on German sources and so failed to achieve a respectable balance between the German and Soviet perspectives. The earliest of these volumes did contain some Soviet materials collected and preserved by German wartime intelligence collection organs, and later volumes incorporated some materials produced by Soviet authors in the early 1960s, after Khrushchev loosened the reins on Soviet historiography. These works also included studies by Westerners who had spent considerable time in the Soviet Union during the war. Among the best and most substantive of these works that contain material on 1941 are Alan Clark's survey of the war, *Barbarossa* (1965), Earl Ziemke's *Stalingrad to Berlin* (1968) (in the CMH series), Paul Carell's more journalistic account, *Hitler Moves East* (1965), Harrison Salisbury's *The 900 Days* (1969), and Albert Seaton's *The Russo-German War* (1971).

THE SOVIET SCHOOL

Although relatively few of the voluminous quantity of published Russian-language works have been translated into English, the vast array of Soviet secondary materials must be addressed because it served as the stimulant for subsequent Western scholarship on the subject. Since de-Stalinization, or roughly 1958, Soviet historiography has produced a massive number of survey histories, operational studies, memoirs, and unit histories associated with the war. Included in this number were two major, officially sanctioned survey histories and several encyclopedia series. The 6-volume *History of the Great Patriotic War*, which appeared between 1960 and 1965, was a classic example of the de-Stalinization process and Khrushchevian glasnost. It introduced readers to hitherto forbidden topics, such as more detail on the 1941 catastrophe, and to a limited number of wartime defeats, such as the May 1942 Khar'kov disaster, which became the "Potemkin village" for failed Soviet wartime operations. Between 1973 and 1982, the Soviets produced a 12-volume *History of the Second World War*, which, while according the Red Army and Soviet state with the leading role in war, finally introduced Russian readers to Allied operations. Characteristic of the Brezhnev period, these volumes were less candid than their 6-volume predecessor.

The most substantive effort to produce a comprehensive encyclopedia of military history took place during the period 1976 through 1980, when the Ministry of Defense produced the 8-volume *Soviet Military Encyclopedia*, edited under the supervision of then Marshal I. V. Ogarkov. A companion single-volume encyclopedia of the Great Patriotic War appeared in 1985. Although of immense use to researchers, these volumes are in Russian and bear the same negative characteristics as other books published during the period. The Ministry of Defense began preparing a new, more candid version of the multivolume encyclopedia in 1990 but ceased publication of the work when the Soviet Union crumbled in 1991.

The best and least politicized of these secondary sources appeared during the height of the 1960s' "Thaw." Thereafter, works were of mixed value depending on the degree of license accorded each author and the sensitivity of the subject each addressed. As a general rule, those in favor were permitted to write with greater candor, as were those writing utilitarian accounts for Soviet Army officer education. Regardless of historical license, certain topics, such as the Red Army in 1941, many combat defeats, including Barbarossa, correct correlations of forces, and politically sensitive operations, remained forbidden. On the other hand, some wartime controversies that served current political needs were thoroughly aired (such as the Zhukov–Konev debate, which paralleled political infighting in the contemporary Soviet political hierarchy).

A limited number of these works, such as memoirs by senior commanders, G. K. Zhukov, A. M. Vasilevsky, I. S. Konev, K. K. Rokossovsky, A. I. Eremenko, K. A. Meretskov, and V. I. Chuikov, an invaluable study of the General Staff at war by S. M. Shtemenko, and a few operational studies on politically safe operations, such as Kursk, appeared in English translation. Soviet authorities heavily edited all memoirs, and only today are the expurgated portions of these memoirs appearing. Although much of the fact in these memoirs is correct, interpretations often are not, and they are as notable for what they do not say as for what they accurately report. The best and most accurate operational and tactical studies remained inaccessible because they were written in Russian. The authors of both genres generally skirted the most controversial issues and, at times, dissembled regarding the nature of and blame for major operational or strategic failures (for example, Zhukov's account of his defeat in the November 1942 Operation Mars and Konev's failure to describe his military career prior to January 1943). A notable exception to this rule were many memoirs and studies published during the Khrushchev "Thaw," from roughly 1960 to 1963, which were marked by unprecedented candor.

THE EMERGENCE OF A SYNTHESIS

A few Western historians, by virtue of their wartime service, keen linguistic talents, or unique access to Soviet sources, were able to synthesize Soviet materials and present a unique picture of the wartime Red Army. In so doing, they formed the Soviet school of war historiography in the West. Foremost among this small group were Malcolm Mackintosh and John Erickson, whose work in the 1960s began to etch a "face" on the hitherto featureless Red Army and added detail to equally shadowy Red Army operations. They did so shortly after Soviet historians began writing with greater candor about the war. Mackintosh's interest and knowledge of the Red Army resulted from his wartime association with it. Erickson's work resulted, in part, from his unique access to senior Red Army commanders during the early 1960s "Thaw" in Soviet historical writing, when the term glasnost (openness) was first used. For many years, Mackintosh's single-volume history of the Red Army, *Juggernaut,* was the most reliable single volume on the subject. Erickson's seminal study, *The Soviet High Command,* which appeared in 1962, provided unprecedented detail about the Red Army's development from 1918 through 1941 and "seized the commanding heights" regarding the Red Army in 1941. His subsequent massive and classic tomes, *The Road to Stalingrad* and *The Road to Berlin,* provided rich details of Soviet participation in the war. Yet even Erickson would admit that, although much of his work has withstood the archival test, he would have preferred to have had greater access to Soviet archives at the time he was writing his works.

In the 1980s, fueled by improved access to Russian-language sources, increased Soviet historical candor, and intensified interest in Soviet affairs by Western scholars, historiography on the war has matured and become better balanced. Scholars have been able to integrate Russian materials with and test them against German and Japanese archival sources to produce a more balanced interpretation of the war. Among those whose efforts have stood out are Christopher Bellamy, Alan Fugate, Geoffrey Jukes, Michael Parrish, Walter Dunn, and a growing number of younger historians. Also, my study of Soviet intelligence and deception opened new vistas to an understanding of the nature and impact of wartime military operations. My survey history of the war, *When Titans Clashed,* exploited both German and Soviet records to uncover previously forgotten major operations and cast new light on those that were already well known. Jukes and Fugate provided more detailed accounts of Operation Barbarossa and the titanic Battle of Kursk, and Bellamy prepared a superb survey of the history of Soviet wartime artillery. Parrish paved the way for the work of these historians by preparing massive seminal bibliographical studies of Soviet historical materials on the war, and Dunn published his massive study of Red Army force structure. Little work has been done on the Soviet Navy; however, Van Hardesty published the first thorough account of the Red Air Force at war. Important contributions to the emerging field of Soviet military biography include Richard Armstrong's portrayal of Soviet Army tank commanders, Harold Shukman's edited anthology on wartime Soviet military leaders, and Otto Chaney's revised biography of Marshal Zhukov. Reconstruction of the social composition of the Red Army and the soldier's human condition began with Roger Reese's study of the Soviet soldier on the eve of war. Although as yet unpublished, N. Ramanichev's manuscript mines voluminous archival materials that supplement and substantiate Reese's conclusions.

*Voenno-istoricheskii zhurnal* [Military-historical journal], abbreviated as *VIZh*
*Voennaia mysl'* [Military thought]
*Izvestiia TsK KPSS* [News of the Communist Party Central Committee]
*Novaia i noveishaia istoriia* [New and recent history]

Alferov, S. "Strategicheskoe razvertyvanie sovetskikh voisk na zapadnom TVD v 1941 godu" [Strategic deployment of Soviet forces in the Western TVD in 1941]. *VIZh* 6 (June 1981): 26–33.

Andriushchenko, N. K. *Na zemle Belorussii letom 1941 goda* [On Belorussian lands in the summer of 1941]. Minsk: Nauka i tekhnika, 1985.

Anfilov, V. A. *Nachalo Velikoi Otechevstvennoi voiny* [The beginning of the Great Patriotic War]. Moscow: Voenizdat, 1962.

———. *Proval blitskriga* [The failure of Blitzkreig]. Moscow: Nauka, 1974.

———. *Nezabyvaemyi sorok pervym* [Unforgettable 1941]. Moscow: Sovetskaia Rossiia, 1989.

Aptekar', P. A. "Opravdanny li zhertvy? O poteriakh v sovetsko-finliandskoi voine" [Were the casualties justified? Concerning losses in the Soviet-Finnish War]. *VIZh* 3 (March 1992): 43–45.

Arbatov, Georgi. *The System: An Insider's Life in Soviet Politics.* New York: Random House, 1992.

Armstrong, Richard. *Red Army Tank Commanders: The Armored Guards.* Atglen, Pa.: Schiffer Military/Aviation History, 1994.

Babich, Iu. P., and Baier, A. G. *Razvitie Vooruzheniia i organizatsii sovetskikh sukhoputnykh voisk v gody Velikoi Otechestvennoi voiny* [Development of the weaponry and organization of Soviet ground forces during the Great Patriotic War]. Moscow: Voenizdat, 1990.

Bagramian, I. Kh. *Istoriia voin i voennogo iskusstva* [A history of wars and military art]. Moscow: Voenizdat, 1970.

———. "Kharakter i osobennosti nachal'nogo perioda voiny" [The nature and peculiarities of the initial period of war]. *VIZh* 10 (October 1981): 20–27.

———. *Tak nachinalas' voina* [How the war began]. Kiev: Dnipro, 1975.

Baskakov, V. "Ob osobennostiakh nachal'nogo perioda voiny" [Concerning the peculiarities of the initial period of war]. *VIZh* 2 (February 1966): 29–34.

Beliaev, V. I. "Usilenie okhrany zapadnoi granitsy SSSR nakanune Velikoi Otechestvennoi voiny" [The strengthening of security of the western borders of the USSR on the eve of the Great Patriotic War]. *VIZh* 5 (May 1988): 50–55.

Bellamy, Chris. *Red God of War: Soviet Artillery and Rocket Forces.* London: Brassey's, 1986.

Bezymensky, L. "Sobiralsia li Stalin kapitulirovat' v 1941 godu?" {Did Stalin intend to capitulate in 1941?]. *Novoe vremia* [New Times] 13 (March 1992): 46–48.

Bialar, Seweryn, ed. *Stalin's Generals.* New York: Pegasus, 1969.

Biriuzov, S. "Pervye dni voiny" [The first days of war]. *VIZh* 10 (October 1960): 14–28.

————. "Uroki nachal'nogo perioda Velikoi Otechestvennoi voiny" [Lessons of the initial period of the Great Patriotic war]. *Voennaia mysl'* 8 (August 1964): 3–63.

Blau, George. *The German Campaign in Russia: Planning and Operations, 1940–1942*. Department of the Army Pamphlet 20-261a. Washington, D.C.: Government Printing Office, 1955.

Bobylev, P. N. "Repetitsiia katastrofy" [A rehearsal for catastrophe]. *VIZh* 6 (June 1993): 10–16.

Bordiugova, G. A., and V. A. Nevezhin, eds. *Gotovil li Stalin nastupatel'nuiu voinu protiv Gitlera? Nezaplanirovannaia diskussiia: Sbornik materialov* [Did Stalin prepare an offensive war against Hitler?: An unplanned discussion: A collection of materials]. Moscow: AIRO-XX, 1995.

Borozniak, A. I. "22 iiunia 1941 goda: Vzgliad s 'toi' storony" [22 June 1941: A view from 'that' side]. *Otechestvennaia istoriia* [Patriotic history] 1 (January 1994): 148–156.

Borshchov, A. D. "Otrazhenie fashistskoi agressii: Uroki i vyvody" [The repulsion of fascist aggression: Lessons and conclusions]. *Voennaia mysl'* 3 (March 1990): 15–22.

Carell, Paul. *Hitler's War on Russia 1941–1943*. London: Harrap, 1964.

Chaney, Otto P. *Zhukov*. Norman: University of Oklahoma Press, 1971. Expanded second edition in 1996.

Cherednichenko, M. "O nachal'nom periode Velikoi Otechestvennoi voiny" [Concerning the initial period of the Great Patriotic War]. *VIZh* 4 (April 1961): 28–35.

Cheremukhin, K. "Boevye deistviia sovetskikh voisk v pervye dni voiny na zapadnom napravlenii" [Combat operations of Soviet forces in the first days of war along the western axis]. *Voennai mysl'* 7 (July 1956): 49–64.

Cimbala, Stephen J. "Intelligence, C3, and the Initial Period of War." *The Journal of Slavic Military Studies* 4, 3 (September 1991): 397–447.

Clark, Alan. *Barbarossa: The Russian-German Conflict 1941–45*. New York: William Morrow, 1966.

Danilov, V. D. "Sovetskoe glavnoe komandovanie v preddverii Velikoi Otechestvennoi voiny" [The Soviet High Command on the threshold of war]. *Novaia i noveishaia istoriia* 6 (June 1988): 3–20.

Dunn, Walter S., Jr. *Hitler's Nemesis: The Red Army, 1930–1945*. New York: Praeger, 1994.

Eremenko, A. I. *The Arduous Beginning*. Moscow: Progress, 1966.

Erickson, John. *The Road to Stalingrad*. London: Weidenfeld and Nicolson, 1975.

————. *The Soviet High Command 1918–1941*. London: Macmillan, 1962.

Eliseeva, N. E. "Plans for the Development of the Workers' and Peasants' Red Army (RKKA) on the eve of war." *The Journal of Slavic Military Studies* 8, 2 (June 1995): 356–365.

Evseev, A. I. "O nekotorykh tendentsiiakh v izmenenii soderzhaniia i kharaktera nachal'nogo perioda voiny" [Concerning some tendencies in the changing form and nature of the initial period of war]. *VIZh* 11 (November 1985): 11–20.

Fugate, Brian I. *Operation Barbarossa: Strategy and Tactics on the Eastern Front*. Novato, Calif.: Presidio, 1984.

Gareev, M. A. "Eshche raz k voprosu: Gotovil li Stalin preventivnyi udar v 1941 g." [Once again on the question: Did Stalin prepare a preventive attack in 1941]. *Novaia i noveishaia istoriia* 1 (January 1994): 202.

Gerard, Beth M. "Mistakes in Force Structure and Strategy on the Eve of the Great Patriotic War." *The Journal of Slavic Military Studies* 4, 3 (September 1991): 471–486.

Glantz, David M. *A History of Airborne Forces.* London: Frank Cass, 1994.

———. *The Military Strategy of the Soviet Union.* London: Frank Cass, 1992.

———. "Observing the Soviets: U. S. Army Attaches in Eastern Europe During the 1930s." *The Journal of Military History* 55, 2 (April 1991): 153–184.

———. *The Role of Intelligence in Soviet Military Strategy in World War II.* Novato, Calif.: Presidio, 1990.

———. *Soviet Military Deception in the Second World War.* London: Frank Cass, 1989.

———. *Soviet Military Intelligence in War.* London: Frank Cass, 1990.

———. "Soviet Mobilization in Peace and War, 1929–1942: A Survey." *The Journal of Slavic Military Studies* 5, 3 (September 1992): 323–362.

Glantz, David M. ed. *The Initial Period of War on the Eastern Front, 22 June–August 1941.* London: Frank Cass, 1993.

———. *The 1984 Art of War Symposium: From the Don to the Dnepr: Soviet Offensive Operations—December 1942–August 1943: A Transcript of Proceedings.* Carlisle, Pa.: U.S. Army War College Center for Land Warfare, 1984.

Glantz, David M., and Jonathan House. *When Titans Clashed: How The Red Army Stopped Hitler.* Lawrence: University Press of Kansas, 1995.

Gor'kov, Iu. A. "Gotovil li Stalin uprezhdaiushchii udar protiv Gitlera v 1941 g." [Did Stalin prepare a forestalling attack against Hitler in 1941]. *Novaia i noveishaia istoriia* 3 (March 1993): 29–39.

*The Great Patriotic War of the Soviet Union 1941–1945.* Moscow: Progress, 1974.

Grechko. A. "25 let tomy nazad" [25 years ago]. *VIZh* 6 (June 1966): 3–15.

Grigorenko, Petro. *Memoirs.* New York: Norton, 1982. Translated by Thomas P. Whitney.

Guderian, Heinz. *Panzer Leader.* New York: Ballantine, 1965.

Gusarov, F. F., and L. A. Butakov. "Tekhnicheskoe prikrytie zheleznykh dorog (po opytu pervogo perioda Velikoi Otechestvennoi voiny)" [Technical cover of the railroads (based on the experience of the first period of the Great Patriotic War)]. *VIZh* 4 (April 1988): 51–58.

Hardesty, Van. *The Red Phoenix: The Rise of Soviet Air Power 1941–1945.* Washington, D.C.: The Smithsonian Institute Press, 1982.

Heinrici, G. *The Campaign in Russia.* London: Frank Cass, forthcoming.

Iakovlenko, I. I. "O prikrytii gosudarstvennoi granitsy nakanune Velikoi Otechestvennoi voiny (po opytu Kievskogo Osobogo voennogo okruga)" [Concerning the covering of the state borders on the eve of the Great Patriotic War (based on the experience of the Kiev Special Military District)]. *VIZh* 5 (May 1987): 84–87.

Iakushevsky, A. S. "Faktor vnezapnosti v napadenii Germanii na SSSR" [The factor of surprise in Germany's attack on the USSR]. *Voprosy istorii* [Problems of history] 1 (January 1990): 3–15.

———. "Osobennosti podgotovki vermakhta k napadeniiu na SSSR" [Peculiarities of Wehrmacht preparations for the attack on the USSR]. *VIZh* 5 (May 1989): 63–75.

Iazov, D. T. "Vperedi byla voina" [War lay ahead]. *VIZh* 5 (May 1991): 4–14.

*Istoriia Vtoroi mirovoi voiny 1939–1945* [A history of the Second World War 1939–1945]. 12 vols. Moscow: Voenizdat, 1973–1982.

Ivanov, S. P. *Nachal'nyi period voiny* [The initial period of war]. Moscow: Voenizdat, 1974.

Ivanov-Skuratov, A. "Napadenie lzhe-Suvorova na Rossiiu" [The attack of the false Suvorov on Russia]. *Na boevom postu* [At the combat post] 8–9 (August–September 1992): 30–32.

Ivashov, L. G. "Oborona strany i zakon: Pravovye osnovy podgotovki Vooruzhennykh Sil SSSR k otrazheniiu agressii" [The nation's defense and the law: The legal basis of the preparation of the armed forces of the USSR to repel aggression]. *VIZh* 8 (August 1992): 10–18.

Ivashutin, P. I. "Dokladyvala tochno (vospominaniia o minuvshei voine)" [It was reported accurately (recollections about the past war)]. *VIZh* 5 (May 1990): 55–59.

———. "Strategiia i taktika verolomstva" [The strategy and tactics of treachery]. *VIZh* 6 (June 1991): 4–11.

Kagan, Frederick. "The Evacuation of Soviet Industry in the Wake of 'Barbarossa.'" *The Journal of Slavic Military Studies* 8, 2 (June 1995): 387–414.

Khor'kov, A. G. "Iz opyta otmobilizovaniia sukhoputnykh voisk" [From the experience of mobilizing ground forces]. *VIZh* 4 (April 1982): 53–60.

———. "K voprosu o nachal'nom periode voiny" [Concerning the question of the initial period of the war]. *Voennaia mysl'* 8 (August 1984): 25–34.

———. "Nakanune groznykh sobitii" [On the eve of threatening events]. *VIZh* 5 (May 1988): 42–49.

———. "Nekotorye voprosy strategicheskogo razvertyvaniia Sovetskikh Vooruzhennykh Sil v nachale Velikoi Otechestvennoi voiny" [Some questions concerning the strategic deployment of the Soviet armed forces in the beginning of the Great Patriotic War]. *VIZh* 1 (January 1986): 9–15.

———. "Preventivnyi udar: Mify i real'nost'" [Preventive attack: Myths and reality]. *Tyl vooruzhennykh sil* [Rear services of the armed forces] 6 (June 1991): 3–9.

Kipp, Jacob W. "Barbarossa, Soviet Covering Forces, and the Initial Period of War: Military History and AirLand Battle." *The Journal of Slavic Military Studies* 1, 2 (June 1988): 188–212.

Kir'ian, M. M. "Nachal'nyi period Velikoi Otechestvennoi voiny" [The initial period of the Great Patriotic War]. *VIZh* 6 (June 1988): 11–17.

———. "Surovye uroki nachala Velikoi Otechestvennoi voiny" [The harsh lessons of the initial period of the Great Patriotic War]. *Voennaia mysl'* 5 (May 1981): 67–72.

Kirshin, Iu. Ia., and N. M. Ramanichev. "Nakanune 22 iiunia 1941 g. (po materialam voennykh arkhivov)" [On the eve of 22 June 1941 (According to materials from military archives)]. *Novaia i noveishaia istoriia* 3 (March 1991): 3–19.

Kolchigin, B. "Mysl' ob ispol'zovanii armii prikrytiia v nachal'nom periode Velikoi Otechestvennoi voiny" [Ideas about the use of covering armies in the initial period of the Great Patriotic War]. *VIZh* 4 (April 1961): 35–37.

Komal, F. B. "Voennye kadry nakanune voiny" [Military cadre on the eve of war]. *VIZh* 2 (February 1990): 21–28.

Korkodinov, P. "Fakty i mysli o nachal'nom periode Velikoi Otechestvennoi voiny" [Facts and notions concerning the initial period of the Great Patriotic War]. *VIZh* 10 (October 1965): 26–34.

Korzun, L. "Rol' voennoi strategii v podgotovke strany k voine" [The role of military strategy in preparing the country for war]. *VIZh* 7 (July 1982): 46–53.

Kozlov, M. M. *Velikaia Otechestvennaia voina 1941–1945: Entsiklopediia* [The Great Patriotic War 1941–1945: An encyclopedia]. Moscow: Soviet Encyclopedia, 1985.

Krikunov, V. P. "Frontoviki otvetili tak!: Piat' voprosov General'nogo shtaba" [Front soldiers thus answer!: Five questions of the General Staff]. *VIZh* 3 (March 1989): 62–69, and 5 (May 1990): 23–32.

Krivosheev, G. F. "Nakanune" [On the eve]. *VIZh* 6 (June 1991): 41–44.

———. *Grif sekretnosti sniat: poteri vooruzhennykh sil SSSR v voinakh, boevykh deistviiakh i voennykh konfliktakh* [The seal of secrecy removed: USSR armed forces losses in wars, combat operations, and military conflicts]. Moscow: Voenizdat, 1993.

Kuchikhin, A. N. "Sovetskie nemtsy: Otkuda, kuda, i pochemu? [Soviet Germans: whence, whither, and why?]. *VIZh* 8 (August 1990): 32–38, and 9 (September 1990): 28–38.

Kurkotkin, S. "Perevod ekonomiki strany s mirnogo na voennoe polozhenie v gody Velikoi Otechestvennoi voiny" [Conversion of the country's economy from a peacetime to a wartime footing during the Great Patriotic War]. *VIZh* 9 (September 1984): 3–11.

Kuznetsov, I. I. "Generaly 1940 goda" [The generals of 1940]. *VIZh* 10 (October 1988): 29–37.

Livin, G. A., and I. I. Volkodaev. "Planiroval li Stalin voinu protiv Germanii?" [Did Stalin plan war against Germany?]. *VIZh* 6 (June 1991): 26–33.

Losik, O. A. *Stroitel'stvo i boevoe primenenie sovetskikh tarkovykh voisk v gody Velikoi Otechestvenoi voiny* [Formation and combat use of Soviet tank forces during the Great Patriotic War]. Moscow: Voenizdat, 1979.

Mackintosh, Malcolm. *Juggernaut: A History of the Soviet Armed Forces*. London: Secker and Warburg, 1967.

McMichael, Scott R. "National Formations in the Red Army, 1918–1938." *The Journal of Slavic Military Studies* 3, 4 (December 1990): 613–644.

Makovsky, V. B. "Prikrytie gosgranitsy nakanune voiny" [The covering of the state borders on the eve of war]. *VIZh* 5 (May 1993): 51–58.

Malafeev, A. M. "Uroki nachal'nogo perioda Velikoi Otechestvennoi voiny" [Lessons of the initial period of the Great Patriotic War]. *Voennaia mysl'* 9 (September 1991): 8–17.

Manstein, Erich von. *Lost Victories*. Chicago: Henry Regnery, 1958.

Matsulenko, V. "Nekotorye vyvody iz opyta nachal'nogo perioda Velikoi Otechestvennoi voiny" [Some conclusions from the experience of the initial period of the Great Patriotic War]. *VIZh* 3 (March 1984): 35–42.

Mellenthin, F. W. von. *Panzer Battles*. Norman: University of Oklahoma Press, 1956.

Mel'tiukhov, M. I. "Spory vokrug 1941 goda: Opyt kriticheskogo osmysleniia odnoi diskusii" [The argument around 1941: The test of a critical understanding of a single discussion]. *Otechestvennaia istoriia* [Patriotic history] 3 (March 1994): 4–21.

———. "22 iiunia 1941 g.: Tsifry svidetel'stvuiut" [22 June 1941: Numbers bear witness]. *Istoriia SSSR* 3 (March 1991): 16–28.

Murin, Iu. G. "Nakanune: 22 iiunia 1941 g. neopublikovennoe interv'iu marshala Sovetskogo Soiuza A. M. Vasilevskogo" [On the eve: 22 June 1941, an unpublished interview with Marshal of the Soviet Union A. M. Vasilevsky]. *Novaia i noveishaia istoriia* 6 (June 1992): 3–11.

*Narodnoe khoziaistvo SSSR v Velikoi Otechestvennoi voine, 1941–1945* [The economy of the USSR during the Great Patriotic War, 1941–1945]. Moscow: IITs Goskomstata SSSR, 1993.

Nekrich, A. M. "1941, 22 iiunia" [1941, 22 June]. In Vladimir Petrov, *Soviet Historians and the German Invasion*. Columbia: University of South Carolina Press, 1968.

Nevezhin, V. A. "The Pact with Germany and the Idea of an 'Offensive War (1939–1941).'" *The Journal of Slavic Military Studies* 8, 4 (December 1995): 809–843.

Nikitin, A. "Perestroika raboty voennoi promyshlennosti SSSR v pervom periode Velikoi Otechestvennoi voiny" [Renewal of the work of the USSR's military industry in the first period of the Great Patriotic War]. *VIZh* 2 (February 1963): 11–19.

Ogarkov, I. V., ed. *Sovetskaia voennaia entsiklopediia* [Soviet military encyclopedia]. 8 vols. Moscow: Voenizdat, 1976–1980.

Osipov, A. "Agressiia ili 'preventivnaia' voina?" [Aggression or "preventive" war?]. *Zarubezhnoe voennoe obozrenie* 4 (April 1991): 3–6.

Parrish, Michael. *The USSR in World War II: An Annotated Bibliography of Books Published in the Soviet Union, 1945–1975, with an Addendum for the Years 1975–1980.* 2 vols. New York: Garland, 1981.

Pastukhovsky, G. P. "Razvertyvanie operativnogo tyla v nachal'nom periode voiny" [Deployment of the operational rear in the initial period of war]. *VIZh* 6 (June 1988): 18–27.

Patychenko, Iu., and P. Knyshevsky. "Mestnaia ekonomicheskaia baza nakanune voiny" [The local economic base on the eve of war]. *Tyl vooruzhennykh sil* [Rear services of the armed forces] 11–12 (November–December 1990): 25–28.

Pavlovsky, I. G. *Sukhoputnye voiska SSSR* [Ground forces of the USSR]. Moscow: Voenizdat, 1985.

Perechnev, Iu. G. "O nekotorykh problemakh podgotovki strany i Vooruzhennykh Sil k otrazheniiu fashistskoi agressii" [About some problems in preparing the nation and armed forces to repel fascist aggression]. *VIZh* 4 (April 1988): 42–50.

Petrov, V. L. "Strana gotovilas' k otrazheniiu agressii" [The country prepared itself to repel aggression]. *VIZh* 6 (November–December 1995): 4–9.

Phillips, Richard H. "Soviet Military Debate on the Initial Period of War: Characteristics and Implications," *The Journal of Slavic Military Studies* 4, 1 (March 1991): 30–61.

Platonov, S. P., ed. *Vtoraia mirovaia voina 1939–1945 gg.* [The Second World War 1939–1945]. Moscow: Voenizdat, 1958.

Proekter, D. M. "22 iiunia 1941 goda: piat'desiat let spustia" [22 June 1941: fifty years later]. *Voennaia mysl'* 6 (June 1991): 15–25.

Ramanichev, N. "The Red Army, 1940–1941: Myths and Realities." Manuscript (1996) written from archival materials and translated by R. Harrison.

Reese, Roger R. *Stalin's Reluctant Soldiers: A Social History of the Red Army, 1925–1941*. Lawrence: University Press of Kansas, 1996.

Rzheshevsky, O. "Kak nachinalas' voina" [How the war began]. *Partinaia zhizn'* [Party life] 13 (1989): 69–73.

Samuelson, Lennart. "Mikhail Tukhachevsky and War-Economic Planning: Archival Revelations and Historical Reconsiderations on the Prewar Soviet Military Build-up." *The Journal of Slavic Military Studies* 9, 4 (December 1996), in press.

Sandalov, L. M. *Na moskovskom napravlenii* [On the Moscow axis]. Moscow: Nauka, 1970.

———. *Perezhitoe* [One's past]. Moscow: Voenizdat, 1961.

Savushkin, Robert. "In the Tracks of a Tragedy: On the 50th Anniversary of the Start of the Great Patriotic War." *The Journal of Slavic Military Studies* 4, 2 (June 1991): 213–251.

Seaton, Albert. *The Russo-German War 1941–1945*. New York: Praeger, 1971.

Shkadov, I. "Bespristrastno pisat' istoriiu" [To write history impartially]. *Zarubezhnoe voennoe obozrenie* [Foreign military review] 5 (May 1991): 3–6.

Shtemenko, S. M. *The Soviet General Staff at War, 1941–1945*. 2 vols. Moscow: Progress, 1970.

Shukman, Harold, ed. *Stalin's Generals*. London: Weidenfeld and Nicolson, 1993.

Solnyshkov, Iu. S. "Po povodu stat'i generala-polkovnika Iu. A. Gor'kova" [Concerning the article of Colonel General Iu. A. Gor'kov]. *Novaia i noveishaia istoriia* 1 (January 1994): 239–240.

Sorokin, K. L. *Trudnye dni sorok pervogo* [The difficult days of '41]. Moscow: Voenizdat, 1991.

Suvorov, Viktor. *Den'-M: 6 iiulia 1941* [M-Day: 6 July 1941]. Moscow: Vse dlia Vas, 1994.

———. *Icebreaker: Who Started the Second World War?* Trans. Thomas B. Beattie. London: Hammish Hamilton, 1990.

Svechin, A. A. *Strategy*. Minneapolis: East View Press, 1982.

Tarleton, Robert E. "What Really Happened to the Stalin Line, Parts I and II." *The Journal of Slavic Military Studies* 5, 2 (June 1992): 187–219, and 6, 1 (March 1993): 21–61.

Temirbiev, S. "Tak kto zhe nachal voiny?" [So who began the war?]. *Armiia* [Army] 8 (August 1993): 16–20.

Tsukertort, I. "Germanskii militarizm i legenda o 'preventivnoi voine' gitlerovskoi Germanii protiv SSSR" [German militarism and the legend of the "preventive war" of Hitlerite Germany against the USSR]. *VIZh* 5 (May 1991): 16–21.

Ukolov, A. T., and V. I. Ivkin. "O masshtabakh repressii v Krasnoi Armii v predvoennye gody" [Concerning the scale of repression in the Red Army in the prewar years]. *VIZh* 1 (January 1993): 56–63.

Van Dyck, Carl. "The Timoshenko Reforms, March–July 1940," *The Journal of Slavic Military Studies* 9, 1 (March 1996): 69–96.

Vasilevsky, A. M. *A Lifelong Cause*. Moscow: Progress, 1976.

*Velikaia Otechestvennaia voina Sovetskogo Soiuza* [The Great Patriotic War of the Soviet Union]. 6 vols. Moscow: Voenizdat, 1960–1965.

Vladimirsky, A. V. *Na kievskom napravlenii* [On the Kiev axis]. Moscow: Voenizdat, 1989.

*Vnutrennie voiska v gody mirnogo sotsialisticheskogo stroitel'stva, 1922–1941 gg.* [Internal forces in the years of peaceful socialist construction, 1922–1941]. Moscow: Voenizdat, Iuridicheskaia literatura, 1977.

Voinovich, Vladimir. *The Life and Extraordinary Adventures of Private Ivan Chonkin.* Translated by Richard Lourie. New York: Farrar, Straus and Giroux, 1977.

Volkogonov, D. *Triumf i tragediia: I. V. Stalin: Politicheskii portret* [Triumph and Tragedy: I. V. Stalin: A political portrait]. 4 pts. Moscow: Novosti, 1989.

Volkov, A. A. *Kriticheskii prolog: Nezavershennye frontovye nastupatel'nye operatsii pervykh kampanii Velikoi Otechestvennoi voiny* [Critical prologue: Incomplete front offensive operations of the first campaigns of the Great Patriotic War]. Moscow: AVIAR, 1992.

Watt, Donald Cameron. "Who Plotted Against Whom? Stalin's Purge of the Soviet High Command Revisited." *The Journal of Slavic Military Studies* 3, 1 (March 1990): 46–65.

Werth, Alexander. *Russia at War, 1941–1945.* New York: Dutton, 1964.

Zakharchuk, M., and V. Golotiuk. "Nakanune voiny" [On the eve of war]. *Protivo-vozdushnaia oborona* [Air defense] 6 (June 1992): 46–52.

Zakharov, M. V. *General'nyi shtab v predvoennye gody* [The General Staff in the prewar years]. Moscow: Voenizdat, 1989.

———. "Nachal'nyi period Velikoi Otechestvennoi voiny i ego uroki [The initial period of the Great Patriotic War and its lessons]. *VIZh* 7 (July 1971): 3–14.

Zaloga, Steven J. "Technological Surprise and the Initial Period of War: The Case of the T-34 Tank in 1941." *The Journal of Slavic Military Studies* 6, 4 (December 1993): 634–646.

Zaloga, Steven J., and James Grandsen. *Operation Barbarossa.* London: Arms and Armor Press, 1985.

Zaloga, Steven J., Jim Kinnear, and Peter Sarson. *KV-1 and 2 Heavy Tanks, 1941–1945.* London: Osprey, 1995.

Zhukov, G. *Reminiscences and Reflections.* 2 vols. Moscow: Progress, 1985.

Zimarin, O. A. "Mif 'Ledokola'" [The "Icebreaker" myth]. *VIZh* 4 (July–August 1995): 32–36.

Zolotarev, V. A., ed. *Velikaia Otechestvennaia voina 1941–1945 gg.: voenno-istoricheskie ocherki v chetyrekh knigakh, Kniga pervaia: surovye ispytaniia* [The Great Patriotic War 1941–1945: military-historical essays in four volumes, volume one: harsh trials]. Moscow: Biblioteka Mosgorarkhiv, 1995.

## Primary Sources: Archival, Semi-Archival, and Documentary Materials

Prior to the mid-1980s, the predominant mass of primary materials on the Soviet-German war was German in origin. The few Soviet archival materials to reach Western hands did so through wartime and postwar intelligence channels. These included selected volumes of Soviet war experience analysis that the Germans captured during wartime. For example, three early volumes concerning operations during the

Stalingrad period fell into German hands and then into U.S. intelligence channels. These were translated and circulated through U.S. Army senior service schools. Because they were fragmentary in nature and their provenance was unclear, until the 1980s virtually no one exploited them. They remained buried in the libraries for 40 years until discovered and published in the 1980s.

In addition, many issues of wartime Soviet military journals also fell into German and Western hands, including scattered issues of the General Staff journal *Military Thought* and *Armored and Mechanized Journal*. These suffered the same fate as the war experience volumes. Finally, random lectures on wartime operations prepared for delivery at Soviet postwar military educational institutions and copies of Soviet wartime regulations made their way west through similar channels. As interesting as these documents were, their disposition in obscure library files and their fragmentary nature diminished their importance and impact. In no way could these documents challenge the stranglehold on historiography of the more numerous German primary sources.

GERMAN

There exist vast quantities of German archival materials, which provided the fodder historians used to reconstruct the history of the war on the German Eastern Front. Much of this material was captured by the Allied armies at war's end, and U.S., British, and now German archival repositories have made most of this material readily accessible to historians. Extensive archival sources that fell exclusively into Soviet hands, however, remain inaccessible to Western scholars. Among the most valuable German primary source materials are the postwar compilations of German archival materials issued in book form and the voluminous German military unit records maintained in Western archives, including the U.S. National Archives in Washington, D.C., and the German Militargeschichtlichen Forschungsamt in Freiberg and Berlin. Some of this material contains assessments of the Red Army on the eve of war.

Surviving OKH (High Command of the Army) records are fragmentary since the Soviet Army captured many German unit war diaries, particularly later in the war, and some German forces destroyed their records to prevent them from falling into Soviet hands. Still other unit records were destroyed by Allied fire while being removed from Berlin after the Nazi government's collapse. The mass of surviving archival material includes a significant number of personal diaries interspersed among thousands of unit records at every level of army command, some of which contain information on 1941. The most interesting high-level diary is the diary of the chief of the German General Staff, Franz Halder, in which he recorded his impressions of the war in the East until Hitler removed him from office in September 1942.

Among the most important series of OKH and German Army unit records available to scholars on microfilm is the National Archives Microfilm (NAM) series T-78, the records of Foreign Armies East (Fremde Heere Ost). This series contains German wartime intelligence materials and assessments of all aspects of the Soviet armed forces and Soviet military-industrial activity. Most interesting are the assessments of Soviet (and German) military strength, strategic and operational intentions, and industrial war production; Red Army order of battle, force composition, and morale; and biographical materials on the Soviet political and military leadership on the eve of and during the first months of war. In addition, the NAM series T-311, of German Army Groups, NAM series T-312 and T-313, of armies and panzer armies, also contain fragmentary intelligence data on the 1941 Red Army.

Even today, new primary source materials that will enrich existing German archival holdings are appearing. Hundreds of postwar memoir studies have lain fallow while accounts by more famous and popular German commanders occupied the historical limelight. These newly discovered memoirs and studies include massive manuscripts written during the immediate postwar years by less famous German military leaders under the auspices of U.S. military historical organizations, in particular, the Historical Division of U.S. European Command. Most prominent in this extensive group of German-language manuscripts is the extensive memoir by the German defensive specialist G. Heinrici, which has just been rediscovered and is now being prepared for publication.

Supplementing these works are the personal memoirs of a host of German military leaders and private soldiers, which have been retained since the war in private family holdings. When released for publication or exploited by scholars, these promise to offer a far more personal view of the war from those who fought and suffered in it. In addition, extensive Finnish, Hungarian, Italian, and Rumanian archival holdings supplement these German records.

SOVIET

The closed nature of Soviet society and ideological restrictions on the writing of history have complicated the definition and classification of Russian-language primary source materials. Prior to 1987, the Soviet government limited access to their archives to a handful of "official" historians. When granted, access was carefully controlled. The Soviets limited their official "release" of archival materials to specially selected documents on specific themes, which Party authorities cleared for publication and published to achieve desired political effects. This material was published in historical studies, many of military operational nature, or in the memoirs of notable Soviet wartime leaders. The Party permitted military historians to write on narrow topics from a restricted data base of officially approved sources. While many of the facts contained in these military histories, studies, and memoirs were accurate, certain topics, such as casualties, embarrassing defeats, and the actual correlation of forces between the warring sides were either severely proscribed or routinely distorted. History also served starkly utilitarian ends, such as the advancement of specific political aims or military education. Almost coincidentally, and somewhat ironically, Soviet commitment to sound education in the realm of military science had the beneficial effect of producing even greater candor, although even here within severe constraints.

Because of the unavailability of archival materials, detailed military studies prepared for the purposes of military education and memoir materials, which the Soviets used as vehicles for discussing controversial military and even political issues, fell into a category midway between what Westerners considered as primary and secondary source material. If properly juxtaposed against Western primary sources, these military studies and memoirs served as proxies for actual primary sources, but proxies that had to be handled critically and with care.

The Red Army General Staff Historical Section prepared a variety of studies during and after the war on the basis of archival materials. The Soviet Army used these publications, which were classified as top secret and secret, in Army education and training. In the main, these studies incorporated archival materials directly and accurately and were generally honest and primary in nature. Like their unclassified counterpart studies, however, they avoided controversial political issues and tended to avoid politically sensitive defeats. A few of these wartime studies fell into the hands of German intelligence during the war and, hence, into Western hands after the war ended. Many more were released during the Gorbachev period of glasnost and after the fall of the Soviet Union. The Soviet Army General Staff ceased preparation and publication of these studies in the mid-1960s, when the function of historical analysis was passed to the Ministry of Defense's newly created Military History Institute. Henceforth, studies prepared by the politicized institute lacked the depth, accuracy, and candor of their earlier General Staff counterparts.

Another category of primary sources is the numerous classified military publications that were used for educational purposes at the many Soviet military educational institutions, such as the Voroshilov General Staff Academy and the Frunze Academy. Although Soviet authors wrote these studies on the basis of archival materials, they were subject to the same general constraints as General Staff writers, and the studies varied in accuracy based on contemporary political exigencies. During the 1950s and 1960s, when historical glasnost prevailed, these studies were fairly accurate and consistent with archival materials. Ultimately, however, by the mid-1970s, after the Brezhnev regime had discarded glasnost, the accuracy, candor, and value of these materials had declined to the level of standard secondary sources.

Military archival materials released thus far fall into several distinct categories. The first, most accurate, and most useful are series of works that various directorates of the General Staff prepared for publication between 1942 and 1968. While preparing these series, the Red Army (and Soviet Army) General Staff made a genuine attempt to establish the truth about the course and consequences of wartime military operations and to harness that truth in the service of improving future Soviet Army combat performance. For the most part, when these studies are compared with German and Japanese archival records, their general accuracy and candor are generally vindicated. There were, of course, topics that the General Staff could not address, including some of the most sensitive failed wartime operations (such as the Liuban operation in early 1942, with its Vlasov connection, Operation Mars, the failed companion piece to the Stalingrad operation, and the abortive Belorussian operation of fall 1943). Also prohibited were politically sensitive topics, such as discussions and disputes between Stavka members (Stalin in particular): the General Staff, and field commands, which were numerous throughout the war, and the motives for controversial political and military decisions. Most important from the standpoint of this volume, discussion of the circumstances surrounding the Barbarossa catastrophe was also severely restricted. This sad reality was altered, however, when, in the late 1980s and after the fall of the Soviet Union, the nature of and responsibility for Barbarossa became a topic of burning interest.

The principal General Staff sources are the *Sborniki* (Collections) of materials prepared by the Soviet (Red) Army General Staff. These General Staff studies, prepared by the Directorate for the Study of War Experience and the Military-historical Directorate, include four distinct collections, three of which contain raw materials on wartime tactical issues and processed studies of military operations. The fourth, entitled *Sbornik boevykh dokumentov Velikoi Otechestvennoi voiny, Vypusk 1–43* (Collection of combat documents of the Great Patriotic War, issues 1–43). abbreviated *SBDVOV* and classified secret, relates directly to the circumstances of 1941. This series, which was published between 1947 and 1960, supplemented the other war experience volumes and contained directives and orders from the Stavka as well as combat documents relating to the activities of all branches and types of Soviet forces. The first 30 volumes ("issues") focused on functional combat themes, with 3 volumes covering key Stavka orders and the histories of the first guards divisions.

The subsequent issues, numbered 33–43, were perhaps the most informative and interesting portions of the documents series and most relevant to the Red Army in 1941. These were compilations of combat orders and reports of *fronts,* armies, and corps during the period 22 June–5 November 1941, assembled in the fashion of force war diaries. Although their component documents were selective, coverage was thorough, and they provided a most vivid, candid, and probably accurate portrait of the condition of the Red Army in June 1941 and combat during the difficult initial period of war. Unfortunately, the General Staff halted its chronological treatment of documents in the mid-1960s, when it had reached late fall of 1941.

The General Staff also prepared many studies on wartime operations during wartime or during the immediate postwar years. These General Staff materials, prepared and published during or immediately after the war, were all classified, and their high quality, candor, and accuracy reflected the best traditions of General Staff work. They were, in essence, utilitarian and designed to teach the Red Army how to better conduct combat operations. Other General Staff or Ministry of Defense–derived publications, including wartime and postwar issues of journals (*Voennaia mysl'* [Military thought]) and studies prepared by the Voroshilov General Staff Academy and Frunze Academy during and shortly after the war, achieved this same high quality. Although accurate in the main, these works leave out statistical data, in particular relating to correlation of forces and means. Most important, while most of this addressed the most important wartime operations, few, if any, concerned the outbreak of war in 1941. That also changed in the late 1980s, with the internal publication of a variety of studies on 1941, most reflecting Soviet concern for the topic, the initial period of war. The most important work of this genre was a 1989 Voroshilov Academy study, *Nachal'nyi period Velikoi Otechestvennoi voiny: Vyvody i uroki* (The initial period of the Great Patriotic War: Conclusions and lessons).

Another vehicle for primary source releases was a variety of military and political journals. The most important is the organ of the General Staff itself, *Voennaia mysl'* (Military thought), which was published as a controlled publication from 1937 through 1989 and publicly thereafter. Other journals include the open-source *Voenno-istoricheskii zhurnal* (Military-historical journal), the armed forces historical journal which has been published since 1939, and *Izvestiia TsK KPSS* (News of the

Communist Party Central Committee), which Party First Secretary Gorbachev used as a prime vehicle for his glasnost program in the late 1980s. Both journals provided a key conduit for the release of documentary archival materials from the mid- and late 1980s.

The most notable series of released archival documents in *VIZh*, which pertained to the Red Army in 1941, are the series "Pervye dni voiny v dokumentakh" (The first days of war in documents), 5–9 (May–September 1989); "Voennye razvedchiki dokladyvali . . ." (Military intelligence reported), 2–3 (February–March 1989); and "GKO postanavliaet . . ." [The People's Commissariat of Defense decrees), 2–5 (February–May 1992). The most important releases in the now defunct *Izvestiia TsK KPSS* include the extensive documents collection published under the rubric "Iz istoriia Velikoi Otechestvennoi voiny" (From the history of the Great Patriotic War) in 1–12 (January–December 1990) and 1–8 (January–August 1991). Unfortunately, the failed coup and outlawing of the Communist Party ended the publishing life of this journal and the release of this document series.

Finally, Stalin suppressed many books published in the Soviet Union during the 1920s and 1930s shortly after their publication. Hence, they were unavailable in the West. These, too, essentially can be categorized as primary sources. Included in their number were controversial works by key interwar theorists such as A. M. Zaionch-kovsky, A. A. Svechin, M. N. Tukhachevsky, E. A. Shilovsky, and G. Isserson, all of which are now released and provide a superb window on the Red Army before the outbreak of war.

It is important to note that most of these materials, General Staff studies and books, other institutional studies, and journals alike, although technically archival, are in some way *processed*, and that process has often affected their content. In addition, these are *released* materials, which have only recently found their way to the West largely through commercial conduits. Although release of these materials is welcome, the larger question regarding direct archival access in the Western sense of the word remains unanswered. Russian authorities have frequently announced that the archives are open for foreign scholars, but that access is still severely limited and in no way comparable to access to Western archives.

In general, classified or restricted Soviet studies published between the mid-1960s and the late 1980s, which supposedly exploited archival materials, as well as secondary studies and memoir literature, lacked the substance and accuracy of their wartime and postwar counterparts and their glasnost successors. Although many of their operational and tactical details and their narrative account of events were generally accurate, they exaggerated enemy strength and covered up the worst aspects of Soviet combat performance, in particular, specific details regarding the many Soviet combat disasters, especially the circumstances of 1941. Moreover, their political content was far more pervasive and strident than that found in the earlier General Staff volumes. This was particularly disturbing regarding educational materials used at the Voroshilov and Frunze academies up to the late 1980s.

Voroshilov Academy publications, issued since 1942 in a variety of formats under the imprimatur VAGSh, include texts, studies, analytical works, and lectures delivered at the academy. Some of these are multivolume surveys of the history of war and military art, such as a two-volume work edited by the eminent military historian I. E.

Shavrov, which were published in revised versions every few years. The most interesting and valuable are the wartime volumes and the collections *(sborniki)* of wartime materials. In general, the Voroshilov materials are more scholarly in nature and, hence, less inaccurate and political. The studies and lectures from the period after 1968, however, contain the same inaccuracies found in other Soviet publications. Frunze Academy publications, which have not been released in as great a number as the Voroshilov materials, share the same characteristics of their Voroshilov counterparts. Studies by these military educational institutions prepared after 1989 have corrected many of these earlier deficiencies.

Several special publications recently released by the Central Archives of the Soviet Army are of particular interest to the study of the Red Army in 1941. The first of these are the mobilization regulations *(ustavy)*, issued in the years immediately preceding the war, and the Red Army's mobilization journal. Although these records cast considerable light on Soviet mobilization capabilities and procedures, the critical appendices linking mobilization and war plans have been removed. The second striking document is the transcript of proceedings of the controversial December 1941 Conference of the High Command. Release of this lengthy document ends years of speculation regarding what was said, and by whom, at this critical session, which followed the completion of the last major Soviet war games before the German June 1941 attack.

Finally, the collections of selective documents published in recent journals seem to be authentic and represent a genuine effort to begin an increased flow of released archival materials. By their very nature, however, they are selective, and the flow of materials has noticeably decreased since the downfall of Gorbachev and the collapse of the Soviet Union. It remains to be seen whether this trend will be reversed.

Compared with the past state of Soviet historiographical work on the subject of the Red Army in 1941, what has transpired in recent years regarding release of archival materials has been revolutionary. However, just as the new Russian revolution is in its infancy, so also is the revolution in historiography. The archival materials that have been released thus far appear prodigious compared with the meager archival materials previously available (through captured German records). They are, however, really very limited compared with what certainly exists behind still-closed doors. Thus, while there is much to celebrate, there is also much to anticipate.

*Voenno-istoricheskii zhurnal* [Military-historical journal], abbreviated as *VIZh*
*Voennaia mysl'* [Military thought]
*Izvestiia TsK KPSS* [News of the Communist Party Central Committee]
*Novaia i noveishaia istoriia* [New and recent history]
*Kommunist vooruzhennykh sil* [Communist of the armed forces]

"19–30 iiulia 1941 g." [19–30 July 1941]. In "Iz arkhivov partii" [From the Party archives]. *Izvestiia TsK KPSS* 8 (August 1990): 208–223.
"3–29 avgusta 1941 g." [3–29 August 1941]. In "Iz arkhivov partii" [From the Party archives]. *Izvestiia TsK KPSS* 9 (September 1990): 215.
"1–13 sentiabria 1941 g." [1–13 September 1941]. In "Iz arkhivov partii" [From the Party archives]. *Izvestiia TsK KPSS* 10 (October 1990): 207–223.

"1–15 oktiabria 1941 g." [1–15 October 1941]. In "Iz arkhivov partii" [From the Party archives]. *Izvestiia TsK KPSS* 12 (December 1990): 203–218.

Anfilov, V. A. "Krasnaia armiia za god do fashistskoi agressii" [The Red Army during the year before the fascist aggression]. *VIZh* 3 (May–June 1996): 28, and 4 (July–August 1996): 18–23.

*Boevoi sostav Sovetskoi armii* [Combat composition of the Soviet Army]. 3 pts. Moscow: Voenno-nauchnoe upravlenie General'nogo Shtaba [Military-scientific directorate of the General Staff]. 1963–1972. Classified secret, declassified in 1964.

"Boevye dokumenty po oboronitel'noi operatsii v Litve i Latvii provodivsheisia s 22 iiunia po 9 iiulia 1941 g. voiskami Severo-Zapadnogo fronta" [Combat documents on the defensive operation in Lithuania and Latvia which was carried out from 22 June through 9 July 1941 by the forces of the Northwest Front]. In *Sbornik boevykh dokumentov Velikoi Otechestvennoi voiny: vypusk 34* [A collection of combat documents of the Great Patriotic War: issue 34]. Moscow: Voenizdat, 1958. Classified secret, declassified in 1964. Prepared by the Military-scientific Directorate of the General Staff.

Dashichev, V. I. *Sovershenno sekretno! Tol'ko dlia komandovaniia* [Top secret! Only for commanders]. Moscow: Nauka, 1967.

———. "Strategicheskoe planirovanie agressii protiv SSSR" [Strategic planning of aggression against the USSR]. *VIZh* 3 (March 1991): 10–30.

"Dokumenty i materialy: Staroe, no groznoe oruzhie" [Documents and materials: Old, but terrible weapons]. *VIZh* 9 (September 1988): 23–32.

"Dokumenty po boevym deistviiam voisk brianskogo fronta na orlovskom i kurskom napravleniiakh s 16 avgusta po 29 oktiabria 1941 g." [Documents on the combat operations of Briansk Front forces on the Orel and Kursk axes from 16 August through 29 October 1941]. In *Sbornik boevykh dokumentov Velikoi Otechestvennoi voiny: vypusk 43* [A collection of combat documents of the Great Patriotic War: issue 43]. Moscow: Voenizdat, 1960. Classified secret, declassified in 1964. Prepared by the Military-scientific Directorate of the General Staff.

"Dokumenty po boevym deistviiam voisk iugo-zapadnogo i iuzhnogo frontov v zapadnoi Ukraine i Moldavii s 22 iiunia po 11 iiulia 1941 g." [Documents on the combat operations of Southwestern and Southern Front forces in western Ukraine and Moldavia from 22 June through 11 July 1941]. In *Sbornik boevykh dokumentov Velikoi Otechestvennoi voiny: vypusk 36* [A collection of combat documents of the Great Patriotic War: issue 36]. Moscow: Voenizdat, 1958. Classified secret, declassified in 1964. Prepared by the Military-scientific Directorate of the General Staff.

"Dokumenty po boevym deistviiam voisk iugo-zapadnogo napravleniia s 11 iiulia po 25 iiulia 1941 g." [Documents on the combat operations of Southwestern Direction forces from 11 July through 25 July 1941]. In *Sbornik boevykh dokumentov Velikoi Otechestvennoi voiny: vypusk 38* [A collection of combat documents of the Great Patriotic War: issue 38]. Moscow: Voenizdat, 1959. Classified secret, declassified in 1964. Prepared by the Military-scientific Directorate of the General Staff.

"Dokumenty po boevym deistviiam voisk iugo-zapadnogo napravleniia s 26 iiulia po 6 avgusta 1941 g." [Documents on the combat operations of Southwestern Direction forces from 26 July through 6 August 1941]. In *Sbornik boevykh dokumentov Velikoi Otechestvennoi voiny: vypusk 39* [A collection of combat documents of the Great Patriotic War: issue 39]. Moscow: Voenizdat, 1959. Classified secret, declassified in 1964. Prepared by the Military-scientific Directorate of the General Staff.

"Dokumenty po boevym deistviiam voisk iugo-zapadnogo napravleniia na pravo-berezhnoi i levoberezhnoi Ukraine s 6 avgusta po 25 sentiabria 1941 g." [Documents on the combat operations of Southwestern Direction forces in right-bank and left-bank Ukraine from 6 August through 25 September 1941]. In *Sbornik boevykh dokumentov Velikoi Otechestvennoi voiny: vypusk 40* [A collection of combat documents of the Great Patriotic War: issue 40]. Moscow: Voenizdat, 1960. Classified secret, declassified in 1964. Prepared by the Military-scientific Directorate of the General Staff.

"Dokumenty po boevym deistviiam voisk iuzhnogo fronta v Donbasse s 26 sentiabria po 5 noiabria 1941 g." [Documents on the combat operations of Southern Front forces from 26 September through 5 November 1941]. In *Sbornik boevykh dokumentov Velikoi Otechestvennoi voiny: vypusk 42* [A collection of combat documents of the Great Patriotic War: issue 42]. Moscow: Voenizdat, 1960. Classified secret, declassified in 1964. Prepared by the Military-scientific Directorate of the General Staff.

"Dokumenty po boevym deistviiam voisk zapadnogo fronta na smolenskom napravlenii s 12 avgusta po 13 sentiabria 1941 g." [Documents on the combat operations of Western Front forces on the Smolensk axis from 12 August through 13 September 1941]. In *Sbornik boevykh dokumentov Velikoi Otechestvennoi voiny: vypusk 41* [A collection of combat documents of the Great Patriotic War: issue 41]. Moscow: Voenizdat, 1960. Classified secret, declassified in 1964. Prepared by the Military-scientific Directorate of the General Staff.

"Dokumenty po boevym deistviiam voisk zapadnogo fronta s 22 iiunia po 5 iiulia 1941 g." [Documents on the combat operations of Western Front forces from 22 June through 5 July 1941]. In *Sbornik boevykh dokumentov Velikoi Otechestvennoi voiny: vypusk 35* [A collection of combat documents of the Great Patriotic War: issue 35]. Moscow: Voenizdat, 1958. Classified secret, declassified in 1964. Prepared by the Military-scientific Directorate of the General Staff.

"Dokumenty po boevym deistviiam voisk zapadnogo fronta i fronta reservnykh armii (rezervnogo fronta) s 3 iiulia po 7 avgusta 1941 g." [Documents on the combat operations of Western Front forces and the front of reserve armies (Reserve Front) from 3 July through 7 August 1941]. In *Sbornik boevykh dokumentov Velikoi Otechestvennoi voiny: vypusk 37* [A collection of combat documents of the Great Patriotic War: issue 37]. Moscow: Voenizdat, 1959. Classified secret, declassified in 1964. Prepared by the Military-scientific Directorate of the General Staff.

Dokumenty po ispol'zovaniiu bronetankovykh i mekhanizirovannykh voisk Sovetskoi Armii v period s 22 iiunia po sentiabr' 1941 g. vkliuchitel'no" [Documents on the employment of armored and mechanized forces of the Soviet Army in the period 22 June through September 1941, inclusive]. In *Sbornik boevykh dokumentov Velikoi Otechestvennoi voiny: vypusk 33* [A collection of combat documents of the Great Patriotic War: issue 33]. Moscow: Voenizdat, 1957. Classified secret, declassified in 1964. Prepared by the Military-scientific Directorate of the General Staff.

Eliseeva, N. E., and I. M. Nagaev. "Germanskii militarizm i legenda o 'preventivnoi voine' gitlerovskoi Germanii protiv SSSR" [German militarism and the legend about Hitlerite Germany's preventive war against the USSR]. *VIZh* 3 (March 1991): 4–8.

Evgen'ev, I. Z. "Iz arkhivov GRU RKKA: Voennye razvedchiki dokladyvali. . . ." [From the Red Army GRU archives: Military scouts reported . . .]. *VIZh* 2 (February 1992): 36–41, and 3 (March 1992): 40–42.

Gishko, N. S. "GKO postanavliaet . . ." [The State Defense Committee decrees . . .]. *VIZh* 2 (February 1992): 31–35, 3 (March 1992): 17–21, and 4–5 (April–May 1992): 19–23.

Gor'kov, Iu. A., and Iu. N. Semin. "Konets global'noi lzhi, operativnye plany zapadnykh prigranichnykh voennykh okrugov 1941 goda svidetel'stvuiut: SSSR ne gotovilsia k napadeniiu na Germaniiu" [The end of a global lie, the 1941 operational plans of the western border military districts bear witness: The USSR did not prepare for an attack on Germany]. *VIZh* 2 (March–April 1996): 2–15, 3 (May–June 1996): 17, and 4 (July–August 1996): 2–17.

———. "Strategicheskie proshchety verkhovnogo? . . ." [Strategic errors of the High Command? . . .]. *VIZh* 8 (August 1992): 19–32.

*Istoriia voin, voennogo iskusstva i voennoi nauki, T. 2: Uchebnik dlia Voennoi akademii General'nogo shtaba Vooruzhennykh Sil SSSR* [A history of wars, military art, and military science, vol. 2: A textbook for the Military Academy of the USSR armed forces General Staff]. Moscow: Voroshilov Academy of the General Staff, 1977.

Ivashov, L. G. "Ne predstavliali sebe . . . vsekh trudnostei, sviazannykh s etoi voinoi" [No one imagined all of the difficulties associated with this war]. *VIZh* 4 (March 1993): 7–12, 5 (May 1993): 45–50, and 7 (July 1993): 35–40.

"Iz arkhivov Ministerstva oborony SSSR: 'My gotovy. Vse pogruzheno. Zavtra vystupaem'" [From the USSR Ministry of Defense archives: "We are ready. Everything is loaded. Tomorrow we go forward"]. *VIZh* 1 (January 1990): 19–26.

"Iz tainykh arkhivov spetssluzhb reikha: Plany fashistskoi imperii" [From the secret archives of the Reich's special services: The plans of the fascist empire]. *VIZh* 5 (May 1990): 39–45.

Khor'kov, A. G. *Analiz boevoi gotovnosti voisk zapadnykh prigranichnykh voennykh okrugov nakanune Velikoi Otechestvennoi voiny* [An analysis of the combat readiness of western military district forces on the eve of the Great Patriotic War]. Moscow: Voroshilov Academy of the General Staff, 1985. For official use only.

———. *Boevaia i mobilizatsionnaia gotovnost' prigranichnykh voennykh okrugov nakanune Velikoi Otechestvennoi voiny* [The combat and mobilization readiness of the border military districts on the eve of the Great Patriotic War]. Moscow: Voroshilov Academy of the General Staff, 1985. Classified secret, but now declassified.

Kiniakin, I. "Boevaia podgotovka VMF nakanune voiny" [The combat preparations of the fleet on the eve of war]. *Morskoi sbornik* [Naval collection] 6 (June 1991): 6–26.

Kirshner, L. A. *Kanun i nachalo voiny: Dokumenty i materialy* [On the eve and in the beginning of war: Documents and materials]. Moscow: Lenizdat, 1991.

*Komandovanie korpusnogo i divizionnogo zvena Sovetskoi Vooruzhennykh Sil perioda Velikoi Otechestvennoi voiny, 1941–1945* [Corps and divisional commanders of the Soviet armed forces in the Great Patriotic War, 1941–1945]. Moscow: Frunze Academy, 1964. Classified secret, declassified in 1964.

Kostetsky, V. "Proshu raz"iasnit': 'Ia besedoval s germanskim poslom Ott . . .'" [I ask you to explain: "I met with the German ambassodor Ott . . ."]. *Armiia* [Army] 1 (January 1992): 25–28.

*Nachal'nyi period Velikoi Otechestvennoi voiny: Vyvody i uroki* [The initial period of the Great Patriotic War: Conclusions and lessons]. Moscow: Voroshilov Academy of the General Staff, 1989.

"Nachalo voiny (22–30 iiunia 1941 g.)" [The beginning of war (22–30 June 1941)]. In "Iz arkhivov partii" [From the Party archives], *Izvestiia TsK KPSS* 6 (June 1990): 196–222.

"Nachalo voiny (1–18 iiulia 1941 g.)" [The beginning of war (1–18 July 1941)]. In "Iz arkhivov partii" [From the Party archives], *Izvestiia TsK KPSS* 7 (July 1990): 193–218.

"Nakanune voiny (documenty 1935–1940 gg.)" [On the eve of war (Documents 1935–1940)]. In "Iz arkhivov partii" [From the Party archives], *Izvestiia TsK KPSS* 1 (January 1990): 160–215.

*Nastavlenie po mobilizatsionnoi rabote mestnykh organov voennogo upravleniia NKO SSSR* [Instructions on the mobilization work of local organs of military control of the People's Commissariat of Defense of the USSR]. Moscow: Voenizdat, 1941. Secret, but now declassified.

*Nastavlenie po mobilizatsionnoi rabote voiskovykh chastei, upravlenii i uchrezhdenii Krasnoi Armii* [Instructions on the mobilization work of force units, directorates, and institutions of the Red Army]. Moscow: Voenizdat, 1940. Secret, but now declassified.

"O podgotovke Germanii k voine" [About Germany's preparations for war]. In "Iz arkhivov partii" [From the Party archives], *Izvestiia TsK KPSS* 5 (May 1990): 206–214.

Pavlov, V. P. "Moskve krichali o voine" [They shouted to Moscow about war]. *VIZh* 6 (June 1994): 21–26.

Petrov, B. N. "Oborona Leningrada, 1941 god" [The Defense of Leningrad in 1941]. *VIZh* 4–5 (April–May 1992): 14–17.

Pron'ko, V. A. "Pod lozungom 'Parazity u vlasti'" [Under the slogan "Parasites in power!"]. *VIZh* 9 (September 1993): 93–96.

———. "Proshu raz"iasnit': Plany agressii protiv SSSR" [I ask you to explain: The aggressive plans against the USSR]. *Kommunist vooruzhennykh sil* 8 (August 1991): 26–34.

Ramanichev, N. "Pochemu Stalin ne veril razvedke?" [Why didn't Stalin believe the intelligence?]. *Kommunist vooruzhennykh sil* 8 (August 1991): 12–17.

Stepanov, A. S. "O masshtabakh repressii v Krasnoi Armii v predvoennye gody" [Concerning the scale of repression in the Red Army during the prewar years]. *VIZh* 2 (February 1993): 71–80, 3 (March 1993): 25–32, and 5 (May 1993): 59–65.

Suvenirov, O. F. "Pogibli v gody bezzakoniia" [They perished in the lawless years]. *VIZh* 2 (February 1993): 81–83, 3 (March 1993): 33–34, 5 (May 1993): 66–68, 6 (June 1993): 81–83, 7 (July 1993): 45–46, 8 (August 1993): 69–72, 9 (September 1993): 47–50, 10 (October 1993): 87–91, 11 (November 1993): 90–93, and 12 (December 1993): 84–86.

———. "Vsearmeiskaia tragediia" [An all-Army tragedy]. *VIZh* 3 (March 1989): 39–47.

Vilenko, S. V., and A. V. Kostenetsky. "Plan 'Barbarossa'" [Plan "Barbarossa"]. *VIZh* 3 (March 1991): 3–47.

Vishlev, O. V. "Pochemu zhe medlil Stalin v 1941 g.? (Iz germanskikh arkhivov)" [Why did Stalin tarry in 1941? (From German archives)]. *Novaia i noveishaia istoriia* 2 (February 1992): 70–96.

*Vnutrennie voiska v Velikoi Otechestvennoi voine 1941–1945 gg.* [Internal troops in the Great Patriotic War 1941–1945]. Moscow: Iuridicheskaia literatura, 1975.

Voiushin, V. A., and S. A. Gorlov. "Fashistskaia agressiia: O chem soobshchali diplomaty" [Fascist aggression: What the diplomats reported]. *VIZh* 6 (June 1991): 13–23.

"V pervye dni voiny: Iazykom dokumentov" [In the first days of war: In the language of documents]. *Pogranichnik* [Border guard] 6 (June 1991): 13–46.

Zhuravlev, V. P., A. S. Anufriev, and N. M. Emel'ianova. "Iz arkhivov Ministerstva oborony SSSR: Pervye dni voiny v dokumentakh" [From the archives of the USSR Ministry of Defense: The first days of war in documents]. *VIZh* 5 (May 1989): 42–56, 6 (June 1989): 22–35, 7 (July 1989): 22–34, 8 (August 1989): 30–31, and 9 (September 1989): 15–21.

Ziuzin, E. I. "Iz arkhivov Ministerstva oborony SSSR: Gotovil li SSSR preventivnyi udar?" [From the USSR Ministry of Defense archives: Did the USSR prepare a preventive attack?]. *VIZh* 1 (January 1992): 7–29.

———. "Iz fondov voennykh arkhivov: Gotovil li SSSR preventivnyi udar?" [From the military archives fonds: Did the USSR prepare a preventive attack?]. *VIZh* 4–5 (April–May 1992): 10–12.

———. "Upriamye fakty nachala voiny" [Stubborn facts of the beginning of the war]. *VIZh* 2 (February 1992): 14–22.

Zolotarev, V. A., ed. "Nakanune voiny: Materialy soveshchaniia vysshego rukovodiashchego sostava RKKA 23–31 dekabria 1940 g." [On the eve of war: Materials of a meeting of the Red Army higher leadership, 23–31 December 1940]. In *Russkii arkhiv: Velikaia Otechestvennaia, T. 1* [Russian archives: The Great Patriotic, Vol. 1]. Moscow: Terra, 1993.

Zolotov, N. P., and S. I. Isaev. "Boegotovy byli . . ." [They were combat ready]. *VIZh* 11 (November 1993): 75–77.

# Index

Voroshilov General staff Academy, 29,
39, 65
VOSO. *See* Military communications
service
Voznesensky, N. A., 89
VV. *See* Internal Forces
VVS. *See* Air forces

War games, 95, 244
secret (1941), 7, 10, 52
War guilt, 1, 2
Weimar Republic, 1
Western axis, 192, 210–211, 215, 222
Western Front, 11, 15, 18(table),
20(table), 90, 113, 114, 126
airborne force, 148
air forces, 212, 226(table)
armies, 129, 206, 210, 226(table)
aviation division, 188, 199
losses, 130, 132, 200–201
order of battle, 262–264, 267
PVO, 182(table), 200–201
radio section, 211
Signal Directorate, 212
Western Special Military District, 11,
12(map), 17, 45, 103
aircraft, 13, 21(tables), 188, 199,
204(table)
artillery, 173, 180–181(table),
183(table)
borders, 95
combat readiness, 153(table), 165,
173, 178, 183(tables), 199–200,
206, 219–220, 246, 252
commanders, 48–51(photos), 118
communications, 200
deployment, 97, 173
engineers, 165, 180–181(table)
fuel, 178
German attacks on, 199
and German troop buildup, 242, 243,
251

German violation of airspace, 239
maneuvers, 123(photo)
MC, 118–119, 155–156(tables), 246
Signal Directorate, 212
soldiers, 65, 66, 70(photo),
153(table), 173
tanks, 153(table), 155–156(tables)
transport, 183(table)
Western Theater, 10, 11, 12(map), 14,
18(table), 84, 87–88, 90, 92, 93,
176
Workers' and Peasants' Military Naval
Fleet (RKVMF). *See* Naval forces
Workers' and Peasants' Red Army
(RKKA). *See* Red Army
Workers' battalions, 175
Workers' divisions, 217
World History Institute (Russian
Federation Academy of Science),
7
World War II, 1. *See also* Soviet-
German war

Yugoslavia, 243, 244

Zaitsev (captain), 238
*Zastav,* 179
Zhdanov, G. M., 89
Zhigarev, P. F., 189, 190, 201
Zhukov, G. K., 5, 7, 41, 42–43, 44, 53,
122(photo), 234
criticism of, 57, 58
head of General Staff, 25, 42,
46(photo), 93, 95, 103
and intelligence reports, 238,
241–242, 251, 254, 255
on Mekhlis, 54
preemptive attack proposal,
244–245, 327(n34)
on Timoshenko, 41–42
Zhukovsky Air Academy, 39
Zotov (colonel), 225